CW00540255

FISHER, CHURCHILL
AND
THE DARDANELLES

Fisher,
Churchill
and
The Dardanelles

by

GEOFFREY PENN

LEO COOPER

First Published in Great Britain 1999 by
LEO COOPER
an imprint of Pen & Sword Books
47 Church Street
Barnsley, S. Yorkshire, S70 2AS

ISBN 0 85052 646 9

Copyright © Geoffrey Penn 1999.

A CIP record for this book is available from the British Library

Typeset in 10/12.5pt Plantin by
Phoenix Typesetting, Ilkley, West Yorkshire.

Printed in England by Redwood Books, Trowbridge, Wiltshire.

CONTENTS

1. *J'Ordonne ou Je Me Tais*   1
2. Cicerone   27
3. The Wicked Folly of it All   50
4. *Lui Seul*   67
5. The Old Broom   87
6. Breaking the Deadlock   105
7. The Dardanelles   128
8. The Resignation   164
9. The Fall of Icarus   198
10. Vindication   221
11. Epitaph   240
     Source Notes   245
     Bibliography   263
     Index   271

MAPS

1. Fisher's Baltic Scheme   16
2. The Dardanelles   119
3. 18 March, 1915   150
4. Gallipoli, Military Operations, 1915   165

ACKNOWLEDGEMENTS

I have to express my very sincere thanks to the third Lord Fisher, DSC, for his unfailing courtesy, for lending me memorabilia of his grandfather and photographs for illustrations. He has never attempted to influence me, but has always been kind and helpful and give me much of his time at his home.

I am very grateful, too, to Vice Admiral Sir Louis Le Bailly, KBE, CB, and Professor Ian Beckett, formerly of The Royal Military Academy, Sandhurst, both of whom read right through my original massive manuscript, a feat of endurance, and made many useful suggestions; to Doctor Ruddock Mackay who lent me his Index to the Lennoxlove Papers and made several good suggestions. His biography of Fisher is an achievement. To Barbara Grey of Canberra A.C.T. for acting as my liaison officer with that beautifully organized museum, the Australian War Memorial, Canberra; to David K. Brown RCNC, who has helped with advice on matters of naval architecture; to Commander W.J.M. Faulkner, Royal Navy, for confirming my views on naval gunnery; to Peter Kent of the Imperial War Museum; to the Warminster Public Library and Mobile Library for obtaining numerous books and papers fo rme, saving me hours of travelling; to the staff at the Public Record Office, always so helpful.

I owe a debt of gratitude to the authors and publishers of the many books I have consulted and from which I have quoted, for permission to do so. The extracts from the works of Winston Churchill are reproduced with permission of Curtis Brown limited, London, on behalf of the estate of Winston Churchill. Copyright Winston S. Churchill. The extracts from the works of Randolph Churchill and Martin Gilbert are reproduced with permission of Curtis Brown Limited, London, on behalf of C& T Publications Limited. Copyright C & T Publications Limited.

Without Professor Arthur Marder's *British Naval Policy, 1880–1905: The Anatomy of British Sea Power,* (Putnam, 1941), *Fear God and Dread Nought, The Correspondence of Admiral of the Fleet Lord Fisher of Kilverstone.* 3 Vols., (Cape,

1952–59), *From the Dardanelles to Oran; Studies of the Royal Navy in War and Peace, 1915–1940)*, (Oxford University Press, 1974), *From the Dreadnought to Scapa Flow*, 5 Vols., (Oxford University Press, 1961–70), and *Portrait of an Admiral: The Life and Papers of Sir Herbert Richmond*, (Cape, 1952), this book would never have appeared.

I have also to thank the Navy Records Society for permission to quote from several of their excellent volumes, the accuracy of which can seldom be surpassed.

If I have missed any authors and publishers I hope they will accept my apologies for the oversight. There are some I have failed to trace and to them I also offer my sincere apologies.

Geoffrey Penn

1

J'ORDONNE, OU JE ME TAIS.

John Arbuthnot Fisher was born in 1841 in Ceylon, son of William Fisher, ADC to Sir Robert Wilmot-Horton, the Governor. William married Sophie Lambe, daughter of a London wine merchant, and that year the Governor died; Captain Fisher left the Army and purchased a coffee plantation. With no school, Fisher had a splendidly wild and free early childhood. At the age of six he travelled home alone for his education, a two-day journey by bullock cart and a sea passage of about a hundred days. He never again saw his father, whose plantation failed, leaving him almost penniless. Fisher's godmother, Lady Wilmot-Horton, the Governor's widow, had moved to her estate at Catton Hall, Burton on Trent, where he spent most of his school holidays and had happy days.

The boy entered the Navy at the age of 13. From that day he seemed to have a premonition that he was destined to prepare the Service for the next war. Certainly he was ambitious, but he was also prescient. Indeed he seems to have been a man with foresight far greater than the average and throughout his long career, spanning over sixty years, he was the leader in naval progress – in torpedoes, gunnery, mines, strategy and tactics. He welcomed steamships when others sneered at them as 'tin kettles'; he was the main influence in introducing submarines when others scoffed at them; his great new battleship, *Dreadnought*, and its successors, the 'battlecruisers', fast ships with the same armament as the battleships, and later the 'Super-Dreadnoughts', the latest with 15-inch guns (the largest fitted up to that time), placed the Royal Navy ahead of any other. He introduced the turbine and oil fuel. To his contemporaries this was a matter for bitter recrimination, arguments, fallacy, sophism, and sheer stupidity.

The Navy Fisher joined was in a state of lethargic resistance to change. The long wars were over and since 1815 there had been little to do except beautify their ships, keep the decks spotless, the sails white and the sheets taut. Firing practices were desultory, regarded as an unnecessary burden, and it was common routine to throw overboard the quarterly allowance of practice ammunition to avoid spoiling the elegance of the ship. Guns, through disuse, were often in no state to be fired and sometimes dangerous.

As steam replaced sail more than due respect was paid to the admirals, who regarded their ships and fleets as their private playthings to enhance their personal magnificence. If the officer knew the right people, promotion was automatic and mainly went to the titled and well-connected. Every admiral, on hauling down his flag at the end of an appointment, could nominate an officer for promotion, usually either a relation or one whose social connections could enhance his position or advance members of his family. It was not unusual for one admiral to nominate the son of another, who in turn nominated his son. The Admiralty had no say in the matter and could not dispute a nomination. After service in the Royal yachts promotion always followed. Nepotism reigned supreme.

Once an officer attained the rank of captain, promotion was routine on reaching the top of the seniority list, provided he served a short period at sea – the length of one normal commission abroad. From then on his future was assured and he rose in his turn through the ranks of rear-admiral, vice-admiral and admiral as he reached the top of every list until he retired at a fixed age, when he continued to rise in rank on the retired list. The lists of officers were overfull and many of them spent much time on half-pay, enjoying the pleasures of their country estates. The Navy was overburdened with unintelligent and inexperienced officers who had seldom bothered to study their profession.

On promotion to admiral, officers were expected suddenly to know what tactics to employ, what strategy to devise and how to handle a fleet, without ever having studied them and without consulting any of their subordinates. No officer below the rank of captain and few even then, expected to be consulted; there was no staff, and if admirals had any plans they kept them to themselves.

Yet many officers in the senior ranks posed as expert tacticians and attempted to prove to a gullible public that progress was retrogression, that wars were not won by material factors, but solely by the blood and guts of the British sailor. They called themselves the 'Historical School' and the genuinely progressive officers as the 'Matériel School', whom they despised. Their leader was the influential and wealthy Lord Charles de la Poer Beresford, son of the Marquess of Waterford, a Member of Parliament while also holding his commission in the Navy. Blessed with little brain, he gathered round him a coterie of opponents of technological progress, ambitious officers who desired to maintain the comfortable *status quo,* and who kept him informed from within the Admiralty and the fleets at sea, so that he was in a position to speak in Parliament with apparent authority.

Fisher and Beresford were poles apart and in the course of time became bitter enemies, Beresford attempting to use his influence in Parliament to gain a position of power, even the political post of First Lord of the Admiralty, while Fisher's ambition was to place the Navy far ahead of any other. With his uncanny foresight, in 1904 he predicted the outbreak of the First World War to within two months, and forecast the German use of U-boats when no other man believed in them. Long before the war Fisher thought out strategies which might have greatly shortened it. Beresford's fight to gain ascendancy in the Navy threatened to destroy all Fisher's efforts and would have left the Service far behind others, especially Germany.

After appointments as Director of Naval Ordnance, Third Sea Lord, C-in-C Mediterranean, and Second Sea Lord, serving as Britain's naval representative on the first Hague Conference and as a member of Lord Esher's committee on the reform of the War Office, Fisher gained the office of First Sea Lord. Frustrated, Beresford contrived to instigate an inquiry into Admiralty policy. The report of the inquiry made minor criticisms of Fisher which upset him greatly and he believed he should relinquish his office, but King Edward VII supported him wholeheartedly and wrote that 'even under pressure' he was not to think of resigning. But Fisher wanted to retire without opening the way to any of the reactionaries. The problem was to find an officer with similar views to his own and sufficient seniority. He decided that the only candidate with these qualifications was Admiral Sir Arthur Knyvet Wilson, VC, who had remained aloof from the controversies and was due to retire in March, 1907. With the King's support, Wilson was promoted to the rank of Admiral of the Fleet, which gave him a further five years' service. The Liberal First Lord, Reginald McKenna, supported Fisher's choice and it was agreed that he would resign a year before his seventieth birthday, to give Wilson two years in office.

Of Wilson one admiral wrote: 'He was, without exception, the least egotistical of human beings, but at the same time a man of extraordinary tenacity and indomitable pluck . . . He was undoubtedly the finest admiral of his day in command of a fleet, and he had been for five years in command of our largest fleets. He was scrupulously just and level-headed. He had no communication whatever with the Press; but unfortunately he was not himself an adept at argument, and therefore he was always at a disadvantage when dealing with politicians.'[1] Beresford whose aim, as we have seen, was to occupy the post of First Lord himself, with one of his adherents as First Sea Lord, embodied hostility to all Fisher had done. Wilson's succession was announced on 2 December, 1909, eliminating all Beresford's adherents. Beresford disclosed that he was certain of his election as MP for Portsmouth and a change of government; he was to become First Lord, 'to keep Wilson right'!

Fisher resigned his post as First Sea Lord on his 69th birthday and, despite the odium to which he had been subjected, his departure was greeted with dismay by many men-in-the-street, to whom he was a hero in his own time, regarded with something of the adulation bestowed on Nelson, exemplified by the flower seller from whom he bought a button-hole. She had never met him before, but refused payment from her hero. He had never commanded a great fleet in wartime and in this respect had never been tested, but few of his contemporaries, least of all himself, had any doubt that he would have discharged the task admirably. 'Oh my! That I was born too soon!' he wrote. His opponents blamed him for the break-up of the Band of Brothers spirit that had characterized the Navy. The unity that Marder describes as 'Nelson's principal legacy to the Navy, had been replaced by disharmony and embittered recrimination, of which he was the centre.' But the Band of Brothers spirit was not Nelson's legacy to the Navy; it did not long survive his death. It was replaced by a spirit of esotericism, nepotism, Buggins' turn, an inner wheel. 'Interest' was almost the only path to promotion and only the very best broke through this barrier, while incompetent men with influence rose without effort. During the nineteenth century and the first decade of the twentieth the Navy needed shaking out of its lethargy, its complacency. Fisher did all this and more; he reorganized the Navy, its personnel and its material; he revised its tactics and strategy to utilize the new technology; he kept the Navy ahead of others; he recognized the future of the new elements of the air and submarines and started the methods of utilizing these new dimensions. In his pursuit of perfection for the Navy, he was often tactless; ('ruthless, relentless, remorseless' he repeatedly called himself). He had to battle against privilege, prejudice, vested interest and resistance to change; if his methods were brutal, he would never have succeeded without brutality. Beresford was far more guilty of destroying any remnant of the Band of Brothers spirit. Both were brought up in an age of huge grandeur, which increased as the years of peace passed; Beresford admired and envied such splendour; he looked forward all his life to enjoying it and when his turn came, it was Fisher who spoilt all that.

What pleased Fisher most was the flood of letters he received from within the Service. He wrote, 'I had thought myself very much alone but my eyes have been opened by such a mass of telegrams and letters from all ranks and classes in the Navy, and of course, one thinks of Elijah when he once felt lonely and saw all those chariots of fire around him when his eyes were opened.'

But even as he packed his belongings in the Admiralty, his prime consideration was for the Navy he loved so much. He wrote, 'I've had a sad day. I've parted from my moorings this morning and the Admiralty knows me no more!' And of those girding him 'to speak and blast my enemies', he responded, '*I will not.* It might be a great personal triumph, but the Navy would be shown to be so strong as to give good cause . . . to build fewer ships. So I welcome hate and odium like the early Christians did the lions – they knew the end was good!'

Professor Arthur Marder wrote:

'By 1910 Fisher's work had been done. A tornado of energy, enthusiasm and persuasive power, a man of originality, vision and courage, a sworn foe of all outworn traditions and customs, the greatest of naval administrators since St Vincent, "Jacky" Fisher was what the lethargic Navy had been in dire need of. His five years' tenure of the post of First Sea Lord was the most memorable and the most profitable in the modern history of the Royal Navy. He fell on the old regime with a devastating fury. During those strenuous years there was no rest for anyone connected with the Service. "It was as though a thousand brooms were at work clearing away the cobwebs". In the teeth of ultra-conservative traditions, he revolutionized the Navy, cramming in a few years the reforms of generations and laying foundations that could never be destroyed. He gave his countrymen a new Navy, stronger and better organized than he found it, impregnated with the spirit of progress and efficiency, and purged as if by fire of "those obese and unchallenged old things that stifled and overlay" it in the past.' [2]

And Churchill wrote:

'There is no doubt whatever that Fisher was right in nine-tenths of what he fought for. . . . After a long period of unchallenged complacency, the mutter of distant thunder could be heard. It was Fisher who hoisted the storm signals and beat all hands to quarters. . . . But the Navy was not a pleasant place while this was going on.' [3]

But Fisher's work was not done. He was to return again to the Navy in war, when the country's need was greatest – and had he been heeded, perhaps the war would have been shortened, perhaps many lives would have been saved.

On promotion, Wilson was not immediately employed and was left on half-pay, but in April, 1909, was brought back to Admiralty as a member of the Committee of Imperial Defence (CID) to bring him up to date with current thinking. His talents were for command afloat; he had little experience as an administrator and did not relish the task. But he had a beneficial effect in healing the wounds of the Navy.

He was a short, stocky bachelor, with a grizzly beard and piercing blue eyes, careless in dress, with a love of outdoor pursuits. Physically tough, he was kindly, but totally committed to the Navy, known to the sailors as 'Old 'Ard 'Eart', because, devoted to duty himself, he tolerated no less from others. But he was quite unable to delegate, treated the Sea Lords as his lieutenants, and was thoroughly obstinate. Rear-Admiral Sir Francis Bridgeman (later Admiral Sir Francis), Second Sea Lord, said, 'There is no joy to be found in serving either with him or under him. Deadly dull and uncompromising, as you know. He will never consult anyone and is impatient in argument even to being impossible.' [4] He continued Fisher's policies and would accept no change. After the turbulent Fisher years, the Navy needed peace; Wilson was perhaps exactly who was wanted.

Despite McKenna's prophecy, 'You will be First Sea Lord again within a year, and bigger than ever,'[5] which he disbelieved, Fisher felt a sense of relief at being free of the burdens of office and retired to Kilverstone Hall, his son's house near Thetford, Norfolk. 'So Jacky Fisher is growing roses is he? Well all I've got to say is those roses will damn well have to grow!' So said an officer who knew him well.[6] Industrialists approached him with lucrative offers, publishers clamoured for his memoirs which he refused, though he started to put his papers in order, but soon lost interest 'I want no flatulent panegyrist to make me out a plaster saint, nor a boudoir pimp . . . to represent me with a forked tail and horns'.[7] Such a man could hardly forget his life's work, yet he saw he must keep out of Wilson's way, leaving him to control the Service without his towering presence. He was still on the active list, could be employed until his seventieth birthday and at the earnest request of Asquith, who had become Prime Minister in April, 1908, was still a member of the CID, though he deliberately attended none of its meetings.

King Edward's death on 6 May, 1910, deeply affected him ('I've lost the greatest friend I ever had!'). The General Election only a few weeks after his retirement caused him some anxiety and he wrote to Arnold White, *Daily Mail* Naval Correspondent, and by now an old friend:

> 'Things look ugly. The one to be sorry for is [Arthur] Balfour [then leader of the opposition] if Asquith turned out at once. However I'm a pure outsider! There will be desperate efforts to supplant Wilson by [Admiral Sir Reginald] Custance, [a supporter of Beresford and enemy of Fisher, who posed as a knowledgeable tactician and strategist, but whose ideas were transparently faulty] so I hear from many quarters; but McKenna will be the real loss to the Navy. The sacred fire of efficiency burns brightly in him, and he's a born fighter and a good hater, which I love (as Dr. Johnson did) with all my heart.'[8]

When he officially retired on his 70th birthday he received a shoal of letters from admirers, including many of his former opponents, who, with the change to the secretive Wilson, appreciated Fisher's forcefulness. In February he departed with Lady Fisher for an extended tour of Austria and Italy. Despite constant pleadings from McKenna and others he refused to return until Wilson retired in March, 1912.

Wilson was immediately faced with the 1910–11 Navy estimates and in December came news that Austria had laid down two more dreadnoughts. One capital ship was brought forward from the 1911–12 programme, making ten in two years. The Navy estimates had now risen to £40m, amid arguments in Parliament and the Press. Winston Churchill, now Home Secretary, deplored naval expenditure and tried to prove Germany would have fewer ships by April, 1912, than had been calculated. McKenna fought the Cabinet, but, unable to get guidance from Wilson, constantly consulted Fisher, who wrote on

5 August, 1910, to Lord Esher, who had become a personal friend since they had served together on the Committee to reform the War Office:

> 'McKenna has just been here on his second visit. . . . He has shown me various secret papers. He is a real fighter and the Navy haters will pass over his dead body! . . The lights begin to twinkle on the rocks . . . .
>
> 'The insidious game is to have an inquiry into Ship Designs, which means delay and no money.'[9]

However hard he tried to keep out of the limelight, his advice was sought by politicians and journalists, while his opponents kept up a barrage of disparagement. 'I am content to be vilified if the country wins by it,' he wrote.[10] Then, on 26 January, the day after his official retirement, 'With much reluctance I paid a second visit last week to England; however, it was a very good thing that I went, as I was able to "direct the whirlwind and control the storm". But it does sicken me to cross the trail of these pimps and intriguers and unabashed liars. Still, as McKenna truly says, I'm bound to do my best for the Navy, and so I went, and saw, and conquered! (So I think).'[11]

The invasion lobby, led by Lord Roberts, who foresaw invasion by Germany, was again active and friends begged Fisher to return and take an active part in affairs. Beresford was openly attempting to remove McKenna, whom he rightly saw as a staunch supporter of Fisher's policies, distastefully using the Archer-Shee case in an attempt to dislodge him.[12] Fisher wrote to Arnold White:

> 'It would be simply silly of me to return to England to knock the bottom out of an empty bomb that can't explode. No! The danger is an organised attack to get McKenna knocked out. Extremes have met. Socialists and Tories, from widely different motives, want to get him out of it! But they won't.
>
> 'They made sure they had him on the Archer-Shee case, but he is a stronger man than ever because of it. You can't do a man a greater service than to attack him unsuccessfully. I'll be back all right in 1912.'[13]

On 1 October, 1911 he wrote to Esher: 'I keep on being pestered to come home. *I won't.* Whatever may be his peculiarities, the Limelight must be kept on A.K.Wilson. If I came home it would be shifted on to me, and also his status in the Committee of Imperial Defence is immensely magnified by my abstention from its sitting.'[14] Again, the same month from Lucerne: 'I yesterday had a long letter from McKenna begging me to return and "put the gloves on again" and in view of his arguments I am going to do so when A.K.Wilson vanishes next year. It is, however, distasteful to me. I have had a lovely time here.'[15]

In July, 1910, the German Chancellor, Bethmann-Hollweg, hinted that he might be prepared to retard the rate of ship construction. Asquith fell for the offer and a year and a half of fruitless negotiation followed, Germany providing ammunition to the British disarmament campaign. Churchill vehemently opposed the building programme, which, he wrote to the King, was 'un-exampled'. Fifteen capital ships would be built in 'scarcely a year'. This was nonsense, for such a programme could not possibly be achieved. He urged that German dreadnought construction was at an end and the maximum fleet they could have by April, 1912, would be only 13, certainly not the 17 or 21 forecast by the Admiralty, while Britain would have at least twenty. McKenna was attacked by the opposition for leaving the Navy too weak, and by his own left for spending too much. In February, 1911, he dropped his guard in the House and admitted that the forecast figure of 17 German dreadnoughts in 1912 would not be achieved until 1913 and she would have 21 in 1914, not 1913. Churchill demanded a reduction in the Navy estimates, the argument continuing throughout the year, and when the 1911–12 estimates were announced, they were called 'enormous', 'alarming' and 'provocative' in view of the 'over-building' since 1909.

Germany's military preparations came to a head in 1911 with the Agadir Crisis. The agreement signed by France and Germany in 1909 recognized the independence of Morocco, but accepted that France had a responsibility for the maintenance of law and order, which the Sultan was unable to enforce, so France occupied Fez. Germany became more suspicious and, to placate her, France started to withdraw, but she had a new government every six months, while Britain was preoccupied with a constitutional crisis and a serious railway strike. Germany saw her opportunity and, with a thinly veiled demand for the partition of Morocco between Germany, France and Spain, sent the gunboat *Panther* to Agadir, then a sparsely inhabited settlement, to 'protect her merchants' there, of which there were none. The obvious aim was to establish a naval coaling station. Britain ranged herself alongside France and war seemed imminent. Half the High Sea Fleet had been transferred from Kiel to Wilhelmshaven, where two docks capable of taking dreadnoughts had been completed, another was in hand and the harbour was being reinforced at Brunsbüttel.

On 23 August, 1911, Asquith called a meeting of the CID to consider the crisis, when the differences between the War Office and the Admiralty were quickly revealed. Major-General Henry Wilson (later Field Marshal Sir Henry), Director of Military Operations, a Francophile and much under the influence of Foch, was determined that the six divisions of the British Army should be thrown immediately to fight on the French left. He was 'strongly opposed to any investigation of plans for the attack of colonial possessions [which] were certain to lead to dispersion of force in "sideshows" to the detriment of the continental expedition on which his heart was set'.[16] He had no understanding of the Navy, whose role he saw as wholly defensive and subsidiary to the Army. A month before the meeting, without consulting the Admiralty, he had, with the French, nominated specific days after mobilization, and French ports where the divisions were to be landed. He expected there would be 40 divisions in the German main attack, against which the French could produce 37 or 39. Thus the six British divisions were crucial. Arthur Wilson was asked if the Admiralty could transport the BEF across the Channel safely and replied that there was no serious difficulty, whereupon Asquith asked for the strategic views of the Admiralty and the Admiral made three crucial observations. The entire Regular Army should not leave the United Kingdom. The invasion bogey had created pressure which would otherwise confine the fleet to the British coast. Supported by Henry Wilson, he did not foresee a full-scale invasion but small enemy raids, especially on the east coast. He then said the naval strategy was close blockade of the whole of the German North Sea coast, the Elbe, Weser and Jade. Britain would also have to watch the entrance to the Baltic; there was no wish to prevent the egress of the German fleet, but he was anxious to prevent the exit of destroyers and submarines.

Had Wilson stopped at this point he might have persuaded his colleagues, but he went on to advocate the capture of Wangeroog Island, at the entrance to the Jade, Schillinghorn, in the Jade estuary, and the new fort, Büsum, at the entrance to the Weser, which he suggested would tie up ten German divisions, for which only one British division would be required. Vaguely he went on to say that Britain might try to destroy the German fleet at Wilhelmshaven and it would be necessary to take Heligoland with Marines, as a prerequisite to the close blockade of the German coast. Thus Fisher's principle that command of the sea must be established before troops could be landed and the concept of an attack on Schleswig-Holstein, with the probable crippling of the German Navy and outflanking of their army, was presented so ineffectually that it was damned from the start. The General was lucid and clear, the Admiral tongue-tied and obscure, ill-prepared for questions and badly briefed. He was attacked from all sides; without a moment's consideration the generals pronounced his military operations impossible. Field Marshal Sir William Nicholson, now Chief of the Imperial General Staff, whom Fisher had disliked, said with contempt that, with excellent rail communications, such operations were outdated, though they might have been valuable a century earlier. But Arthur Wilson continued to get himself further into the morass; the fleet might have to enter the Baltic and therefore have to capture Fehmarn Island, Swinemünde and Danzig. The generals took the opportunity so ably presented to throw cold water over the whole plan, gave it no serious consideration and made no attempt to discuss it or even suggest the staffs should study it; the Army was wholly unready for such an assault, had never considered it and, with war in immediate prospect, it was now too late. No specialized craft existed, no serious exercises had been carried out in combined operations or landings on a hostile shore since 1904 when Fisher was C-in-C, Portsmouth.

Henry Wilson again demanded an assurance that the six divisions could safely be conveyed to France. McKenna and Arthur Wilson maintained that the enemy fleet must first be disposed of, and now felt unable to give an assurance of safe conduct.

The arrogation of authority by the War Office and Arthur Wilson's failure to consider his plans in detail, to commit them to paper, to have them studied by an Admiralty Staff and properly prepared in conjunction with the War Office, long before the emergency arose, all contributed to the failure to adopt the principle of a sound strategy, but the root cause was the renowned 'leakiness' of Government departments, especially the War Office, and only slightly less, the Admiralty, and this is why Fisher only reluctantly put his thoughts on paper. Wilson followed the same rules, but demonstrated that, for all his tactical ability, he was no strategist and, though he was 'most clear-headed and had the gift of expressing his thoughts readily and exactly in a few words',[17] his written work always convincing, his minutes concise, he was quite unable to debate in such company.

As the meeting broke up, Richard Haldane (later Viscount), Secretary of State for War, informed the Prime Minister that he could not remain unless the Admiralty worked in harmony with the plans of the General Staff, and that to achieve this a proper Naval Staff should be organized. He later wrote to Asquith:

> 'The Fisher method, which Wilson appears to follow, that war plans should be locked in the brain of the First Sea Lord, is out of date and impracticable. Our problems of defence are far too numerous and complex to be treated in that way. They can only be solved correctly by a properly organized and scientifically trained staff, working in the closest cooperation with the military General Staff, *under the general direction of the War Office.*' (my italics)[18]

The italicized words exposed the underlying thinking. The Navy was to be a secondary Service, an auxiliary, its duty confined to transporting the Army. The generals saw Germany, France and Russia as land powers, with massive continental armies; they thought of war only in terms of vast movements across land. It never occurred to them to consider the two Services operating together, nor the war at sea, nor the function of the Navy in bringing in food and warlike materials without which the Army would be immobilized; they never appreciated that an island nation could fight a war in solely maritime terms, that without a foothold on the Continent there would be nowhere for the Army to fight. This need not surprise us, for the last great naval battle had been Trafalgar. Waterloo came ten years later; the Crimea, the Sudan, the Zulu and the Boer wars had been mainly Army wars in which the Navy took only a subsidiary role and despite the many skirmishes in which the Navy had taken part they were small by comparison. It was only in the second half of the First World War that other factors were recognized. In the event, as Churchill said, it was Jellicoe who was 'the only man who could lose the war in an afternoon'.[19]

But Haldane was right. Fisher had served on the Esher Committee, which was responsible for creating the War Office Staff, and had founded the Naval Staff College at Portsmouth (not Churchill, as Vice-Admiral Sir Peter Gretton mistakenly asserts [20]), he never accepted a staff in the Admiralty because of lack of security, shortage of competent and trained staff officers, few having yet emerged from the Staff College, (though he had flirted for a time with Battenberg and Beresford's 'War Lord' concept – an additional Member of the Board responsible for operations). But there were many examples in both wars when desk-bound officers in Whitehall completely lost touch with reality, and between the wars absurd staffs were installed afloat. When Admiral Sir Roger Keyes was Commander-in-Chief, Mediterranean, with a fleet then consisting of seven battleships, 12 cruisers and 32 destroyers, there were 31 staff officers in the fleet flagship, Vice-Admiral Kelly had 12 for a battle squadron of six ships and Rear-Admiral Collard proposed a staff of four, though he had no command and virtually no duties. [21]

Wilson said the 'naval War Staff at the Admiralty consisted of himself – assisted by every soul inside the Admiralty,' and added 'including the charwomen who emptied the waste-paper baskets full of the plans of amateur strategists – Cabinet or otherwise'. [22] Nevertheless, it was Fisher's great mistake not to embrace a naval staff. Had he done so and proper plans been prepared in writing for presentation to the Cabinet and had it been possible to keep them secret, the whole course of the war might have been altered. In 1889 a somewhat unsatisfactory Act had been passed to protect official secrets, but a sub-committee of the CID under Haldane drafted the Official Secrets Act, including the D-notice system, passed during the Agadir Crisis, and though the Privy Counsellors' oath of confidentiality dates back to the 13th century, Asquith, for example, did not hesitate to breach it frequently. He wrote private letters to Venetia Stanley during Cabinet meetings, even in wartime, giving details of the discussion and sent her secret papers, including copies of letters from Sir John French, in command in France, clearly marked 'Secret'. [23] A strong man like Fisher need not have feared a naval staff, as long as his Parliamentary colleague was a man like McKenna, and as long as he kept firm control and clearly defined their accountability to him as First Sea Lord, and no one else. The myth that his objection to a naval staff was based on love of power has echoed down history from Beresford and his friends and is still believed by some misinformed historians today.

After the Agadir Crisis Churchill reversed his view on Germany and systematically criticized the War Office and the Admiralty, especially the latter. He now no longer demanded reductions in estimates, but denounced naval strategy, policy and even tactics, of which he had no knowledge whatever. As Home Secretary he was only marginally concerned in defence matters, but bombarded Asquith and others with criticisms of McKenna, using the collective responsibility of the Cabinet and his duty for law and order as his excuse. In September, 1911, he wrote to Asquith:

> 'Are you sure that the ships we have at Cromarty are strong enough to defeat the whole German High Sea Fleet? If not they shd. be reinforced without delay. Are 2 divisions of the Home Fleet enough? This appears to be a vital matter.
>
> 'I cannot measure the forces, but the principle is clear that the fleet concentrated in the North Sea shd. be strong enough without further aid to fight a decisive battle with the German Navy.
>
> 'And something must be allowed for losses through a torpedo surprise.
>
> 'Are you sure the Admiralty realise the serious situation of Europe?'[24]

The same day he wrote to McKenna, tortuously arguing that his responsibility for law and order could be affected by the price of foodstuffs, in turn influenced by the safe arrival of ships, and therefore proposed compensation for losses of merchant ships in wartime. The next day he wrote to Lloyd George, Chancellor of the Exchequer: 'Seely [Under-Secretary at the Colonial Office and an old friend from Harrow] tells me that having to make some official enquiries at the Admiralty today he found that practically everybody of importance & authority is away on his holidays, except Wilson himself who goes tomorrow. The War Office cannot understand this at such a time, & Sir William Nicholson expressed his surprise to Admiral Wilson last night that he should find it possible to leave the office so denuded.'[25]

Lloyd George who, with Churchill, only two years earlier had thought four dreadnoughts enough, wrote to Churchill on 15 September: 'I had a long talk with Balfour. He is very much worried – as you are – about the Navy. He is by no means happy about the Admiralty. He has no confidence in Wilson's capacity for direction and leadership. He thinks the Admirals too cocksure. If there is war, he will support us.'[26]

Churchill wrote a long memorandum forecasting the events of the war, which in the event proved accurate, for it took no cognizance of any strategy other than the battering ram on the Western Front.[27]

His stratagem worked. As Haldane wrote, 'Asquith does not seem to have resented the fact that his Home Secretary was concerning himself so vigorously in military and in naval matters. On the contrary, Churchill's activities convinced him that he must replace McKenna at the Admiralty.'[28] Haldane also wanted to be First Lord. 'It was as I thought. Churchill was importunate about going himself to the Admiralty.'[29] Asquith left them to argue it out, Haldane urging his experience at the War Office. But Churchill's rhetoric won the argument, he and McKenna exchanging offices, just what 'the young man in a hurry' wanted.

Churchill had first met Fisher in January, 1907, when Fisher wrote 'I had two hour *tete à tete* with Winston Churchill, wanting to do battle on my behalf,' and again in April at Biarritz, where both were guests of the King. Fisher described the young politician as 'quite the nicest fellow I ever met and such a quick brain that it's a delight to talk to him'. The King was amused: 'I call them the "chatterers",' he told Lady Londonderry.[30]

Churchill wrote:

> 'He was then First Sea Lord and in the height of his reign. We talked all day long and far into the nights. He told me wonderful stories of the Navy and of his plans – all about dreadnoughts, all about submarines, all about the new education scheme for every branch of the Navy, all about big guns, and splendid Admirals and foolish miserable ones, and Nelson and the Bible, and finally the island of Borkum. I remembered it all. I reflected on it often. I even remembered the island of Borkum when my teacher had ceased to think so much of it.'[31]

Fisher inspired Churchill's lifelong interest in the Navy, but was deceived by his wish to 'do battle' for him; Churchill was then interested only in reducing naval estimates. Fisher maintained a vigorous correspondence with him, much of it designed to educate him in naval matters, but always keeping McKenna informed. But on taking up his new appointment Churchill at once called for advice from Fisher, writing when the change was announced: 'I want to see you vy. much. When am I to have that pleasure? You have but to indicate your convenience & I will await you at the Admiralty.'[32]

Fisher refused to respond, recognizing Churchill's shabby behaviour to McKenna, but after a second appeal and with McKenna's encouragement he agreed. He wrote to Esher:

> Reigate Priory, Surrey,
> 29th October,
>
> 'I am here three days with Winston and many of the Cabinet. I got a very urgent letter to come here and I think my advice has been fully and completely digested; but don't say a word please to a soul! I am returning direct to Lucerne on Wednesday after Tuesday at Kilverstone.'[33]

Fisher enjoyed himself, but was anxious both to avoid overshadowing Wilson and betraying McKenna: 'These are ticklish times indeed! I have got to be extremely careful. I must not get between Winston and A.K.W. in any way – it would not only be very grave, but fatal to any smooth working. So I begged Winston not to write to me. With extreme reluctance I went to Reigate as I did, but McKenna urged me on the grounds of the good of the Navy, and from what Winston has since said to a friend of mine I think I did right in going.'[34]

Despite Randolph Churchill's unworthy statement in his biography of his father that Fisher 'did not scruple to leak information to the Press . . . whenever he thought it could help his cause against the enemy, his colleagues or his Chief,'[35] Churchill wrote of Fisher at this meeting, 'he conceived himself bound in loyalty to Mr. McKenna', and disclaimed responsibility for the two politicians exchanging offices. Loyalty was one of Fisher's most enduring characteristics. Nor did Churchill admit to consulting Beresford, who wrote to Sturdee, his former Chief of Staff, that Churchill had invited him to the Admiralty and 'was sure that I could help him in his new difficult duties, etc'.[36]

> 'Although my education had been mainly military . . . I intended to prepare for an attack by Germany as if it might come the next day. I intended to raise the fleet to the highest possible strength and secure that all that strength was immediately ready. I was pledged to create a War Staff. *I was resolved to have all arrangements made at once in the closest concert with the military to provide for the transportation of a British Army to France should war come.*' (my italics)[37]

Though Churchill had adopted Fisher's dictum 'instant readiness for war', the Army was far from being a 'projectile to be fired by the Navy'. The following month Fisher had become concerned at the turn of war policy and wrote to Esher: 'I shouldn't have written again so soon except for just now seeing in a Paris Newspaper that Sir John French, accompanied by four officers, had landed at Calais en route to the French headquarters and expatiating on the evident intention of joint military action! Do you remember the classic interview we had with the late King in his cabin? If this is on the Tapis again, then we have another deep regret for the loss of that sagacious intuition.'[38]

This was bound to cause Fisher concern. He was confident that the Agadir Crisis would not lead to war; he was equally sure that war would come when the Kiel Canal and the German North Sea harbours were ready. The War Office had shown their hand and the policy, revealed so openly to Germany, would inevitably be carried through when the day came.

He saw the British contingent in France as negligible in comparison with the French Army and was opposed to it being placed under French command. The French had only one aim: to defend France and prevent a repetition of the German success of 1870. They had no imaginative plans for offensive, only to retreat in the face of the enemy until his lines of communication were overextended and then to riposte. The static trench warfare that developed in 1915 was not foreseen; a war of movement was envisaged, but the principle of a frontal defence, designed only to throw the Germans out of France, did not appeal to Fisher, who believed it would be inconclusive, solve nothing in the long run and make no use of the huge capacity of the Navy. Indeed, it appeared to him that the two Services were to be fighting quite independently; the War Office still gave no regard to their employment together, apart from the Navy ferrying transports across the Channel. The Army had not even considered the use of naval gunfire to soften up the enemy near the coast. As Liddell Hart, the noted military historian, put it:

'The reforms by which the Army had been brought into line with continental models had one defect, accentuated by the close relations established between the British and French General Staffs since the Entente. It induced a 'continental' habit of thought among the General Staff, and predisposed them to the rôle, for which their slender strength was unsuited, of fighting alongside an Allied Army. This obscured the British Army's traditional employment in amphibious operations through which the mobility given by command of the sea could be exploited. A small but highly trained force striking 'out of the blue' at a vital spot can produce a strategic effect out of all proportion to its slight numbers.'[39]

The assumption was that the Navy was confined to defence against invasion, and of the colonies and British trade. Even the eagerly anticipated new Trafalgar was defensive, to eliminate these dangers by destroying the new German Navy. The continental school wanted to confine the Navy to the long-drawn-out exercise of economic pressure, yet the Army would win the war in a few months, before maritime economic pressure had any hope of an effective contribution.

With the exceptions of Corbett, the naval historian, Captain G.A.Ballard, Director of Naval operations until July, 1906, Captain E.J.W.Slade, formerly Director of Fisher's War College, and Hankey, then Assistant Secretary of the Committee of Imperial Defence, who was young and as yet uninfluential, and to some extent Esher, Fisher was almost alone in thinking of a strategy wider and more imaginative than the frontal attack. In Carlsbad and Lucerne he had met many influential Germans. He believed that Britain should fight at a moment of her own choosing, rather than wait until Germany was ready to attack. 'The Germans are in a blue funk of the British Navy,' he wrote to Esher.[40]

He believed the British Army should not be transported to France merely to create what he foresaw as an indecisive stalemate, but should be landed in Belgium or in Germany itself, in the Baltic or in Schleswig-Holstein. 'The Germans are quite assured that 942 German Merchant steamers will be "gobbled up" in the first 48 hours of war and also the damned uncertainty of when and where 100,000 troops embarked in transports and kept "in the air" might land! NB There's a lovely spot only 90 miles from Berlin! Anyhow they would demobilise about a million German soldiers!'[41]

In Fisher's War Plans, compiled in 1907, in which he was assisted by Corbett, Ballard, Slade and Hankey, it was proposed that a base should be established at the north end of Sylt, and British forces should work down the coast to Brunsbüttel so as to force the High Sea Fleet to sea. 'If we can at the same time damage the canal, so much the better, as it will open up a wider field for action, and will enable us to enter the Baltic and operate on those

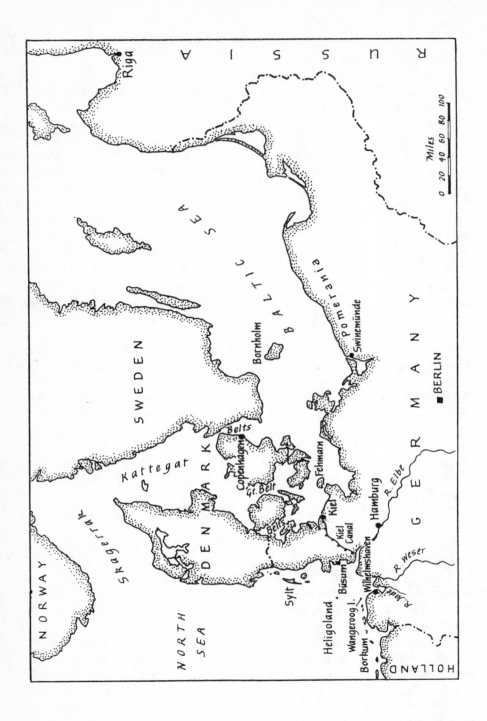

coasts. We should then be within 80 miles of Berlin, and may bring considerable pressure to bear in that direction.'[42]

> 'I wrote my opinions,' sneered Repington, military correspondent of *The Times,* 'of Sir John Fisher's attitude to Lord Esher, and saw Clarke [Secretary of the CID] at his house . . . It would not have mattered to me had he confined himself to naval operations. But he wished to impound our Army to use it for naval ends. He was all for scratching in the Baltic and wished the Army to help him and not the French. . . . I learnt that Sir John French was for the Fisher plan, and at this time opposed union with the French on French soil. This was very exasperating and I objected that nothing counted in comparison with weight at the decisive point, and that fooling in the Baltic was the sort of stuff amateurs were teaching the Navy, whose leaders seemed to be completely ignorant of strategy and of the necessity of making as sure as our means allowed the victory of France in the first great shock of battle.'[43]

Repington wielded considerable influence in Army and political circles and his remarks, written in 1922 after the results of 'weight at the decisive point' were fully and bloodily known, typify the inflexible and unimaginative attitude of many of the generals, to whom he had free and easy access and who, despite his earlier removal from the Army, did not hesitate to impart confidential information to him. There were some generals besides French who strongly supported Fisher. Lieutenant-General Sir Gerald Ellison, then Haldane's military secretary, wrote in 1926:

> 'Two names will ever remain associated with the strategical conception which more than aught else contributed to the downfall of the Central Powers. . . . Fisher was no dreamer. Time and again he had been proved in practice to be right, after his plans had encountered most bitter opposition in many quarters, both naval and political. He himself had no doubts as to the ultimate success of the North Sea-Baltic scheme and [Arthur] Wilson shared his views. . . . The fear the Germans had of a vigorous initiative on our part in the North Sea is, in itself, the most complete justification of the Fisher-Wilson strategy.'[44]

Grand Admiral von Tirpitz, who had raised the German Fleet and commanded it until 1916, confirmed Ellison's view:

> 'The possibility . . . that a battle might occur on the initiative of the enemy and not on ours . . . constituted a danger for us. The English only needed to conduct a feint attack on our coast. An attack, for example, on Borkum or Sylt might easily force a battle on us. For such an attack they could bring up their whole fleet, including a number of their coastal vessels. We should then be fighting near our own ports, but against an overwhelming

superiority of forces and at a point which could be rendered most unsafe and so unfavourable by mines and submarines. . . . The English did not even seek battle under these favourable circumstances.'[45]

During the early stages of the war Churchill supported Fisher's plan, but in *The World Crisis,* to justify his Dardanelles campaign, he suggested that Fisher's ideas were impracticable. Many historians have accepted Churchill's version, supported as it was by the generals and Fisher's enemies. So the Baltic scheme has been discounted, though Churchill raised the idea again in the Second World War. Roskill, the official war historian, wrote: 'As in World War I Churchill regarded the Baltic as the best Theatre for launching the "naval offensive" which he was always seeking.'[46] Churchill explained: 'On the fourth day after I reached the Admiralty [September, 1939] I asked that a plan for forcing a passage into the Baltic should be prepared by the Naval Staff. . . . On September 12 I was able to write a detailed minute to the authorities concerned.'[47]

After a pessimistic report from Admirals Sir Reginald Drax and Sir Gerald Dickens, who said that offensive action would not be possible for six months, Churchill brought Lord Cork back to the Admiralty to plan the scheme. Churchill's plan differed little from Fisher's and his assumption of expertise is amusing:

> 'Both Lord Cork's ideas and mine rested upon the construction of capital ships specially adapted to withstand air and torpedo attack. . . . I wished to convert two or three ships of the "Royal Sovereign" class for action inshore or in narrow waters by giving them super-bulges against torpedoes and strong armour-plated decks against air bombs. For this I was prepared to sacrifice one or even two turrets and seven or eight knots speed.'[48]

He was in fact converting the battleships into shallow-draught monitors. His minute of 12 September clearly shows it was Fisher's scheme he had in mind:

> 'DNC [Director of Naval Construction] thinks it would be possible to hoist an 'R' ['Royal Sovereign'] 9 ft., thus enabling a certain channel where the depth is only 26 ft. to be passed. . . . The objective is the command of a particular theatre [the Baltic] [*sic*] which will be secured by the placing [in it] [*sic*] of a battle squadron which the enemy ships dare not engage. . . . The presence of this fleet in the theatre would hold all enemy forces on the spot. . . . They would have to arm the whole northern shore against bombardment, or possibly, if the alliance of the Scandinavian Powers was obtained, *military descents.*'[49] [my italics]

The German invasion of Denmark frustrated these plans, otherwise Churchill would have pressed, as he did the Dardanelles, for 'military descents' on the

Pomeranian coast, exactly as Fisher had intended. Properly planned, the idea was completely feasible.

The inspiration may not have been original, for at the Hague Conference Fisher had become on intimate terms with General Gross Von Schwartzhoff, the German military delegate (the Kaiser said he was greater than Moltke), who had told him the supremacy of the Royal Navy gave the British Army power far beyond its strength, because it could be put ashore anywhere, in Antwerp, Flushing or Pomerania. At the time of the Agadir Crisis Churchill had a discussion with Sir Henry Wilson and wrote to Lloyd George: 'He entirely agrees that great strategic advantages wd. be immediately derived from our being able to move into a friendly Belgium to threaten the German flank. . . . [Henry] Wilson said in conversation that Anglo-Belgian cooperation, promptly applied to the German flank, might mean the subtraction of as much as 10 or 12 divisions from the decisive battle front.'[50] One is therefore at a loss to understand Henry Wilson's disparagement at the meeting of the CID on 23 August, unless it was pure inter-service rivalry or the joyful anticipation of a glorious military escapade on the Continent.

Germany still had a relatively insignificant fleet. Nevertheless, Fisher believed it should be destroyed in harbour immediately on the outbreak of war. A.K.Wilson shared his views and planned accordingly, though keeping his ideas to himself and his bungled explanation at the CID had nullified them; they were never seriously considered again.

Repington, much influenced by the Beresford faction, wrote to Cabinet Ministers claiming the Admiralty had no war plans and challenging them to disclose them, an absurdity – war plans disclosed were not much use – but Fisher later revealed they included a descent on Kiel.

On 21 July, 1914, Lloyd George warned Germany in a speech in the Mansion House, which he had previously discussed with Churchill, Grey and Asquith:

> 'If a situation were to be forced upon us in which peace could only be preserved by the surrender of the great and beneficent position Britain has won by centuries of heroism and achievement – by allowing Britain to be treated, where her interests are vitally affected, as if she were of no account in the cabinet of nations – then I say emphatically that peace at that price would be a humiliation intolerable to a great country like ours to endure.'[51]

Balfour then warned Germany that Party strife would not weaken Britain's resolve, and German warlike ardour was checked, though it was diverted from France to Britain. 'It is not by concessions that we shall secure peace, but by the German sword,' said a member of the Reichstag, to the delight of the Crown Prince. The German newspaper *Germania* said, 'England poses as the arbiter of the world. It cannot go on. The conflict between us, far from being settled, is now more than ever inevitable.'

If Churchill shared many characteristics with Fisher, he shared many more with his predecessor of 1868–71, Hugh Childers. Above all he was domineering and the organization of the Admiralty did not suit him. It is most simply expressed by the full title of the Board: 'The Lords Commissioners for Executing the Office of Lord High Admiral'. They were a board, a Commission for performing a single function and, though each Sea Lord had a specific responsibility, they were, like the Cabinet, jointly and severally responsible for all decisions, though the First Sea Lord had always borne an overall professional responsibility, especially in the fields of strategy, tactics and the Navy's readiness for war, while the First Lord, as political head, represented the Navy in Parliament and relayed Cabinet decisions to the Board. The Terms of the Letters Patent stated that he was 'responsible to the Crown and Parliament for all the business of the Admiralty'. Much depended on the interpretation of these words and few First Lords had ever countered the professional opinions of the Sea Lords, unless there were overwhelming political reasons, Childers being perhaps the only civilian exception. The Admiralty, one of the largest spending Departments in the country, had been virtually outside the control of the Treasury, and it was with a mandate from Gladstone to end this that Childers was appointed. In less than a month an Order in Council gave a seat on the Board to the Controller, Vice-Admiral Sir Robert Spencer Robinson, the title of whose office had been significantly changed from that of Surveyor in 1860, the year before he took office and he was the only Liberal on the Board. Trouble was inevitable, especially as Robinson, a disagreeable and ambitious man, was less than five months junior to the First Naval Lord, Vice-Admiral Sir Sydney Dacres, with whom he disagreed on nearly every subject. To make matters worse, Childers removed the Controller from Somerset House to Spring Gardens, from which the Lords of the Admiralty were evicted and the Board almost abolished altogether, its meetings reduced to extremely infrequent half-hour sessions to give formal approval to decisions already made by Childers. Instead, he sent for each member individually, making decisions without consulting the other members of the Board. The members of the Board 'were in and out of his private room all day long', and often important decisions were made without Dacres even seeing the papers, with which, when he demanded to see them, he often violently disagreed. 'This state of things went on from day to day, and naturally led to warm discussions and to much that was unpleasant, which was followed by constant threats of resignation.'[52]

Knowing his character, Asquith would have done well to have examined and revised the Admiralty Patent when Churchill became First Lord, for he never understood the organization and thought of himself, not as a political chairman of a board, but rather as the Chief Executive of the Service, to whom he regarded all the other members as subordinate and responsible. Few welcomed his appointment, *The Spectator* saying, 'He has not the loyalty, the dignity, the steadfastness and the good sense which makes an efficient head of a great office.

He must always be living in the limelight, and there is no fault more damning in an administrator.'[53] Most of the Navy agreed, as also did the *National Review*, which referred to him as 'a windbag . . . a political gambler of the worst type' and 'a self-advertising Mountebank'. 'I fear Winston as First Lord of the Admiralty,' wrote Esher, 'Will he play up? He has one eye undoubtedly on the Navy and to be a popular First Lord, but the other, not unnaturally, is on the radical tail.'[54] George Riddell (later Baron) proprietor of the *News of the World* and a man of immense curiosity who garnered wide political knowledge of which he kept careful record and was admitted to the inner circle, wrote in his diary, 'He has not got the art of playing in conjunction with others. He does not understand the method which made the Welsh footballers so successful . . . passing the ball to one another.'[55]

Churchill's eloquence and personal charm enabled him to overcome resistance based on knowledge and experience, reducing naval officers, untrained in the art of debate, to stuttering, incoherent and frustrated impotence. His attitude is revealed in his own words: 'I convened a formal meeting of the Board, at which the Secretary read the new letters patent, constituting me its head, and I thereupon, in the words of the Order in Council, became "responsible to Crown and Parliament for all the business of the Admiralty".'[56] Randolph Churchill perpetuates the distortion:

> 'Nonetheless, this seemingly wide power was *shackled* [my italics] by provisions which made action difficult without consent of the Board of Admiralty. Some of the members, accustomed to the more easy-going ways of McKenna, grew restive under their new civilian chief. They did not scruple to let their views become known to the Opposition, though not, it must be admitted in the peculiarly peccant and aggravated form which had distinguished Sir John Fisher.'[57]

Churchill thought of sea warfare as a cavalry officer. In spite of advice to the contrary, it was characteristic that he should choose as his Naval Secretary the histrionic Beatty, who had thrown him a bottle of champagne from a Nile steamer during Kitchener's 1898 Expedition to Khartoum. Beatty, a rich socialite who had refused a sea-going appointment as a flag officer, was generally regarded as having been over-promoted and likely to be placed on the retired list as soon as he reached the top of the list of rear-admirals. He was a great hunting man and the son of an officer of Churchill's Hussar regiment. 'Churchill said, "I would like to see this young admiral who refuses good appointments". When Beatty came into his room, Winston said to him, "You seem to be very young to be an admiral." Beatty replied, "And you seem to be very young to be First Lord of the Admiralty".'[58]

Of him, Churchill wrote:

> 'It became increasingly clear to me that he viewed questions of naval strategy and tactics in a different light from the average naval officer; he

approached them, as it seemed to me, much more as a soldier would. His war experience on land had illuminated the facts he had acquired in his naval training . . . His mind had been rendered quick and supple by the situations of polo and the hunting field and enriched by varied experiences against the enemy on Nile gunboats and ashore.'[59]

Most naval officers would regard such a testimonial as detrimental to their professional reputations, but Beatty was hardly as enthusiastic about Churchill: 'Oh dear! I am so tired and bored with the whole thing . . . and the party on board [*Enchantress*, the Admiralty yacht] bores me to tears. Winston talks about nothing but the sea and the Navy and all the wonderful things he is going to do. Mrs Winston is a perfect fool.'[60] The appointment, although that of only a relatively junior rear-admiral, was an important one, carrying responsibility for advising on the selection of flag officers for senior appointments.

Within days Churchill was floundering about upsetting everybody in the Navy from top to bottom. The 36-year-old ex-Hussar subaltern was not lacking in self-confidence, vitality, hard work and eloquence, but lacked appreciation of the sensitivities of admirals old enough to be his father. He set out to familiarize himself with the Navy and spent eight of the 33 months before the outbreak of war at sea in the Admiralty yacht, often accompanied by his family and guests, which no doubt gave him pleasure, but he also visited dockyards, naval establishments and nearly every one of the bigger ships. Yet he failed totally to understand the function of the First Lord, so well recognized by McKenna, who saw it as his duty to listen to advice from the naval officers with their collective years of experience in a complex profession, to listen to their reasoning, resolve any conflicting views and represent the Board in Parliament, but not to take charge of the Navy. As the German Naval Attaché put it: 'According to many, through his lack of tact, he injures discipline, through his ambition for popularity with the lower ranks, especially the lower deck'.[61] Visiting a ship, he ordered the commander to fall in his ship's company for inspection and proceeded, in front of their men, to cross-examine the officers as to whether they knew their names. The Attaché said the First Lord left the commander and officers in a state of 'choking wrath'. J.S.Sanders, Balfour's secretary, wrote, 'Winston . . . has been sending the most peremptory orders to the Sea Lords'.[62]

Churchill soon began to interfere in specialist matters. He could not wait to have issues discussed and thought out properly, and before many months was ready to argue on strategy and tactics. Jellicoe, then Second Sea Lord, wrote:

'It did not take me long to find out that Mr. Churchill . . . was very apt to express strong opinions upon purely technical matters; moreover, not being satisfied with expressing opinions, he tried to force his view upon the Board. It is quite true Mr. Churchill proved himself to be a very clever and able First Lord in some directions, but his fatal error was his inability to realise his own limitations as a civilian with, it is true, some early experience of military service, but quite ignorant of naval affairs.'[63]

At the annual manoeuvres in 1912 Churchill issued wireless instructions to Commanders-in-Chief and, on return to harbour, 'he lectured to the flag officers on how the manoeuvres should have been conducted, and this even before the umpire had concluded his report!'[64] (Not quite as bad as Childers who attempted to take command of the fleets during manoeuvres, with near disastrous results!)

Beatty was relieved in November, 1912, by Rear Admiral Dudley de Chair, who wrote:

'Several of my seniors urged me to try to keep him steady, and, as they expressed it, "Never leave his side," and to remember I was there as the keeper of his conscience. . . .

'He would look into my room at the Admiralty sometimes, and say, "Naval Secretary, I am going this weekend for a cruise in the *Enchantress* – please give the necessary orders, and you need not accompany me." I used to reply that as long as he would promise not to visit any ships or dockyards, it was all right; otherwise I must be with him.

'Winston Churchill thoroughly enjoyed these trips in the Admiralty yacht, and he generally invited important members of the Cabinet to accompany him on his visits to the Fleet. Many a time the Prime Minister, Mr. Asquith, and F.E.Smith (later Lord Birkenhead) were among the guests I met.

'Asquith also enjoyed these outings, and there I had the opportunity of seeing him informally. I must say I was not impressed; he seemed to me to be a poor leader (God help us all in case of war!) – always so undecided, and apparently hesitant in weighing the pros and cons of any problem he was asked to decide. . . .

'Winston Churchill certainly made us realise that he was clever and hard-working, but he was also impulsive, headstrong and even at times obstinate. As a result of this I, as Naval Secretary, found it difficult to keep the balance even, especially as he thought he knew more about the naval personnel than any of us in the Admiralty, who had been all our lives in the Service.' [65]

Had Churchill been blessed with a strong First Sea Lord from the outset, things might have been different; had he been pulled up short right at the beginning his talents might have been better used.

Thus the stormy years of Fisher were followed by the stormy years of Churchill, and everything Fisher had planted was pulled up to see if the roots were growing. Wilson's determination to retain in his head all strategic plans, and not to consider for a moment the creation of a War Staff, were too much for Churchill, whose brief from the Prime Minister was precisely to achieve this. Churchill recognized the need for a proper war staff capable of working out plans for war. As long as the Admiralty was controlled by a Fisher, with his ability forcefully to explain his views, and his immense capacity for work, the old system could be *made* to work. But Wilson's incoherence made him helpless under cross-examination by the dialectician, Churchill, who determined to rid himself of this unyielding colleague. The creation of a war staff was not only a duty, but an opportunity to enhance his reputation. 'After we had had several preliminary talks and I found we were not likely to reach an agreement, I sent him a minute about the creation of a Naval War Staff, which raised an unmistakable issue. He met it by a powerfully reasoned and unqualified refusal, and I then determined to form a new Board of Admiralty without delay.' [66]

Wilson's 'powerfully reasoned' paper pointed out that, when stripped of hyperbole, Churchill's proposal amounted only to the addition of a Chief of Staff, interposed between the heads of departments and the First Sea Lord. 'An adviser without responsibility can only produce irritation when his advice does not happen to agree with the officer who has the responsibility.' Wilson pointed out the difference between Army warfare and that of the Navy. The Army needed a staff to work out all logistic and other problems, but the staff of the Navy was the Navy itself.

The First Sea Lord became heavily engaged in matters of administration and politics. Either these matters had to be removed from the First Sea Lord, enabling him to concentrate on plans for war, or the latter had to be undertaken by a staff to free him for the daily administration of the Service, making him little more than a political cipher or clerk. Neither solution could ever be satisfactory, for the administration of the Navy is inextricably bound with instant readiness for war, so the First Sea Lord must be the final arbiter of both, and had Wilson been more politically astute, he would have agreed to the formation of a War Staff, expanding the strategical planning departments, but ensuring that he himself was designated its head. But this is reckoning without Churchill, who would not have hesitated to bypass the First Sea Lord, and later did exactly that, leading to disaster.

Wilson was due to retire in March, 1912, and it might have been thought wise to leave him in office until his successor found his feet, but his supersession was announced on 28 November, just a month after Churchill's arrival. Their parting was cold and Wilson refused a peerage. But obviously Churchill had made up his mind to remove Wilson at once. His few days with Fisher at Reigate had filled him with enthusiasm:

'I found Fisher a veritable volcano of knowledge and inspiration; . . . Once he began, he could hardly stop. I plied him with questions and he poured out ideas. It was always a joy to me to talk to him on these great matters, but most of all he was stimulating in all that related to the design of ships. He also talked brilliantly about Admirals. . . .

'I began our conversation with no thought of Fisher's recall. But by the Sunday night the power of the man was deeply borne in upon me and I had almost made up my mind to do what I did three years later, and place him again at the head of the Naval Service. . . . All the way up to London the next morning I was on the brink of saying 'Come and Help me,' and had he by a word seemed to wish to return I would surely have spoken. But he maintained a proper dignity, and in an hour we were in London. Other reflections supervened, adverse councils were not lacking, and in a few days I had definitely made up my mind to look elsewhere for a First Sea Lord.

'I wonder whether I was right or wrong.'[67]

Churchill selected the uninspiring Sir Francis Bridgeman, who had been Second Sea Lord until the previous January. Though a supporter of Fisher's reforms, he appeared unforceful and pliable, which he himself attributed to modesty, and seemed far more likely to give way to Churchill than his predecessors. However, Churchill was not satisfied with a change of the First Sea Lord only. Vice-Admiral Sir George Egerton, the Second Sea Lord was replaced by Prince Louis of Battenberg, while the Fourth Sea Lord, Rear-Admiral Charles Madden, who was due to leave in any case in January, was relieved by Captain William Pakenham, who had so distinguished himself as Attaché in Japan. Rear-Admiral Charles Briggs, the Controller, who had taken over from Jellicoe, had only been in office for a year, so was retained.

Churchill had discussed his new Board with Fisher, who wrote to his daughter in Law:

> '*Yes, I have really had an immense triumph over* [the constitution of] *the Board of Admiralty.* The King quite thought he had arranged for [Admiral] Sir John Durnford to be First Sea Lord. *This is very Private, of course,* and [Admiral] Sir John Fullerton actually telegraphed out to Eric [his son, Admiral Fullerton] in the *Triumph* that it was all settled . . . No one expected any of the new men. I would have gone further and have got rid of the one that has been kept, as he is a poor fool. . . . dear old Wilson was not a Machiavelli, and these lawyers in the Cabinet just walked round him! . . . Winston Churchill has again, two days ago pressed me to pay him another visit. I don't thinks it's judicious. I am letting it stand over. The greater your friends the more careful you ought to be of their susceptibilities. Bridgeman, Battenberg and Pakenham all know I got them there. I don't want to rub their noses in it. The greatest triumph of all is getting Jellicoe Second-in-Command of the Home Fleet. He is the future Nelson, *SURE.* '[68]

All these plans aimed at getting Jellicoe into position to take command of the Grand Fleet with which Churchill agreed. He was prepared to be guided by Fisher, who wrote to Pamela McKenna:

> 'Now I will give you the whole effect of what has happened in one word!
> JELLICOE
> I say Nunc Dimittis! For in two years he will be Commander-in-Chief of the Home Fleet at the same time as Battenberg becomes First Sea Lord, owing to Bridgeman's age retirement. The battle of Armageddon comes along in September 1914. That date suits the Germans, if ever they are going to fight. Both their Army and Fleet then mobilised, and the Kiel Canal finished, and their new building complete. *So I sleep quiet in my bed.*[69]

Fisher's suggestion of Bridgeman's appointment as First Sea Lord was, however, not only a manoeuvre to get Jellicoe into position as Admiralissimo in the conflict he dated so accurately, but also because the former supported the Selborne-Fisher Scheme which unified the deck and engineering branches of the Service to the chagrin of the reactionaries now again under attack.[70] Bridgeman, conscious of his refusal to succeed Fisher in 1910, acknowledged his letter of congratulation:

> 'You may perhaps wonder why I came! Two reasons forced me to do it: First, within the Admiralty there were designs for wrecking the whole scheme of education. That had to be stopped, and I saw no means of doing so other than coming here myself. Second, I do feel that I was perhaps needlessly standing in the way of younger men, who it's very desirable should go ahead! So long as I remained [in the Home Fleet], there could be no real advancement for, say Jellicoe. Directly I go, he comes automatically to command the 2nd Division, and a splendid opportunity for him!'[71]

Fisher had written in late November: 'My two private visits to Winston were fruitful. I tell you (AND YOU ONLY!) the whole secret of the changes! *To get Jellicoe Commander-in-Chief of the Home Fleet, prior to October 21, 1914, which is the date of the Battle of Armageddon . . . Everything revolved around Jellicoe!*[72]

Fisher never had any inclination to 'lag superfluous on the stage'. He was enjoying himself and he maintained an interest in naval affairs mainly to ensure the exclusion of the reactionaries who would have lost the war. In January he wrote to Esher: 'Winston urges me to come back, but he forgets the greatest of all the Napoleonic sayings: *"J'ordonne, ou je me tais"*. Besides, you see, I was first violin. However, Winston is *splendidly receptive.*[73]

2

CICERONE

Churchill's purpose in appointing Bridgeman was mainly to create a naval staff. The majority of naval officers opposed it as a deprivation of authority and responsibility from the Board and admirals, increased centralization and bureaucracy run by a theoretically-minded staff, perhaps with limited sea service and unfamiliar with prevailing conditions.

Churchill, under pressure from the Cabinet and the CID, especially Haldane, and with support from Battenberg, and, surprisingly, from Fisher, in January, 1912, renamed the Navy War Council the 'Admiralty War Staff'. He also created a 'Chief of the War Staff' whom he wished to make responsible to himself – exactly what Fisher and Wilson had feared. Fortunately Battenberg, supported by Haldane, was strong enough to prevent this potentially disastrous move and the office was placed under the First Sea Lord. Under the Chief of Staff came three main divisions, Operations, Intelligence and Mobilization, whose task was to study preparations for war and advise the First Sea Lord, who remained responsible for operational matters. Outside the Service the move was welcomed, though Beresford said it did not go far enough; he wanted the staff to be given executive responsibility.

When Selborne had visited Fisher in Malta in 1901, the latter had pressed for a Naval War College. He used the War College as a staff, which, remote from the Admiralty, would remain advisory, reducing the danger of direct reporting to the First Lord. A 'Staff Course' was now set up at Greenwich to train officers of the rank of commander and below in staff work, but there were few officers capable of running such a course and strategic thinking was generally lacking. A major problem remained in the status of the proposed Chief of Staff. There was confusion of thought. Wilson had warned Churchill that divorce of the office from that of First Sea Lord was unworkable, while Battenberg, when later First Sea Lord, refused to lower the position of his office by becoming Chief of Staff *to a civilian* First Lord.[1] Churchill wanted to make operational decisions with a staff directly responsible to him. There could never have been any question but that operational control was a matter for a professional naval officer, who had to be the First Sea Lord. Churchill himself wrote, 'But it takes a generation to form a General Staff. No wave of the wand can create those habits of mind in seniors on which the efficiency and even the reality of a staff depends'.[2] It is difficult to see how he believed he had those habits of mind. Inexperience of staff work supported this view, for in the event many staff proposals were turned down either because of expense or impracticability – the very thing they should have researched. Despite the view of Julian Corbett that at the outbreak of war 'there is no doubt that the machinery for setting our forces in action had reached an ordered completeness in detail that has no parallel in our history',[3] they achieved little before the war. They proposed the system of distant blockade, but the difficulties of close blockade had been pointed out in the Report of the Three Admirals in 1889: and they added that distant blockade 'would not answer the case'.

Wilson was a strong advocate of close blockade and believed the problem of torpedo boats could be overcome. In 1897 Admiral Von Knorr had presented a memorandum at a special audience with the Kaiser in which he said that 'the relatively short German coast line literally invited a close blockade'.

Despite Churchill's arrogation of power and his search for a submissive First Sea Lord, he was pleased to be advised by Fisher, who in turn was happy to guide him from outside the Admiralty. He knew that once he accepted an official position things would change, but the more his advice was sought, the more he admired Churchill.

When First Sea Lord, Fisher had endeavoured to improve the lot of the sailor and redress the grievances brought to his attention by Lionel Yexley, editor of the journal *The Fleet*. Ironically, it was due almost entirely to Churchill and Lloyd George that the one area in which he had been able to make little progress was that of pay, but now he was out of office he was able to press his radical young disciple to rectify a position he had long seen as urgent. Churchill took the matter up with vigour and was obliged to argue ferociously with his old colleague, now Chancellor of the Exchequer, with whom, in a letter he never sent, he threatened a break:

> 'My naval advisors take a serious view of the decision of the Cabinet about the Pay of the Men; and I may at any time be confronted with the resignation of the Sea Lords in a body. . . . I fully share their view that the scheme we had passed with so much care was an extremely moderate one. . . . It is not possible that these proposals shd be confined to the crude or arbitrary limit of £300,000 p.a.
>
> 'If you wd like to discuss this with me before it is brought before the Cabinet I am at your service. . . .
>
> 'From what you said the other morning about my 'having looked out

for opportunities to squander money', it has occurred to me that you may perhaps prefer that final decision on the Pay question shd. be deferred until the estimates can be surveyed as a whole. . . .

'If we are to separate it had much better be on the great issue of retrenchment v. National Defence, than on a small matter of £170,000 a year for Sailors' Pay.'[4]

Churchill was successful, and sailors' pay was increased by 3d a day to 1s 11d (£4–36 in 1990's values) and that of Petty Officer by 6d a day to 3s 2d. But it is of interest that, despite all his claims to social welfare, Lloyd George should have resisted so paltry an increase for grossly underpaid servicemen, and that Churchill his fellow champion, should have to be persuaded by Fisher and threatened with resignation by the Sea Lords.

Churchill encouraged the flood of eight- to ten-page outpourings from Fisher; 'Keep continually sending,' he wrote, and Fisher sent him 'every sort of news and counsel, from blistering reproach to supreme inspiration',[5] largely in response to his requests for guidance from the ageing but ingenious admiral.

He followed up many of Fisher's reforms of naval discipline, setting up a committee under Rear-Admiral Frederic Brock, most of whose recommendations on summary punishments were accepted, and naval detention quarters were set up so that men no longer served sentences in civil prisons.

But in April, 1912, Churchill made three appointments for which he gave his reasons to Fisher, who angrily replied criticizing them and saying their relationship must cease. The three admirals were Meux, Sir Berkeley Milne and Custance. Meux was to be C-in-C Portsmouth instead of remaining on half-pay and it was rumoured that the King had sent for Churchill and insisted on the appointment, which opened the possibility of Meux becoming First Sea Lord. He would have reversed all Fisher's reforms. Milne, whose promotion in the Service, had also been influenced by the King, had been appointed C-in-C Mediterranean. Fisher reposed no confidence in him as a wartime commander and he was senior to Jellicoe, whom Fisher wanted to be the senior officer afloat in 1914. He wrote to Churchill:

'I consider you have betrayed the Navy in these three appointments, and what the pressure could have been to induce you to betray your trust is beyond my comprehension. *You are aware that Sir Berkeley Milne is unfitted to be the senior Admiral afloat, as you have now made him.* You are aware that Sir E Poë should have been Commander-in Chief at Portsmouth, failing your promise to Admiral Egerton, and you must have been as cognizant as I am of Custance's views and animus . . .

'I am glad you appreciate Jellicoe. You have practically annihilated him by your appointments of Meux and Milne. *I can't believe that you foresee all the consequences!*

'There are splendid officers of superior rank in the Navy, but alas! in a naval disaster there is no time to send for a Roberts to retrieve the incompetency of a Buller. *You have arranged a Colenso.*[6] A NAVAL COLENSO IS IRREPARABLE, IRREMEDIAL, ETERNAL.'[7]

These were prophetic words. Milne's naval Colenso occurred under three years later, and it *was* irreparable.

Custance was to preside over a committee to consider 'the whole question of the entry and education of cadets and midshipmen', His bitter attacks on the Selborne-Fisher scheme convinced Fisher that severe damage was inevitable, but to his surprise, little change was proposed, Custance, with unaccustomed broadmindedness, now taking the view that 'whether we like it or whether we do not, we are committed to the new scheme for years to come and I maintain that it is our duty to our country and to our Service to assist in carrying it out to the utmost of our ability.'[8]

Randolph Churchill asserts that his father 'was a proud man and must have wanted Fisher's services very badly to have put up with such an insult', but Winston had not seen Fisher's letter to Esher in which he said, 'Winston . . . feared for his wife the social ostracism of the Court and succumbed to the appointment of the two Court favourites.'[9] Fisher's letter to Churchill also gave him sound advice about new ships.

Churchill's speech introducing the Navy estimates in March, 1912, was praised, though in fact he merely adopted McKenna's programme, so heartily endorsed by Fisher. But Churchill always prepared his speeches with great care and this was masterly compared with those of McKenna, always inhibited by Churchill's anticipated criticism. The speech was welcomed on all sides. Repington effused pompously: 'The point of your great speech on March 18 which appeals to me most is that in which you guarantee to meet at [our] average moment the naval force of an enemy at his selected moment. There is a whole world of difference between this and the past.'[10] Repington was so wrong. The phrases were direct quotation from Fisher; they were among his favourite catchphrases!

But Churchill had no intention of leaving Fisher to sun himself abroad when he could be so great a prop. In May, 1912, he, with Asquith and their families, cruised the Mediterranean in *Enchantress* and in Naples Fisher received a letter, followed by a telegram, that they would arrive for discussions later that month. Esher, Jellicoe and Hankey had all written to Fisher urging the value of his good relations with Churchill and, despite his caution, he was flattered by this attention. He was so controversial a figure that it was announced that from Genoa the yacht would go to Malta and was later claimed to have been driven into Naples by bad weather, though Fisher read in a newspaper that 'it was well known that he was running the Navy and the Admiralty all the time'. Asquith and Churchill asked him to make himself available for four days of discussion, with the main object of persuading him to become chairman of a Royal

Commission on oil fuel for the Navy, covering the oil resources of the world and their relation to Britain and the Navy in particular. But though of vital importance, this was partly a device to get Fisher back to the United Kingdom so that Churchill could consult him. It did not require four days to discuss this single issue, nor did it require the presence of the Prime Minister, and it could have been dealt with by correspondence. Beatty, who accompanied the party, misjudging the whole affair, wrote to his wife, 'That old Rascal Fisher arrived on board directly we got here, looking very well and young, never stopped talking and has been closeted with Winston ever since. Wasn't that something to come to Naples for? Do not mention in conversation to *anyone* that F. is in close confidence with Winston'.[11] Fisher, cautious and reluctant to be dragged back, had twice refused to accompany the Ministers in the yacht to Alexandria, and at first refused to go on board, but 'If Mahomet comes to the mountain, why the mountain can't well help it!' Many other subjects were discussed and on 17 June he wrote to his son, 'I'm worn out with writing. Eight sheets to Sir Francis Hopwood yesterday – nine to Winston today in answer to a long and pressing letter from him received this morning. . . . I'm extremely reluctant to give up my freedom.'[12]

So Fisher was persuaded to continue his reforms from the anonymity of retirement. Churchill, in *The World Crisis*, does not hesitate to claim them as his own and, though it was he who pushed them through a reluctant Cabinet and Parliament, they stemmed from Fisher.

Churchill was pressing:

> 'This liquid fuel problem has got to be solved . . . the natural, inherent, unavoidable difficulties are such that require the drive and enthusiasm of a big man . . .
>
> No one else can do it. . . . Perhaps no one else but you can do it at all. It means that you will have to give your life and strength, and I don't know what there is to give you in exchange or return.
>
> 'When you have resolved the riddle, you will find a very hushed, attentive audience. But the riddle will not be solved unless you are willing, for the Glory of God, to expend yourself upon its toil. I recognise it is little enough I offer you. But your Gifts, your Force, your Hopes, belong to the Navy, with or without return, and as your most sincere admirer and as Head of the Admiralty, I claim them now for the Navy, knowing well you will not grudge them. You need a plough to draw, your propellers are racing in the air![13]

Despite the mixed metaphors, this was a carefully calculated appeal, designed to flatter and persuade the susceptible Fisher, who was at home and hard at work before the month was out.

Though not wealthy, Fisher had a few shares in the Shell Oil Company which he at once sold at a loss. Churchill's prime concern was a reliable source of oil in wartime, but Fisher persuaded him to add oil engines and the Royal Commission on Oil and Oil Engines was formed with George Lambert, Civil Lord of the Admiralty, Jellicoe, Engineer Vice Admiral Sir Henry Oram, Engineer-in-Chief of the Fleet, Alexander Gracie and Alfred Yarrow, the last two having served on the Dreadnought Committee. Wilson had gone, so Fisher returned to the CID, where he had a 'regular set-to' with Lloyd George over the defence of Cromarty, which he considered strategically better placed than Rosyth.

Churchill's enthusiasm for oil stemmed from Fisher, who, as early as 1886, was known in the Navy as 'the Oil Maniac'. There were two main problems, first the technical one of burning oil in HM Ships, which Fisher was convinced, after experience in *Dreadnought*, presented little difficulty, the second the problem of ensuring supplies for Britain, who had none of her own, apart from minor quantities of shale oil in Scotland.

The advantages of oil fuel were such that conversion of the fleet was imperative. The operation of coaling ship was a lengthy, arduous and thoroughly inconvenient process, while the embarkation of oil fuel was simple, fast and easy. By attaching 9-inch hoses from the tanker or shore storage tanks, it could be pumped aboard with ease in a few hours, and as soon as the hoses had been detached the fleet could be on its way. Coaling at sea was hazardous and difficult. In any seaway the collier and the warship, lying alongside each other were often damaged, injuries were common and the operation frequently abandoned, so that it could never be relied on. With oil, fuelling at sea became a practical proposition, even under way, the two ships standing off each other.

The operation of stoking a ship with coal can only be visualized by those who have experienced it. The furnaces were often between 15 and 20 feet long and it was essential that the coal should be spread evenly over the surface, so a stoker had to handle a heavy shovel full of coal which he had to throw into the back of the furnace, itself white hot, radiating intense heat into his face, so much so that he wore a mask of wet sackcloth draped in front of his face, with holes cut in it for the eyes, so as to prevent scorching of the skin. As the ship gathered speed, more and more coal had to be shovelled into the furnaces, which inhibited rapid acceleration until the fresh fuel was well ignited and hot, leaving her performance entirely at the mercy of the skill, determination and physical strength of the stokers. The reverse process, slowing down, was even more difficult, for fires had to be 'drawn', heaps of blazing hot coal raked out on to the deckplates. Under the furnaces were ashpans, which had to be emptied with a flat rake and the red-hot ash drawn out on to the plates in front of the boiler. Clinker formed in the furnace and had to be removed by two instruments, a 'slice' and 'devil', the former made of wedge-shaped steel about a foot long and four inches wide, on the end of a steel bar about $1^1/_2$ inches diameter and long enough to reach the back of the furnace. This heavy tool had to be lifted on to the lip of the furnace and then run backwards and forwards along the firebars, under the coals, to dislodge the sticky, white-hot clinker. The 'devil', so called because it consisted of two horns on the end of a somewhat lighter steel bar, but also long enough to reach the back of the furnace, was then used to draw the clinker gradually forward until the stoker, peering in from behind his mask, scattered it on the plates in front of the boiler. After each of these operations the white-hot products were then hosed down to dowse them, the resulting sulphurous, stinking smoke and steam entirely filling the boiler room with its choking stench.

While this process of 'cleaning fires' was being carried out additional coal could not be added to the furnaces and the ship slowed down. The accumulation of ashes and clinker had to be removed by means of an 'ash-hoist', a small steam engine that hoisted the hot, wet, dirty load on a wire whip to the upper deck, whence it was pitched overboard. Some ships were lucky enough to be equipped with an 'ash-ejector', utilising a high-pressure water nozzle to eject the ashes through a pipe leading out of the ship's side from a trough into which they were shovelled.

All the while, the coal in the bunkers had to be 'trimmed', that is, to be shovelled across from the remote corners of the bunkers to the bunker doors where it could be reached from the stokehold floor, the 'trimmers' standing on the coal while they heaved it across. The operational speeds of ships and fleets were wholly dependent on the stokers and in a chase the fate of the ship or the outcome of a battle depended upon how long they could maintain this outstandingly arduous work, while, as they piled more coal on the furnaces, clouds of black smoke were unavoidable, giving away their position to the enemy.

Oil fuel, by comparison, was simple. If additional speed was needed more sprayers were ignited on the boiler front, simply by opening a valve and increasing the oil pressure by speeding up the pump. The controls were all to hand and the number of men needed vastly reduced. This in turn produced savings, increasing accommodation space, making more room for guns or equipment or saving weight for extra armour or larger machinery to provide higher speeds. The problem of trimming disappeared and ballasting could be achieved merely by pumping oil from one tank to another. By proper control of the combustion air supply the ship could steam with virtually no smoke, remaining invisible over the horizon.

There was never any comparison between the two; oil was vastly superior. The major problem therefore was to ensure supplies. The Burmah Oil Company, virtually the only source within the British Empire, had already been formed. Undeveloped resources were known to exist in Trinidad and a Mr. W.Knox D'Arcy had obtained certain concessions in Persia (Iran) where he had recognized that extensive resources remained untouched.

When Fisher had become First Sea Lord in 1904, strongly supported by Selborne, Pretyman, Financial Secretary, and Gordon Miller, Director of

Contracts, he had pioneered oil fuel in the Navy. Churchill appreciated Fisher's arguments and his invitation to become chairman of the Commission was an immense step forward, demonstrating wisdom of a high order.

Much of the work of the Commission was secret, not only for obvious defence reasons, but for commercial and political ones. Fisher determined to convince the Burmah Oil Company to come to the assistance of D'Arcy in the development of his concessions, for which he had inadequate capital. The British Government entered into a long-term contract with the newly-formed Anglo-Persian Oil Company, securing a large proportion of the Company's output, and the whole in time of war; the Government invested £2m for further development, securing a controlling interest in the company, which subsequently became the British Petroleum Company, probably the most profitable investment ever made. Not only did foreign governments and commercial interests try to thwart the scheme, but at home, coal-owners and mining unions joined in an unlikely alliance to prove it a retrograde step, arguing that it was suicidal to depend on fuel supplies unavailable from home, and attempting to prove that vast dangers from explosion existed. The result was only achieved just in time, in July, 1914.

Fisher's proposals regarding oil engines were less realistic. He believed oil engines would not only provide greater power and speed, but could be run for long periods without maintenance. 'Motor battleships! No funnels – no smoke – no engineers – no stokers – only a d——d chauffeur and prodigious economy!' Such was never the case; oil engines were suitable for merchant vessels, small craft and submarines but the only nation that built large warships powered by oil engines was Germany, between the wars. Even Fisher recognized, belatedly, that the motor battleship was 'obsolete for war before she has been begun, as we have got to turn her into a submersible – not that there is any difficulty in that,'[14] and in the 1990s some former Soviet Union submarines are of 30,000 tonnes, far bigger then the battleships of Fisher's day.

More pregnant was Fisher's vision of the gas turbine, at least 25 years before Whittle. He pressed Sir Charles Parsons, whose firm developed the turbine, on the subject: 'I wish you could see your way to the continuance of the Turbine in connection with the internal combustion principle. *Remember we can't have funnels for future fighting!* And we want the armament amidships, or more amidships than boilers will allow of. It means victory to see the enemy before they see you and to be absolutely devoid of a puff of inadvertent black smoke through some accident with the oil-spraying apparatus.'[15] But Parsons said, 'I do not think the internal combustion turbine will ever come in. The internal combustion turbine is an absolute impossibility.'[16] It is difficult to understand how Fisher thought he could dispense with funnels of some kind; the exhaust gases from turbine, boiler or oil engines would have to disposed of, and some discharge remained essential, though he may have been thinking of exhausting at the side of the ship rather than building the tall funnels then necessary for natural draught.

He was on firmer ground when he suggested a pipeline under the English Channel to supply oil for ships and transport, thirty years later to become 'Pluto', attributed by Churchill to Mountbatten's staff.[17] Perhaps they had read Fisher's letters on the subject.

His enthusiasm for submarines was unabated and again demonstrated his foresight. In January, 1911, he wrote to A.G.Gardiner visualizing Britain possessing 100 submarines:

> 'There is a momentous change coming in sea fighting. . . . We have got a submarine that carries two 4-inch guns and goes 21 knots and can cross the Atlantic and wants no convoy and can live by herself for 2 months! *Do you see the outcome?* . . . For invasion is a simple impossibility in the face of submarines!'[18]

Again on 31 January:

> 'You never said anything more to the point when stating that some fool, zealot or traitor gives us away to foreigners. A zealot lately did this in [the case of] the *Lion*. . . . I only hope our submarine secrets may not get out. The Germans and others have several more to go to the bottom before they reach our present position. P.S. – The one absorbing anxiety is, shall we go ahead as we ought to in the development of submarines and internal combustion propulsion? *These are the two burning naval questions of the day; all the rest, rot.* '[19]

In June, 1912, Churchill discussed with Fisher the removal of all the pre-dreadnought battleships in the Mediterranean, which had stimulated attack on the First Lord in the Press and by the opposition, even from Esher, and in the Cabinet, especially by McKenna and Harcourt. Churchill asked him to prepare a memorandum for use in the Cabinet, in which he included: 'The immense development of the submarine precludes the presence of heavy ships of war or the passage of trade through the Mediterranean Sea. . . . As to the policy of reducing the Mediterranean Fleet, the matter is most simple. The margin of power in the North Sea is irreducible and requires this addition of the Mediterranean battleships. . . . It is futile to be strong in the subsidiary theatre of war and not overwhelmingly supreme in the decisive theatre. The moral effect of an omnipresent fleet is very great, but it cannot be weighed – at least in the Cabinets of the powers – against a main fleet known to be ready to strike and to strike hard.' [20]

Foreseeing the unrestricted submarine campaigns of 1914–18 and the need for British submarines to be sufficient in number and power to bottle up the High Sea Fleet in its harbours, in July,1912, Fisher attended a meeting of the CID at which Churchill outlined his memorandum, and he seized the opportunity. The danger to transports from submarine and torpedo attack was 'so serious that any idea of invasion anywhere in face of them was out of the question'. His aim was to discredit the invasion lobby while a massive submarine force accompanying the Grand Fleet would inhibit attack by the German Fleet. Fisher assured Asquith that he had absolute faith in the power of the submarine against large warships, to which McKenna observed that, if this was correct, the North Sea was unsuitable for battleships. Fisher replied that the British Battle Fleet would not be in the North Sea, but off the north coast of Scotland. The emergence of the German Fleet would be met by submarines and destroyers, but 'if it came out far enough it would then have to fight our battle fleet', foreshadowing the disposition adopted, Keyes with his submarines and Tyrwhitt with his destroyers and light cruisers operating from Harwich, while the Grand Fleet remained at Scapa Flow in the far north.

Churchill, defeated by a knowledgeable man, lamely remarked that the 'Board of Admiralty did not entirely accept Lord Fisher's views on submarines'. Neither Bridgeman nor Battenberg, both of whom were in attendance, made any comment. 'Perhaps,' writes Ruddock Mackay in his biography of Fisher, 'they had already fallen into the habit of waiting for the First Lord to speak on the fundamentals of naval strategy.'[21] But Fisher, as a full and uninhibited member of the CID, spoke up fluently and freely, which we should remember in relation to his position later.

Fisher's views on the danger to Britain of the German submarines and the dearth of her own preoccupied him. With increasing endurance, submerged in daylight and surfacing at night to charge batteries, they could maintain close blockade, while the surface fleet was kept out of harm's way until required to launch the major attack he envisaged, which itself would be accompanied by submarines. If, as was increasingly accepted, enemy submarines were capable of preventing a close blockade by surface ships, British ones would make invasion impossible. This required a huge construction programme, and he was concerned that few in the Admiralty or Cabinet seemed to see this need. He was assisted by the appointment in April, 1913, as one of the secretaries of the Oil Commission, of Captain S.S.Hall (later Admiral) who had been Inspecting Captain of Submarines, and a staff including Captain Philip Dumas (later Admiral), former naval attaché in Berlin, and Engineer Lieutenant C.J.Hawkes. In August, 1912, Hall wrote a paper entitled *The Question of the Submarine Menace*[22] and Fisher pursued the matter with enhanced vigour, discussing it with Balfour and starting on a new paper himself. His draft was ready in May and he sent copies to Balfour, Hankey (who was now Secretary of the CID), Jellicoe and Sydenham. Balfour answered:

'You know how long, and how earnestly, I have preached the case of submarines. The question that really troubles me is not whether our submarines could render the enemy's position intolerable, but whether their submarines could render our position untenable. If it be true (a) that a large type of submarine can, so far as its seagoing qualities, etc. are concerned, blockade a hostile port for very long periods, and (b) that it cannot be driven off either by other submarines or by any other known method of attack, how are we to prevent a blockade of *all* our ports in time of war? In other words, what is to prevent the Germans sealing up every port, military or commercial, round our whole coast – and this whatever our superiority in battleships and cruisers might happen to be? That's the question *I* want answered!'[23]

Fisher persuaded Balfour that submarines 'must increase the hazards of that very hazardous operation' of invasion, and Balfour agreed that Germany's short seaboard 'renders it easier for us to blockade them than for them to blockade us', but pointed out that the consequences were greater for Britain as an island than for mainland Germany and she might be surrounded by seas in which no enemy's battleship could live, nor enemy troops cross, but which would yet be as little under her control, for military or commercial purposes, as if she were the inferior maritime power. 'If there was any chance of such an extreme hypothesis being realised, we should not only be useless allies to any friendly power on the continent, but we should have the utmost difficulty in keeping ourselves alive.'[24] Fisher answered that he was preparing a further memorandum on these points, and was obtaining information from Krupp himself, through an intermediary, but *'The appalling thing is our admirals are so blind to these developments!* but it has always been so'. The Admiralty had recognized the objections to petrol engines in submarines but since Fisher's departure there had been, as Marder said, 'No driving force at the Admiralty'. In June, 1913, he wrote to Jellicoe that Krupps were making hundreds of submarine engines

> *'of a far larger power than ours in our submarines.* . . . I am extremely anxious about the Admiralty development of the submarine. *The more I hear, the more d——d fools they seem to be!* I've written a memorandum on the subject, but if I sent it to Winston, it would mean open war with the Admiralty, so I withhold it. The most fatal error imaginable would be to put steam engines in a submarine. The "oversea" submarine now building by Vickers should not be exceeded in size, or you won't be able to use them in the North Sea, *besides other vital reasons'.*[25]

And to Hopwood:

> 'Kindly mark my words that the coming German submarines (with a radius of action extending to the Argentine, and a 4-inch gun) will effectually blockade all our principal ports. . . . *The oil engine will govern all sea fighting, and all sea fighting is going to be governed by submarines,*

and yet like d——d fools we are only spending as much money on them as the Germans and we are behind them in the oil engine, and so like the French we are fatally hankering after steam engines in submarines.'[26]

There was still doubt as to how submarines should be employed. Some, like Admiral Sir Percy Scott, the greatest gunnery expert in the Navy, thought they presaged the end of the big ship. Balfour raised this in August and Fisher pointed out that the 'root of the matter is surface speed . . . which will enable it to overhaul or circumvent a Battle Fleet . . . This speed can be obtained at the present time and in the immediate future by no other path except those of size and steam'. Although he enthusiastically agreed that 'a fast Battle Fleet which can be accompanied always by submarines under all circumstances would possess an overwhelming fighting advantage', he had already stated his objection to steam (and was to be proved right in the disastrous K and M classes).

He envisaged another type of submarine with great endurance armed with 'a 3-inch gun and a large supply of small-size Whitehead torpedoes (say 10-inch)' for trade protection, but reminded Balfour that 'the latest approved design of submarine is about the limit of size for use in the North Sea to enable her to dive under a dreadnought in those shallow waters. Also be it remembered very distinctly that the increasing size of the submarine is solely and wholly dependent upon the development of its engine . . . due to requirements of weight, space, and engine foundation.'

The most important point raised by Balfour, however, was one Fisher had already considered. Regarding blockade by submarine he asked, 'What would be the effect on freights produced by the knowledge that the approaches of our half dozen chief ports were infested by submarines?' He had not hitherto contemplated unrestricted submarine warfare and was primarily thinking of the impact on freight and insurance rates. 'Should we not, among other things, have to reconsider our views about the capture (or rather the destruction, for a submarine could not capture) of private property at sea?' [27]

Fisher suggested

> 'diverting our commerce to our far western ports in war time, and developing the port and railway facilities of such harbours as Plymouth, Falmouth, Bristol, Channel ports, Fishguard, Holyhead, etc . . . Again it will be impossible for submarines to deal with merchant ships in accordance with international law. Is it presumed that they will disregard this and sink any vessel heading for an English commercial port? . . . No means can be suggested at present of meeting it except by reprisals. All that would be known would be that a certain steamer did not arrive or that some of her boats [had been] picked up with a few survivors to tell the tale.'[28]

Against this Jellicoe wrote a marginal note: 'I cannot conceive that submarines will sink merchant ships without warning.'! Sydenham was of a like view: 'I cannot believe that submarines will sink unarmed ships and I do not see how they can easily convoy them into port. In more barbarous days, unarmed ships were not summarily sunk, and modern sentiment could not stand such proceedings.'[29] However, Sydenham advocated the most realistic method of dealing with submarines yet postulated: 'An aeroplane sights a submarine on the surface. It can be over it before submergence is complete. If it can skim low enough to drop a high explosive charge over the submarine, the latter is doomed. If located with sufficient accuracy the submarine's course under water can be followed. An accurately dropped high explosive with delayed fuze would end the career of the submarine.'[30] In 1903 A.K.Wilson had suggested the use of nets to catch submarines, when they could be destroyed by 'depth bombs', carrying 300 pounds of TNT detonated by a hydrostatic mechanism (depth charges). But Sydenham was over-optimistic, for contemporary aircraft were too slow to be over a submarine before submergence was complete unless the submarine had failed to sight them, and one 'high explosive charge' would not do the damage he suggested. Tracking submarines under water was only possible when near the surface in very calm and clear water.

Churchill got wind of Fisher's paper, which was prepared for the CID, and which Fisher assiduously kept from him, knowing that he would manipulate it, but he extracted a copy from Keyes, now Commodore, Submarines, and wrote indignantly to Fisher, 'Surely this is the very letter or paper about which you spoke to me some time ago, and which you said you were going to show me?' Fisher wrote to Jellicoe from Marienbad:

> 'He presses me for the third time to go and stay with him in *Enchantress, but I'm not going!* I don't care about being mixed up with the job lot he gets on board with him such as Custance & Co., and also he's playing up to certain people who don't have my sympathies at all, never have, and never will! . . . He said to me before I came here, "did I object to Custance?" I told him I did, and all his retrograde opinions and d——d underhand tactics in the past in association with Beresford (all of whose letters he wrote for him in concert with Sturdee!).'[31]

In November the paper was ready and he passed it to Julian Corbett, asking him to 'make it a work of art, *as the subject deserves it!* . . . When I became First Sea Lord, everyone thought me a lunatic for developing the submarine, and I had to hide the money in the Estimates. In consequence we now have 3,000 trained submarine officers and men, and are 2 keels to one against Germany and MORE SO. *Its's wonderful what they did in these last manoeuvres!*'[32] Corbett did more than improve Fisher's style, making several suggestions on content, adding that he too believed the enemy 'would not incur the odium of sinking merchant ships out of hand'.

In December, 1913, the paper was complete and a copy went to Churchill, who on 1 January, 1914, having 'read and re-read with the closest attention the brilliant and most valuable paper on submarines which you have drawn up *for the Admiralty*' (my italics) he had asked his naval colleagues 'to study it forthwith'. But he went on: 'There are a few points on which I am not convinced. Of these the greatest is the question of the use of submarines to sink merchant vessels. I do not believe that this would ever be done by a civilised Power. . . . [in retaliation] it would be justifiable, and indeed necessary . . . to spread pestilence, poison the water supply of great cities . . . unthinkable propositions and the excellence of your paper is, to some extent, marred by the prominence assigned to them.'[33] Like Balfour, Churchill confused the unpalatable with the impossible. Fisher had said the only available countermeasure was reprisal; so it was, but this did not imply that Fisher thought in such terms any more than he would have 'boiled prisoners in oil'. Fisher fiercely underlined the last sentence of Churchill's letter. Keyes too, believed unrestricted submarine warfare 'impossible and unthinkable'.[34]

Churchill agreed with one feature of Fisher's paper : 'Like you, I am disquieted about our submarine development and it is clear that in the near future we must make an effort on a greatly increased scale to counter the enormous programmes in which Germany has been indulging for the last 6 years.'[35] But there was little sense of urgency in the Admiralty's collective mind. Fisher wrote to Jellicoe at the end of the month: 'I told him [Churchill] last week for the twentieth time since he became First Lord that the weak point of his administration is the neglect of submarines; four years ago to-day I left the Admiralty, *and then we had 12 more submarines than we have now,* and the Germans were at zero; now they are fulfilling their programme of having SEVENTY-TWO, whilst 19 of ours are in their last stages!'[36] Mackay says Fisher's usual complaint about the Germans having more submarines than the British is a 'misleading line of thought; . . . German commerce could best be throttled by British surface vessels. More British submarines would not do much to counteract the U-boats'.[37] But large numbers of submarines in the Heligoland Bight and off the German bases would have menaced the High Sea Fleet and achieved close blockade.

Under Churchill, little research was done in the Admiralty into countermeasures and less to providing escort vessels to institute convoy. Fisher remained virtually the only man who believed Germany capable of unrestricted submarine warfare. Impatient at its cool reception, he sent a copy of his paper to Asquith and in a covering letter wrote:

'In my opinion the statements therein contained are irrefutable. . . . I venture to ask your earnest attention thereto. Those who lecture in International Law say the civilised world will hold up its hand in horror at such acts of barbarism as a submarine sinking its prey, but yet an enemy can lay mines without outraging propriety! After all, submarines can exercise discretion – mines can't! It is patent to all that the operation of "visit" is attended with grave risk nowadays. A few worthless tramp steamers sent out, accompanied by one or two submarines illustrate this! Up comes the cruiser to "visit" the tramps, the submarine would give the *coup-de-grâce* to the cruiser. Therefore, when declaring a blockade it will have to be stated that "owing to danger now attending the process of 'visit and search' no passes will be issued, and any vessel breaking blockade, inwards or outwards will be sunk".'[38]

This is precisely what happened in due course. The idea of 'stop and search' involved warships stopping in mid-ocean while an inspection party boarded the merchant ship to satisfy themselves that contraband of war was not being carried. This was fine before the age of submarines, but wholly impracticable afterwards. But Asquith took little interest. As Mackay says, his copy of the paper 'is unsullied by any mark or comment'![39] On 25 May, 1914, Fisher wrote to Jellicoe, 'The Prime Minister has asked me to dine with him, but I've declined. I let fly at him about submarines and he is evidently *greatly moved! But he entreated me to say nothing! Burn this.*'[40] Indeed, nothing happened at all. Had Fisher still been at the Admiralty, no doubt vigorous efforts would have been made to devise methods of dealing with enemy submarines. As it was, with a succession of unconcerned First Sea Lords, from whom authority had been removed by a domineering amateur, it was decided that zig-zagging, high speed and destroyer screens would protect the fleet and this was all that was required. Nothing was done to protect merchant ships; no arrangements were made to reintroduce convoy, no programme of construction of escort vessels was embarked upon. '*It is not invasion we have to fear but starvation,*' wrote Fisher.

When the Royal Commission on Oil Fuel was disbanded at the end of February, 1914, the members signed a tribute to Fisher expressing their deep sense of the dignity, conspicuous ability, and impartiality with which he had conducted the proceedings, and the national value of his services.[41]

The Commission had far-reaching consequences. It was oil fuel that permitted the construction of the 'super-dreadnoughts' *Queen Elizabeth, Warspite, Barham, Valiant* and *Malaya,* for the weight of coal they would have had to carry to give them acceptable endurance and speed would have been prohibitive.

But Churchill's attempts to take personal control of the Navy led to great dangers, loss of morale and bitterness. This was exemplified when Churchill visited Sheerness where lay HMS *Hermes,* headquarters ship for the Royal Naval Air Service, under Captain Gerald Vivian, who had given his decision on the use of some ground on the shores of the Medway. A young lieutenant had other views, and with crass stupidity, expressed them to the First Lord, who sent for Vivian and told him the lieutenant's arguments were to be accepted. Vivian would have been supported by the entire Navy (except the young officer!) had he point blank refused the First Lord's order for which there was no authority under King's Regulations. Vivian sent for the lieutenant and told him in blunt language how improper his conduct had been, whereupon he told Vivian that 'if he did not get what he wanted he would write to the First Lord, and that he [the First Lord] had told him so'. The Captain complained indignantly to Admiral Sir Richard Poore, Commander-in-Chief, the Nore, who reported the matter to Jellicoe (as Second Sea Lord responsible for personnel, and also at that time, for the RNAS). Churchill heard of the correspondence, possibly from the young officer, and compounding his offence, demanded of Jellicoe that he send him immediately any communication on the subject from Poore. When Poore's letter arrived Jellicoe felt that the strong terms used were such as to exacerbate the situation and returned it to Poore, suggesting in a private letter, some amendments. Somehow Churchill discovered this and, as if the matter was not already bad enough, arranged for the Post Office to search for the letter and return it direct to him. Having read Jellicoe's private letter, though unbelievably claiming not, he announced his intention to order Poore to haul down his flag, which further exceeded his authority, since this was a matter for the Board as a whole. Jellicoe assured Churchill that in that event he would resign and make his reasons public. The Third and Fourth Sea Lords, Sir Archibald Moore (who had relieved Briggs) and Pakenham, supported Jellicoe and also threatened resignation. All four Sea Lords signed their resignations and so did Poore, but Battenberg was talked out of it by the persuasive First Lord. It is said that Churchill resolved the matter by informing the Sea Lords that criticisms of his methods would result in his own resignation. If so it is curious that they did not persist and challenge his threat, for it seems more likely that the resulting political storm would have forced his resignation, and by maintaining their resolve, they might have induced the First Lord to take up his legitimate position. As it was, Poore was persuaded to withdraw his letter and, astonishingly, express his regret. Vast pressure was put on him not to resign. The lieutenant was lectured by the First Sea Lord, who told him his conduct had been improper (his discharge from the Navy might have been more appropriate). Sir Francis Hopwood, the Additional Civil Lord, afterwards wrote: 'Winston would not be flattered if he knew the arguments used by the Naval Lords (sic) to keep the Commander-in-Chief from going. They were in short that he (Churchill) was so much off his head over the whole business that Poore need take no notice of it! We thought Poore would ask for a Court Martial, in which case the whole business would have turned on the accusation of the Commander-in-Chief against the First Lord, and the latter would really have been on his defence.'[42]

The story leaked and the Press and Opposition took issue with Churchill.

The Globe wrote: 'The methods of Mr. Churchill are wholly unfitted for the great Service, of which for the time being, he is the responsible head'.

But for sheer arrogance it would be hard to excel his letter to Rear-Admiral Arthur Limpus, who in early December, 1913, wrote as head of the British Mission in Turkey, in a personal letter to the First Lord, an account of the progress of negotiations with the Turks for certain defence contracts in fierce competition against the Germans. They had continued for over two months, were complicated and of vital importance since they were likely to decide for years to come whether Germany or Britain predominated in influence over the Turks. He tried to reduce the complexities to as brief an explanation as possible, and Churchill was apparently unable to understand them, though there was no necessity for him to concern himself personally in the detail. To Limpus, a man of 50, who 'had been in the Navy since Churchill was two years old', he wrote like a pompous schoolmaster:

> 'I find it necessary to criticise the general style and presentment of your letters. A flag officer writing to a member of the Board of Admiralty ought to observe a proper seriousness and formality. The letters should be well written or typed on good paper; the sentences should be complete and follow the regular English form. Mere jottings of passing impressions hurriedly put together without sequence, and very often with marked confusion, are calculated to give an impression the reverse of that which is desirable. You do not do yourself justice in these matters. No one can be so busy as not to be able to cast a letter to a superior in proper form. You should make up your mind beforehand exactly what you mean to say, and study to say it in the clearest and shortest way, if necessary redrafting your letter. In your latest communication three letters appear to be mixed up without beginning or end. Knowing the good work which you did in South Africa and your zeal in your Turkish mission, I am able to dispel from my mind the impression which the chaotic character of your correspondence would otherwise convey.'[43]

Even the amenable Bridgeman found Churchill's interference unacceptable. Without consulting the naval members, he issued orders and sent telegrams to the fleet. He sent for anyone in the Admiralty and discussed details of their work without mention to their superiors. Bridgeman had hesitated to accept his post in the first place; but within ten months he and the rest of the Board were in strident discord with their political head, whose vehement dogmatism and firm belief that he knew more than the professionals exasperated them. The First Lord used peremptory language that outraged his colleagues so much that the whole Board threatened resignation and Bridgeman told Churchill in unvarnished language that, unless he changed his attitude, they would all resign, that the First Lord was not empowered to give a single order outside the Admiralty building without the consent of the Board, and the manner in which he addressed his colleagues was improper. Churchill fought back, but Bridgeman threatened to take the matter first to the Prime Minister and if necessary to the King, whereupon Churchill, to Bridgeman's embarrassment, burst into tears, which he explained was due to ill health. The ruse worked, and Bridgeman eased the pressure.

A month later, on leave at his home in Yorkshire, Bridgeman caught a chill, with a touch of bronchitis. He had recently had appendicitis, and this was just the opportunity Churchill wanted. Bridgeman was not as acquiescent as he had anticipated and on 28 November, 1912, he told the King that Bridgeman's health was breaking down, writing to the admiral a letter of sympathy in which he said he had been 'meaning to write to you for some time about your health which causes me concern, both as a colleague and a friend. . . . I have seen how heavily the strain of your great office has told upon you and I know that only your high sense of duty and your consideration for me have enabled you successfully to overcome your strong inclination to retire.'[44] Gretton describes this as a 'tactful' letter to a man 'with whom he had no specific quarrel'.[45] Perhaps 'crafty' would be a better word, and certainly the quarrel was heated.

Bridgeman had no such inclination. He assured Churchill that he was now fully recovered, but added that he would think the matter over. Churchill immediately wrote to the King asking for approval for Bridgeman's promotion to Admiral of the Fleet and for Prince Louis of Battenberg to succeed him. Bridgeman's doctor had passed him fit and before he had received Churchill's letter calling for his resignation he wrote to the First Lord that he would return to the Admiralty in the new year. But Churchill insisted on his resignation, which took effect on 2 December, and denied flatly that there had been any conflict between the two. The matter became public; threatening letters were exchanged between the two and Churchill, with astonishing ignorance of the King's constitutional position, asked him to intervene, which naturally he refused to do. 'There is absolutely no truth in the idea that any difference in policy or procedure or any divergence or incident between us influenced me at all. Honestly, I only thought about your health and the European situation and what would happen if war began and you broke down.'[46] This was transparently untrue, for a newspaper correspondent found the Admiral in vigorous health, riding to hounds three days a week. The matter became a Party political one, leading to heated debates in the Commons, Beresford and Bonar Law fighting on behalf of Bridgeman and attacking the First Lord unmercifully. Beresford described Bridgeman's treatment as 'a disgraceful affair', Churchill having threatened to quote from a private letter from Bridgeman to Battenberg, obtained by Beatty. There followed an increasingly bitter correspondenc between the two men. Beresford was later to describe Churchill as 'a Lilliput Napoleon – a man with an unbalanced mind, an egomaniac – whose one absorbing thought was personal vindictiveness.'[47]

The King approved the appointment of Battenberg, who proved another rather ineffectual man (Beatty thought him lazy), though he was well thought of in naval circles for his ability as a commander afloat. The affair did the Navy no good, morale being further damaged, but this was by no means the worst. When Jellicoe became Second Sea Lord in the new Board he was maddened by 'Churchill's meddling'.

Fisher urged Churchill to maintain the British lead by increasing gunpower. In 1909 he had introduced the 13.5-inch guns in place of the 12-inch guns of *Dreadnought*. This was a far bigger step forward than it might seem, for the shell of the 12-inch gun of *Dreadnought* weighed 850 pounds, while that of the 13.5-inch gun weighed 1,400 pounds, over 40% more than the biggest German projectile. Increased weight of projectile resulted in smaller loss of velocity during traverse to the target, so the projectile arrived at the target with higher velocity, the range was substantially increased, and the heavier bursting charge did more damage to the enemy. The 'Bellerophons', laid down in 1906-07, (virtually repeat 'Dreadnoughts') had a main armament of ten 12-inch guns, whose broadside weighed a total of 6,800 pounds, whereas the German *Nassau*, built in the same period with twelve 11-inch guns, had a broadside of 5,280 pounds. *Orion*, laid down in November, 1909, had ten 13.5-inch guns, with a broadside of 12,500 pounds and the *Kaiser* of the same year had ten 12-inch guns and a broadside of 8,600 pounds. Thus Britain's lead was not confined to numbers of ships or endurance but the effectiveness of their armament. Fisher and Jellicoe had fought a lonely battle to introduce the 13.5-inch gun against massive opposition. Twenty years before, 13.5-inch guns had been used, but had been unsuccessful due to excessive wear in the barrel caused by the large charge, and it was this that created the opposition. But the new gun had longer barrels, which, with slower burning powder, reduced the wear to an acceptable level, further advancing the lead *Dreadnought* had gained.

Fisher urged Churchill to progress to the next stage, the 15-inch gun, with a projectile weighing 1,950 pounds, giving the 'Queen Elizabeths', with their eight guns, a broadside of 15,600 pounds, whereas *Kronprinz* (renamed *Kronprinz Wilhelm* in 1918) had ten 12-inch guns of little more than half. Higher speeds gave ships with long range the ability to open fire outside enemy range, and to withdraw or close at will. The 'Queen Elizabeths' were designed for a speed of 25 knots; *Kronprinz* for only 21. Thus the 'failures' at Jutland were not due to insufficient accuracy, weight of armament or range, but to badly manufactured armour-piercing shells, which failed to penetrate the superior Krupp armour of the German ships. The naval historian who describes this as 'pure Beatty-ite red herring' should think again! The Royal Arsenal, in testing shells (not the Admiralty as another asserts), fired them at right angles to the armour; but in action, shells have to penetrate at an oblique angle, (for example a shell fired at 12-inch armour, striking at 70° to the surface must penetrate 35 inches of plate). In 1910 Jellicoe, when Controller, arranged for HMS *Edinburgh* an obsolete ship, to be fitted with modern armour plates and had firing trials carried out at her with 12-inch armour-piercing shells, as a result of which the Director of Naval Ordnance, on 18 October, 1910, requested the joint services Ordnance Committee to design armour-piercing shells for guns 12-inches and above which would penetrate thick armour at oblique angles. Jellicoe shortly afterwards left the Admiralty for a seagoing command and no action was taken until Dreyer became DNO in 1917, when efficient armour-piercing shell was provided to the Grand Fleet. The Germans, who were at the receiving end, testified to the magnificent shooting of the Battle Fleet at Jutland, Scheer stating in his dispatch that 'they fired with remarkable rapidity and accuracy'. When the range opened out, Scheer was at times unable to return the accurate fire of the 15-inch guns of the four 'Barhams' which were out of his range. Four salvos from *Iron Duke* made a number of hits on *Wiesbaden* at a range of 11,000 yards. Of 43 rounds fired in under five minutes by *Iron Duke* at *König* in the night action, the Germans confirmed there were seven or eight hits.

After the war Jellicoe discussed the subject with Commander Paschen, gunnery officer of *Lützow*, who stated that against armour, British shell burst outside and had no effect. Soon after the battle, Dreyer had written officially to Jellicoe: 'We have many people engaged trying to make out that our AP shell, filled with Lyddite, which burst half-way through the plate are just as good as the German shell filled Trotyl, with delay-action fuse, which burst their shell well inside our ships, It seems a pity not to be willing to learn.' [48] A Swedish officer said that he had been told by German officers that the British heavy shell broke up on their armour and the effect was *lächerlich* (laughable), and Tirpitz in his memoirs wrote of 'secret' German armour-piercing shell.

Randolph Churchill falls into a common error:

> 'The *Dreadnought* gave the Royal Navy an important advantage over the German Fleet, but it also weakened the overall superiority which rested on the total number of ships of all sizes and armaments. It made the German battleships obsolete; it did the same thing for all existing British battleships, and we could never gain so great a preponderance as we had with the old battleships.'[49]

This was the Beresford philosophy; it was comparable to saying that ships of the Nelson era in sufficient numbers could defeat *Dreadnought*. Between *Dreadnought* of 1906 and Churchill's accession Fisher had masterminded a programme of 20 battleships, the latest with a broadside of 14,000 pounds, nine battlecruisers, the last with a designed speed of 28 knots and a broadside of 11,200 pounds. During this period Germany had built sixteen battleships, the latest with a speed of $21^1/_2$ knots and a broadside of 9,040 pounds and five battlecruisers, the last (*Seydlitz*) with a speed of 27 knots and a 6,720-pound broadside. However, Randolph Churchill misquotes his father: 'This tremendous new Navy, for it was nothing less, was a providential aid to the

Admiralty when more than two years later the real German submarine attack began. Its creation on such a scale is one of the greatest services that the nation has owed to the genius and energy of Lord Fisher.'[50] This extract referred to Fisher's building programme in 1914–15, not his earlier period in office, and there was nothing 'providential' about it; its aim was Fisher's strategic concept.

Fisher pressed Churchill to maintain the momentum. On 13 December, 1911, he wrote to Jellicoe, then Controller:

> 'My heart is set on a new type and it is practicable.
> 'Cost: £1,995,000.
> Speed: 30 knots.
> 'Armament: Eight 15-inch guns and 10 submerged tubes. *Reduce armour* and let 'SIZE AND SUBDIVISION' be immensely developed. . . . I hear from Elswick [Ordnance Co.] no anxiety whatever in manufacturing 15-inch guns without a trial gun. *But, really, speed is absolutely everything!* . . . speed enables you to fight WHEN you like, WHERE you like, and HOW you like! And this armament . . . makes an increase of *63* percent in gun-power! Also I strongly advocate oil alone! Consider the reduction in personnel and the increased radius of action and no going back to harbour to coal! *The advantages are prodigious.* . . . Do ram this down Winston's throat.'[51]

This is almost an exact description of *Queen Elizabeth*, yet another product of Fisher's ingenuity. Yet Churchill did not hesitate to claim for himself credit for the introduction of the 15-inch gun:

> 'I immediately sought to go one size better. I mentioned this to Lord Fisher at Reigate, and he hurled himself into its advocacy with tremendous passion. "Nothing less than the 15-inch gun could be looked at for all the battleships and battlecruisers of the new programme. To achieve the supply of this gun was the equivalent of a great victory at sea; to shrink from the endeavour was treason to the Empire. What was it that enabled Jack Johnson to knock out his opponents? It was the big punch. And where were those miserable men with navies of futile popguns crowding up their ships?" No one who has not experienced it has any idea of the passion and eloquence of this old lion when thoroughly roused on a technical question.'[52]

But Churchill had been only four days in office. 'Quite ignorant of naval affairs', his unsubtle inference that the idea was his own and that he had, in those four days, considered in detail all the immense variety of highly specialized problems for the tactician, the engineer, the gunmaker, the ammunition manufacturer and especially the naval architect, is the height of absurdity. Nor can he have had discussions with the experts and put forward their views, for

Rear-Admiral G.H.Moore, who had taken over as DNO from Bacon, when confronted with the proposal, had serious misgivings, advocating the construction of a test mounting and trials lasting about a year, necessitating arming the 'Queen Elizabeths' with the well-tried 13.5-inch guns, with which there was every probability that Germany would have caught up. The idea came from Fisher, despite Churchill's transparent claim, 'I think it necessary to place on record the fact that my sole naval adviser on every measure taken prior to the declaration of war was the First Sea Lord.'[53]

The denial of his mentor by praising him for his 'passion and eloquence when thoroughly roused *on a technical question*' (my italics) implied that Fisher's talents were confined to technicalities, lacking ability in tactics and strategy, which Churchill and Fisher's enemies successfully propagated, deceiving many naval historians – a good example of Churchill's rhetorical sophism, for the whole concept of the 'Queen Elizabeths', like *Dreadnought*, was based on tactical and strategic considerations.

Now the problems were borne in on Churchill: 'The ordnance Board were set to work and they rapidly produced a design. Armstrongs were consulted in deadly secrecy and they undertook to execute it. I had anxious conferences with these experts, with whose science I was of course wholly unacquainted. . . . For, after all, if the guns had failed, the ships would have been fearfully marred. I hardly remember to have had more anxiety about any administrative decision as this. I went back to Lord Fisher. He was steadfast and even violent. So I hardened my heart and took the plunge. The whole outfit of guns was ordered forthwith.'[54]

The original idea had been for ships armed with ten 13.5-inch guns, providing a broadside of 12,500 pounds. This was now to be ten 15-inch guns and a speed of 21 knots. Fisher urged, and Churchill accepted, that eight 15-inch guns, providing a broadside of 15,600 pounds, an increase of nearly 25%, would result in saving in weight allowing engines capable of achieving 25 knots, sufficient to overtake the enemy and cross the bows of his leading ship – 'crossing the T'. *This* was the fast division.

None of these facts prevented Randolph Churchill from claiming for his father credit for all the progress made on the advice of his cicerone:

> 'The 15-inch gun, the Fast Division and oil were the three major advances which the First Lord initiated and over whose development he presided. But he also inherited one legacy from Lord Fisher, the *Dreadnought*, which had become in the public mind the principle advance in naval technology and guarantee of British naval superiority. This was an exaggeration, as the existence of these 'all big-gun battleships' at once made the smaller British as well as German warships less effective.'[55]

Thus did the Churchills join Fisher's detractors with a flawed argument, even sometimes repeated today.

But as Marder says: 'It took still greater courage for the First Lord on Fisher's advice but against the advice of responsible experts, to order all the 15-inch guns at once instead of waiting for a trial gun to be constructed and tested before placing orders for the lot. This would have meant losing a year.'[56]

It would also have meant losing the war.

3

THE WICKED FOLLY OF IT ALL.

'In the month of June, 1914, a group of Englishmen, who for ten years, amid ridicule and contumely, had foretold a world war, became suddenly aware that the pretext had been found by the rulers, soldiers and professors of modern Germany.'[1]

In that brilliant June there was rejoicing at Kiel, where the dredging and widening of the canal was complete and a glorious celebration accompanied the ceremonial reopening by the Kaiser, whose yacht *Hohenzollern* cut the ribbon across the lock. Four great modern dreadnoughts and three cruisers represented Britain at the round of parties, official calls, dances, sports matches and gun salutes that marked the occasion, while each navy tried to learn as much about the others as possible.

On 28 June celebrations came to an abrupt halt. The Archduke Franz Ferdinand, heir to the Austrian throne, was assassinated by a Serb from Bosnia. Austria looked with suspicion at Serbia, who would dearly have liked to regain her lost province. Russia had proclaimed herself protector of the Slavs and herein lay the real danger. In 1909 Germany had assured Austria-Hungary of support, but when she now asked the Kaiser what position he would adopt in a conflict with Serbia, he believed Russia would not join in and assured her of support whatever occurred, since termed a 'blank cheque'.

As Esher wrote, 'During the three years preceding the War, that odd Ministerial breed generated by English faction professed opinions cynically adverse to the group to which Fisher and Lord Roberts, Henry Wilson and Douglas Haig belonged. The party then in power were never tired of declaiming against these men as thinkers who thought wrong, for it was the strange passion of liberalism from 1900 to 1914, to dub as militarist a man who ventured to allude to the German Menace, and who urged that the nation should prepare to meet it.'[2]

The German High Command saw little prospect of war with Britain. It was war with Russia they wanted at this juncture, and British intervention in continental war would be of small consequence. The *Admiralstab* had a different view. They knew of Fisher's ideas of a 'Copenhagen' and believed that the German fleet could not be absent from home waters on a planned cruise to Norway. The Kaiser ordered Ingenohl, the German Commander-in-Chief, to take the fleet into the Baltic and prepare for an attack on Russia. Ingenohl objected: 'When I pointed out the danger of England taking part in the war, and the consequent necessity of having, at all events, the battleships in the North Sea, the Kaiser answered emphatically that there was no question whatever of England's intervention.'[3]

Austria sent an ultimatum to Serbia on 23 July, which Asquith described as 'bullying and humiliating', with which Serbia 'cannot possibly comply', demanding an answer in 48 hours. Serbia appeared ready to compromise, but Austria, with confidence of German support, was resolved upon humiliating surrender. She declared war on Serbia on 28 July and two days later Belgrade was occupied. Germany sent an ultimatum to Russia on 31 July and the following day declared war. To avoid war on two fronts, the Schlieffen plan demanded prior defeat of France by invasion through Belgium and, as France showed no sign of abrogating her treaty with Russia, Germany also declared war on her on 3 August.

On 25 July St Petersburg had appealed to Britain to take a firm stand alongside Russia and France, urging that this would avoid war. Asquith was preoccupied with the Irish Home Rule Bill and the necessity of keeping his cabinet together. With no Cabinet Secretariat and no agenda, matters were raised at meetings on an *ad hoc* basis, so others were unable to brief themselves. Germany's belief in British neutrality was realistic; two-thirds of the Cabinet favoured it, Asquith, Grey and Churchill leading the minority. Few knew of Britain's commitment to France, and Germany announced on 2 August that she intended to march through Belgium. Britain was one of the signatories of the 1839 guarantee of the neutrality of Belgium and the next day sent an ultimatum to Germany expiring at midnight. Germany declared war on Belgium and no reply was received to the British ultimatum. Only Morley and Burns resigned.

It was remarkably fortunate that, instead of the usual annual manoeuvres, it had been decided in 1914, for purely economic reasons, to carry out test mobilization of all reserves, and the ships, now fully manned, were assembled for a great naval review. The operation began on 12 July and five days later the largest assembly of ships ever seen lay at Spithead: 24 dreadnoughts, 35 pre-dreadnoughts. and 123 smaller vessels. After the review, on 20 July the ships began to disperse, the three main fleets taking part in combined exercises, and on 24 July the Admiralty signalled Sir George Callaghan, Commander-in-Chief, that the 'first fleet squadrons will all disperse on Monday 27th in accordance with your approved programme'.

Grey records that on the Saturday Churchill suggested that the fleet should not be demobilized, and told the First Lord that he agreed. Churchill had planned to spend Sunday 26 July at Cromer with his family and arranged a special operator in the telegraph office to ensure a continuous service. At 9 o'clock 'the next morning' he telephoned the First Sea Lord and there were no developments; he asked Battenberg to telephone him at 12 noon and went on to the beach with his children. At noon Battenberg told him 'various items of news that had come in from different capitals, none, however, of decisive importance, but all tending to a rise in temperature'.

'I asked him whether all the reservists had already been dismissed. He told me they had. I decided to return to London. I told him I would be with him at nine, and that meanwhile he should do whatever was necessary. Prince Louis awaited me at the Admiralty. . . . The First Sea Lord told me that in accordance with our conversation he had told the fleet not to disperse.'[4]

Dudley de Chair, Churchill's naval secretary, relates a different story:

'On Saturday, July 25, the Austrian ultimatum to Serbia was fixed to expire. The Ministers of the Crown, including Asquith, . . . Grey . . . and Churchill, had left London and gone away for the week-end. Prince Louis, First Sea Lord, remained at the Admiralty. He wrote to a friend the following letter during that critical time: "Ministers with their week-end holidays are incorrigible. Things looked pretty bad on Saturday, on which at 6 pm the Ultimatum expired. Asquith, Grey, Churchill and all the rest left London. I sat here all Sunday, reading all the telegrams from Embassies as they arrived. On Monday morning the big fleet at Portland had orders to disperse, demobilise and give leave. I took it upon myself to countermand everything by telegraph on Sunday afternoon. When the Ministers hurried back late that evening they cordially approved my action." '[5]

Battenberg cancelled the demobilization, restricted leave and ordered all ships to complete with coal. The Navy was ready for war when, on 2 August, Germany marched into Belgium, expecting to take Paris within a month.

The results of the Long Peace and the inexperience of many admirals now became apparent. When Fisher had written so strongly to Churchill objecting to the appointments of Milne, Custance and Meux his judgment was once again demonstrated. In the event the appointments of Meux and Custance did not matter, but that of Milne was to influence the whole course of the war.

On Monday 27 July Churchill sent to all Commanders-in-Chief a signal preparing them for all eventualities: 'This is not the warning Telegram, but European political situation makes war between Triple Entente and Triple Alliance Powers by no means impossible. Be prepared to shadow possible hostile men-of-war and consider dispositions of ships under your command from this point of view.'[6]

The *Admiralstab* had dispatched to the Eastern Mediterranean, under the command of the brilliant and courageous Rear-Admiral Wilhelm Souchon, the battlecruiser *Goeben* armed with ten 11-inch guns, accompanied by the light cruiser *Breslau* with twelve 4.1-inch guns. The former was designed for a speed of 28 knots in a short run over the measured mile, though it is unlikely that the stokers could long have sustained such speeds in the summer heat of the Mediterranean. *Breslau* was designed for 27 knots. *Goeben,* suffering serious boiler problems, was refitting at Pola. Souchon cut the work short in mid-July and, with *Breslau* in company, sailed south out of the trap of the Adriatic.

Milne's command was more than adequate to deal with them. He had the three battlecruisers, *Inflexible* (flag), *Indomitable* and *Indefatigable,* each armed with eight 12-inch guns and designed for 25.5 knots, though they too had all achieved 28 knots, and *Indomitable* maintained 27 knots at the Battle of the Dogger Bank.[7] He had the 1st Cruiser Squadron under Troubridge consisting of the armoured cruisers *Defence* (four 9.2-inch, ten 7.5-inch guns), *Black Prince, Duke of Edinburgh* (six 9.2-inch and ten 6-inch each) and *Warrior* (six 9.2-inch and four 7.5-inch) together with the four light cruisers *Chatham, Dublin, Gloucester* and *Weymouth* and a flotilla of destroyers.

Milne went to Malta to coal and store, where, on 29 July, he received the official Warning Telegram, followed the next day by a further signal from Churchill, explaining the probable line-up of the powers and continuing:

> 'It is especially important that your squadron should not be seriously engaged with Austrian ships before we know what Italy will do. Your first task should be to aid the French in the transportation of their African Army by covering and if possible bringing to action individual fast German ships, particularly *Goeben,* who may interfere with that transportation. You will be notified by telegraph when you may consult with the French Admiral. Do not at this stage be brought to action against superior forces, except in combination with the French, as part of a general battle. The speed of your Squadrons is sufficient to enable you to choose your moment. We shall hope later to reinforce the Mediterranean, and you must husband your forces at the outset.'[8]

The version of this message that appears in *The World Crisis* is heavily edited, though it changes the sense little. Churchill claims that 'So far as the English language may serve as a vehicle of thought, the words employed appear to express the intentions we had formed.'[9] Many might think them verbose and, addressed to a commander-in-chief, unnecessarily detailed, especially the penultimate sentence. Packed with ambiguities and uncertainties, this message contravened the first rules of naval signalling – brevity, accuracy and clarity, especially when wireless was unreliable, many phrases having to be repeated. Milne's actions were immediately circumscribed. He was not to risk an encounter with the Austrian ships; did this mean he was to keep away from the

Adriatic? He was not to be brought to action by superior forces; how does one define superior forces? If the whole of Milne's fleet encountered them, German ships would not be superior, but against the light cruisers alone they would be. Souchon might attack the French troopships, but Milne was not to contact the French Admiral. He was to 'husband his forces'. What did this mean – avoid action?

Milne understandably assumed he was to give the highest priority to the protection of the French troopships. If he had not been forbidden to communicate with the French admiral, he would have discovered that the movements were to take place in convoy when an adequate force was available. If Churchill had restricted himself to providing information and left the strategic decisions to the man on the spot it would not have been difficult to deduce the courses of action open to Souchon. He could attack the French troopships, he could make for the open Atlantic, (a forlorn prospect with three battlecruisers to oppose him), he could shelter in the Adriatic, linking up with the Austrian fleet, or he could go to the Dardanelles. Milne can hardly be blamed that the last possibility did not occur to him, though Sir Louis Mallet had warned the British Government that Enver Pasha was mobilizing his army under the German General Liman von Sanders, of which Churchill was aware. Milne replied that he intended to keep his entire fleet at Malta to assist the French when required.

Souchon coaled at Brindisi on 31 July and Milne sent the light cruiser *Chatham* to keep watch on the southern end of the Straits of Messina to report if Souchon attempted to avoid him at Malta by passing through the Straits. Souchon moved round to Taranto on 2 August where he topped up with coal. That afternoon Milne received from the Admiralty:

> '*Goeben* must be shadowed by two battlecruisers. Approaches to Adriatic must be watched by cruisers and destroyers. Remain near Malta yourself. It is believed that Italy will remain neutral, but you cannot yet count absolutely on this.'[10]

Milne was informed of Souchon's movements through British consuls, yet he then sent Troubridge with his 1st Cruiser Squadron, *Indomitable, Indefatigable,* the light cruiser *Gloucester* and eight destroyers, (almost his entire fleet) to seal the southern end of the Straits of Otranto, firmly shutting the stable door after the horse had bolted. That evening Milne and all other Cs-in-C were informed they could enter into discussions with French naval officers. A common signal cipher, agreed with the French, had been issued to Milne in a sealed packet, which he was informed he would be instructed to open in a period of tension likely to lead to war in alliance with the French. He appears to have received no such instruction and, instead of using his own initiative, asked the Admiralty for permission to open it. It took twelve hours to obtain confirmation, whereupon Milne signalled the French Admiral

Lapyrère, offering cooperation but with no positive suggestions, to which he received no reply. He then sent the light cruiser *Dublin* to contact the French at Bizerta – by *letter*! At this time Lapyrère was half-way between France and Algiers.

Milne sent another signal to the Admiralty asking if, in the event that Souchon left the Adriatic (which he had already done), should Troubridge's ships, other than the battlecruisers which were to shadow Souchon, maintain the watch on the Adriatic or rejoin his flag to assist the French? 'At 12.50 am on August 3, I emphasized the importance of the *Goeben* compared with all other objectives . . . "Watch on mouth of Adriatic should be maintained, but *Goeben* is your objective. Follow her and shadow her wherever she goes and be ready to act on declaration of war, which appears probable and imminent."'[11]

The position now ought to have been clear to Milne. The Admiralty does not appear to have recognized, despite the consular information, that Souchon had already left the Adriatic. A close watch on Taranto would have been more profitable, but this was now too late. *Goeben* and *Breslau* had already passed through the Straits of Messina the day before, prior to the departure of Troubridge and *Chatham*. They entered Messina and, with the assistance of a sympathetic Italian Navy, again coaled from German merchant ships. *Chatham* arrived at the southern end of the Straits early on 3 August and steamed right through them, to find Messina empty. The birds had flown six hours earlier. Milne learned that morning that Souchon had been been seen at Messina and told Troubridge by signal. The latter asked if the watch on the Adriatic should be maintained and whether he should send the battle-cruisers westward, passing south of Sicily, a clear suggestion of the best course at that time. Common sense should surely have indicated to Milne that Souchon must have left Messina north about, and he could only have turned west, there being no other way to go. A chase to the west was indicated, but he told Troubridge that the watch on the Adriatic should continue and that the dispatch of the battlecruisers should be delayed 'until you get authentic news of the *Goeben*'. Then he received *Chatham's* report and told Troubridge to detach the battlecruisers to chase to the westward, with the likelihood of trapping Souchon between them and the French, leaving Troubridge with his light forces and slow armoured cruisers at Otranto, in accordance with his orders from London, though he might with advantage have reported the situation to Whitehall and suggested that he should join the other two battlecruisers in his flagship; indeed any worthy admiral would have sailed at once to rendezvous with his other big ships en route, leaving the rest of his fleet to block the Straits of Messina and the eighty miles between Cape Bon and Sicily, and reported his actions to the Admiralty as intentions rather than proposals. But with slavish adherence to orders from an office in London, he remained in Malta with the light cruiser *Weymouth* and four of his eight remaining destroyers, and left his second-in-command with the bulk of his fleet at the mouth of the Adriatic, to whom he sent four more of his destroyers, which could better have been sent west.

The Admiralty, assuming that Souchon would make a break for the Atlantic, instructed Flag Officer Gibraltar to patrol the straits with destroyers and signalled Milne to direct his two battlecruisers there, which he relayed to Captain Kennedy in *Indomitable*. In the meantime Souchon had made for the coast of Algeria. At dawn on the 4th *Goeben* bombarded Philippville and *Breslau* Bône. Intended to confuse the Allies, this diversion succeeded admirably. It established Souchon's location in the western Mediterranean, convincing London and Paris that he was either making for Gibraltar or attempting to disrupt the French troop movements. In fact Tirpitz had signalled Souchon that an alliance had been concluded with Turkey and he was to proceed immediately to Constantinople.[12] Directly after the bombardment, he left the coast heading west, and when out of sight turned back on his course and headed east at high speed.

By sheer luck, *Indomitable* sighted both ships and signalled Milne, giving their exact position. The four ships passed each other on opposite courses, their guns loaded, but all trained fore and aft to avoid provocation, and refrained from the customary salute to an admiral, in case the smoke and sound of the saluting guns was mistaken for opening fire. The two British ships turned and followed the Germans. Milne signalled the Admiralty: '*Indomitable, Indefatigable* shadowing *Goeben* and *Breslau* 37° 44' North 7° 56' East.' He failed entirely to indicate the course the German ships were steering. To this signal Churchill replied: 'Very good. Hold her. War Imminent.' He followed this up after consultation with Grey and the Prime Minister: 'If *Goeben* attacks French Transports, you should at once engage her'.[13] The Cabinet refused to ratify this signal authorizing an act of war before its declaration, and Churchill was obliged to cancel it that afternoon. Just over an hour earlier, Battenberg, with Churchill's agreement, had signalled Milne: 'Italian Government have declared neutrality. You are to respect this neutrality rigidly and should not allow any of His Majesty's ships to come within six miles of the Italian coast.'[14] Churchill says: 'This certainly as it turned out was to complicate the task of catching the *Goeben;* but not as it will appear, in a decisive manner'.[15] How decisive will be seen.

The British battlecruisers were longer out of dock than the Germans and did not yet have additional wartime complements, both factors contributing to their poor performance compared with *Goeben* in which every available man, including officers, went below to fire the boilers, only the watch off duty being available to fight the ship, and, despite having three boilers out of action, the Germans steadily outpaced the British ships until, at 4.30 pm Kennedy reported to Milne that he had lost sight of his quarry. *Dublin*, a ship of the same designed speed, which had joined the battlecruisers, lost sight of the Germans at 9 pm.

Tirpitz wrote:

'There was a naval agreement, concluded in time of peace, between Austria, Italy and ourselves, according to which, in the event of war, our combined naval forces were to be mustered in the Straits of Messina against the double alliance. . . . When the *Goeben* and *Breslau* arrived at Messina . . . they met neither Italians nor Austrians and the former, who had declared strict neutrality scarcely allowed them one coaling at Messina. Enemy ships were patrolling at both ends of the straits.'[16]

The last sentence was mistaken. Kennedy intended to continue east and close the northern entrance to the Straits of Messina, but due to the restriction on approaching within six miles of Italian territory, Milne ordered him to rejoin his flag to the west of Sicily, where he patrolled on the assumption that Souchon would again head west. The Italians allowed Souchon to coal again from German merchant ships, though due to the fatigue of his men he was unable to top up to more than two-thirds of his capacity and remained in the port for 36 hours for his exhausted ship's company to recover from their superhuman efforts, while Von Wangenheim, the German Ambassador, frantically negotiated with the Turks to allow him into the Dardanelles. The *Admiralstab* signalled to Souchon: 'For political reasons entry into Constantinople is not yet possible. You should proceed to Pola or the Atlantic'. Tirpitz adds:

'In the evening the news arrived that the Austrian Commander-in-Chief, owing to the position, the distance and the state of readiness of his fleet, was unable to help – a typical instance of our political preparation for the war. Under the circumstances Admiral Souchon was informed by telegraph that he might himself choose in what direction he should break through. He thereupon . . . chose the way to Constantinople.'[17]

Milne stationed *Gloucester* (Captain Howard Kelly) at the southern end of the straits, but decided that *Goeben* must eventually turn west. It might be judged that with three battlecruisers to the west of Sicily, Souchon would have been quite foolish to do so; it should now have been obvious to Milne that he would turn east. At last Milne arrived at this conclusion and returned westward round the coast of Sicily to Malta to coal, before resuming the chase, taking 17 hours to cover the 250 miles distance, a speed of under 15 knots. In fact there was no need to go to Malta at all, for subsequent careful research by Captain John Creswell shows that the battlecruisers had adequate fuel to reach the eastern Mediterranean and return at high speed. Moreover, no ship now guarded the northern exit from the straits, though Souchon did not know this. He sailed south through the straits and turned east, followed at 7.30 pm on 6 August by Howard Kelly in *Gloucester*, who signalled to Milne that Souchon was heading east and rounding Cape Spartivento. In an attempted bluff, the Germans turned north into the Adriatic, but were unable to shake off the tenacious *Gloucester,* and Souchon resumed his course towards Cape Matapan, while Troubridge sailed for the mouth of the Adriatic to meet him, on the assumption that he was heading for Pola. About midnight he realized Souchon's intentions and headed south to intercept. During this run south, his Flag Captain, Fawcett Wray, remembering Milne's instruction from the Admiralty not to engage a superior force persuaded the tired Troubridge to give up the chase. Details of this tragic incident, leading to Troubridge's court-martial, need not be discussed here, but Wray, an outstanding gunnery officer, convinced him that the enemy ships constituted a superior force. With their greater speed they could circle round him at the range of their guns while he could never bring his own into range. At the court-martial, Wray, giving Troubridge loyal support, made a convincing case.

Gloucester continued shadowing as far as Matapan, but Milne had ordered her not to proceed further and she gave up the chase, signalling Milne the exact location, course and speed of the enemy. He therefore knew perfectly well that Souchon was heading for the Aegean and not the Adriatic. Milne sailed from Malta just after midnight on 7/8 August, having remained there for over twelve hours doing nothing except unnecessary coaling. 'We followed the enemy ships at a leisurely pace to the Dardanelles,' wrote Vice Admiral B. B. Schofield, then a midshipman in *Indomitable.* [18] It was leisurely indeed; this time, in just under 24 hours, Milne had covered 270 miles, a speed of under 12 knots. Souchon had been for several hours at Denusa, in the Aegean, where he again took a little coal and remained until the early morning of 10 August.

A confusing succession of signals then reached Milne as to whether or not Austria was at war with the Allies, which caused the dilatory admiral further delay by altering course towards the Adriatic. By 5 pm on 10 August, Souchon had reached the Dardanelles; Milne had just rounded Matapan. Churchill had arranged his 'naval Colenso'.

It is about 900 miles from the west of Sicily to Denusa. Had Milne left Sicily for the Aegean at once, instead of going to Malta to coal, he would have had to maintain a speed of under 20 knots to catch Souchon at Denusa. Had he maintained a higher speed, of which he was entirely capable, he could have entered the Aegean and reached the Dardanelles first and with his three battle-cruisers destroyed the German ships.

Tirpitz records the result:

'A decisive turn was given to the whole Turkish question by this break-through. Before the war our Eastern policy had always seemed mistaken to me, as Germany's only real prospects of release from encirclement were to be found through Russia; but once we were actually at war with Russia all considerations of this sort vanished. I accordingly supported Turkey so far as lay in my power. Her weakness made it impossible for her to remain neutral in the long run, and the arrival of our vessels made it possible to ensure she came in on our side instead of against us . . . our navy took a leading part in the famous defence of the Dardanelles, thus assisting in the saving of Constantinople. On this depended victory or defeat on the Balkan front, which was so important to the Central Powers. The approach from the Mediterranean remained closed. The maintenance of communications with Asia Minor rendered possible our serious threats against the English in Egypt and Mesopotamia, which drew off in that direction strong English armies and transport vessels.'[19]

When war broke out Britain had no idea of the enormity of the struggle before her. Most believed it would be over in a few months with the defeat of Germany. Custance, now retired, replying to a question on 1 August, answered, 'Oh, these things are generally over in a few months!' The Government was unwilling to embark on greater expenditure than they thought essential to achieve this easy victory. Vital weeks were wasted in attempting to limit expenditure and days were occupied in deciding whether the War Office plan of 1911 should be adhered to, how many troops should be sent to France and how many retained for defence against the invasion that any thinking naval officer knew to be impossible. Since the resignation of Seely as War Minister, Asquith had assumed the office in addition to Prime Minister. Now it became imperative to fill the vacancy and Asquith had given the matter no thought whatever. Kitchener happened to be in England, about to return to Egypt, so, under pressure from Haldane and Northcliffe, on 5 August Asquith appointed him Minister for War.

The inscrutable Kitchener, who, by long association with the Middle East, India and Africa, had developed their circumlocutory speech and habit of thinking, was welcomed with great satisfaction. He was slim and erect, a fine figure, massive, unbending and uncommunicative, giving an impression of masterly self-assurance and inspiring confidence to no ordinary degree. He disliked ceremony, believed only in verbal orders and hated the written word. Like Fisher, he worked early and late, never spared himself, had no patience with men who failed him, ensured the success of those who served him, but, unlike Fisher and like Wellington, was 'never seen to address or even notice a private soldier'. He had little knowledge of tactics, took no interest in modern weaponry, the reorganization of the War Office or the recently formed Territorial Force. Nevertheless, such was his resounding reputation that politicians and public took his word on military matters almost as holy writ. As Esher put it: 'When Kitchener of Khartoum took control of the War Office on the 5th of August, 1914, there was a sigh of relief, for here was a man in the right place – a man whose antecedents exposed this crucial office to no risks, a man upon whose tried proficiency the Army and the nation could rely at the moment of greatest trial.'[20]

The War Office plan to fight on the French left was now questioned by Haig and others, including Sir John French, who was to command, and suggested the Army's dispatch to Belgium where it would stiffen Belgian morale and fight with the Belgian Army, itself about the same size as the British. As A.J.P. Taylor wrote:

'When the British entered the war they imagined they had a free hand to decide their strategy. Their Expeditionary Force, though small . . . could be sent anywhere, thanks to the power of the British Navy. . . . Could the expeditionary force be delayed while alternatives were considered? . . . Or strike at Germany's heart by landing in Schleswig?' If France collapsed, could Britain extricate the BEF? 'Sir Henry Wilson of the War Office pulled the great men up short. Even the British Expeditionary Force, small as it was, could not move except to a prepared timetable; and only one had been prepared. . . . It was irrelevant to complain that this would not help Belgium. . . . It was this plan or nothing. The Council of War, and after it, the Cabinet, reluctantly agreed. Thus the British policy lost its freedom of action from the start. . . .[21]

'The fact that such questions were asked, for the most part by general officers who were destined to hold high positions throughout the war, seems to indicate that the Army as a whole was less convinced than has generally been assumed that the official plan was the best one. The overwhelming factor was, however, that the plan for co-operation by our Expeditionary Force on the left of the French Army had been worked out by the two staffs in great detail, and this could not be said of any other plan.'[22]

Here was an example of staff work adopting the very rigidity Fisher had so acutely feared; immutable plans had been prepared before the facts could be ascertained; Henry Wilson's determination condemned Britain to a plan that neither fulfilled her purpose in going to war nor made any use of her greatest asset, the Navy. Esher wrote in his journal on 6 August:

'I have always thought the strategy of tacking the small British Army on to the French was arguable. We often have discussed it. Presently, if the Germans get held up, the threat of a landing of 150,000 men at some unknown points on German soil is bound to exercise a moral effect and the military diversion that might well be the turning point in a campaign. By the precipitate alignment of our Army to that of the French, we forego the advantages of sea power. This strategy is adopted in the belief that the French armies cannot hold their own against the Germans and that the small force we are able to throw into the earlier battles of the war is bound to make a vital difference to the campaign. We shall never know, as whatever happens, our military historians are in honour bound to show that Germany was vanquished or France saved by Sir John [French] and his gallant four or five divisions.'[23]

Kitchener recognized that the war would not be 'over by Christmas'. He forecast, to the disbelief of the politicians, that it would last for three years. He adopted the continental view, for the success of which a huge mass army was necessary. The German advance pivoted about their left flank in conformity with the Schlieffen plan until it lay along the line of the Marne. The right flank was in sight of the Eiffel Tower and the left on the Vosges mountains. On 24 August, the first day of the retreat from Mons, orders were issued that no more transports were to sail for Boulogne or Havre; on 29 August the disembarkation base was transferred to St. Nazaire, and by 5 September Calais, Boulogne, Dieppe, Havre and Rouen had been evacuated, lengthening the lines of communication by over 500 miles. Astonishingly, though he diverted men to Antwerp and East Prussia, with all the Channel ports and the coast as far west as Havre evacuated by the Allies, Moltke made little attempt to capture them when they were there for the taking, perhaps one of the greatest blunders of the war. A month later it cost many German lives. The advance was so rapid that a 30 mile gap formed between the armies of Von Kluck and Von Bülow. Here the French stood, while Manoury's 6th Army attacked Kluck's right flank. The British Army turned under Kluck's guns and poured into the gap. The Allied armies pushed the Germans back to the Aisne and each side attempted to turn the other's flank. Paris had been saved and now the Channel ports and Antwerp became of cardinal importance as the Army's foothold on the continent and as the German advanced naval base. Who commanded them commanded the Channel. The race for the sea began.

Antwerp, bravely defended by the Belgians, was a fortress guarding the Channel, threatening the flank and rear of the German Army. Fisher had written in his war plans of 1907:

'Germany may pass over into Belgium, in order to gain possession of Antwerp, but if she shows any signs of doing this, we should be able so to reinforce the Belgian troops as to render such an attempt impossible . . . In any case we must be prepared to control the approaches to Antwerp . . . we must throw such forces into Antwerp that the strongly fortified positions round it may be perfectly secure.'[24]

Castlereagh had written in 1814, that 'to leave Antwerp in the hands of France would be little short of imposing on Great Britain the charge of a perpetual war establishment, for a constant vigilance and a state of constant readiness, would be needed.'[25] This applied equally to Germany. Fisher's plan would have changed the whole course of the war, but it was now too late; four divisions were to embark for France and two would remain behind to defend the country against invasion. The British Army was already committed, serving only as a small part of the French Army.

Appreciating the importance of Antwerp, the Admiralty had sent spare guns and a few marines there at the outbreak of war and on 7 September Churchill, influenced by Fisher, wrote to Asquith, Grey and Kitchener: 'The Admiralty view the sustained and effective defence of Antwerp as a matter of high consequence. It preserves the life of the Belgian nation; it safeguards a strategic point which, if captured, would be of the utmost menace.'[26]

Belgium appealed to Britain to send 25,000 troops to defend a line from Ostend to Antwerp to keep open her supply routes along the coast. The only troops available were the two regular divisions Kitchener saw as necessary against invasion and had refused to send. The Territorials, for which Kitchener had a hearty contempt, were not then liable for overseas service, and he refused to send them either.

The theory of the amphibious outflanking coastal attack was given convincing support when the Belgian Army fell back to defend Antwerp. On 24 August they made a sortie, attacking the right wing of the German Army in a convincing attempt to ease pressure on the Allied left flank at Mons. The Germans were obliged to detach four reserve divisions and three Landwehr brigades to check it. On 7 September news reached King Albert that the Germans were sending part of this force to the front in France and he launched a further sortie on the 9th, the critical day of the Battle of the Marne. This action was initiated solely by the King. The dispatch of three German divisions to France was cancelled, the German command was alerted to the baneful menace of Antwerp, compelling them to reduce the fortress and seize this potential British landing place.

On the outbreak of war the Admiralty had established a number of naval air stations round Dunkirk and, as a defence against isolated marauding Uhlan patrols, had landed a force of marines equipped with armoured omnibuses and cars (all available Rolls Royce vehicles had been commandeered for the purpose). But by now heavy German forces were descending on the area and they could no longer offer an adequate defence. Thus Dunkirk too was exposed.

Kitchener called for the French to provide a regular division to join with a small British force to mount the relief of Antwerp through the region of Dunkirk. But on 2 October a telegram was received from the British Minister in Antwerp that the Belgians were withdrawing along the coast to Ghent and it was unlikely that Antwerp could hold out for more than a few days.

According to Churchill, he was recalled from a projected visit to Dunkirk for a meeting the following night at Kitchener's house, with Battenberg, Grey and Sir William Tyrrel of the Foreign Office, resulting from which a telegram was sent to Antwerp urging the Belgian Government to hold on and promising that a brigade of Royal Marines would arrive the next day. In the meantime the French promised two Territorial divisions, with artillery and cavalry, indicating their optimistic hope that the advance of Joffre's armies would relieve Antwerp.

At the meeting in Kitchener's house Churchill said it was agreed that 'some person in authority' should visit Antwerp to discover the true position and he appears to have volunteered with alacrity, setting off at 1.30 am, according to Asquith, 'with Grey's rather reluctant consent'.[27] Sir Francis Hopwood (later Lord Southborough) put it more strongly: He left 'in spite of the remonstrances of his two colleagues'.[28] His aim was to persuade the King and Government to hold on. Churchill says, 'The First Sea Lord consented to accept sole responsibility in my absence',[29] a somewhat condescending reference to a full admiral! Though Grey rather diffidently supported Churchill's version, Esher's was different;

> 'One night he [Kitchener] was in bed asleep when Mr Churchill, then First Lord of the Admiralty, bursting into the room, pleaded for the War Minister's permission to leave at once for Antwerp. In spite of the late hour, Sir Edward Grey arrived in the middle of the discussion, and while he was engaging Lord Kitchener's attention, Mr. Churchill slipped away. He was next heard of when a telegram from Antwerp was put into Lord Kitchener's hands in which his impetuous colleague asked bravely to be allowed to resign his great office, to be given command of a Naval Brigade . . . Lord Kitchener was not upset, but he was not unmoved.'[30]

Churchill arrived at Antwerp at 3 pm the following day, to find the outer forts falling to the German 17-inch howitzers, Antwerp short of food and ammunition and the water supply cut off. Dispirited by what they saw as their allies' failure to support them, the Belgian Army fought bravely. The Scheldt closed by the strict Dutch interpretation of neutrality, the only line of retreat was along the narrow strip of country parallel to the Dutch frontier and the coast. If Ghent fell, this strip too would be closed, and it was held by only two Belgian infantry and one cavalry division. Churchill explained the Allies' intention to relieve Antwerp, the Belgians agreed to continue their resistance for the time being and Churchill telegraphed to Kitchener that Antwerp might hold out for ten days, provided an assurance of relief was given within three. He asked him to instruct the Admiralty to send both the untrained and ill-equipped naval brigades, with 2m rounds of ammunition; 2,000 marines, he said, were arriving that evening. They actually arrived on the morning of 4 October and went immediately into the ill-defended and unprepared lines.

The Naval Brigades had been formed by Churchill on the outbreak of war, mostly from reserve officers and men, who had trained in their own time. Churchill said they were intended for service afloat, or in defence of the Home Ports. Kitchener and most others regarded them as Churchill's private army. Richmond, now Assistant Director of Naval Intelligence, was appalled. 'I really believe Churchill is not sane,' he wrote on 20 August, 'His entire energies have since last Monday been devoted to forming a naval battalion for shore service. . . . What this force is to do, Heaven only knows.' Churchill appointed Fisher and Beresford as Colonels-in-Chief, which both greeted with wry amusement. The sketchy training of the naval brigades, which Hankey said were 'quite unfit to take the field'[31] was exemplified by Asquith's son, Arthur, and many of his friends who had been commissioned from civilian life only three days before they went to Antwerp. 'For the Reservists, as I myself encountered them, were indeed a lamentable spectacle of unpreparedness. They lacked almost every aid that a soldier in the field should possess. They carried their ammunition in their pockets and their bayonets stuck into their gaiters. They had next to no supply service and were clearly unfit for anything but garrison duty behind fortifications.'[32]

That morning Kitchener's reply to Churchill's telegram said a force of 18,000 British infantry with 63 guns, 4,000 cavalry with 12 guns and a naval detachment of 8,000 men would disembark at Zeebrugge on 6 and 7 October. The French were sending 15,000 infantry with two squadrons of cavalry and the Fusiliers Marins Brigade, 8,000 men, to arrive between 6 and 9 October.

Several competent Belgian and British generals, including General Paris of the Royal Marines, were at Antwerp, and Sir Henry Rawlinson was on the way to take command, yet Churchill's self-confidence prompted him to telegraph the Prime Minister:

'If it is thought by HM Government that I can be of service here, I am willing to resign my office and undertake command of relieving and defensive forces assigned to Antwerp in conjunction with Belgian Army, provided I am given necessary military rank and authority, and full powers of a commander of a detached force in the field. I feel it my duty to offer my services, because I am sure this arrangement will afford the best prospects of a victorious result to an enterprise in which I am deeply involved. I should require complete staff proportionate to the force employed, as I have had to use all the officers now here in positions of urgency. I wait your reply. Runciman would do Admiralty well.'[33]

This Asquith described as a 'real bit of tragicomedy'. He wrote to Venetia Stanley, a cousin of Clementine Churchill;

'Of course without consulting anybody I at once telegraphed to him warm appreciation of his mission and his offer, with a *most decided* negative, saying that we could not spare him at the Admiralty etc. I had not meant to read it at the Cabinet, but as everybody, including K. [Kitchener] began to ask how soon he was going to return, I was at last obliged to do so, carefully suppressing the last sentence! I regret to say that it was received with a Homeric laugh.'[34]

Asquith had already sent Churchill's telegram to Kitchener, who astoundingly wrote in the margin, 'I will make him a Lieut.-General if you give him the command'. This from a man who despised the territorials as amateurs! Churchill interpreted it as support: 'I have since learned that Lord Kitchener wrote proposing that it should be and wished to give me the necessary military rank.' 'Lovers of the curious in history,' wrote Beaverbrook, 'may regret that the occasion was lost for producing the spectacle, unprecedented in modern times, of a Cabinet Minister stepping direct from the council chamber to high command in the field.'[35]

On 6 October the Germans overran the exhausted Belgian Army in the outer defences and Rawlinson ordered a general retirement to the inner lines of forts. The town was now exposed to heavy bombardment and the Belgian Government withdrew to the left bank of the Scheldt. Churchill returned to England. On 8 October the last Belgian troops and the naval brigades retreated to Ghent and Ostend. The inexperience of the naval brigades led one of them to march in the wrong direction, ending up in Holland, where they were interned for the rest of the war.

It seems surprising that Fisher's foresight was ignored. If Britain had gone into the Scheldt it is most unlikely that Germany would have declared war on Holland; she was much more useful as a neutral. Nor would Holland have joined Germany to become a German vassal. Antwerp would have been saved, German communications might have been cut and the German Navy would have been forced back to its nearest base at Wilhelmshaven, 230 miles further east. All this was thrown away. Eleven Territorial divisions were available in England, but while the Germans threw in all their forces, Kitchener considered them still unfitted for active service, in contrast with Churchill's Naval Brigades. Antwerp fell on 10 October and Rawlinson's force, which landed at Ostend and Zeebrugge on 5 and 6 October, was too late to do more than cover the escape of the Belgian Army. However, even this feeble amphibious effort retarded the German advance. It gave time for the transfer of the main British force from the Aisne to the new left of the Allied line and their heroic stand at Ypres, aided by the French and Belgians along the Yser to the sea, held the Germans, but by so narrow a margin that Antwerp must be regarded as the deciding factor.

Now the more intelligent strategists and politicians began to see the force of Fisher's arguments. Hankey noted: 'For my part, I had never been a partisan of the plan of committing our expeditionary force into the main theatre at the outset of the war,'[36] and Esher wrote:

'For four years I fought in the Defence Committee and out of it to prevent committing our Expeditionary Force to an alignment with the French and in favour of using our sea power and our sea base. Ah, well! We are caught now in the meshes of this business, so we must win through as best we can. But think of it! Suppose we had, at any time, been free to launch our whole force from any of the northern ports on the right of the Germans!!'[37]

'The fall of Antwerp,' wrote Churchill to Sir John French, was a great and untimely injury to the Allied cause. I do not agree with the policy that abandoned it; and I fear you will now have the army which was before Antwerp to meet almost immediatel.y'[38]

Richmond said of Antwerp:

> 'I don't mind his tuppenny rabble going, but I do strongly object to 2,000 invaluable Marines being sent to be locked up in the Fortress & become prisoners of war if the place is taken. They are our last reserve. No Board of Admiralty with two pennyworth of knowledge & backbone would have allowed marines to be used in such a way ... our invaluable marines and several seamen gunners, will be interned in Holland or locked up in a German fortress. It is a tragedy that the Navy should be in such lunatic hands at this time.'[39]

Beatty said that Churchill had made 'such a darned fool of himself over the Antwerp débacle. The man must have been mad to imagine he could relieve [Antwerp] ... by putting 8,000 half-trained troops into it'.[40] Marder says Churchill's critics 'ascribed the "failure" to the vanity and mock heroism of the First Lord, a charge with more than a shred of truth.'[41] Even Asquith saw the absurdity, though he did nothing.

> 'Strictly between ourselves, I can't tell you what I feel of the *wicked folly* of it all. The marines of course are splendid troops and can go anywhere and do anything; but nothing can excuse Winston (who knew all the facts) for sending in the other two naval brigades. ... As a matter of fact, only about one quarter were reservists and the rest were a callow crowd of the rawest, most of whom had never fired off a rifle, while none of them had ever handled an entrenching tool.'[42]

4

LUI SEUL

The Channel ports, after Moltke's blunder, now had to be saved. On 16 October Joffre telegraphed Kitchener: 'Now that the operations extend up to the coast of the North Sea between Ostend and the advanced defences of Dunkirk, it would be important for the Allied Navies to participate in these operations by supporting our left wing and acting with long-range guns on the German right wing. The Commander of the naval forces would then act in concert with General Foch through the Governor of Dunkirk.'[1] The next day British destroyers were ordered to bombard the coast. Fast destroyers towed steel frameworks with small platforms on top. These were planted in shallow water and a spotting officer and signalman left on the platform, the latter passing the spotting corrections to the ships over the horizon. On completion, the destroyer would rush in, pick up the spotting party and sink the platform. The Germans never detected them[2] and on 18 October Rear-Admiral Hon. Horace Hood was appointed to command a special force of shallow draught monitors, *Humber, Severn* and *Mersey,* purchased on the outbreak of war from Brazil, each with two 6-inch and two 4.7-inch guns, escorted by four destroyers. With aerial reconnaissance, many enemy batteries were located and harassed.

There now began increasing numbers of messages to Hood 'from First Lord', which was at least unconventional; any messages should have been 'from Admiralty'. Hood maintained the proper procedure in addressing all his messages to 'Admiralty'.

The enemy advantage in U-boats immediately caused great concern. Jellicoe and Beatty wrote separately to Churchill complaining of lack of submarine defences, the latter suggesting Cromarty was the most satisfactory harbour. As he succinctly put it, 'We have no place to lay our heads.'[3] In these conditions the fleet proceeded to the north coast of Ireland to carry out maintenance and gunnery practice. It was an unhappy choice, for on the way *Audacious,* launched only in 1912, with ten 13.5-inch guns, was sunk by a recently laid mine. Already in the first two months of the war six ships had been lost. *Aboukir, Cressy* and *Hogue,* 14-year-old 12,000-ton 'Bacchante' class cruisers, were patrolling in the Broad Fourteens. Extreme weather forced their destroyer screen to return to harbour and speed was reduced to 10 knots. The flagship *Euryalus* (Rear-Admiral Arthur Christian) had returned to harbour to coal, leaving Captain John Drummond of *Aboukir* in command. Bad weather was assumed to prevent submarine attacks, so Drummond steamed at this slow speed without zig-zagging. At dawn on 22 September *Aboukir* was torpedoed by an obsolescent coastal submarine. The other two ships returned to pick up survivors and while stationary were torpedoed and sunk by the same submarine. The squadron had made regular patrols of the Dogger Bank area and the Broad Fourteens. Churchill wrote that during a visit to the Grand Fleet on 17 September he had heard them referred to in a casual remark as the 'live bait squadron'. 'I there-upon reviewed the whole position in this area. I discussed it with Commodore Tyrwhitt and Commodore Keyes.'[4] He neglects to mention that on his visit to the Grand Fleet he was accompanied by Keyes, Tyrwhitt and Sturdee. Keyes had written in a letter to Captain Arthur Leveson, Director of Operations, almost a month before the sinking: 'For heaven's sake take those 'Bacchantes' away! How can the atmosphere there be the right one? I have been into it twice, feeling buoyant and confident and come out of it feeling depressed and unhappy . . . the Germans must know they are about, and if they send out a suitable force, God help them!'[5] It was Keyes who had used the phrase 'live bait squadron' and he discussed the matter with Churchill on the return journey from Loch Ewe. On arrival at the Admiralty, although 'It was no part of my duty to deal with the routine movements of the fleet,'[6] Churchill wrote a memorandum to Battenberg: 'The force available for operations in the narrow seas . . . should have effective support, either by two or three battle-cruisers or battleships of the Second Fleet, working from Sheerness. . . . Battlecruisers are much to be preferred. The Bacchantes ought not to continue on this beat. The risk to such ships is not justified by any services they can render. The narrow seas, being the nearest point to the enemy, should be kept by a small number of good modern ships.'[7]

He continues that Prince Louis agreed and gave orders to the Chief of Staff, Sturdee, to 'make the necessary redistribution of forces. With this I was content, and I dismissed the matter from my mind, being sure that the orders given would be complied with at the earliest moment. Before they could take effect, disaster occurred.'

His memorandum has repeatedly been quoted by Churchill's apologists as evidence that he had foreseen the danger. Gretton says, 'If the War Staff had listened to the First Lord the tragedy would have been avoided'.[8]

Such is not the case. Jellicoe and Beatty, who had already vociferously complained that their forces were too weak, would have resisted to the utmost

68

the removal from the Second Fleet of 'two or three battlecruisers or battle-ships,' which would have depleted it unacceptably, and had such ships, no better protected against submarines than the cruisers, been similarly operated they and not the cruisers would have been lost. This would have been a disaster of the first magnitude, reducing the Grand Fleet to equality or even inferiority to the High Sea Fleet at its 'selected moment'. The tragedy would not have been avoided; it would have been compounded. But in any case there is no way in which heavy ships could have been redistributed in time. The minute is therefore wholly irrelevant.

'Pending the introduction of the new system the Admiralty War Staff carried on with the old.'[9] On 19 September the ships were redeployed to the Broad Fourteens. The signal for this action was originated by Sturdee and approved by Battenberg. Churchill claims that he never saw this signal, implying that he would have seen the danger. He also said that the ships were among the oldest cruisers of the Third Fleet and 'contributed in no appreciable way to our vital margins'.[10] 1,459 valuable officers and men were killed, certainly contributing to our vital margins, but had the battlecruisers been substituted, the loss of life would have been even greater, not to mention the ships.

The Press placed the blame squarely, if a little unfairly, on Churchill, Thomas Gibson Bowles, a Conservative MP and authority on Maritime Law, attributing it to 'the interference of a civilian Minister in naval operations and the overriding of the judgment of skillful and experienced Admirals'.[11]

Churchill had prepared his exculpation long before he wrote *The World Crisis*. Repington records in his diary for Wednesday 29 September, 1915:

'Dined with Winston, Lady Randolph. . . . Lady R's house. . . . Soon after dinner, W. and I adjourned to his study upstairs and went through all his alleged failures at the Admiralty. He showed me that he had been the first to suggest the withdrawal of the patrol . . . and this was because he heard a young officer . . . talk about the "live-bait squadron". . . . It appeared to me that Prince Louis of Battenberg had been playing a very restricted part, and that the Secretary of the Admiralty had been acting as a kind of Chief of Staff to Winston, with whom a great deal of the initiative originated. I told him if he had been content to administer his department, and not to dabble in strategy, he would have been still at the Admiralty.'[12]

Churchill questioned Sturdee on the matter; he was evasive and Richmond wrote:

'It is utterly sickening that such carelessness should be the cause of this waste of life. To my mind it is simply criminal. . . . The attitude of the Chief of Staff seemed to me to be that it was hard luck on *him*. Leveson said in my hearing that "it couldn't be helped." I wrote a paper to Leveson some time ago urging that it was dangerous to put vessels on a regular patrol where their movements could be reported, but nothing came of it. I have now sent in another this morning to repeat it.'[13]

Asquith wrote to Venetia Stanley:

'We have just had some very bad news: the worst I think since the war began. Three good and powerful cruisers . . . were sunk this morning in the North Sea. . . . The Navy is not doing very well just now: there are nearly half a dozen German cruisers, *Emden, Dresden, Karlsruhe* etc. which are at large on the high seas and in all parts of the world are sinking or capturing British merchantmen. Things came almost to a climax in the Cabinet today when we learned that the New Zealanders absolutely declined to dispatch their expeditionary force – all in transports ready to sail tomorrow or next day – unless we can provide them with a sufficiently powerful escort. . . . Unfortunately on this day, when of all others he was most needed, Winston is away on one of his furtive missions – this time again to Dunkirk.'[14]

A few days earlier *Pegasus,* a cruiser with 4-inch guns lying in an open road-stead off Zanzibar cleaning boilers, was sunk by *Königsberg,* utterly outranged. Richmond wrote, 'I cannot help thinking it smacks of carelessness. . . . I do know, however, that her captain pointed out the danger . . . & that the Admiralty replied that she must "take her chance". Such a bankruptcy of strategy I have never seen.'[15] *Pathfinder* had also been sunk because she had inadequate lookouts and *Hawke,* a cruiser of 7,350 tons, was sunk in the North Sea by a submarine, with only 31 survivors.

These disasters had three elements: the inexperience and insufficient study of war by seagoing officers, their ignorance of elementary principles after so many years of peace and the blindness of the Admiralty in its equal ignorance, compounded by the master hand of the overbearing Churchill. Keyes' verdict was, 'The sinking of the *Pathfinder, Aboukir, Hogue, Cressy* and *Hawke* . . . was about as simple an operation for a submarine captain as the stalking of tame elephants, chained to trees, would be to an experienced big game hunter, who wished to kill them unseen and unsuspected.'[16]

Asquith attached more importance to the financial and political consequences:

'28th October, 1914

'The disaster of which I wrote to you in veiled language yesterday was the sinking of the *Audacious* – one of the best and newest of the super-dreadnoughts, with a crew of about 1,000 and ten 13.5-inch guns, off the north coast of Ireland. . . . It is far the worst calamity the navy has so far sustained, as she cost at least 2½ millions. It is cruel luck for Winston.

'Poor boy! He has just been here pouring out his woes. . . . After a rather heated discussion in the Cabinet this morning, we resolved *not* to make public the loss at this moment. . . . Of course you will say nothing about the *Audacious* till it is public property.'[17]

The sinking had been visible to some merchant ships and several thousand people, including passengers in SS *Olympic,* (which had taken her in tow), who had photographed her. The loss was not announced for five weeks, because Churchill could see his political situation was precarious.

> 'My own position was to some extent impaired. The loss of the three cruisers had been freely attributed to my personal interference. I was accused of having overridden the advice of the Sea Lords and having wantonly sent the squadron to its doom. Antwerp became a source of severe reproach. One might almost have thought I had brought about the fall of the city by my meddling. The employment of such untrained men as the naval brigades was generally censured. The internment in Holland of three of their battalions was spoken of as a great disaster entirely due to my inexcusable folly. . . . In spite of being accustomed to years of abuse, I could not but feel the adverse currents that flowed about me. One began to perceive that they might easily lead to a practical result.'[18]

The nation had expected a new Trafalgar. The disappointment was due to the strategy of the High Sea Fleet which pinned down the Grand Fleet at Scapa, while the widely spread colonial Empire demanded protection in a hundred places against commerce raiders.

The censorious mood of the country was directed at Churchill and Battenberg, whose German antecedents were held against him. It was not surprising that when the war was going badly the employment in the supreme naval appointment of a man of German origin should be questioned. Letters of protest appeared in the Press, hundreds were written to the King and Queen and rumours of gigantic absurdity spread by word of mouth. Beresford remarked that, despite Battenberg's ability, 'He is a German and should not be occupying his present position'. This was nothing new. Ironically, in view of Beresford's obsequiousness to the Kaiser, Battenberg had written to Fisher in 1906:

> 'I heard by chance what the reasons were which Beresford and Lambton [Meux] and all that tribe gave out *Urbi et Orbi* against my going Second Lord – or any other Lord and Fleet Command presumably – viz, that I was a damned German who had no business in the British Navy, and that the Service, for that reason did not trust me. I know the latter to be a foul lie . . . it was however such a blow to me that I seriously contemplated resigning my command there and then.'[19]

Fisher had forecast something of the sort in 1910, 'ill-deserved, but none the less effective!'[20]

This was convenient to Churchill. Demands for his resignation grew, especially after Antwerp, which made him a figure of ridicule. He therefore did little to dispel the mounting depression of Battenberg, an insufficiently strong character to resist subordination by the autocratic First Lord. Vice-Admiral Sir Cecil Colville wrote to the Second Sea Lord that talk about Prince Louis being a spy was 'rot. But from all one has heard and knows, it is pretty well self-evident he had become a nonentity and a simple tool in W.C's hand,'[21] and Fisher wrote to Jellicoe that Battenberg was a 'cipher and Winston's facile dupe'.[22] He lacked energy and never took control of his office and though a competent naval officer, never had the virility to lead. His German origins and royal connections made him diffident in argument. He was seen in his office in the morning, leisurely reading *The Times*. He wrote few minutes or memoranda and earned the sobriquet 'Quite concur' from his habit of writing these words on every paper placed before him.

Churchill attempted to engineer Battenberg's resignation, justifying himself by the gutter press attacks, though the motive was certainly different. Churchill's marred reputation, ostentation and ambition led to mistrust in the Cabinet and even more so among the opposition; his position was delicate. The public wanted a scapegoat; it had to be either Churchill or Battenberg. He wrote to Prince Louis and asked him to resign. Oliver confirmed that he delivered the note on Churchill's behalf and Fisher later told the Dardanelles Commission that he had been nominated to succeed Battenberg on 20 October, though he did not actually do so until the 30th.

Churchill had remained in contact with Fisher, who was content to guide the vigorous and aggressive First Lord. The ageing admiral still enjoyed massive support in the country, remaining a popular hero and it was convenient to Churchill when Battenberg resigned on 28 October on the grounds that his German birth impaired his usefulness on the Board of Admiralty. He accepted the resignation graciously, but with alacrity.

> 'Lord Fisher used occasionally to come to the Admiralty and I watched him narrowly to judge his physical strength and mental alertness. There seemed no doubt about either. . . . I therefore determined to act without delay. I sought the Prime Minister and submitted to him the arguments which led me to the conclusion that Fisher should return and that I could work with no one else. I also spoke to Sir Arthur Wilson as his principle coadjutor. . . . Having formed my conviction, I was determined not to remain at the Admiralty unless I could do justice to it.'[23]

But it was more the knowledge that Fisher was the only man who could restore confidence and save him. 'He was, as has been here contended, the most distinguished naval officer since Nelson. The originality of his mind and the spontaneity of his nature freed him from conventionalities of all kind. His genius was deep and true. Above all he was in harmony with the vast size of events. Like them, he was built on a titanic scale.'[24]

Beatty saw through the gambit: 'Prince Louis departed not for the reason given but to save the politicians.'[25] Who else could have saved Churchill? Jellicoe was still urgently needed in the Grand Fleet. Beatty was almost unknown to the public and far junior to less able admirals; Wilson had neither the glamour to appeal to the public nor, after his incompetent handling of the Agadir Crisis, the confidence of the Cabinet. But Fisher had it all; 'the most distinguished naval officer since Nelson' and the public knew it. As to his fitness, Major General Callwell, then Director of Military Operations, early in 1915 found him younger than he had seemed during his Mediterranean command fifteen years earlier: 'He covered the ground at such a pace that I was speedily toiling breathless and dishevelled far in the rear . . . to have a hotch-potch of Shakespeare, internal combustion engines, principles of the utilisation of sea power, holy writ and details of ship construction dolloped out on one's plate, and to have to bolt it there and then.'[26]

The King had grave doubts and suggested alternatives, including his old friend Meux or Sir Henry Jackson. Sturdee was also proposed. Churchill rejected all three. The King approached Asquith who backed up Churchill and said if Fisher were not recalled Churchill would resign. The King, never a supporter of Churchill, suggested this might offer a solution. Asquith argued that Churchill had a most intimate knowledge of the Navy and his services in his present position could not be dispensed with. Wilson was also rejected. 'Winston's real trouble,' wrote Asquith, 'is about Prince Louis and the succession to his post. . . . W. proposes to appoint Fisher . . . but Stamfordham . . . declares the King's unconquerable aversion to Fisher. (He – the King – was always a Beresfordite in the old quarrels) and suggests nonsense people. . . . I said that nothing would induce me to part with W.'[27] The King gave in, but protested that Fisher was 'not trusted in the Navy.' a statement soon proved groundless, the Navy showing great satisfaction at the appointment, as did the Press, taking the view that Fisher would restrain Churchill. Even Fisher's antagonists accepted the appointment for this reason. Churchill's thinking was quite the reverse. 'I took him,' he told Violet Asquith in May, 1915, 'because I knew he was *old and weak* and that I should be able to keep things in my own hands.'[28]

Beatty wrote to his wife:

'They have resurrected old Fisher. Well, I think he is the best they could have done, but I wish he was 10 years younger. He still has fine zeal, energy and determination coupled with low cunning, which is eminently desirable just now. He also has courage and will take any responsibility. He will recognise that his position is absolutely secure and will rule the Admiralty and Winston with a heavy hand. He has patriotism and is a firm believer in the good qualities of the Navy, that it can do anything and will go anywhere, and please God, we shall change our present method for a strong offensive policy. He is head of the Navy now and as such must, in this great and terrifying crisis be supported by every officer and man in the Fleet and out of it. I think in circumstances such as they are, if he is not too old, he will be able to do more than any other man that I know of. At least the situation cannot be worse than it was before. I trust old Charles Beresford will have the decency to sink his differences with him and not stump about the country endeavouring to calumniate him, as he has done in the past.'[29]

Wemyss was among the few opposed to the appointment and accurately foresaw a breach: 'They will be as thick as thieves at first until they differ on some subject, probably as to who is going to be number one, when they will begin to intrigue against each other.'[30]

Retrospectively, so did Beaverbrook:

'Churchill co-opted Fisher to relieve the pressure against himself, but he had no intention of letting anyone else rule the roost. Here, then were two strong men of incompatible tempers both bent on an autocracy. It only required a difference of opinion on policy to produce a clash, and this cause of dissension was not long wanting.'[31]

The appointment necessitated other changes at the Admiralty. Churchill offered Wilson the appointment of Chief of Staff, but he turned it down. Determined to accept no official position, he came back as an unpaid adviser and undertook a wide range of special duties, providing valuable service.

Churchill's verdict was:

'Fisher and Wilson had outlived their contemporaries and towered above the naval generation that had followed them. It was to these two great old men and weather-beaten sea dogs, who for more than half a century had braved the battle and the breeze, and were captains afloat when I was in my cradle, that the professional conduct of the war was now to be confided.'[32]

Fisher found a discouraging situation. The ferrying of 12 ships a day carrying troops and supplies to France was vital; the great Battle of Ypres was being fought to save the Channel ports; many German raiders were at sea, Spee's squadron, *Emden*, *Dresden*, *Karlsruhe* and numbers of armed merchant cruisers raiding British ships across the globe, their uncertain movements demanding a disproportionate number to protect British interests. Yet the Grand Fleet had to be maintained for the new Trafalgar against the High Sea Fleet. All the regular Army was now overseas, the Territorial Force half-trained and the newly recruited civilian army an embryo only. The fear of invasion revived, and troopships carrying men from Australia, Canada, New Zealand, South Africa and India were joined by those bringing home the regular British garrisons from all parts of the world; they all had to be defended, all to be escorted. The submarine menace had been disregarded until it forced its unwelcome attention on the Government, who had failed to provide adequate funds for escort vessels. The defences of Scapa, Cromarty and Rosyth were inadequate, despite Fisher's earlier warnings, and Churchill described the menace as 'exaggerated in our minds'. There was no effective defence against submarines, no way of detecting them under water; the only method of attack was to keep the boat submerged until forced to surface as her batteries ran out, and then to sink her by gunfire or ramming, the latter often doing more damage to the attacker than the attacked. Boom defences were installed at Cromarty and later at Scapa, where three of the entrances were sealed by concrete-filled blockships. These defences took many anxious weeks.

Fisher and Churchill admired each other greatly and sometimes they were in complete accord; at others the two men, too much alike, found one another impossible. Fisher returned full of hope. The lethargy, paralysis and lack of imagination that dogged his predecessor had done little to progress the war.

During the early months there was no War Council, no organized system of managing the war. There were *ad hoc* consultations between Asquith and Kitchener and the First Lord separately, and sometimes all three together. Occasionally the Foreign Secretary was brought in, but there were no regular meetings, no attempts to determine clear policies. Not until the end of November was a War Council established and it had no meetings until January the following year. Even then it failed to endorse or understand the role Fisher saw for the Navy. Bacon called it 'an anaemic body that shunned issues and avoided, whenever it was possible, giving clear-cut decisions'. Fisher 'saw what he considered to be golden opportunities slipping by for want of the adoption of a cut and dried policy.'[33]

He arrived at the Admiralty like a whirlwind and immediately stirred it to feverish activity; inertia disappeared and vital energy took its place. 'One felt at once,' wrote Asquith, 'the difference made by the substitution of Fisher, for poor L.B. – *élan,* dash, initiative and new spirit.'[34] But behind all this lay a worry; Wilson had made it clear that the segregation of the Chief of the Naval Staff from the office of First Sea Lord was unworkable and the system had produced almost daily friction. As long as a subservient man like Battenberg was in office it could work, for Churchill used his dominating personality to force his views. He had installed a 'War Group' in the Admiralty, consisting of himself, Battenberg, Wilson, Sturdee as Chief of Staff and sometimes Sir Henry Jackson, like Wilson, brought back from retirement. Churchill dominated the group, whose value would have been great if it had been presided over by a strong First Sea Lord, with responsibility for operations. Wearied by verbal batterings, his colleagues often gave in and, after meetings, Churchill, in his own hand, drafted orders to carry out decisions, often misunderstanding professional views, and sometimes slanting messages to accord more closely with his own, while ignorance of naval language and signalling terminology led to misunderstandings and ambiguities.

Fisher insisted on a pact with Churchill that neither would take any important step without consulting the other and at first it was adhered to, but before long was observed only on one side. Fisher was a man of great loyalty and his devotion to Churchill may have influenced him to accept this unsatisfactory situation. His loyalty to McKenna had inspired him to seek the latter's agreement before he would accept re-appointment. Now he extended this loyalty to Churchill.

Churchill was accustomed to having his own way. By appeals to Fisher's patriotism and fidelity, by subtle cajolery, he thought he could handle him, while Fisher thought he was strong enough to handle the young politician. Both were wrong. The situation was fraught with bitter dangers and Fisher soon recognized that his tenure might be short. 'I am working hard,' he wrote, 'I'm in the position of playing a game of chess very badly begun. . . . I've got rid of the fools, but it's long and arduous to get back to a good position with a consummate good player for an enemy! *But I'm trying!*'[35]

He returned in a crisis. Von Spee was in the Pacific with two armoured cruisers, *Gneisenau* and *Scharnhorst,* built in 1907, with eight 8.2-inch and six 5.9-inch guns, with three light cruisers, *Nürnberg, Leipzig* and *Dresden,* each with ten 4.1-inch guns. The force on the south-west coast of South America was inadequate. Rear-Admiral Sir Christopher Cradock flew his flag in the armoured cruiser *Good Hope* built in 1902, with a mixed armament of two 9.2-inch and sixteen 6-inch guns. Commissioned on 2 August, 1914, with 90% reservists, she had only once carried out a full-calibre shoot. A legacy of the nineteenth century, half her 6-inch batteries were too low in the ship to be used in a seaway. In company with her were the cruiser *Glasgow*, the armoured cruiser *Monmouth* built in 1901 with fourteen 6-inch and ten 4-inch guns and the armed merchant cruiser *Otranto,* a converted liner with eight 4.7-inch guns, intended only as a commerce raider or to protect allied merchant ships. *Good Hope* had two guns larger than any of the enemy's but their range was only 12,500 yards, compared with 17,826 yards of the sixteen biggest guns of the enemy. All the remaining British guns were of shorter range. Except *Glasgow,* all ships were slower than the Germans, who could therefore choose the range. The British squadron was hopelessly outclassed.

The Admiralty knew Von Spee would attack British ships off South America carrying grain and nitrates, the latter essential for the manufacture of explosives, and it was obvious that Cradock must be reinforced. The Admiralty, influenced by Jellicoe, were preoccupied in keeping the Grand Fleet intact, enticing the High Sea Fleet to action in the North Sea. Jellicoe protested vehemently whenever it was proposed to remove any ships from his fleet. The Admiralty therefore decided to dispatch *Indomitable* with her eight 12-inch guns and 16,400 yards' range from the Mediterranean. But at Gibraltar she was turned back in response to increasing pressure from Turkey on the Russians. With pathetic futility, they substituted the battleship *Canopus*. With four 12-inch and twelve, 6-inch guns she had a designed speed of 18 knots. Churchill assumed Cradock would 'come to no harm so long as he had *Canopus* with him' and described her as 'a citadel around which all our cruisers in those waters could find absolute security'.[36] '*Scharnhorst* and *Gneisenau*,' he said, 'would not dare come within range of her four 12-inch guns.' This was absurd. *Canopus* was 15 years old and for two years had been in care and maintenance; she was due for scrapping in 1915. When mobilized in July, 1914, she had achieved 17 knots, but even the slowest of the German ships, *Nürnberg*, could make 23 knots (Churchill gives 22). Churchill said *Canopus* could achieve 15$\frac{1}{2}$ knots, but even this was a gross exaggeration. Jellicoe said she 'could steam 15$\frac{1}{2}$ knots for 3–4 days if she did not break down'.[37] She was suffering from leaking condensers and her engineer commander reported that she should be limited to 12 knots. Her captain advised Cradock accordingly. The engineer commander was invalided shortly afterwards with a nervous breakdown, probably resulting from the strain of running a ship in that condition. Marder quotes a letter from Rear-Admiral S. P. Start, who was senior engineer under him, and he said that due to his mental condition, the engineer commander was making 'false reports' on the state of the machinery or much exaggerating them, and the ship was capable of 16$\frac{1}{2}$ knots. But leaking condensers at relatively high speed would have disabled the boilers and engines, and despite his sickness, the engineer commander was probably right. *Canopus* was fitted with water-tube boilers and reciprocating engines, a combination most susceptible to such damage. In any case the slightly higher speed would have made little difference, leaving a huge disparity when compared with the German ships. Furthermore, Start said,

> 'Our fighting value was very small – our two turrets were in charge of Royal Naval Reserve lieutenants, who had never been in a turret before, and the only rounds we had fired . . . were two six-pounders to stop a merchant vessel. The four 12-inch guns were of an obsolete design, with a maximum range of 14,000 yards, only 500 yards more than that of the two German cruisers, [he was wrong] with their total of sixteen 8.2-inch guns.'[38]

The likelihood of this slow, clumsy ship getting anywhere near the enemy to use her heavy guns was nil and the higher speed of the enemy ships gave them the choice of range. With their sixteen 8.2-inch guns they would have destroyed her in minutes. 'This', says Marder, 'was the vessel described by Churchill as a "citadel".' Yet Churchill's unrealism was matched by Oliver, his naval secretary, who minuted on 29 October, 'The situation on the West Coast seems safe'. He based this on the fact that a Japanese battleship, *Idzumo*, and a cruiser, *Hizen*, with a British light cruiser, *Newcastle*, were in the North Pacific approaching the west coast of South America. Oliver suggested that this squadron would 'force' Spee southward into Cradock's arms. In all the huge space of the wide Pacific there was no earthly reason for this assumption; Spee had the whole ocean to choose from and could easily have avoided Cradock, which in any case was precisely what he did not want, his object being to destroy him. Oliver confused the hunter with the hunted, the hounds with the fox. With *Canopus* in company Cradock had no hope of catching the enemy, tied as he was to a 12-knot burden; without her he was outgunned and outranged, so he could never get near the enemy to use his two 9.2-inch guns. Worse, Cradock's orders were confused. On 5 October Churchill made to him:

> 'It appears from information received that *Gneisenau* and *Scharnhorst* are working across to South America. *Dresden* may be scouting for them. You must be prepared to meet them in company. *Canopus* should accompany *Glasgow, Monmouth* and *Otranto* and should search and protect trade.'[39]

It was not possible to protect trade and simultaneously bring a superior squadron to action. As Tromp had said some 250 years earlier, 'I wish to be so fortunate as to have only one of the two duties, to seek out the enemy, or to give convoy; for to do both is attended by great difficulties.' In September *Defence* had been ordered to join Cradock, but was recalled to the Mediterranean. He was in a dilemma, exacerbated by a string of contradictory and confusing signals stemming from indecision at the Admiralty. On 8 October he pointed out that, in the vastness of the Pacific, Spee's strong squadron could evade him and reach the Atlantic, where it could with impunity destroy the Falklands, English Bank and Abrolhos coaling bases. A strong squadron was required each side of South America. He reported that *Dresden* had visited Orange Bay early in September and that *Scharnhorst* had been joined by *Nürnberg, Dresden* and *Leipzig*. He intended to concentrate all his forces, including *Canopus*, at the Falklands and pitiably asked: 'Does *Defence* join my command?' To this Churchill showed his ignorance of naval warfare and minuted Battenberg:

> 'First Sea Lord.
>
> 'In these circumstances it would be best for the British ships to keep within supporting distance of one another, whether in the straits or near the Falklands, and to postpone the cruise along the West coast until the present uncertainty about *Scharnhorst-Gneisenau* is cleared up
>
> 'They and not the trade are our quarry at the moment. *Above all we must not miss them.*'[40] (my italics)

He was sending Cradock on a suicide mission. Battenberg ineffectually minuted, 'Settled'. In a meeting between Churchill and Battenberg, the politician made dispositions much better left to Cradock, who, he decided, should concentrate his squadron at the Falklands, except *Glasgow*, who should be sent round the west coast to look for *Leipzig*, presumably assuming the latter was still on her own, and 'protect trade on the west coast of South America as far north as Valparaiso'. *Defence* would join Rear-Admiral Archibald Stoddart in *Carnarvon* in forming 'a new combat squadron on the great trade route from Rio' and *Albion* would join the flag of C-in-C, Cape. A message was sent to Cradock accordingly, which added that Stoddart, on the East Coast would have *Cornwall*, *Bristol*, *Orama*, and *Macedonia* as well. *Essex* was to remain in the West Indies. Thus the forces concerned were scattered all over the Pacific and Atlantic, predominantly the latter. Not only was Cradock's force helpless, but Stoddart's was comparable. *Defence* had four 9.2-inch guns, also outranged, and her speed only just matched that of the German ships. The only ship with a speed greater than the Germans was *Bristol*, with only two 6-inch and ten 4-inch guns. Thus, if Spee escaped into the Atlantic, he would have destroyed Stoddart with as much ease as Cradock.

On 18 October Cradock informed the Admiralty that he believed *Karlsruhe* was joining the five German ships. Churchill argued that had Cradock remained concentrated on *Canopus*, 'even though his squadron speed should be reduced to 12 knots', all would have been well. But Cradock had said in his signal of the 18th: 'I trust circumstances will enable me to force an action, but fear that strategically, owing to *Canopus*, the speed of my squadron cannot exceed 12 knots'.[41] Cradock was a brave fighting admiral and, leaving *Canopus*, he would undoubtedly have attacked the enemy with his cruisers hoping to disable the enemy ships, slowing them down to give *Canopus* a chance to reach them, even if it meant the almost certain loss of all his ships.

Fisher joined the Admiralty 48 hours before the Battle of Coronel and instantly appreciated the peril of the situation. *Defence* was immediately ordered to join Cradock. Churchill claims this was only done when Spee's squadron was positively located early on 3 November. But there seems no valid reason why *Defence* should not have joined Cradock earlier, and Bacon was convinced that it was due to Fisher's arrival that this belated and inadequate action was taken. But the opposing squadrons met on 1 November; *Good Hope* and *Monmouth* were sunk and Cradock lost his life.

Churchill said Cradock had 'let himself be caught or has engaged recklessly with only *Monmouth* and *Good Hope*'. This version was adopted by the Cabinet: 'The mishap is the more regrettable as it would seem that the Admiral was acting in disobedience of his instructions, which were expressly to the effect that he must concentrate his whole squadron, including *Canopus* and *Defence*, and run no risk of being caught in a condition of inferiority.'[42] The Cabinet was guilty of a clear deception, for on 28 October the Admiralty had denied Cradock the reinforcement of *Defence* and when this decision was reversed, Churchill himself said, 'We were already talking to the void'. *Defence* was unavailable and *Canopus* was useless. All the more inexcusable therefore is Churchill's statement:

> 'I cannot therefore accept for the Admiralty any share in the responsibility for what followed. The first rule of war is to concentrate superior strength for decisive action and to avoid division of forces or engaging in detail. The Admiral showed by his telegrams that he clearly appreciated this. The Admiralty orders explicitly approved his assertion of these elementary principles.'[43]

Asquith, of course, was completely taken in. On 4 November he wrote:

> 'If the admiral had followed his instructions, he would never have met them with an inferior force but would have been by now the other side of South America with the *Canopus* and *Defence* in overwhelming superiority. I am afraid the poor man has gone to the bottom; otherwise he richly deserves to be court-martialled.'[44]

Beatty's assessment is more accurate :

> 'Poor old Kit Cradock has gone poor chap. He has had a glorious death, but if it had only been in victory instead of defeat . . . his death and the loss of the ships and the gallant lives in them can be laid to door [*sic*] of the incompetency of the Admiralty. They have as much idea of strategy as the Board School boy, and have broken over and over again the first principles. It is inconceivable that their intelligence does not make them see it. . . . No one trusts the Admiralty. They have made so many mistakes that should never have been made.'[45]

When Cradock had suggested two squadrons he had made it perfectly clear that each should be strong enough to defeat Spee, instead of which the Admiralty divided the available ships into two inadequate squadrons under him and Stoddart. It was the Admiralty and not Cradock who had totally disregarded the first principle of war – concentration. Richmond wanted to send out *Defence* with two other ships of the same class and blamed Sturdee for failing to achieve 'a real concentration of strength'. Beatty and Richmond were justified. In three months of war seven British ships had been sunk, without any compensating successes. The *Kaiser Wilhelm der Grosse,* a large armed merchant cruiser, was playing havoc on the west coast of Africa, *Emden* and *Königsberg* similarly in the Indian Ocean.

This was the picture when Fisher arrived at the Admiralty and Churchill showed him round the War Room, going over the map showing the positions of all British ships. Four days later came the news of Coronel and all vacillation disappeared. *Invincible* and *Inflexible*, two of Fisher's dreadnought battle-cruisers, each armed with eight 12-inch and sixteen 4-inch guns, the former with a range of 16,400 yards, were detached from the Grand Fleet and ordered to sail at once for the Falkland Islands. Churchill claimed he was already considering sending a battlecruiser, quoting his memorandum of 4 November in which he asked the Director of the Operations Division how long it would take various ships to reach Punta Arenas, Rio and Abrolhos. 'But I found Lord Fisher in a bolder mood.' That day the two battlecruisers were ordered to sail. The ships arrived at Devonport on 8 November and were ordered to coal and sail in three days. The Admiral Superintendent protested that they could not be ready until two days later because *Invincible's* boilers required brickwork repairs. Fisher was with Churchill when his message came in and dictated a reply which is reproduced in Churchill's hand in *The World Crisis*. It is a classic example of Fisher's style and instructs that, if necessary, dockyard workers were to sail with the ship to complete the repairs. The Admiral Superintendent came to the Admiralty to protest and was sent away by the new First Sea Lord with the information that by the time he returned to his yard the ships would have sailed. Such were Fisher's methods and such was the way in which he brought new urgency to the whole Navy. But so lax was security that it rapidly became known in Plymouth that the ships were on their way to the South Atlantic.

It is not surprising that Fisher regarded Sturdee with suspicion and as incompetent. As Chief of Staff he had been quite impossible, lacking in imagination, with little appreciation of necessary measures, a classic example of the peacetime admiral. He claimed and was credited with a degree of tactical ability (Chatfield said he was 'a good strategist and tactician' and Jellicoe said he had 'made a special study of tactics'), but in practice he showed little sign of either at any time. Richmond, his assistant, said in his diary:

> 'Sturdee takes any suggestions as personal insults to his own intelligence, so it is hopeless trying to do anything through him. . . . I have only one thing left and that is to try and show Winston the madness of it all. But he is absorbed in naval brigades, the defence of Antwerp & the flying corps, & high sea-strategy is a thing he does not understand – nor any sea-strategy for the matter of that. . . . When I suggested the other day that the officers on watch in the Chart Room should be acquainted with the position of our ships in home waters in order that they might be able to apply any intelligence that came in, all I got was a snub for criticising "the Department of which I am the Head". Oliver showed me a telegram which he had written for dispatch on 4th October, but which was not sent until the 8th, having been held up by the C.O.S.'[46]

When Fisher told Sturdee he intended sending two battlecruisers to the South Atlantic, Sturdee said he had suggested the same thing himself, but the idea had been turned down by Churchill in deference to Jellicoe's fear of depletion of the Grand Fleet. Jellicoe, knowing Fisher, and recognizing that he had a different master now, raised no objection. Fisher was aghast at Sturdee's apparent weakness, jumped at the opportunity to get rid of him and declared he would not tolerate 'that damned fool' for another day. Churchill's solution was simple and neat. He told Sturdee: 'The destruction of the German squadron concentrated on the west coast of South America is an object of high and immediate importance and I propose to entrust this duty to you'.[47] Sturdee hoisted his flag in *Invincible*, his orders clear, in unmistakable Fisher language:

> 'To proceed to South American waters. Your most important duty is to search for the *Scharnhorst* and *Gneisenau* and bring them to action. All other considerations are to be subordinated to this end.'[48]

Stoddart's squadron, now consisting of *Carnarvon*, *Cornwall*, *Kent*, *Bristol* and *Orama*. were to join Sturdee at Abrolhos. Thence the force was to proceed directly to the Falklands. Considering the speed with which the decisions had been made, the orders to Devonport Dockyard and the atmosphere of urgency, which Sturdee was present to see, it should surely have been clear to him that speed in bringing the German ships to action was vital. Moreover, though he had not been specifically instructed to observe wireless silence or to keep his movements secret, such instructions to a competent admiral were superfluous, even insulting. His conduct on passage is therefore puzzling.

On 17 November he called at the Portuguese Cape Verde Islands to coal and his visit was immediately telegraphed to South America. As he crossed the Atlantic at a leisurely pace to conserve coal, totally ignoring his orders, he repeatedly stopped to examine merchant ships, who could have passed information of the contact. He ordered battle practice firings and, having fouled one of *Invincible's* propellers with a target-towing wire, stopped his entire force for twelve hours while he cleared it, instead of sending on the remaining ships and catching them up later, for which his powerful ship had the speed, and the strength to defend herself.

The two battlecruisers arrived at Abrolhos on 26 November, where the rest of the squadron awaited them and Sturdee announced his intention of awaiting the arrival of the store ship, due about the 29th, and completing with stores before proceeding. Luce, the captain of the *Glasgow*, which on Cradock's order had escaped destruction at Coronel when defeat was certain, managed to persuade him to sail a day early, pointing out that Spee would be certain to attack the Falklands. A message was sent to Spee by German agents in South America informing him of Sturdee's presence; fortunately it never reached him. But the squadron arrived at the Falklands four days later than it need, which, but for bad weather delaying Spee, would have meant the destruction of the coal stocks there, and the Germans' escape into the open Atlantic. Without coal, Sturdee's position would have been grim; he could have been destroyed in harbour.

In the meantime the Admiralty telegraphed *Canopus* on 4 November, informing Captain H.S.Grant of the loss of *Good Hope* and *Monmouth* and instructing him to join *Defence* off Montevideo. He replied that further boiler defects made this impossible, whereupon he received:

> 'You are to remain in Stanley Harbour. Moor the ship so that the entrance is commanded by your guns. Extemporise mines outside the entrance. Send down your topmasts and be prepared for bombardment from outside the harbour. Stimulate the Governor to organize all local forces and make determined defence. Arrange observation stations on shore by which your fire on ships outside can be directed. Land guns or use boats' torpedoes to sink a blocking ship before she reaches the Narrows. No objection to your grounding ship to obtain a good berth.
>
> 'Should *Glasgow* be able to get sufficient start of enemy to avoid capture, send her on to the River Plate; if not moor her inside *Canopus*. Repair your defects and wait orders.'[49]

Grant had no means of knowing that Fisher had returned to the Admiralty and until that moment had no suspicion of it. Yet he turned to his commander and said, 'Fisher wrote that telegram!'[50] He recognized the style, the thoroughness; who but a professional like Fisher would have thought it out so thoroughly or told him to strike topmasts so that he could not be sighted so far away?

Sturdee reached the Falklands on 7 December, where Grant had beached *Canopus,* laid mines, set up spotting posts and landed 12-pounders with a detachment of Royal Marines. But Sturdee believed Spee was still off the west coast of South America and decided to go there. His ships would remain at the Falklands long enough to coal – about 48 hours. He left only the helpless AMC *Macedonia* to patrol outside the harbour.

In the early hours of the next morning Spee arrived; at 9 am *Gneisenau* sighted the tripod masts of the battlecruisers, but her captain refused to believe that such ships could be in the South Atlantic and continued towards his target. An hour earlier Grant's lookouts on the hills had spotted the Germans. *Canopus* signalled 'Enemy in sight', but it took another four hours before Sturdee's ships were ready to sail. In the meantime, *Canopus* opened fire. Spee then signalled his ships to break off action. Had he realized the British ships were still alongside their colliers, their decks littered with coal sacks and trolleys and almost helpless, he could have closed the harbour and raked them with fire. One by one the British ships left harbour and the chase began. All Spee's ships were sunk, except *Dresden*, which escaped to the south-west. Sturdee mounted a desultory search for her, which he abandoned after one day and she made her way to Punta Arenas where she coaled to capacity. Sturdee, learning this, sent *Inflexible, Glasgow* and *Bristol* after her but she had already departed before their arrival.

Fisher blamed Sturdee and criticised his movements after the battle, wanting him to remain in the South Atlantic to search for and destroy *Dresden*, but largely due to inefficient handling of his squadron, involving many changes of course and positioning himself where there was severe interference from funnel smoke, Sturdee had used three-quarters of the two battlecruisers' ammunition (1,174 rounds), so they had to come home to replenish. On learning that *Dresden* had coaled at Punta Arenas, the Admiralty told Sturdee he could use his discretion as to the return of the battlecruisers, but to press the chase of *Dresden*. He at once answered that he would sail for England in *Invincible*, leaving *Inflexible* to continue the search, but only until 29 December, when she would coal at the Falklands and return home. Information in the Admiralty indicated that the enemy intended to send one or more battlecruisers to intercept Sturdee. Ammunition was sent to the Cape Verde Islands, minimising danger to the two ships, though Churchill's implication that they were now safe ignores the long hazardous journey from the South Atlantic while short of ammunition; more daring by Germany might have produced a different result.

Fisher wanted Sturdee to continue the search, transferring his flag to one of the cruisers, but Churchill argued that this would leave Sturdee with a squadron less prestigious than his rank warranted, which in wartime seems rather unimportant! His real reason, we may guess, was that he wanted to make political capital from the public acclaim awaiting the hero of the Falklands, which would redound to his advantage. Fisher was furious and, ordering Sturdee to return at once, added, 'Report fully reasons for the course you have followed since the action'.[51]

Sturdee returned to a hero's welcome with both battlecruisers, leaving the remnants of his force to hunt *Dresden*. Fisher bitterly resented the adulation of a man he despised. Had Spee not turned and fled when he did he could have destroyed the British squadron, tilting the close naval balance between Jellicoe and Von Pohl. Indeed, luck was with Sturdee. Richmond said it was 'an irony that Sturdee, the man who more than anyone else is responsible for the loss of Cradock's squadron, should be the person who profits principally by it, and should be made a national hero! . . . the enemy come in sight . . . running into his arms and saving him the trouble of searching for them. He puts to sea with his squadron of greatly superior force . . . and has only to steer after them and sink them, which he not unnaturally does. If he didn't he would indeed be a duffer. Yet for this simple piece of service he is acclaimed as a marvellous strategist and tactician! So are reputations made!'[52] Even Asquith saw reality:

'One of the false reputations of the war threatens to fall to the luck of Admiral Sturdee. He had to be hustled away with his ship from Devonport and if he had loitered there, as he wished, he would have been from twelve to twenty-four hours too late to encounter the Germans at the Falklands. He certainly ought to have chased and caught the *Dresden* which is now at large, no one knows exactly where and he seems from today's papers to have made a singularly foolish speech . . . at Montevideo.'[53]

On 3 January Fisher sent to Sturdee: 'Explain why neither *Inflexible, Invincible* nor any other vessel proceeded immediately on completion of the action to Punta Arenas to cable the Admiralty and also to obtain information from British Consul.'[54] Sturdee replied with impertinent abruptness: 'Reasons for action taken were given in my reply to your signal of 18 December'[55] whereupon Fisher responded, 'Your previous reply does not answer the question' to which Sturdee, with the dignity of a man returning to a hero's welcome and in an unassailable position, stiffly answered: 'Their Lordships selected me as C-in-C to destroy the two armoured cruisers and I endeavoured to the best of my ability to carry out these orders. I submit that my being called upon in three separate telegrams to give reasons for my separate action was unexpected.'[56] To this Fisher replied : 'Last paragraph of your signal is improper and such observations must not be repeated'.[57]

Fisher's complaints were fully justified; the search for the *Dresden* continued for nearly another three months and occupied substantial numbers of Allied warships urgently needed elsewhere. She disappeared for nearly a month and was at last located when 'Blinker' Hall in Room 40 deciphered an enemy telegram sent by an agent in South America, whereupon she was sunk by *Glasgow* and *Kent*.

On his arrival home Sturdee was sent for by the King, created a baronet and received volumes of letters of congratulations, invitations to speak and biographical articles in the Press. Fisher, still burning with rage at his incompetence, kept him waiting for several hours for an interview that lasted only five minutes and was restricted to a discussion of the failure to sink *Dresden*. Though Churchill welcomed the political value of the acclamation of the hero, he too gave him only five minutes, though he did, against Fisher's vehement advice, give Sturdee command of a battle squadron in the Grand Fleet. Perhaps this was politically necessary, for had he not done so the Press would have demanded to know why not. Thus do the Press and politics command war!

Fisher would have done better not to have attacked Sturdee, though thoroughly justified. It would have been more effective to have allowed him his hour of glory and then made sure analysis of his actions spoke for themselves. Churchill at least, recognized where the credit lay and wrote to Fisher:

'My dear,
'This was your show and your luck. I should only have sent one greyhound [battlecruiser] and *Defence*. This would have done the trick.
'But it was a great coup. Your flair is quite true. Let us have some more victories together and confound all our foes abroad – and (don't forget) at home.'[58]

The victory restored the confidence of the Navy, and of the nation in the Navy. Had Sturdee's many errors resulted in disaster the consequence would have been shattering and the whole course of the war might have been altered. Fisher later listed the possible consequences of failure:

'1. We should have had no munitions – our nitrate came from Chili (*sic*).
2. We should have lost the Pacific – the Falkland Islands would have been another Heligoland and a submarine base.
3. Von Spee had German reservists, picked up on the Pacific Coast, on board to man the fortifications to be erected on the Falkland Islands.
4. He would have proceeded to the Cape of Good Hope and massacred our squadron there, as he had massacred Cradock and his squadron.
5. General Botha and his vast fleet of transports proceeding to the conquest of German South West Africa would have been destroyed.
6. Africa under Hertzog would have become German.
7. Von Spee, distributing his squadron on every ocean, would have exterminated British trade.'[59]

Exaggerated perhaps, for Spee would have been running short of ammunition, stores and coal before all this could be accomplished. But even a fraction of it would have been disastrous for Britain.

> '*Les coups de canon des Falklands ont rêsonné sur toutes les terres, sur toutes les mers Britannique. Parmi les détonations sourdes de la mer du Nord, le vieux Fisher les a reconnus. Il n s'étonne point: il les attendait lui, lui seul.*'[60]

But Falklands did something else; it proved Fisher's battlecruiser concept. No other ships with adequate fire-power could have reached the South Atlantic in time.

5

THE OLD BROOM

The new spirit pervading the Admiralty was a morale boost to the Navy and the nation, though many unexpected problems arose. The failure of the Germans to take the Channel ports suggested they would attempt some other means of cutting supply lines. They had not yet ventured an incursion into the Channel, but an alternative might be to induce Britain to retain troops at home by sporadic raids on her coast, reviving the threat of invasion – the strategy Fisher had urged against them. The distribution of British ships rested on preventing the High Sea Fleet from emerging north-about into the Atlantic, and enticing the enemy to a great action. On 3 November German battleships and battlecruisers bombarded Yarmouth. Such action against a small fishing port was pointless and was assumed to be a diversion for a much bigger enterprise.

The Grand Fleet was in Lough Swilly in Northern Ireland, the 3rd Battle Squadron in the Irish Channel and the nearest part of the Grand Fleet, Beatty's battlecruisers, at Cromarty. The Channel was entirely undefended except for Hood's forces off the Belgian coast and Burney's depleted Second Fleet. Moreover, Jellicoe was absent from his fleet at the Admiralty for discussions. However, the German action underlined Fisher's view that the disposition of the fleet was far from satisfactory and it was for this reason that Jellicoe was present. Supported by Wilson, Fisher wanted to bring the 3rd Battle Squadron (the eight 'King Edward VIIs') to Portland to defend the Channel and move the 5th Battle Squadron (the 'Formidables') with the two 'Lord Nelsons' to join the Harwich force, providing against incursions into the Channel, cutting off the retreat of German forces to their bases and giving extra security against raids or invasion of the east coast.

The news of Coronel arrived on the 4th, necessitating the dispatch of *Invincible* and *Inflexible*. Fisher also sent *Princess Royal* to Halifax, in case Spee moved into the Atlantic. Naturally Jellicoe resisted depletion of his fleet, and neither Churchill nor Battenberg appreciated his problems. Exposed in the unsuitable base at Scapa, lacking facilities and subject to the severe northern weather, ship after ship was out of action permanently or temporarily. In August the destroyers *Rifleman* and *Comet* collided in fog with considerable damage; *Bellerophon* collided with a merchant ship; *Orion* had condenser defects, *Ajax* burnt out a boiler, *King Edward VII*, *Dominion* and *Hibernia* suffered cracked gun tubes. In September the AMC *Oceanic* went ashore in fog, a total loss. Westerly gales caused damage to several ships, including *Iron Duke,* Jellicoe's flagship, which took in water through casemates. Jellicoe wrote that at the end of October:

'The Grand Fleet was considerably weakened at this time apart from the loss of *Audacious*. The *Ajax* had developed condenser defects; the *Iron Duke* had similar troubles; the *Orion* had to be sent to Greenock for examination of turbine supports. . . . *Conqueror* was at Devonport refitting, and the *New Zealand* was in dock at Cromarty. The *Erin* and *Agincourt,* having been newly commissioned, could not yet be regarded as efficient. . . . The margin of superiority was, therefore, unpleasantly small in view of the fact that the High Sea Fleet possessed 88 destroyers and the Grand Fleet only 42.'[1]

Not only was Scapa Flow unsuitable, but was too far north, days, rather than hours from the areas where action was likely, a lesson Britain should have learned in 1796–97 when French ships lay in Bantry Bay for 17 days without opposition. Fisher examined the disposition of every ship throughout the world and found weaknesses everywhere. His prewar warnings to get Rosyth and Cromarty defended were now seen as prophetic; ironically it was he who had to deal with the omission. The bombardment of Yarmouth did him some service, for it proved to be no more than a feint, but demonstrated these weaknesses. On 12 November he sent Jellicoe a telegram explaining all dispositions in detail and informing him of German plans to send two battlecruisers to assist Spee and release the fast liners in New York, designed for conversion to commerce raiders. Jellicoe was more determined than ever to maintain his fleet in the North but it was agreed that the 'King Edwards' would go to Rosyth. Jellicoe released the two 'Inflexibles' without further demur.

German strategy was working, for a strong Grand Fleet in the north militated against protecting the eastern seaboard and English Channel. Hence superior British forces were distributed more widely than German. On 16 December Hartlepool, Whitby and Scarborough were bombarded, though this time, due to good intelligence, Beatty was brought out and nearly achieved success against enemy battlecruisers, frustrated by poor visibility. But the High Sea Fleet had also put to sea, while the Grand Fleet remained in harbour, so the ending might have been less happy had the High Sea Fleet not turned tail on the Kaiser's orders. Jellicoe's caution in remaining in the North was, he believed, justified and his opponents forget that this was the first war in which submarines, torpedoes and mines were to take a major part. Many German cruisers carried 70 to 120 mines[2] which were intended to be strewn in his path in minefields about two miles long and he was acutely aware of the danger from submarine traps set by the Germans, who might, in a chase, draw him over them or over the mines. Beatty supported him and both opposed the use of the Forth and the Humber because of the danger of being 'mined in' and claimed that, anyway, there was insufficient space for their ships. Fisher believed they should come south where they would be able to make contact with the enemy at a much earlier stage in an operation. Hindsight distorts judgment, but Fisher was probably right, though the risks Jellicoe saw were real.

Fisher's vexation at the escape of the *Dresden* was understandable, for, apart from the AMCs *Kronpriz Wilhelm* and *Prinz Eitel Friedrich,* of all Germany's ships on the scattered oceans, only *Karlsruhe* and *Dresden* remained unaccounted for, and we now know that the first was sunk on 4 November by an internal explosion due to unstable ammunition. As late as January, 1915, Britain had 41 ships abroad hunting the raiders in all the wide seas.

Churchill's policy regarding new construction was influenced by his belief in a short war and his prewar philosophy of economizing to provide social services, (repeated so disastrously between the wars, with the Geddes axe, the Washington and London Naval Treaties, the 'ten year rule' and in the 1990s by the facile belief that war was now over, which all the experience of mankind has shown to be false). Priority was given to ships that could be completed within six months, but, with growing stalemate on the Western Front and the refusal of the German Fleet to offer battle, this was extended to ships that could be completed in 1915; work on other ships was suspended. Like Kitchener, Fisher foresaw a long war and was determined to suffer no shortage of ships and to build specifically for offensive operations. He at once reviewed the building programme and was far from satisfied, especially with regard to submarines, few having been ordered because of a wrangle over patent rights.[3]

Fisher's constant pressure before the war for increased building and modernization of submarines had fallen on deaf ears. In July, 1914, he had been staying in *Enchantress* at Portsmouth with Churchill, who arranged for Keyes, then Inspecting Captain of Submarines, to show him over the submarine base, Fort Blockhouse. Wrote Keyes:

> ' "Why had we not built more submarines?" [he asked], I said I considered he was responsible. . . . He had given Vickers . . . an absolute monopoly, all Vickers' resources had been devoted to building small submarines, which, in my opinion would be of little value to us in war. Vickers and Chatham Dockyard, the only Government establishment equipped to build submarines, had been given orders for "oversea" submarines to their full building capacity, but they had entirely failed to keep pace with

our requirements, with the result that we had fallen behind Germany, who had avoided our mistake and built nothing but "overseas" submarines for some years. I said I had made every possible effort to get the monopoly broken, in order to increase the field of production, but could get no definite action taken until Churchill came. Then we had to wait two years before we could build elsewhere to any but foreign design. His policy had in fact, had disastrous effects on our capacity to build'.[4]

Keyes' rudeness to a distinguished officer teemed with inaccuracies; at the outbreak of war the number of operational British submarines had actually declined while Germany's had increased.[5] On his arrival back in the Admiralty, Fisher sent for the papers and was handed a bundle a foot thick, which he promptly put on his office fire. The next day he called a conference and appointed Captain S.S.Hall, Keyes' predecessor, to his personal staff. Keyes attended this meeting and 'learnt at first hand the admiral's forceful way of getting things done'. Fisher announced his intentions and told the Superintendent of Contracts that 'he would make his house a dunghill if he brought any red tape into the business'. He meant to have submarines built within eight months, and if they were *not* he would commit hari-kiri. Keyes' engineer officer, sitting next to him, remarked in an audible whisper, 'Now we know exactly how long he has to live!' Keyes sniggered and Fisher, fixing him with a ferocious glare, said, 'If anyone thwarts me, he had better commit hari-kiri too'.[6] More than 30 submarines were ordered within a week and during his short tenure at the Admiralty, 64 were laid down. They were completed within the time he set.

> 'Lord Fisher hurled himself into this business with explosive energy. He summoned around him all the naval constructors and shipbuilding firms of Great Britain, and in four or five glorious days, every minute of which was pure delight to him, he presented me with schemes for a far greater construction of submarines, destroyers and small craft than I or any of my advisors had ever deemed possible.'[7]

While in the United States for his son's wedding, Fisher had met Mr Schwab, Chairman of the Bethlehem Steel Corporation, who arrived in England in *Olympic* and asked to meet Fisher with certain propositions regarding the construction of submarines and other vessels. Jellicoe informed Churchill, and Fisher invited Schwab to the Admiralty. Churchill wrote: 'Mr Schwab was at that time passing through England on his return to the United States. *We* invited him to the Admiralty; and he undertook to build twenty-four submarines – twelve in Canada and twelve in the United States – the bulk of which were completed in the incredibly short period of six months . . . and the subsequent work was carried out with wonderful thoroughness and punctuality by the immense organization of the Bethlehem Steel Corporation'. (my italics)[8] Many of these submarines were actually completed in five months.

Richard Hough has drawn attention to Churchill's ability to ensure 'for him all possible credit. With his admirals, who were not usually concerned with the written record and posterity, Churchill acquired the practice of committing to paper an idea put up to him in these terms: "As you know, since I discussed with you the matter of . . ." and then requesting a memorandum on the subject'.[9] The use by Churchill of the first person plural above is an example of how he appropriated credit for actions with which he had little connection. There is no evidence that he had ever heard of Schwab.

Early in December Fisher abolished the ineffective appointment, 'Captain Supervising Modified Sweeps', and put in its place a 'Submarine Attack Committee' under Captain Leonard Donaldson, the one passive and the other offensive, the committee's function to devise new methods of attack. Home waters were divided into 23 patrol areas, whose ships, equipped with rapid communication, were to prevent minelaying and reconnaissance. Net detecting devices, supported by floats, were introduced in the hope that submarines would be entangled in them and betray their presence by the movement of the floats. Trawlers and yachts were fitted with electrically detonated charges towed astern, though, in the absence of satisfactory methods of detection, this was ineffective. Churchill claimed the submarine threat had been surmounted, the mine peril overcome and that 'blisters' on ships sides made them 'torpedo-proof'.

The monitors *Humber, Severn* and *Mersey* had been commandeered and gave good service. Schwab offered Fisher and Churchill four twin 14-inch turrets almost complete for the Greek battleship *Salamis*, building in Germany. The immediate decision was made to purchase these and build four monitors round them. In December Churchill wrote one of his 'As you know . . .' notes:

'We ought . . . to order more 'Styx' class for heavy inshore work. There are, for instance, the four reserve 13.5-inch guns of the *Audacious*, which should certainly be mounted in new monitors. . . . We require now to make ships which can be built in 6 or 7 months at the outside, and which can certainly go close inshore and attack the German fleet in its harbours. These are special vessels built for a definite war operation. and we must look to them in default of a general action for giving us the power of forcing a naval decision at the latest in the autumn of 1915. . . . Our thought is proceeding independently on the same lines. I propose . . . that in addition to the 4 Schwab monitors, we prepare 8 more . . . armed either with 13.5-inch or 15-inch guns.'[10]

A belated acceptance of Fisher's 'Copenhagen' concept, this would also have made possible the attacks on the German coast he had so long planned. But they were appropriated elsewhere.

For a few hours Fisher was closeted with the constructors, planning the new ships. The battleships *Repulse* and *Renown* had been suspended because armour plate and building resources were in short supply. Much material had been provided, and they would be more use as battlecruisers in service than battleships on the drawing board; they joined the Grand Fleet in 1916. By reducing the armament by one turret each and providing only 6-inch side armour, he produced much faster ships, of shallower draught. The two 15-inch turrets removed from *Repulse* and *Renown* were installed in new monitors, as were the eight 12-inch turrets of the four 'Majestics' whose completion was distant, and the 9.2-inch guns of the old 'Edgars', which had been paid off because the ships were beyond repair. These were installed in monitors drawing only 6' 6", suitable for the Baltic. Ten 6-inch guns, mounted too low in the ships, had been removed from the 'Queen Elizabeths'. These were installed in yet shallower draught monitors. In addition were ordered 12 large river gunboats and 240 'protected self-propelled lighters' for landing troops under fire, fitted with internal combustion engines, forerunners of the landing craft of the Second World War.

'Thus in the autumn of 1914, under the various programmes, *culminating in the great Fisher impetus* (my italics) we set on foot the following enormous fleet, all due to complete by the end of 1915:

Battleships and battlecruisers of the greatest power	7
Light cruisers	12
Destroyers of the largest class and leaders	65
Overseas submarines	40
Coastal submarines	22
Monitors – heavy	18
medium	14
light	5
Sloops and smaller anti-submarine vessels	107
Motor launches	60
Ex-Lighters with Internal Combustion engines	240

'This tremendous new Navy, for it was nothing else, was a providential aid when more than two years later the real German submarine attack began. Its creation on such a scale is one of the greatest services which the nation owed to the genius and energy of Lord Fisher. Probably Fisher in all his long life never had a more joyous experience than this great effort of new construction. No man knew better than he how to put war thought into a ship. Shipbuilding had been the greatest passion of his life. Here were all the yards of Britain at his disposal and every Treasury barrier broken down.'[11]

Despite his gracious tribute to Fisher, Churchill's first paragraph claimed for himself much of the credit for the new programme. In fact he still believed the war would be over by the end of 1915 and he had 'misgivings on the score of expense'.[12] Fisher was, he said, 'very difficult to feed. In a day he would sketch the design of a capital ship. In a week he would devour a programme and come back asking for more. . . . He was far more often right than wrong, and his drive and life-force made the Admiralty quiver like one of his great ships at its highest speed.'[13]

There was nothing 'providential' about this 'tremendous new Navy', Fisher saw the need to combat the growing menace of U-boats when others, including Churchill, thought it defeated;[14] with the object of introducing convoy, Fisher built 107 anti-submarine vessels which the politicians, under pressure from Lloyd George and Churchill, had refused before the war; he planned an assault on the German mainland which could have changed the course of the war, when others thought only of defence of British shores, and the gigantic, heart-breaking, fruitless bloody, muddy slogging match on the Western Front. Moreover, to describe shipbuilding as the 'greatest passion of his life' is, perhaps intentionally, grossly to underestimate him. All his shipbuilding was directed to strategic and tactical purposes.

In 1911 Arthur Wilson had written in an undated memorandum for the CID:

'It is certain that if a British force is landed on French soil to assist the French Army, it cannot be withdrawn without great damage to our pride and national honour, and the tendency will be to make increasing sacrifices in men and material to support it. Hence . . . the navy can expect to get very little, if any, support from the Army . . . and joint action of any kind will become impossible. . . .

'If the proposed landing of the Expeditionary Force gave any hope of ensuring the final victory to France, and of marching in triumph to Berlin, it might be considered worth while to forego the cooperation of the Army with the Navy. . . .

'If our Army is once committed to action with the French they [the Germans] will know they have nothing to fear, and the Coast Army can be used, either as reserves for the main Army or to return to their occupations as required. To keep these men mobilised would of itself be a blow to the resources of Germany.

'If the Army decides to act with the Navy, one division embarked in transports and acting with the Navy, would keep the whole Coast Army, whatever its strength, on the move and compel them to keep it fully supplied with transport and stores, and above all with skilled officers who they would very much prefer to employ with the main army.'[15]

As 1914 faded, a stalemate developed from which none could see an escape, except Fisher and Churchill, whose views differed but shared a common purpose. The German Fleet remained sheltered in its harbours. Its mere existence pinned down the Grand Fleet. With the new undetectable vessels Germany could starve her enemy and deny him the munitions of war.

Fisher pressed for an attack on the Belgian coast. Sir John French supported him, but the Allies would not agree. Belgium could see her cities again ravaged; France saw only a weakening of her defence. To the Navy the Belgian coast was vital. Had Germany seized Calais and Boulogne and used them as submarine bases, the Channel would have been virtually impassable. If the 250,000 men eventually found for the Dardanelles had been employed in attacking Belgium from the sea, it seems probable that Germany, already fighting on two fronts and barely holding her own, would have found a third too great a strain. In November, 1914, after the successful Ypres battle Sir John French proposed, with the Belgians, to advance along the coast from Nieuport towards Ostend and Zeebrugge, and called for naval assistance. Fisher and Churchill saw this as a possible lead to amphibious warfare. Kitchener and the War Council did not oppose the project, though they did not encourage it, while France objected to an operation by the British so close to the coast in cooperation with the Belgians. So difficult did they find it to forget the quarrels of the past that they believed Britain intended to remain in possession of that part of the continent after the war. Joffre preferred a direct assault on Wytschaete Ridge and Messines, where British and French troops 'waded and plodded through the indescribable winter bogs of No Man's Land under cruel rifle and machine-gun fire. None penetrated the enemy's line, few reached the German wire, and those that did remained there till they died and mouldered'.[16]

The Germans were developing Zeebrugge as a submarine base and, inspired by Fisher, Churchill pressed for combined military and naval action to re-capture Ostend and Zeebrugge. Again French supported the proposal, but Kitchener stated in the War Council that he could provide neither men nor ammunition, because another assault on the Allied lines was expected shortly. Joffre opposed the scheme, while Fisher objected to naval action without military cooperation. The flat shores invited an amphibious attack and he believed the guns of the monitors, loaded with shrapnel, could rake the shores in depth, beyond the British troops, providing an opportunity for an outflanking movement. All through December Churchill pressed the matter without success.

His hand was strengthened on 1 January, 1915, when Vice-Admiral Sir Lewis Bayly, in command of the 5th Battle Squadron, was working up in the Channel and *Formidable,* steaming at only ten knots, without zig-zagging, was sunk by a submarine off Start Point. He had been told that U-boats had not penetrated so far west and was ordered to send his destroyer escort back on passing Folkestone. He demanded a court-martial, but was denied one and ordered to haul down his flag which he had only hoisted a few days earlier, despite outstanding previous service in the Grand Fleet.

Churchill continued throughout January to press the idea of the attack. French again argued for an outflanking attack along the coast and for this purpose desired to exchange places with the French forces on the left of the line and work in cooperation with the Belgian Army. The plan was discussed at a meeting of the War Council on 7 January, when, according to Hankey, it received a 'chilly reception', especially from Kitchener, because French wanted to incorporate the new armies into existing experienced formations, rather than throwing them into battle as new, untried units. On these futile grounds and because Kitchener refused him enough guns, the project was rejected, another wasted strategic opportunity which left Zeebrugge in the hands of the U-boat commander. Again was demonstrated the paucity of imagination on the part of the generals, with the shining exception of French, and strangely enough, Roberts.

Hankey says, 'It is not correct that Roberts advocated a landing in Belgium'.[17] But Repington describes how the old warrior arrived at his house during the Battle of the Marne to 'talk strategy' and discussed a plan for a landing on the Belgian coast, 'the outflanking of the German line of battle and the ruin of its communications. . . . He thought that the stroke should be delivered by 150,000 men. . . . We discussed it up and down; the troops, the ships, escorts, landing organisation, forward march and so on and we finally decided that though it was an operation of great risk and difficulty, it was the right stroke to deliver.'[18]

But the General Staff could still appreciate nothing more than their blinkered eyes could see in front of them; neither the danger of submarines to their own operations nor the possibility of combined operations or the thought of outflanking the enemy appealed to their infertile imagination.

Thwarted over Belgium, Fisher tried to animate his plan for a landing in Pomerania, at Stettin, where the flat coast and sheltered waters provided ideal conditions. He wanted the invasion carried out by Russian troops mounted from Riga in the 'ex-lighters', under the protection of both the Russian and British Navies; he would 'saturate' the Baltic with submarines. 'The Baltic project,' he wrote, 'meant victory by land and sea. . . . A million Russian soldiers could have been landed within eighty-two miles of Berlin.'[19]

In 1917 Hankey wrote a memorandum for Lloyd George:

> 'I do not think Lord Fisher's Baltic project, to which he alludes, was ever feasible. As outlined in these papers the project is extremely vague. . . . My own opinion is that the whole plan was a chimera from the very beginning. . . . If we have never been able to knock out from the sea Ostend and Zeebrugge, the defences of which have been wholly extemporised during the war, how could we ever have hoped to penetrate through the narrow passage of the Skager-Rack [sic] Cattegat and the Great Belt, into the heavily mined seas of the Western Baltic?'[20]

It is this memorandum on which has been based the nearly universal belief in the impossibility of the Baltic Scheme. But Hankey later wrote:

'Broadly speaking I held that we should get better value for our small but efficient army by holding it in reserve until some favourable opportunity arose for using it in conjunction with our sea power. To quote from a memorandum I wrote before the war: "But if the Army has been committed to the centre of the campaign at the outset of the war, all possibility of influencing the course of the war in one of the manners suggested – a manner which sea power alone can render possible – disappears, and the advantage of sea power is to a great extent thrown away." From that view I never departed and it was with some regret that I had recorded the conclusions of the Council of War in favour of the dispatch of the expeditionary force to join up with the French Army. For the same reason I was opposed to the dispatch of the VIIth Division and should have preferred to see it kept in hand to form the nucleus of a force which could be utilised to take advantage of our sea power. I felt, rightly or wrongly, that a great opportunity had been lost.'[21]

It is easy to understand Hankey's change of mind, for once the BEF was committed to a continental war, and Germany given the opportunity to mine the western Baltic, the plan became, in his belief, a chimera. His view undoubtedly dated from this decision. Wherever it was launched, Fisher's war plans of 1906 quite clearly envisaged an immediate attack:

'Whatever we do must be done quickly and absolutely secretly. It will be throwing away all chance of success to put the expedition [to Borkum] off until our enemy has time to make all the necessary preparation. The attack should be delivered at dawn of the first day of war, and there should be no hesitation about pushing it home, whether the formal declaration of war has been made or not.'[22]

In other words, a 'Copenhagen', which Hankey supported until the policy of the War Office was adopted, so well presented by Henry Wilson. Esher had written: 'Suppose we had, at any time, been free to launch our whole force from any of the northern ports on the right of the Germans!!'[23]

The British General Staff was dominated by the heroic figure of Kitchener. His voice and his alone represented the view of the War Office and was always accepted as final by the War Council. Churchill could recollect no occasion when the War Council or Cabinet overruled him, and they never made a move without his agreement. But he had enormous weaknesses. He was quite incapable of delegation; the General Staff had declined to a position of a mere supplier of information and compiler of statistics. Most of the more able officers had gone to France, eager not to miss the great adventure that was to be over by Christmas, and their places were taken by retired officers or men who inspired little confidence. They were all terrified of the great Kitchener. None argued with him or made any proposal of their own;

they merely carried out his orders. 'I am not quite sure that he trusted anyone,' said Esher.[24] No one man could carry such a burden and Kitchener failed to provide new ideas, failed to discern anything beyond holding the line on the Western Front. It was left to Lloyd George and Churchill, ironically the two men who had opposed rearmament, to propose alternatives, diversions or new strategies and seldom did Kitchener fail to throw cold water on them. But his outward confidence belied inner misgivings. Grey wrote: 'When the opposing armies had dug themselves in, from Switzerland to the sea . . . no one was more perplexed than Kitchener. "I don't know what is to be done," he said to me more than once; "This isn't war." He must have reached his conclusion about the duration of the war by some flash of instinct, rather than by reasoning.'[25]

Fisher's views remained consistent. The main aim should be to penetrate the Baltic and land on the flat Pomeranian coast. To do this meant passing through the Kattegat and the narrow strait under the eyes of Copenhagen. Denmark, almost defenceless, was troubled at the fate that had befallen Belgium. Moreover many of the Danes from the southern part of the country were of German blood, whose loyalty was doubtful. First, therefore, it was necessary to safeguard Denmark and this could be achieved by an attack on Wilhelmshaven, Bremerhaven and Hamburg, cutting through to Kiel, closing the canal and isolating the narrow neck of land only 60 miles wide connecting the Jutland Peninsula with Germany. Such an action on the German ports would bring German troops rushing to defend their vital naval bases. Then would be the time for a feint on the Belgian coast, which would draw more German troops from the Western and Eastern fronts. Finally the landing on the Pomeranian coast would follow. Each landing would outflank the Germans on both fronts. Churchill said that, given the ability to defend Scandinavia, the position of Germany would have 'become desperate'.

That there were difficulties Fisher was the first to acknowledge. The German naval ports were heavily defended and protected by minefields. But he believed that a carefully planned operation would overcome these problems A long-range bombardment preceded by a well planned minesweeping operation would cripple the German Fleet, and, since the North Sea German ports were obstructed by a bar which could only be cleared by heavy warships a few hours either side of high tide, if the attack was timed with care, the German fleet would be trapped. Churchill supported the plan and, on 19 August, 1914, while Fisher was still his unofficial adviser, he obtained the Prime Minister's permission to send a memorandum to the Grand Duke Nicholas in which he stated the key to the Baltic was the Kiel Canal, which enabled the Germans to deploy their fleet in the North Sea or the Baltic at will. Britain did not possess two fleets, each superior to the German and the options therefore were either to entice the High Sea Fleet to action or to destroy the Kiel Canal by an attack on the Brunsbüttel lock gates at the western end. The operation of sending a British fleet through the Belts into the Baltic, he said, was feasible and transports to carry a large invading army could readily be provided from Britain. Churchill wrote in his memorandum:

'It would be possible, if we had command of the Baltic, to land a Russian army in order:-
(1) To turn the flank and rear of the German armies holding the Dantzig-Thorn [Gdansk-Torun] line, or which were elsewhere resisting the main Russian attack.
(2) To attack Berlin from the North – only 90 miles from Berlin in the direct line.
(3) To attack Kiel and the Canal in force and to drive the German fleet to sea.'[26]

The Grand Duke, in his reply accepting the offer, said, 'We consider that the suggested landing operation, under favourable circumstances, would be quite feasible and fully expedient.'[27]

'These ideas,' says Churchill, 'received a powerful impetus from the arrival at the Admiralty, three months later of Lord Fisher. . . . When I showed him my correspondence with the Russian Government on this subject, he rallied enthusiastically to the idea.'[28] Thus he implied that the idea was new to Fisher!

Fisher's plan was to mount a simultaneous attack on the Frisian coast to close the estuary of the Elbe, and therefore the Kiel Canal, by bombardment and mining. Plans for the military operations after the landing were a matter for the War Office, but no opinion was called for by the War Council.

The triple-pronged attack outflanking both the enemy Eastern and Western fronts – a third front – was the outline of the plan. Careful planning would overcome the problems. It was the only way to breach the developing deadlock in France. It would have hemmed in the German battlefleet, closed her submarine ports and put her army very much on the defensive. There could have been only one retaliation, the emergence of the High Sea Fleet to fight off the invaders, to give battle to the Grand Fleet, which the Royal Navy spent the rest of the war trying to achieve.

The Baltic project was discussed by the War Council twice, first on 1 December, 1914, when it was minuted that Lord Fisher 'pointed out the importance of adopting the offensive. The question of seizing an island off the German coast was adjourned'.[29] We may be quite sure that Fisher said a great deal more than merely point out 'the importance of adopting the offensive'. Bacon says, 'Questions of importance were always being adjourned by the War Council and rarely decided'.[30] It was again discussed on 28 January, 1915. Churchill went further to claim the strategy as his own: 'I told the War Council in his presence during our December discussions, in words which he often afterwards referred to, that there were three phases in the naval war. "First the clearance of the outer seas; second the blocking of the German fleet; and third the entry of the Baltic".'[31] He may well have spoken thus to the War Council in Fisher's presence, but good manners forbade publicly reminding Churchill that these were Fisher's words in his war plans of 1907. At that time he had proposed an attack on Borkum,[32] then unfortified, but conditions had wholly altered. The Germans too had seen the possibilities; Borkum was now a veritable fortress, and he no longer supported his original scheme, practical in 1907, but not in 1914.

Churchill could not see this: 'I even remembered the island of Borkum when my teacher had ceased to think so much of it.' But once an idea took root in Churchill's mind it was very difficult to dissuade him. In 1913, when Fisher explained the strategy to Churchill, the latter had the plans re-examined and updated. The intention was to use the island as a base from which to mount an assault on the mainland. The policy of 1914 of sending the maximum number of troops to France forbade the operation and the Navy in any case was extended in clearing the sea. Wilson and Battenberg still favoured the plan, but conditions had changed; the submarine, the mine, the aircraft and the long-range gun made the operation more hazardous and the possibility of a landing much diminished, which Fisher recognized. A case could be made for an advanced base, but to take the island right under the German nose would involve great secrecy and massive forces. It would give the enemy clear notice of Allied intentions; an immediate counter-attack could be expected and, before the base could be established, German troops would be massed on the adjacent coast and all surprise lost. Borkum is 100 miles from the Kiel Canal and 12 miles off the German shore at its nearest point. Between the island and the mainland are numerous sandbanks, unusual tides and currents. Once established in Borkum, there remained the problem of an opposed crossing to the mainland and a landing resisted in force, followed by a long fighting advance to the canal.

The attack on Borkum was no longer convincing. Better to attack with feints on Pomerania, the Belgian coast and in Schleswig-Holstein, followed by a genuine attack on the Brunsbüttel lock gates and, when the Kiel canal had been closed, penetration into the Baltic through the Skagerrak, timed so that the passage through the Belts at night coincided with the period on either side of low tide when the High Sea Fleet was trapped in Wilhelmshaven; an attack in force on Pomerania and the Grand Fleet stationed so as to meet the enemy when, and if, it emerged to round the Jutland Peninsula to enter the Baltic. With good planning, minesweeping methods and timing, the operation was entirely feasible, representing not only an opportunity to outflank the German Army but to force the High Sea Fleet to action. This would have caused the German High Command some real problems. In those days, before abundant reliable motor vehicles and good roads, the enemy relied on railways, horses and their feet. German railways were highly efficient, the network extensive, strategically planned by Bismarck. Even so, having moved troops, guns, stores and ammunition to Pomerania, back to Belgium and then to Brunsbüttel, only to have to return them to Pomerania would have taxed the ingenuity and strength of any army.

Churchill found the new First Sea Lord less than enthusiastic for the attack on Borkum, but strongly pressing the Baltic project. Apart from Wilson, who still favoured the Borkum scheme, Churchill had no support. All the remaining professionals were now against it and sought alternative means of mounting the Baltic operation. But Churchill had committed himself and was unwilling to admit the changed circumstances. He tried in vain to justify the idea and complained of lack of spirit by his naval colleagues.

> 'Many afternoons there were meeting in the First Lord's room. Fisher, Wilson, Graham-Greene (Secretary) and I [Oliver] and often others discussed future possible and impossible operations. Churchill wanted to land troops at Borkum Island and capture it. Emden was to be captured at the same time – both impossible to hold if captured as we had not the land forces. Fisher wanted to send the Grand Fleet into the Baltic and convey a Russian Army from Petrograd to land and take Berlin. . . .
>
> 'Wilson wanted to bombard Heligoland with the old pre-dreadnought battleships and land and capture it; our old ships with their short 12-inch guns would have stood little chance against the guns of modern batteries. If captured, every time supplies were required would involve a major operation for the Grand Fleet in the minefields, and the island was within gun range of the mainland.
>
> 'I hated all these projects but had to be careful what I said. The saving clause was that two of the three were always violently opposed to the plan of the third under discussion. . . .'[33]
>
> 'Churchill would often look in on his way to bed and tell me how he would capture Borkum or Sylt. If I did not interrupt or ask questions he would capture Borkum in twenty minutes.'[34]

That a tactician of Wilson's ability should advocate the capture of Heligoland is most surprising and, however much Fisher lamented its cession by Salisbury in exchange for Zanzibar, he would never have agreed to assault that impregnable fortress. It stands high and precipitous directly out of the sea, has a flat top and is one of the most easily defended solid rocks in the world.

Apart from *Severn*, *Humber* and *Mersey*, the monitors would not be ready for some months and the 5th Battle Squadron of the eight 'Formidables', each armed with four 12-inch guns, was chosen to form the nucleus of the future bombarding fleet and could in the meantime be used in support of the Army on the Belgian coast.

On 29 December Churchill, in a minute to the Prime Minister, put the case for the Baltic project:

'The invasion of Schleswig-Holstein from the sea would at once threaten the Kiel Canal and enable Denmark to join us. The accession of Denmark would throw open the Baltic. British naval command of the Baltic would enable the Russian armies to be landed within 90 miles of Berlin; and the enemy, while being closely held on all existing lines, would be forced to face new attacks directed at vital points and exhaust himself along a still larger perimeter.'[35]

But he spoilt his case by asserting that the capture of Borkum was a necessary preliminary to closing the Elbe and could be held without compromising the action of the Grand Fleet. Borkum, 80 miles from the Elbe, would not close it.

'During December and January I continued to explore and endeavoured to animate the Baltic project. . . . The detailed scheme of an attack on Borkum, and for holding it after it was captured, might reveal risks and complications which no one would face. Projects of landing large armies in Schleswig-Holstein were obviously at this stage of the most speculative character. . . . But having regard to the First Sea Lord's favourable views, and the obvious greatness of the prize, I continued to press the subject forward and to explore it by every means open to me. . . . But it would have taken the full impulse of the Allies to make the matter move.'[36]

Surely the facts speak otherwise. Churchill was committed to Borkum as a first step, in which he was opposed by all but one admiral. Landing large armies in Schleswig-Holstein was not as 'speculative' as landing in Borkum. Given properly coordinated plans, the Baltic project could have been a success, but Fisher's proposals were not embraced with eagerness. There were difficulties and caution was needed. Two nations were involved, neither familiar with the language or methods of the other, but the main military objection was that no landing could be considered unless the Navy could *guarantee* that their troops, all their equipment and transport could reach shore unmolested, and after disembarkation would not merely have a beachhead, but sufficient area free from hostile fire to form up for battle. In other words, they were only prepared to consider an orderly, unopposed landing and, despite these idealistic conditions, naval opinion was that four divisions could be landed in the first day. General Ellison wrote:

'Fisher was no dreamer. Time and again he had been proved in practice to be right after his plans had encountered most bitter opposition in many quarters, both naval and political. He himself had no doubts as to the ultimate success of the North Sea-Baltic scheme, and Wilson shared his views. . . . Their plan of 1914 was the logical development of the strategical conception that had held good since 1904.'[37]

Fisher wrote in 1917:

> 'Some terrible headlines in the newspapers have upset me! Terribly! "The German Fleet to assist the land operations in the Baltic". "Landing the German Army south of Reval". We are five times stronger at sea than our enemies and here is a small fleet, that we could gobble up in a few minutes, playing the great vital sea-part of landing an army in the enemy's rear and probably capturing the Russian capital [St Petersburg] by sea. This is 'holding the ring' with a vengeance! I hear a new Order of Knighthood is on the Tapis – OMG, (Oh! My God!) Shower it on the Admiralty!!'[38]

In March, 1918, he wrote:

> 'Never was there such criminal folly as the relegation of the Navy into a "subsidiary Service" as so described by Sir Ivor Philipp MP in the House of Commons quite recently. Instead of (with the main help of the Fleet) at the very outset of the war having obtained with the Expeditionary Force possession of Antwerp and the Belgian coast, we had instead thereof the "Massacre of Mons" and our expeditionary force was actually detrained under the fire of the German Army under General Von Kluck. In a printed memorandum prepared in 1914 it was incontestably proved that the Baltic constituted the decisive theatre of the war, but this Navy plan was condemned and turned down, notwithstanding Mr Churchill's representation to the War Council at its ninth meeting at 6.30 pm on 28th January, 1915, and we now see the consequences in two-thirds of Russia being under German domination and Germany with a greater conquest than ever effected by the Roman Empire. . . . But all this that I am saying to you is only a tiny bit of the congenital idiocy that has marked the whole conduct of the war.'[39]

The last word on the refusal to take the offensive came from Germany. When the German Official History appeared, it was revealed that Prince Henry, in command of the Baltic in 1914, asked for reinforcements when he heard rumours of Russian naval activity in the Gulf of Finland. The IVth Squadron and a few heavy cruisers were reluctantly sent through the Kiel Canal, but Von Pohl, Chief of Naval Staff, confided to his diary that the whole project caused him 'grave anxiety'. A few days later Pohl was warned that Britain was starting 'great undertakings' and at once ordered the ships back to the North Sea. Fisher was advocating the operation most feared by the German General Staff .

Tirpitz agreed: 'The English did not even seek battle under these favourable circumstances.'[40] Scheer, too, said in an interview with the American Journalist Cyril Brown: 'If the British Fleet had attacked in the first week of the war, we should have been beaten. Under cover of the British Navy, the Russian Armies, then available in great numbers, could have been landed on the coast of Pomerania and could have easily marched to Berlin.'[41]

Ellison believed the Baltic plan would have brought the war to a conclusion in 1915, and the fact that the scheme has been disparaged and dismissed by so many writers, historians, soldiers and sailors is due in part to the incestuous nature of historical writing, memoirs and biographies, which tend to utilize and repeat each others' conclusions as fact; a classic example is the acceptance of *The World Crisis* as history, and is reflected in Randolph Churchill's work, often used to support the former. Partly, too, it is due to those politicians, generals and admirals who opposed the plan at the time or desired to denigrate Fisher because they had incurred his wrath. In no instance has it been dismissed on informed logic, only bald statements that it was impossible. One of the most common arguments against the Baltic plan is the assertion, originated by Jellicoe, Beatty, Keyes *et al* that the Kattegat, the Skagerrak and the Belts were mined and impenetrable. But Tirpitz says they were not mined until after May, 1915:

'I may mention here that at the outbreak of war we had made an agreement with Denmark, by which the Great Belt was to be closed, under Danish guarantee, to all belligerents. England, however, did not recognise the right of Denmark to do this, and if the English had desired to force their way into the Baltic, they would have had no difficulty in overcoming the weak Danish barriers. This agreement, which was unfortunately approved by myself also in the early days of the war, proved disadvantageous to us, since we felt constrained throughout the war to pay respect to Denmark, while it prevented us from improving, by use of the Kattegat and the Skager Rack [*sic*] our unfortunate position in the Bight of Heligoland.'[42]

Churchill raised the Baltic scheme again in the Second World War. As Roskill wrote, 'As in World War I Churchill regarded the Baltic as the best theatre for launching the "naval offensive" which he was always seeking.'[43] After a depressing report from Admirals Sir Reginald Drax and Sir Gerald Dickens, who forecast that no offensive operations would be possible for at least six months, Churchill wrote:

'On the fourth day after I reached the Admiralty [September, 1939] I asked that a plan for forcing a passage into the Baltic should be prepared by the Naval Staff . . . meanwhile I had long talks with the Director of Naval Construction. . . . on September 12 I was able to write a detailed minute to the authorities concerned.'[44] Churchill recalled Lord Cork and Orrery to prepare plans for the Baltic scheme. 'Both Lord Cork's ideas and mine rested upon the construction of capital ships specially adapted to withstand air and torpedo attack. . . . I wished to convert two or three ships of the "Royal Sovereign" class for action inshore or in narrow waters by giving them super-bulges against torpedoes and strong armour-plated decks against air-bombs. For this I was prepared to sacrifice one or even two turrets and seven or eight knots speed.'[45]

In other words he was converting them to monitors.

'DNC thinks it would be possible to hoist an 'R' [Royal Sovereign class battleship] 9 ft., thus enabling a certain channel where the depth is only 26 ft. to be passed. There are at present no guns commanding this channel, and the states on either side are neutral. . . . The objective is the command of the particular theatre [the Baltic] which will be secured by the placing [in it] of a battle squadron which the enemy heavy ships dare not engage. . . . The presence of this fleet in the theatre would hold all enemy forces on the spot. . . . They would have to arm the whole northern shore against bombardment, or possibly even, if the alliance of the Scandinavian Powers was obtained, *military descents.*[46] (my italics)

6

BREAKING THE DEADLOCK

Stalemate on the Western Front, stalemate on the Eastern Front, stalemate at sea. It was not only the Allies who felt frustrated; Germany too could see no way of solving the intractable problem. Her naval weakness led her to seek every unconventional means of attack. In a memorandum to the Kaiser, Von Pohl reviewed German naval policy, recommending bombardment by airships of military targets in London and the lower reaches of the Thames, as far as possible sparing private property and historic buildings. The Kaiser approved; London itself was not to be bombed, attacks confined to the dockyards, arsenals, docks and military establishments. Such was British intelligence that before the memorandum had been laid before the Kaiser, it was being discussed in the Admiralty.

Most of the Royal Flying Corps aircraft had gone to France and the air defence of Britain placed on the Royal Naval Air Service. This was logical, as the majority of RNAS aircraft were stationed ashore at home. The chief of the Air Department at the Admiralty, Commodore Murray Sueter, said at the end of the year that there were up to 20 zeppelins capable of reaching London, each carrying a ton of high explosives. The airships could travel over Britain by night and be out of sight off the coast by daylight. It would take many months before any defence or retaliation could be developed.

Aircraft were a new dimension in warfare and zeppelins were regarded as the greater menace. In Fisher's opinion they were a deadly threat. In the early days engines were not powerful enough to enable aeroplanes to achieve the height attainable by zeppelins, which carried a much heavier load of bombs. Night flying by aeroplanes was hazardous. There were no observation posts, no network of telephones to report zeppelin movements, no anti-aircraft guns or searchlights. Zeppelins enjoyed an immunity that infuriated Fisher; few believed attacks would be confined to military targets; bombing of civilians was expected at a time when hysterical anti-German feeling was already running high, when 'Hang the Kaiser!' was a slogan, when Swiss restaurants were mobbed because their names had German origins, when many wanted to treat the crews of U-boats as pirates and execute them. In days when men still believed it possible to fight wars as gentlemen, attack upon the civilian population was regarded as savagery. Aerial bombing was new and, though its scale was paltry compared with that of 30 years later, it was regarded as terrifying.

Fisher, deeply concerned at the moral effect air raids would have on the civil population, held that drastic measures were needed and abhorred the lethargy with which the problem was addressed. Churchill took a more rational view. Unimpressed by zeppelins, he believed 'an enormous bladder of combustible and explosive gas' would prove to be easily destructible. 'I was sure the fighting aeroplane rising lightly laden from its base, armed with incendiary bullets, would harry, rout and burn these gaseous monsters.' Certainly these unwieldy craft were at the mercy of the wind and weather and highly inflammable.

'This situation preyed on the mind of the First Sea Lord. He believed that a catastrophe was impending and that he would be held partly responsible. He proposed to me that we should take a large number of hostages from the German population in our hands and should declare our intention of executing one of them for every civilian killed by bombs from aircraft.'[1]

Support for Churchill's claim and the exact nature of the proposal are hard to find, but in the prevailing atmosphere Fisher's view was commonly held. Churchill said he felt sympathy for these 'puppets of fate' and that 'shooting them in droves' would make no difference and only stain Britain's reputation. He expected large-scale attacks on London and accepted that there was no means of defence. He agreed to put Fisher's views to the Cabinet, but modified them to the effect that Britain reserved 'full liberty to regard these persons as hostages in a similar manner to those regularly taken by the Germans in France and Belgium'.

'I was therefore offended,' he writes 'to receive from Lord Fisher the following official minute,' and quotes *the last two paragraphs* of the minute, in which Fisher proffered his resignation. These, quoted in isolation, imply that this was solely because reprisals were not being taken. In fact the full minute read:

'*First Lord.*

'On December 26 the Admiralty had reliable information of a Zeppelin attack on London on the largest scale, with both naval and military German Zeppelins.

'This is January 4, and the public are not aware of what is impending, nor any step taken as reprisals in notifying German Government. There are at least 20 zeppelins available for this attack on London, and each Zeppelin can carry a ton of explosive. It is asserted by the experts that one ton of explosive would completely wreck the Admiralty buildings. This is quoted merely to indicate the terrible massacre resulting from the dropping of these 20 tons of explosive anywhere in the London area.

'There is no defence except reprisals to be officially announced beforehand to the German Government. As this step has not been taken, I must with great reluctance ask to be relieved of my present official position as First Sea Lord, because the Admiralty under present arrangement will be responsible for the massacre coming suddenly upon, and unprepared for by, the public.

'I have allowed a week to elapse, much against my judgment before taking this step, to avoid embarrassing the Government. I cannot delay any longer.

F.'[2]

'I thought it necessary', wrote Churchill, 'to reply as follows:

'*Mr. Churchill to Lord Fisher.*   *January 4, 1915*

'The question of aerial defence is not one upon which you have any professional experience. The question of killing prisoners in reprisal for an aerial attack is not one for the Admiralty, and certainly not one for you to decide. The Cabinet alone can settle such a matter. I will bring your view to their notice at our meeting tomorrow. After much reflection I cannot support it. I am circulating a paper giving the facts about a zeppelin raid as far as we can estimate them.

'I hope that I am not to take the last part of your letter seriously. I have always made up my mind not to dissuade anyone serving in the department over which I preside from resigning if they wish to do so. Business becomes impossible under any other terms.

'But I sympathise with your feelings of exasperation at our powerlessness to resist certain forms of attack; and I presume I may take your letter simply as an expression of those feelings.'[3]

Churchill 'received no reply and work proceeded normally, but it may have counted in the general balance of our relationship.' He must have known that the Prime Minister prevailed upon Fisher to withdraw his resignation.

Churchill put a misleading construction on the matter. The quotation of only the last two paragraphs gave the impression that Fisher was seriously proposing a barbaric act, but the omitted paragraphs show it was a protest at the failure of the Government, and Churchill in particular, to warn the people or to take action for their protection; Churchill's remarks were clearly intended to discredit the Admiral.

A few days later Fisher obtained information of a probable zeppelin attack on an east coast town, to be followed by another on London and he reported it to the War Council on 7 January. They took no action, so again he offered his resignation. His information proved accurate; on the night of 19/20 January bombs were dropped on King's Lynn, Yarmouth and Sheringham. Damage and loss of life was very small, but the effect on the public was comparable with that created in the Second World War by flying bombs. Again Fisher was persuaded to withdraw his resignation. He seems to have foreseen Churchill's tactic, for in 1919 (four years before Churchill's book appeared) he wrote:

AIRCRAFT

'Somewhere about January 15th, 1915, I submitted my resignation as First Sea Lord to Mr. Churchill because of the supineness manifested by the High Authorities as regards aircraft; and I then prophesied the raid over London in particular and all over England, that by and by caused several millions sterling of damage and infinite fright.

'I refer to my resignation on the aircraft question with some fear and trembling of denials; however I have a copy of my letter, so it's all right. I withdrew my resignation at the request of Authority, because Authority said that the War Office and not the Admiralty were responsible and would be held responsible.'[4]

There was certainly more to Fisher's resignation than reprisals; it had more to do with lack of energy over the supply of aircraft. Churchill's memorandum said he was 'circulating a paper giving the facts about a zeppelin raid', which may have satisfied the Admiral, but there is a discrepancy in the dates given by Churchill. He says the information came on 1 January and his memorandum is so dated. Fisher's letter states the information was available on 26 December, and anyway his resignation had more to do with events before its receipt. None would quarrel with Churchill's views on reprisals, nor dispute the Cabinet's responsibility, but no one had suggested 'shooting them in droves'; Fisher was dead when Churchill's book appeared, so we have his word alone. To assert that Fisher had no professional experience of air defence is odd; who had? He probably knew as much as anyone, and simply wanted action.

On the Western Front the stalemate continued, the generals adopting a war of attrition, trench lines running from the Alps to the sea, 350 miles, separated by barbed wire. In the Franco-Prussian war large armies attempted to turn each others' flanks and with increasing power of weapons, frontal attack had been abandoned. In 1915 there was no flank to turn, only the sea at one end and neutral territory at the other, so the generals adopted the use of men as battering rams. Attacks cost two or three lives for every enemy one, with perhaps a few yards of territory gained, only to be surrendered the next day or the next week in a similar battering attack, with similar enemy losses, every attack announced by a bombardment to clear the wire.

On the Eastern Front, during the first three months of the war, the Russians fired off 45,000 shells a day, while output of their factories was less than 1,200; by December they had less than a week's supply left and had suffered 1,350,000 casualties with the loss of over a million rifles. They had over 800,000 trained troops ready for the front, but no weapons, and every Russian gun was silenced.

At sea two great fleets glowered at each other from their harbours, the Germans, at the command of the Kaiser, scurrying back to harbour whenever a major action seemed possible. The most effective action on either side was submarine warfare and mining, mostly by the Germans, since nearly all her merchant ships had been cleared off the oceans, offering few targets.

The Allies fought their separate wars, each independent of the others, each nibbling at the common problem. Communication between politicians, admirals and generals, between governments, was largely by memoranda and telegrams. Churchill said in retrospect that a single prolonged conference in January, 1915, might have brought rich rewards. It might have brought adoption of the Baltic plan.

Wilhelm may have voiced French thoughts as well as German when he called the British a 'contemptible little army', for the French General Staff allocated it a sector considered unimportant. Only when the German attack through Alsace proved a feint and John French, on his own initiative, skillfully moved towards the Channel, outstripping the enemy, did the British Army find itself bearing the main attack. That it held and covered itself in glory does not deny Fisher's prediction in 1909 that it would come near to annihilation.

Moltke, says Churchill,

> 'had not thought it worth while to attempt to stop or delay the transport of the British Expeditionary Force across the Channel. According to the German naval history, "The Chief of the General Staff personally replied that the Navy should not allow the operations that it would otherwise have carried out to be interfered with on this account. It would even be an advantage if the armies in the west could settle with the 160,000 English [British] at the same time as with the French and Belgians".'[5]

Seldom had British armies and navies worked or exercised together, little inter-service planning ever took place and this remained true up to the Second World War when the problem was much exacerbated by the introduction of a third service. The naval rôle, Corbett argued, was not merely to provide transports and protection for the Army, but to take part actively in the assault of enemy territory in support of the Army and to ensure its safe establishment on enemy shores.

Fisher and Churchill both saw how to break the deadlock. If the Army could not perform an outflanking movement, the Navy must do it. Turkey, Greece, Rumania and Bulgaria had declared their neutrality, but the German policy of wooing Turkey and the German-trained Turkish Army, offered Germany and Austria the opportunity to break out into the Balkans and Middle East. The escape of the *Goeben* and *Breslau* into the Black Sea on 27 October gave Turkey the opportunity to strike at her traditional enemy, Russia. The ships were 'purchased' by Turkey and their officers 'commissioned' into the Turkish Navy. They retained their German uniform, but exchanged their service cap for a fez. Germany hoped to penetrate Persia (Iran) through Mesopotamia (Iraq), commercially and politically, make a thrust on the British position in Egypt and threaten India. To these ambitious schemes Constantinople was essential. Germany poured money and munitions into Turkey. For years she had trained and organized the Turkish Army and in December, 1913, Marshal Liman von Sanders arrived in Constantinople, with a staff of seventy carefully selected officers; from August, 1914, German naval and military officers, with mechanics and artisans, bolstered the Turkish forces. German officers were placed in command of the forts of the Dardanelles.

Churchill had visited the city in 1909, met many of the leading political figures and knew the geography of the area. On 1 September he tried to arrange with the War Office for the seizure of Gallipoli with Greek troops, to enable the navy to penetrate the Black Sea through which Russia could be aided and bring welcome supplies of wheat to her allies. The War Office said the difficult operation would require 60,000 men, half to be landed in the initial assault. Diplomatic information came from Greece, still neutral, that she could provide the forces against her historical enemy, but she did not trust Bulgaria, poised at her back door, and guarantees of neutrality would not alter this. On this mistrust the scheme foundered. The Greeks called only for a British squadron of two battlecruisers, one armoured cruiser, three light cruisers and a flotilla of destroyers. Britain could have provided more. Germany had not yet obtained full control of Turkish forces and the Dardanelles were still ill-defended.

Von Sanders and Admiral von Usedom, who arrived in September, became Commanders-in-Chief of the Turkish Army and Navy. During the winter months, despite myths to the contrary, Germans supervised massive Turkish labour battalions building Gallipoli defences. General Sir Ian Hamilton, in March, 1915, estimated that the Bulair lines, at the neck of the peninsula, alone must have occupied 10,000 men for at least a month. From Kilid Bahr to Achi Baba and on the Asiatic side, near Troy, excellent trenches had been dug and barbed wire entanglements erected on the hillside overlooking the obvious landing places. On 29 and 30 October *Goeben* and *Breslau,* supported by units of the Turkish fleet, bombarded the Russian Black Sea ports of Sevastopol, Odessa and Novorossiysk, destroying the oil installations.

Churchill's clear appreciation of the overall Balkan picture was accurately stated in a memorandum to Sir Edward Grey on 23 September. In contrast, the brief, inconclusive and ineffectual discussion of the Baltic project did the proposal no justice. It was never rejected; it was simply left in abeyance, always deferred for discussion another day.

This was typical of the way business was conducted by the War Council. Kitchener represented the General Staff and Churchill the Admiralty, Fisher and Wilson sitting silent, only speaking when called upon, while Churchill pontificated on naval warfare. During his interregnum, when Fisher had been a member of the CID in his own right, he had joined all the discussions, but now he saw himself as an adviser to a civilian minister, emphasized by Asquith seldom addressing questions directly to him or Wilson.

'One of Asquith's objects in setting up the War Council was to enable Ministers to question the Service chiefs. But a First Lord who had taken over so much of what others regarded as the First Sea Lord's rôle, did not encourage his political colleagues to question the latter. Balfour wrote, in September, 1915, that Churchill 'would not have tolerated for a moment the independent examination' of the First Sea Lord by a member of the War Council. Thus it was easy for the Council to gain mistaken impressions about the balance of professional opinion within the Admiralty.'[6]

Fisher and Wilson sat chafing as Churchill confidently expounded on naval professional matters, making incorrect and misleading statements to an even more ignorant Council. Feeling that they were there to answer questions and not to offer unsolicited views, they might as well not have been there. Fisher should have spoken up and ensured he dominated the Council on naval matters. With almost any other First Lord such would have been possible; as Carson was to say when First Lord, 'As long as I am at the Admiralty the sailors will have full scope. They will not be interfered with by me, and I will not let anyone interfere with them'.[7] With Churchill's mastery of rhetoric, however, it would either have led to bitter public disagreement or to Churchill making Fisher seem wrong, when he knew perfectly well he was right.

The arrangement was poor. It was proper that Kitchener, a professional soldier, represented the Army, even if not the best choice, but the Navy's representative was an enthusiastic amateur who had leant heavily on Fisher, with sixty years' experience, including many at the Admiralty under eight First Lords. By now Churchill fancied he had learned enough to express dogmatic views and ignore the advice of admirals who had spent a lifetime in the pursuit of what is, and always has been, a complex profession which cannot be learned without practical experience. Nor could he always distinguish between those who had learned and studied and those who rose with little exertion. Beresford, three weeks after Fisher's appointment, in a debate on the adjournment on 27 November, came generously to his aid: 'There is doubt in the public mind and a want of confidence in the Navy to carry out its duties . . . loss of confidence, in my opinion, is absolutely unwarrantable.' After surveying the disasters before Fisher's recall he continued that the duty of the First Lord was to lay down policy, not to tell the admirals how they should carry out that policy.[8]

At the War Council Asquith was a poor chairman, failed to probe any proposition, never questioned views put forward. Still convinced the war would be short, he remained deeply concerned about party politics and ensured the conduct of the war did not excessively interfere with his social life. He adhered tenaciously to the classicists' commonly held view that the 'trained mind' only could arrive at logical and reasoned judgments, that politicians by the mere fact that they had been elected to Parliament, knew better than the experts. Asquith was completely taken in by Churchill and believed that all the new ideas – many of which were not new at all – emanated from the First Lord personally:

'Then he unfolded to me his schemes for cheating and baffling the submarines. Some of the ships are to be clad in enveloping and protecting 'shoes', others to be provided round their keels and lower parts with 'saddlebags' and beyond all this he is going to establish by means of a huge network of wire and nets, a 'hen-coop' – somewhere off the east coast – with a couple of doors, in which from time to time our big ships can refuge and nestle without any fear of torpedo attack. A little later we hope we may have a still larger 'birdcage' of the same character further north. I like this; it is inventive and resourceful and shows both originality and dash. I laugh at our idiotic outside critics, who long for an expert instead of a civilian at the head of the Admiralty. Nothing truer was ever said than that 'experts are good servants but bad masters'. I am not sure that we are not really suffering from a neglect of this sound maxim at the War Office. The lunatic who edits the *Morning Post* writes me a long private letter this morning urging the supersession of Winston by Jellicoe.'[9]

The 'lunatic' was H.A.Gwynne, who, in criticizing Churchill's conduct at Antwerp, called not for his supersession but for him to be 'controlled'. 'There is an ample field for Mr Churchill's talents which are considerable . . . in securing for the experts of the Navy complete command of resources and complete freedom from political or amateur interference.'[10]

Asquith pretended to take the admirals' silence as acquiescence, but he well knew they violently disagreed. He had already prevailed upon Fisher to withdraw his resignation over air raids and wrote to Venetia Stanley:

'Hankey came to see me to-day to say – very privately – that Fisher, who is an old friend of his, had come to him in a very unhappy frame of mind. He likes Winston personally, but complained that on purely technical naval matters he is frequently over-ruled . . . and he is not by any means at ease about either the present disposition of the fleets, or their movements. Of course he didn't want Winston or indeed anybody to know this, but Hankey told him he should pass it on to me. Though I think the old man is rather unbalanced, I fear there is some truth in what he says, and I am revolving in my mind whether I can do anything and if anything, what. What do you say?'[11]

In fact he did nothing. Surely few Prime Ministers can have behaved more irresponsibly. If Fisher was really 'rather unbalanced', he should have been relieved at once. If there was 'some truth in what he says', emphatically Asquith should have probed the matter to establish the facts, perhaps by questioning Fisher at War Councils. That the Government of the day failed to make good use of so great a man, relying instead on the smooth talk of an ambitious politician, is inexplicable. Fisher was 'the greatest naval officer since Nelson', and, in this task, perhaps better. Nelson never became First Sea Lord and perhaps would not have done well. He was a man of action, not a great administrator. Fisher was both. Had Nelson lived and occupied the office he would perhaps not have remained a national hero; had Fisher died in victorious action, he certainly would.

The War Council met only about fortnightly and possessed no sense of urgency. Its minutes are littered with records of matters 'deferred' or 'adjourned' and astoundingly few of positive decisions or serious consideration of proposals, discussed in the loosest and most casual way.

The purpose of both the proposed attack on the Belgian coast and the Baltic plan was to turn the right flank of the enemy on the western front and their left on the east. Either could have been the last straw for the Germans. The alternative was to turn the other flank by penetrating the central powers through Turkey, a dramatically different scheme. The Belgian coast was only 60 miles from the British and, had it been taken, the nearest German naval bases, Wilhelmshaven, Bremerhaven and Hamburg, would have been 350 miles distant. The British fleet could have concentrated to the north of Holland with short lines of communication comparatively easy to defend. Landing troops at the Dardanelles, nearly 3,500 sea miles from home, involved long lines of communication, necessitating an immense fleet of colliers, transports and store ships (at one stage there were 60 hospital ships there). Landing on the flat shores of Belgium or of Pomerania would have been far easier than on the precipitous Turkish ones and allied military efforts would have been concentrated on the one decisive theatre. Churchill claimed the Dardanelles operation was a 'far smaller and less hazardous business',[12] and expected far less German resistance than in the north. The shortest route through Turkey to attack the eastern flank of the Central Powers was the Dardanelles; this was as obvious to the Germans as to the Allies and they had only one area to reinforce compared with the whole coastline in the north, from Belgium to the Russian flank.

Turkey entered the war on 29 October and on 3 November Britain and France declared war. Two days earlier, on Churchill's instructions, the outer forts of the Dardanelles were bombarded by Allied ships for about ten minutes. The reason given was to test the ranges of the German guns. No more foolish action could have been taken; nothing could be achieved in so short a time and all the action did was to gain credit for Churchill at home for the gesture, while alerting the Turks' German masters, persuading them to reinforce the defences to an even higher state of efficiency and give them three months in which to do so. Churchill claimed that considerable damage was done to the forts and several hundred casualties inflicted.[13] Since the two British and two French battleships fired only 80 rounds between them and the forts were in full working order when the attack came several months later, this seems unconvincing. 'There was a long-range bombardment of the outer forts at daylight on November 3rd,' wrote Lord Cunningham, 'We claimed to have done considerable damage, to have demoralised the Turks and blown up a magazine; but in the light of after events I think we erred on the side of optimism,'[14]

Churchill still supported the Baltic scheme. On 22 December he wrote to Fisher that he was wholly with him but that action to close the canal or defeat the High Sea Fleet in general action was an essential preliminary – which Fisher had already told him! But he continued significantly that the Baltic was the only theatre in which the Navy could shorten the war.[15] Asquith naïvely believed the whole idea was Churchill's. 'Winston,' he recorded in his diary, 'wants, primarily of course by means of the Navy, to close the Elbe and dominate the Baltic. He would . . . invade Schleswig-Holstein, obtain naval command of the Baltic, and thus enable Russia to land her troops. . . . There is a good deal of food for thought.'[16]

But Churchill's attention now began to be diverted to the Dardanelles. The traditional hatred between the Balkan countries, Bulgaria, Rumania, Serbia, each deeply suspicious of the others and covetous of their territory, had been exacerbated by the recent Balkan wars. Serbia was already fighting for survival against Austria. Churchill believed this motley collection of warring states could be persuaded to put aside their internecine differences in their shared hatred of Turkey. Without regard to their equipment, training or mutual distrust, he looked exultantly at the numbers of men they could put into the field, Bulgaria 300,000, Greece 200,000, Rumania 350,000, Serbia 250,000, a total of 1,100,000 men. For a politician who had so recently presented so masterly an appreciation of the Balkans, this was strange. If such unity were possible the political result could have been invaluable. It would have completed the encirclement of the Central Powers as British naval and combined operations in the Mediterranean had Napoleon. 'At one stroke, we could remove all danger to Egypt, secure the Balkan states, win the wavering respect of the Arabs and put an end to the hesitation of Italy.'[17]

On 25 November the War Council briefly discussed the Dardanelles. With Fisher's vigorous support, Churchill suggested that the best method of defending Egypt was by a combined attack on Gallipoli. But Kitchener said the time was not yet opportune and the only futile decision was that horses were to be transported to Egypt 'as opportunity offered', surely a waste of resources when no plans had been laid. Churchill pressed the matter. On 30 November he suggested that enough transports should be retained in Egypt for 40,000 men and, if this was not agreed, asked how much notice the Admiralty could expect for their requirement. Kitchener brushed the question aside with a curt note: 'I will give Admiralty full notice. I do not think transports need be detained in Egypt yet.'[18] He failed to define what 'full notice' meant, but, assuming he knew how long it would take to assemble the transports, he clearly did not see offensive action against Turkey for many months.

While Kitchener and French believed that every possible man should be kept available for the Western Front, the former had other undisclosed plans. The day he wrote this note he disembarked the two Anzac divisions in Egypt, where, under General Sir William Birdwood, they joined one Indian and one Territorial division, with a body of mounted troops. While the British naval squadron kept watch outside the Dardanelles, Birdwood's forces continued their training and waited, and though said to be destined for the Austrian Front, they were really intended for another plan. Kitchener believed the Turks could be dissuaded from attacking Egypt by an assault on Alexandretta. Here a deadly blow could be struck, cutting the Baghdad railway, Turkey's main line of communication eastward. Without adequate transport, Turkish armies would have been confronted with an 80-mile treck across mountainous tracks and their supply problem would have been immense. Furthermore, the local population, mostly Armenian, would certainly have welcomed the British as liberators. Kitchener's plan did not conflict with Fisher's Baltic strategy; the two complemented each other and it was a tragedy that the secretive soldier did not disclose his ideas to Churchill and Fisher, who might have embraced them with enthusiasm. Hindenburg believed the British had wasted an opportunity, suggesting that the fate of Turkey could have been settled by such action, the whole of the country south of the Taurus lost to them, severing the flow of forces to Mesopotamia and the Caucasus. 'Why,' he asked, 'did England never make use of her opportunity here?'[19]

Churchill made no recriminations against the War Office for their inactivity; the need elsewhere appeared too great to find the necessary trained troops, though he knew nothing of Kitchener's plan. Quite a small military force sent to the Dardanelles then would have been worth much more than the huge one that landed in April. But there was no willingness in the War Council for new offensives, only to throw more men into the trenches of Flanders.

At the turn of the year both the Admiralty schemes lay in suspense. Of the two, the Baltic scheme promised the greater results, but demanded immensely detailed planning and coordination between services and allies. The Dardanelles could have succeeded too, if it had been embarked upon at once, properly planned as a combined operation, without providing warning to the enemy by the useless bombardment of the outer forts.

Both Lloyd George and Hankey prepared papers setting forth the arguments for an assault on an alternative front. Churchill avers that they were prepared independently, but it seems a coincidence that both should present much the same argument and both should have been in Churchill's hands before reaching those of the Prime Minister. Both pointed to the stalemate on the Western Front, the pointlessness of attempts to gain a few yards at the cost of many lives and suggested that, if these were abandoned, a smaller force could hold the enemy and release troops for an attack elsewhere. Hankey wrote that if Greece and Bulgaria could be induced to cooperate, Constantinople, the Dardanelles and the Bosphorus could be occupied. He believed that in a few months' time three army corps, including one original first-line army corps, could be devoted to a campaign in Turkey without endangering the position in France, though sea transport might prove a difficulty.

Hankey's memorandum made many suggestions for alternative attacks, including the Baltic plan. Lloyd George wanted to attack Turkey through Syria, though he had no idea where to land the Army or what should be the line of attack and suggested it might be desirable to send an advance force through Salonica to find out. Both were considering an attack by the Army. The politicians' juvenile schemes were undeveloped, ill-considered, vague. 'After reading advance copies of these documents,' Churchill forwarded Hankey's paper to Asquith with a covering note: 'We are substantially in agreement, and our conclusions are not incompatible. I wanted Gallipoli attacked on the declaration of war [with Turkey]. . . . I think the War Council ought to meet daily for a few days next week No topic can be pursued to any fruitful result at weekly intervals.'[20]

Few would disagree. To organize a major war in Asquith's desultory manner was wholly unrealistic. A properly planned amphibious operation at an early stage before Turco-German defences were in place could have taken Gallipoli and entered Constantinople with relative ease, but it would not have enabled the Allies to strike at the heart of Germany. Constantinople is 1,100 miles from Berlin. The mountainous regions of Bulgaria and the Transylvanian Alps stand between it and the Plain of Hungary; the Moravian Heights then block the route to Germany itself.

During the months preceding Turkey's entry to the war, no preparations were made. Churchill had tried to manoeuvre Turkey on to the side of the Allies; when that failed, he attempted the unrealistic task of uniting the remaining Balkan countries against her. Kitchener recognized the threat to Egypt only when Turkey opened hostilities, when it was too late. Turkey thirsted to regain her lost provinces, Egypt and Cyprus from Britain, Salonika and Crete from the Greeks, Tripoli from the Italians. Two expeditions set out, one led by Enver Pasha in an attempt to take the Caucasus from the Russians, against the advice of Von Sanders, who reminded him that he was taking troops across mountains at Sarikamish in mid-winter, when the passes were blocked with snow and he had arranged no supporting lines of supply. Undeterred, Enver claimed that, having defeated the Russians, he would advance upon

India through Afghanistan, and the phlegmatic von Sanders was roused to say, 'Enver gave utterance to fantastic ideas'.

Simultaneously another expedition was mounted by Djemal, Minister of Marine, with the ambitious object of capturing the Suez Canal and throwing the British out of Egypt. This too ended in fiasco, only a few exhausted and demoralized troops reaching the canal, who were easily driven off, fewer still returning alive.

On 2 January St Petersburg telegraphed London that they were being hard-pressed in the Caucasus and asked for assistance. Politically, this was important; to refuse an ally assistance would have been a serious step and this factor was to influence Fisher considerably, for he regarded political matters as outside his province, and was always prepared to consider naval operations mounted for political reasons. The telegram included a passage which asked if it would be possible for Kitchener to arrange a demonstration against the Turks elsewhere, either naval or military, which would cause the Turks to withdraw some of their forces acting against the Russians in the Caucasus.[21] Kitchener sent the telegram to Churchill with a covering note asking if naval action would be possible to prevent the Turks sending more men into the Caucasus.[22]

It should have been obvious that Turkey was incapable of continuing pressure on the Caucasus and simultaneously mounting an expedition against Egypt; either would have been beyond her capability. Yet on 2 January, after receiving the telegram from St Petersburg, Kitchener and Churchill discussed it. Fisher was not asked to join this conversation, but the same day Kitchener summarized the discussion in a Memorandum to Churchill: 'I do not see that we can do anything that will very seriously help the Russians in the Caucasus. . . . In the Caucasus and Northern Persia the Russians are in a bad way. We have no troops to land anywhere. . . . The only place that a demonstration might have some effect in stopping reinforcements going east would be the Dardanelles. . . . We shall not be ready for anything big for some months.'[23]

Kitchener then sent a telegram to the Foreign Office for transmission to St Petersburg: 'Please assure the Grand Duke that steps will be taken to make a demonstration against the Turks. It is however feared that any action will be unlikely to seriously affect numbers of enemy in the Caucasus or cause their withdrawal.'[24]

Churchill admits he had no record of his conversation with Kitchener, whose memorandum clearly stated, 'We have no troops to land anywhere'. Yet the message to the Grand Duke committed Britain to making a 'demonstration'. This could only mean naval action unsupported by troops. Kitchener's enthusiasm for a demonstration is understandable, for it would materially assist his Alexandretta strategy; it was in fact an almost indispensable complement, a feint against the Dardanelles and Aegean Islands. 'The next morning,' wrote Churchill, 'Lord Fisher entered the field. He had been considering all these

117

matters, had read the various Cabinet papers and the Russian telegram, and had full knowledge of my conversation with Lord Kitchener.'[25]

The last sentence cannot be true. Fisher was not present at the conversation and Churchill had no record of it. How then could Fisher have 'full knowledge' of it? Corbett gives quite a different view:

> 'Fisher was more than doubtful. In his opinion the bombardment in November had shown that no possible purpose could be served by repeating it with the squadron . . . on the spot. For effective action a much larger and differently constituted force would certainly be needed. Still he strongly held the view that as an alternative theatre Turkey was the best in the field, *if a sufficient military force was available to cooperate with the fleet.*'[26] (my italics)

The same day Fisher wrote to Churchill that Hankey had told him a meeting of the War Council would take place, which he said would be 'like a game of ninepins! Everyone will have a plan and one ninepin in falling will knock over its neighbour!' He supported the attack on Turkey, but only if it was immediate, and did not believe it would be, forecasting that the Council would adjourn and decide on another futile bombardment. He suggested the appointment of Sir William Robertson in command of 75,000 seasoned troops from Sir John French's command with Territorials from England to be embarked at Marseilles and landed at Besika Bay on the Turkish Asiatic coast, with feints against Haifa and Alexandretta. Simultaneously, the Greeks would take Gallipoli, while the Bulgarians would go for Constantinople and the Russians, Serbians and Rumanians attack Austria. He nominated Sturdee to command a naval force of old battleships to penetrate the Dardanelles. But, he added '*Celerity;* without it, *Failure*'.[27]

Of this memorandum Churchill states 'The letter which he now sent me is of great importance. It reveals Lord Fisher's position fully and clearly. . . . He was always in favour of a great scheme against the Turks. . . . He was always prepared to risk the old battleships *as part of a large naval, military and diplomatic combination.*'[28] (my italics)

The next day Fisher wrote further to Churchill: 'The naval advantages of the possession of Constantinople and the getting of the wheat from the Black Sea are so overwhelming that I consider Colonel Hankey's plan for the Turkish operations vital and imperative and very pressing.'[29]

These minutes have been repeatedly quoted out of context as evidence that Fisher supported the Dardanelles operation and changed his mind at a later stage. But the minutes refer *only* to a combined operation and emphatically not to an unsupported naval operation. Even the combined operation he approached with great caution, and the rough outline he suggested would have required detailed planning. He knew the area better than Churchill. He had studied the problem when Phipps Hornby had forced the Narrows in 1898. He

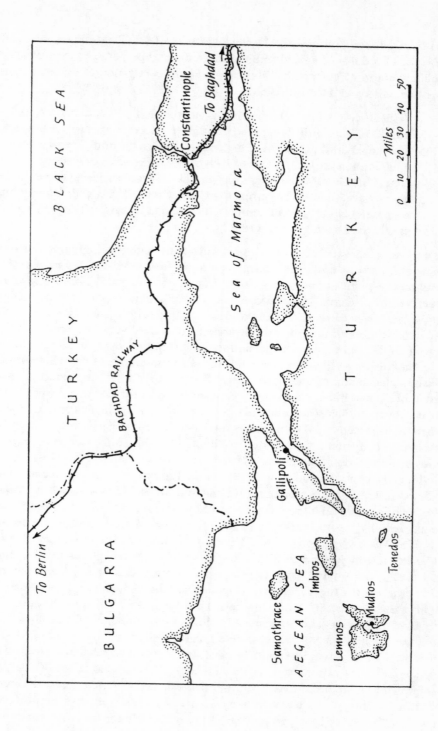

had visited Gallipoli and the Dardanelles while C-in-C, Mediterranean. As First Sea Lord he had agreed with the adverse report prepared by the naval and military committee which had investigated joint occupation of the peninsula. He had written to Tweedmouth on 27 July, 1906:

> 'The forcing of the Dardanelles is, in the first place, a military oper-ation ... and with the altered conditions of German supervision, and German handling of the Dardanelles defences, and German mines and German torpedoes, I agree with Sir John French that we cannot now repeat Sir Geoffrey Hornby's passage of the Dardanelles and even if we get passage, there is the getting back, as Sir John Duckworth found to his cost [see below]. But of course a reasoned argument will be got out to satisfy the Defence Committee.'[30]

The Dardanelles are about two miles wide at the entrance, opening out to a maximum of just under five miles. Ten miles further up the Narrows begin, and at one point are only about one mile wide. It is about eight miles from the Narrows to the Sea of Marmora. Fisher supported a joint operation provided it was carried out without delay and, if British troops were unavail-able, used those of the Allies in the area. Britain should, he believed, hit hard by land and sea in the peninsula and in Syria simultaneously or not at all.

Churchill wrote that there was not the slightest chance of the whole of the Fisher plan being carried into effect. Robertson would 'presumably' have advised against it, his policy being concentration in the decisive theatre. The withdrawal of 75,000 seasoned troops from Sir John French's command and their replacement by Territorials would have been resisted to the point of resignation by the Commander-in-Chief. General Joffre and the French Government would also have protested in a decisive manner.[31]

There is a lot of supposition in this, and a fundamental divergence of view. Churchill was already thinking of a solely naval operation, which he knew Fisher opposed, and if there was never 'the slightest chance' of the Fisher plan being adopted, we may ask why Churchill supported it, and indeed pressed it, until he realized no troops would be forthcoming. Yet he continued: 'Lord Fisher's fourth paragraph [Sturdee's penetration of the Dardanelles simul-taneously with military operations] made its impression on me. Here for the first time was the suggestion of forcing the Dardanelles with the old battleships. This series of weighty representations had the effect of making me move. I thought I saw a great convergence of opinion in the direction of that attack on the Dardanelles which I had always so greatly desired.'[32]

How Churchill could seriously have drawn such conclusions remains a mystery. To extract one aspect from Fisher's plan, the use of the old battle-ships, without all the concomitant essentials was extraordinary. No competent admiral would have advocated a naval attack without military support. At Churchill's request, early in January, Admiral Sir Henry Jackson prepared a

1. Admiral of the Fleet Lord Fisher of Kilverstone.

2. Admiral Sir Arthur Knyvet Wilson, VC, "the finest admiral of his day in command of a fleet" (p.3).

3. Reginald McKenna, First Lord of the Admiralty, April, 1908 to October, 1911.

4. Richard Burdon Haldane "also wanted to be First Lord" (p.12).

5. Admiral Fisher in the Funeral Procession for King Edward VII. "I've lost the greatest friend I've ever had" (p.6).

6. Winston Churchill, First Lord of the Admiralty at the age of 37, on board the Admiralty yacht *Enchantress* in 1912 (see p.22).

7. Herbert Asquith, Prime Minister
   1908-16.

8. David Lloyd George, Chancellor of
   the Exchequer 1908-15.

9. Sir Edward Grey, Foreign Secretary
   1905-16.

10. Fisher in jovial mood.

12. Prince Louis of Battenberg "resigned on the grounds that his German birth impaired his usefulness on the Board of Admiralty" (p.77).

11. Admiral Jellicoe, C-in-C Grand Fleet: "the only man who could lose the war in an afternoon" (p.10).

13. The German battlecruiser *Goeben* (see p.53 *et seq*). (IWM).

14. The battleship *Canopus:* "a citadel around which all our cruisers in those
 waters could find absolute security" (p.77). (Maritime Photo Library).

15. "'The aeroplane ship' *Ark Royal,* an ugly converted steamer with a launching
 ramp forward" (p.138). (IWM).

16. The Turkish Army "was mobilizing . . . under the German General Liman von Sanders" (p.54).

17. "Grand Admiral Von Tirpitz . . . had raised the German Fleet and commanded it until 1916" (p.17).

18. HMS *Queen Elizabeth*, "yet another product of Fisher's ingenuity" (p.47). (IWM).

19. Maurice Hankey, Secretary, Committee of Imperial Defence 1912-38.

20. A. J. Balfour, who succeeded Churchill as First Lord in 1915.

21. Admiral Sir Rosslyn Wemyss "accurately foresaw the breach" between Fisher and Churchill (p.74).

22. Admiral Guépratte, Commander of the French naval force at the Dardanelles.

23. (a) *Bouvet's* magazine explodes and (b) minutes later she sinks (see pp.151-2). (IWM).

24. *Irresistible* sinking (see p.152). (IWM).

25. "*Gaulois* had to be beached on Drepano Island with bows badly damaged by gunfire" (p.152).

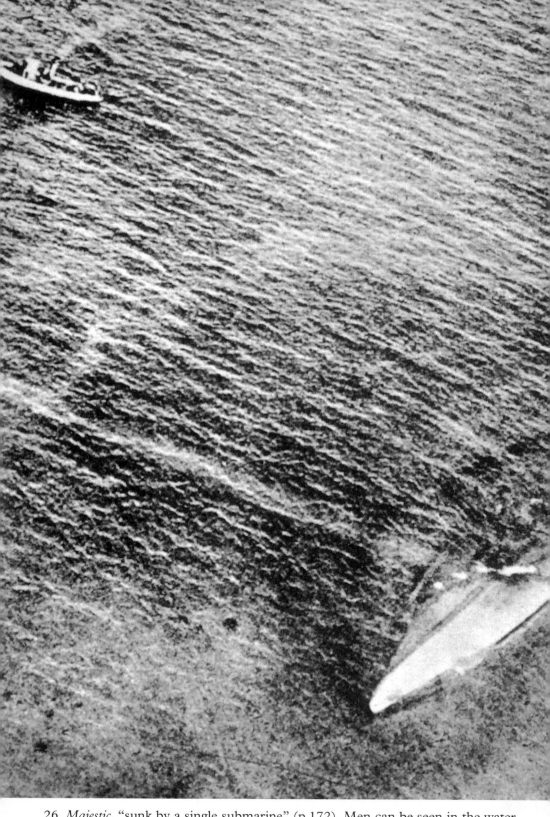

26. *Majestic*, "sunk by a single submarine" (p.172). Men can be seen in the water and on the hull.

27. Keyes, de
Robeck and
Hamilton.

28. "Abandoned":
London Opinion's
graphic comment
on the treatment
of Lord Fisher.

29. "*Triumph*, also at anchor, with anti-torpedo nets out, was sunk by a single submarine" (p.171).

30. Anzac Beach, Gallipoli: no room to land reinforcements or tend the wounded; steep cliffs behind and no water. Other beaches were much the same. (Australian War Memorial negative no. AO5763).

31. Australian soldiers in a bayonet charge at Gallipoli. (IWM).

32. Soldiers suffering from frostbite huddle in a shelter made from biscuit tins. (IWM).

33. *M15*, one of Fisher's monitors intended for the Baltic but diverted to the
Dardanelles. (Maritime Photo Library).

34. "The Field
Marshal was
sent off to
Gallipoli" (p.
218). Birdwood
(left) explaining
the situation to
Kitchener.

35. Kitchener and Birdwood at Russell's Top above Anzac Cove. (IWM).

36. Men being evacuated by raft from Gallipoli. (IWM).

37. Stores about to be burnt. (IWM).

38. "The people, in its silent, stolid, reverent British way, wrote its affection and admiration for 'Jacky Fisher' upon the social history of our time" (p. 241).

memorandum on the practicability of the operation without military assistance. He emphasized that, however successful, the fleet could not hope to obtain any result unless a large military force was available to occupy Constantinople.[33] Corbett wrote that 'naval opinion never doubted the unwisdom of engaging in an undertaking except in combination with a military force. But when the enterprise began to take on the aspect of a serious attempt to force the Straits and reduce Constantinople without military cooperation he began to contemplate it each day with graver apprehension.'[34]

The Dardanelles have always had a strange fascination for politicians. In 1806 Sir John Duckworth was chosen to attack the Dardanelles, which were being reinforced with French assistance, and expressed grave doubts: 'For though I consider it the duty of an Admiral to fight, it is a much more essential and bounden part of his duty to have mind enough not chimerically to sacrifice the force entrusted to his charge.'[35] The politicians had publicly committed him and in February, 1807, he broke into the Sea of Marmora with little loss. Far from fleeing in panic, the Turks redoubled their efforts to defend their city. After eleven days Duckworth was obliged to take his ships down the Dardanelles, suffering much greater damage than on the way in. 'Another week might have made the straits impassable.'[36] 'I must,' said Duckworth, 'as an officer, declare it to be my decided opinion that without the cooperation of a body of land forces it would be a wanton sacrifice of the squadrons ... to attempt to force the passage.'[37] Later that year a naval expedition to Copenhagen accompanied by 27,000 troops, achieved complete success. During the Crimean War it was concluded that possession of the Gallipoli peninsula was essential for a successful penetration of the Straits by a British Fleet.

When Fisher had joined Phipps Hornby in the Russo-Turkish war of 1877–78, even though the Turks were allies, Hornby warned the Foreign Secretary, Lord Derby, that if the Russians occupied the Gallipoli Peninsula with mobile guns he would be unable to keep the strait open for transports, colliers and supply ships. 'Not all the fleets in the world,' he said, could keep the Dardanelles open for the passage of such vessels without troops.

After the bombardment of Alexandria in 1878, Sydenham Clarke, then a Captain, Royal Engineers, had been sent to report on the effect of the naval bombardment and stated (rather unfairly), that the defences were very poor, magazines exposed, and (incorrectly) that there were no rifled guns ashore. But Fisher reported that 'The earthworks have sustained very little damage from our shell, and could be easily and rapidly repaired ...'[38] Percy Scott too, had remarked on the vast number of shell used by the fleet.

In response to a memorandum from Lord George Hamilton in June, 1890, on penetrating the straits, Sir Anthony Hoskins, then Commander-in-Chief, Mediterranean, wrote: 'If, as I presume is the case, the Turkish batteries and gunners are fairly efficient, such an attempt would in all probability end in disaster, and even if by a rush past at night the squadron succeeded in reaching the Sea of Marmara (*sic*) without serious injury, its position would be hazardous in the extreme.'[39]

At the time of the escape of the *Goeben* and *Breslau* Vice-Admiral Sackville Carden, the Admiral Superintendent, Malta Dockyard, had been placed in command of the squadron in the Eastern Mediterranean. He was not an able sea commander and was told 'your sole duty is to sink the *Goeben* and *Breslau*', in which he had not succeeded. Carden was a curious choice for the command. Rear-Admiral A.H.Limpus, who had only just left Turkey, where he had been head of the British Naval Mission, knew the country inside out, had an exact knowledge of the naval defences and was available. He had only the previous year supervised the Turks in laying mines and torpedoes in the Dardanelles against an attempted Italian penetration. Yet with schoolboy chivalry, Limpus was not placed in command because the Foreign Office considered it 'unfair' to the Turks! Carden was brought from Malta and Limpus, the expert, sent there to replace him.

The Germans now clearly expected an attack on the Dardanelles and Von Usedom took measures to ensure the passage could not be forced. The forts either side of the entrance, that Churchill had claimed were so badly damaged during the ten-minute bombardment in November, had been restored and were supported by searchlights. About 2½ miles up the straits thirty-six mobile howitzers (mainly 5.9-inch) and 24 mortars (mostly 8.2-inch) had been installed in batteries at intervals of under one mile, as far as the beginning of the Narrows, about two miles past the 700-foot peak of Achi Baba. On the southern shore five similar mobile howitzer batteries had been installed and were covered by a searchlight. All the batteries were carefully concealed and the Germans had cleverly placed numbers of dummy batteries, discharging black smoke, which later successfully drew the ships' fire. About 8,000 yards from the Narrows, abreast Kephez Bay on the Asiatic shore, was a field of five lines of mines extending for two miles; a mile further up was a similar minefield of five lines, extending into the Narrows, the ten lines consisting of 363 mines, covered by eight batteries on the European side and five on the Asiatic side, comprising seventy-four guns, mostly 3-inch and 4-inch, and eight 90-cm searchlights. In addition, Fort Dardanos (No. 8) overlooked Kephez Bay. At the narrows themselves there were five major batteries, three on the European and two on the Asiatic shore, together with the forts on either side of the Narrows, Chanak and Kilid Bahr, with fixed batteries of heavy guns. The most modern were 35-calibre, hand loaded Krupp guns of 1885, two 14-inch and six 9.4-inch on the European side, and three 14-inch and eight 9.4-inch on the Asiatic side. Limpus had installed torpedo tubes, and nothing was known about further installations after his departure. Although, in fact, the tubes were ineffective, they constituted a worry throughout the campaign. It was a formidable defence system.

On 3 January Churchill asked Carden if he thought it possible to force the Dardanelles. It seems unlikely that Fisher had anything to do with this enquiry, for he knew far more about the subject than Carden. With all the experience and records of the matter in the Admiralty, it seems curious that Carden should have been asked at all. He replied, guardedly, on 5 January: 'I do not consider Dardanelles can be rushed. They might be forced by extended operations with large number of ships.'[40]

To this Churchill responded, 'High authorities here concur in your opinion. Forward particulars showing what force would be required for extended operations, how you think it could be employed, and what results could be obtained.'[41]

'The "high authorities" I had in mind,' wrote Churchill, 'were Sir Henry Jackson and the Chief of the Staff. Lord Fisher had expressed no opinion on the technical question: but of course he saw the telegram.'[42] Of course he had not; he had never been consulted! He 'saw the telegram' after it was sent. The irritations building up between Fisher and Churchill now became acute. Such an operational message was squarely in the province of the First Sea Lord, yet Churchill not only sent it himself but did so without consulting Fisher, almost certainly because he knew he would not agree. Nor in fact did Jackson, who explained to the Dardanelles Commission his insistence on the need for troops. The use of the curious term 'high authorities' raises suspicion that Churchill was avoiding mention of opposition. The normal wording would have been simply 'concur' or 'approved', which would have implied Board approval, necessarily including Fisher. Carden confirmed that he never suspected Fisher had not agreed and the latter told the Commission that he certainly did not.

Churchill claimed that a formal memo from Fisher the next day indicated his support for the operation, whereas it surely indicates the operations now proposed would over-extend British forces. To claim it as support was absurd; Fisher was drawing attention to the folly of embarking simultaneously on so many widely dispersed naval and military operations, all of which were under consideration. He was appealing for rational planning of a firm and realistic policy for fighting the war.

January 6, 1915.

Chief of Staff.
First Lord.

'I think before the proposed bombardment of Zeebrugge is again discussed it should be carefully considered what certain losses we have to face in capture of Borkum; in attack on Dardanelles and forcing the passage; in Baltic operations – and (I HOPE) in landing and covering a British Army landed in the Spring in Schleswig Holstein to advance on the Kiel canal. No one can question that whatever damage is inflicted at Zeebrugge can be quickly repaired by the Germans, unless the Army join with the fleet to hold it. Are we going to bombard it every three weeks? P.S. I strongly supported the previous bombardment at Zeebrugge and would strongly support it now, but have we the margin of ships in view of the impending great operations? *and the men and officers!*[43]

Churchill wrote that this 'very clearly indicates his [Fisher's] position'.[44] Surely it is an insult to the intelligence of his readers to suggest it implies support for the Dardanelles operation without troops.

At a meeting of the War Council on 8 January Lloyd George opened the case for operations in an alternative theatre and there was a succession of discussions on various strategies, each of the politicians and generals vying with each other to produce his own scheme, most of them ill-digested and impracticable. Lloyd George's proposals for an offensive against Austria through the Adriatic met with 'a barrage of criticism'. Kitchener then read a letter from French to the effect that, until success in breaking through the German lines in France was proved impossible, there could be no question of making an attack elsewhere. But if these arguments were not accepted, an attack with Greece and Serbia through Salonika was perhaps the least objectionable. 'To attack Turkey would produce no decisive result, and would play Germany's game.'[45] The War Office had examined all the various proposals. Kitchener estimated that 150,000 troops would be required to capture Gallipoli, reiterated that no troops were available, yet blithely told the Council that it appeared the most suitable military objective! The ninepins were falling.

On 11 January Carden proposed a four-stage operation, with little detail. First, destruction of the outer forts, next action against the straits, then destruction of defences at the Narrows by shelling over the minefield at a range of about 10,000 yards and finally sweeping a passage through the minefield. He provided wordy generalizations and his 'plan' was little more than a verbose expression of the intention to force the Dardanelles. Perhaps his earlier telegram had been intended to placate the Admiralty and he never expected to hear any more of the matter.

It was axiomatic that ships should never attack forts, a lesson Fisher had learned as a midshipman at Peiho. If ships are forced to advance within range of shore batteries of sufficient size to damage them, the advantages all lie with the batteries. The ships, out in the open, can clearly be seen and cannot train their guns on all batteries simultaneously, while all batteries within range can be directed on the ships. Smokescreens can be used, but not from both directions at once. The shore guns, especially mobile batteries, can be placed out of sight behind hills. An observer on the hill can spot the fall of shot and pass corrections to the batteries, while ships stand out in the open sea, the splashes making observation easy. Conversely, the ships cannot accurately spot the fall of shot, every shell sending up clouds of dust and smoke, obscuring the target from ships and aircraft. Moreover, the trajectory of naval guns, designed for sea warfare, is flatter than those for land artillery, so that a small change in elevation results in a substantial difference in the point at which the shell lands. The ship makes a comparatively large target and can be disabled by a hit almost anywhere on the hull; the destruction of a shore battery demands a direct hit on the gun or its mounting. A miss is very much 'as good as a mile'; a shower of sand, stone and rock will be sent up, but when the ship's attention is diverted elsewhere the battery can be dug out and set up again, while all the time, not only is the ship moving, but it is rolling, pitching and yawing, while the shore batteries have steady platforms. Churchill stated that the 15-inch naval gun from a warship at anchor in calm weather and with perfect observation had a greater chance of hitting the targets than the contemporary 15-inch howitzer[46] and 'it was not only possible to hit *forts* at ranges from which they could not reply, but to hit in succession every single *gun* in them'.[47] These statements are ridiculous. It is difficult, therefore, to imagine what Carden had in mind. He could, with his longer-range guns, destroy the forts at the entrance, but only with the expenditure of much ammunition. Once inside, his position would be perilous and what 'action inside the straits' he proposed is far from clear. It is doubtful if the 'destruction of the defences of the Narrows' could be achieved from long range and without entering them, which required the prior sweeping of the minefields, impossible under the guns and searchlights ashore, by day or by night. These had to be destroyed first.

Again Fisher appears not to have been consulted; Wilson certainly was not, and had Fisher been he would almost certainly have discussed the matter with his old and trusted friend. Now Churchill took the matter out of his hands and on 12 January wrote a memorandum stating that forcing the Dardanelles would be a victory of the first importance and change the whole situation of the war in the east. He ordered the allocation of *Ocean, Swiftsure* and *Triumph* (already in or assigned to this theatre) *Vengeance* and *Canopus* (from the Atlantic), *Albion* (from the Cape), *Caesar* and *Prince George* (from Gibraltar), *Victorious, Mars, Magnificent, Hannibal* (already ordered to be dismantled at home), *Queen Elizabeth* (detailed for gunnery trials at Gibraltar), *Inflexible* (ordered to the Mediterranean to relieve *Indefatigable*), *Indefatigable* (already on the spot). He claimed that no capital ship would be ordered from home waters, except four already ordered to be dismantled, and margins necessary in home waters would not be weakened, while this took no account of four French battleships on the spot, and six others reported available. He continued: 'Operations could begin on February 1. . . . All arrangements should be secretly concerted for carrying the plan through, the seaplanes and the ancillary craft being provided. Admiral Carden to command. . . . Definite plans should be worked out accordingly.'[48]

Churchill said, 'Lord Fisher approved this minute.'[49] But he had little option, nor was he asked to approve it. The wording, specifically the last sentence, made it clear the matter was settled, a decision by the First Lord, using his ulti-mate power of veto. Fisher had been overruled. He would never have agreed;

Carden would not have been his choice to command; the motley collection of ships had never worked together. The four 'Victorious' class had been ordered to be broken up because they absorbed disproportionate maintenance resources, were worn out and their personnel was required to man new ships. *Inflexible* was ordered to relieve *Indefatigable* because the latter was seriously overdue for refit; to assert that both could remain was absurd and in any case both were needed at home. The Channel Fleet had been reduced by half. The new battleship *Queen Elizabeth* was programmed to do her gunnery trials at Gibraltar and, in a mood of frustration, Fisher suggested she might as well discharge her shell against the Turks. With hindsight, he should have resigned.

On 13 January Churchill sent for Percy Scott, told him of his plan and offered him the command. Scott emphatically and unhesitatingly refused, saying the operation was impossible. He consented to accompany *Queen Elizabeth* as far as Gibraltar, to assist in calibrating her guns, but would go no further for fear of becoming embroiled.

Kitchener meantime had communicated the decision of the War Council to French, whose proposed advance along the coast, aided by a naval bombardment, was rejected; the main effort must remain alongside the French Army. French, frustrated at the rejection of his plan and the indecisiveness of the Council, returned home and met them on 13 January. The meeting dragged on for several hours, Lloyd George and Balfour holding out against French's plan. At length the War Council turned to the possibility of action in the eastern Mediterranean. The members were tired and the meeting was coming to an ineffectual end, when Churchill, sensing his opportunity with magnificent timing, 'suddenly revealed his well-kept secret of a naval attack on the Dardanelles,'[50] and read out Carden's signal.

'The idea caught on at once,' wrote Hankey. 'The whole atmosphere changed. Fatigue was forgotten. The War Council turned eagerly from the dreary vista of a "slogging match" on the Western Front to brighter prospects, as they seemed, in the Mediterranean. The Navy, in whom everyone had implicit confidence and whose opportunities had so far been few and far between, was to come into the front line. Even French, with his tremendous preoccupations, caught something of the general enthusiasm.'[51] 'Everyone seemed alive to all its advantages,' wrote Churchill, 'If successful, the operation would open communications with Russia, enabling her to export her wheat and to receive munitions.' Churchill made no mention in *The World Crisis* of the fact that the Turks were totally defeated at Sarikamish; of 90,000 only 12,000 returned, the others being killed, captured or dying of hunger and frozen to death. The argument for the Dardanelles campaign had disappeared before it was started, and this information had already reached the Cabinet.

Kitchener and Balfour supported the plan. The Dardanelles Commission recorded:

'The First Lord thought it was possible to convert and extend that demonstration into an attempt to force a passage. . . . The views entertained by Mr Churchill at the time as to the prospect of success of a purely naval operation were somewhat more optimistic than was warranted by the opinion of the experts. Under these circumstances, Lord Kitchener grasped, perhaps rather too eagerly, at the proposal to act through the agency of the fleet alone.'[52]

Fisher and Wilson remained silent; neither was asked his view, nor were any questions addressed to them. 'Neither made any remark and I certainly thought that they agreed,' wrote Churchill.[53] Fisher may have thought he would get an opportunity to go into the details and remark on the expedition later. But Churchill's persuasive powers won the day. The War Council decided that two Territorial divisions should reinforce French for an advance along the Dixmude line to the Dutch frontier, that the Admiralty should consider action in the Adriatic, at Cattaro for instance (Grey's suggestion) and:

That the Admiralty should also prepare for a naval expedition in February to bombard and take the Gallipoli peninsula, with Constantinople as its objective.[54]

This was an extraordinary decision. A combined operation in which the Army took the guns from behind might have enabled the fleet to force the Dardanelles. How the Navy alone was expected to 'take' the Gallipoli Peninsula, fifteen miles long and seven miles wide and 'take' Constantinople 100 miles distant beggars the imagination. Hankey wrote that Asquith had in mind that, after the passage of the fleet into the Sea of Marmora, the garrison would be compelled to surrender. The War Council feebly laid down that if in the spring a deadlock occurred in the West, the new armies would be used 'elsewhere' and a committee was appointed to 'study the matter'. It was already too late.

'Fisher alone, whose silence had not meant consent as was generally assumed, was beginning to brood on the difficulties of his position which were eventually to lead to his resignation.'[55]

That he should have spoken up is obvious.

7

THE DARDANELLES

After the meeting of 13 January Fisher again studied the Dardanelles scheme and confirmed that it was impossible without the Army and, furthermore, would deplete resources at home. Churchill had confined his arguments to capital ships making no mention of the destroyers, minesweepers, colliers, auxiliaries and minor vessels needed. On 19 January Churchill, though only authorized to 'prepare' for an expedition, wrote to the Grand Duke, 'It has therefore been determined to attempt to force the passage of the Dardanelles.'[1] The next day, 'as the result of continued discussion and continued united agreement',[2] he issued a memorandum which said: 'The attack on the Dardanelles should be begun as soon as the *Queen Elizabeth* can get there. . . . All preparations are to proceed . . . in accordance with my minutes of January 12 and 13,' ending with the fiction, 'The First Sea Lord concurs'.[3] Sir Henry Jackson had prepared a detailed plan to accomplish Carden's loose outline, which has been cited as evidence that he supported the scheme, but he later told the Dardanelles Commission that he 'agreed to an attack on the outer forts and nothing more'.[4] It was no duty of Jackson or any other member of the Staff to attempt to dissuade the Cabinet or the First Lord from a decision finally made.

To the Dardanelles Commission Churchill claimed it was not until Fisher's Memorandum of 25 January, discussed below, that he had any indication of the First Sea Lord's opposition. Yet on 19 January Fisher wrote to Jellicoe:

> 'And now the Cabinet have decided on taking the Dardanelles solely with the Navy, using 15 battleships and 32 other vessels, and keeping out there three battlecruisers and a flotilla of destroyers – *all urgently required in the decisive theatre at home!* There is only one way out and that is to resign! But you say "no", which means I am a consenting party to what I absolutely disapprove. I don't agree with one single step taken.'[5]

Two days later he added:

'This Dardanelles operation decided upon by the Cabinet, in its taking away *Queen Elizabeth, Indefatigable* and *Inflexible* and *Blenheim* with a flotilla of destroyers arranged to have been brought home, is a serious interference in our imperative needs in Home waters, and I've fought against it tooth and nail, but of course if the Government of the country decide on a project as a subject of high policy, one can't put oneself to govern the diplomatic attitude of the nation. . . . I just abominate the Dardanelles operation, unless a great change is made and it is settled to be a military operation with 200,000 men in conjunction with the Fleet. I believe Kitchener is coming now to this sane view of the matter.'[6]

Churchill would have us believe that the man who wrote those words did not represent his views to the First Lord. There is no evidence that he put them in writing until 25 January, but the correspondence between them concentrates on weakening the Grand Fleet and on the 22nd he told Jellicoe that the decision on *Inflexible* and *Invincible* was reversed; they would leave the Mediterranean for Scapa, so much discussion must have taken place.

Asquith certainly knew more than he pretended. As Roskill said:

'Hankey was close enough to the Admiralty to know that Churchill was almost the only person there who had ever believed in a solely naval effort. . . . Here as always the chief responsibility for a mistaken decision lay with the Prime Minister. He knew more than his colleagues on the War Council about Fisher's forebodings. If anyone could have restrained Churchill, it was the Premier. But Asquith was not the only member of the Council to disregard warnings which should have been heeded. On 19 March, Hankey recorded laconically in his diary: "On the first day proposal was made I warned PM, Lord K, Chief of Staff, L. George and Balfour that fleet could not effect passage without troops, and that all naval officers thought so."'[7]

Asquith later suggested that Fisher's objections were confined to 'an avowed preference for a wholly different objective'.[8] His objections were the impracticability of the operation and the need to maintain the superiority of the Grand Fleet, without regard to the Baltic scheme. His memorandum of 25 January is worded as a formal step to place his views on record, for which he had the assistance of Hankey and Corbett. Reproduced in *The World Crisis*, it was addressed to Asquith with a copy to Churchill, the latter preceded by a note: 'I have no desire to continue a useless resistance in the War Council to plans I cannot concur in, but I would ask that the enclosed may be printed and circulated to its members before the next meeting'.[9] The memorandum ran to several pages and was a reasoned and convincing document:

'We play into Germany's hands if we risk fighting ships in any subsidiary operations such as coastal bombardment or the attack on fortified places without military co-operation, for we thereby increase the possibility that the Germans may be able to engage our fleet with some approach to equality of strength. The sole justification of coastal bombardment and attacks by the fleet on fortified places, such as the contemplated bombardment of the Dardanelles forts by our fleet, is to force a decision at sea, and so far and no farther can they be justified.'[10]

Fisher had made his objections to the Dardanelles more than clear to Churchill. His views were being ignored and inexorably the matter was proceeding. His memorandum was not circulated to the War Council as he had asked. With breathtaking absurdity, having suppressed all the professional opposition, so clearly expressed in his book, Churchill claimed:

'At no point did lay or civilian interference mingle with or mar the integrity of a professional conception. . . . There can be very little dispute about the facts in the face of the documents. For twenty days the project has been under discussion among the leading naval authorities of the day, and among the members of the War Council. At the Admiralty it has been the question most debated in our secret circles. *So far all opinions are favourable. So far no voice has been raised and no argument advanced against it.*'[11] (my italics)

Churchill's political security, boosted by the Falklands operation, was further strengthened when Hipper again attacked the English East Coast. Due to the intelligence of Room 40 his plans were known in ample time for Fisher to set a trap for him. We need not go into the failure of Beatty's signal organization to close the trap, but the sinking of the *Blücher* and serious damage to two other German battlecruisers at the Dogger Bank allowed Churchill to appropriate credit and his political star ascended still further. He was listened to with attention by fellow politicians at the War Council.

Churchill claimed that Fisher 'changed his mind' about 20 January. This is absurd; Fisher supported the Dardanelles operation until Churchill extracted from his memorandum of 3 January the paragraph relating to the use of old battleships and transformed it into a naval-only action. From then on it met his staunch opposition. He was far from alone in his views. The professional officers in the Admiralty almost all opposed it and the experienced French Minister of Marine, Victor Augagneur, who met Churchill in London on 26 January, informed him that French Naval intelligence reported that an attempt to force the Dardanelles without military support would achieve nothing. Before the next meeting of the War Council on 28 January Fisher wrote to Asquith;

'I am giving this note to Colonel Hankey to hand to you to explain my absence from the War Council. I am not in accord with the First Lord and I do not think it would be seemly to say so before the Council. His reply to my memorandum does not meet the case. I say that the Zeebrugge and Dardanelles bombardments can only be justified on naval grounds by military co-operation, which would compensate for the loss in ships and irreplaceable officers and men. As purely naval operations they are unjustifiable, as they both drain our naval margin. . . . We are at this moment vitally in want of destroyers, wrongly kept at the Dardanelles in opposition to my representations. We are sending our best submarines to the Dardanelles and our largest and most valuable battleship, the *Queen Elizabeth*, with the only 15-inch guns ready at present, besides sending other battlecruisers now there against my protest. . . . I am very reluctant to leave the First Lord. I have great personal affection and admiration for him, but I see no possibility of a union of ideas, and unity is essential in war, so I refrain from any desire of remaining as a stumbling block. The British Empire ceases if the Grand Fleet ceases. No risks can be taken.'[12]

This exemplifies Fisher's poor writing when in haste, comparing unfavourably with that when carefully considered. The portions omitted ramble into irrelevancies about Buller, Colenso and Spion Kop and the habit sometimes gave rise to unjustified doubts about his wisdom.

Before the Council Asquith called Churchill and Fisher to a meeting. The summons came in a cunning note from Churchill

'The Prime Minister considers your presence at the War Council indispensable and so do I. . . . You have assented to both the operations in question, and so far as I am concerned there can be no withdrawal, without good reason, from measures which are necessary, and for which preparations are far advanced. I would infinitely sooner work with you than with Sturdee, who will undoubtedly be forced upon me in the eventuality of which you write so lightheartedly.'[13]

If Fisher's presence at the Council was so essential, it must be asked why his views were not more often sought, and the statement that Fisher had 'assented' to the operation was untrue; he had assented to a combined operation. Finally, the hint that he might be replaced by the inadequate Sturdee would cause the old Admiral deep anxiety.

Fisher was unsubtle. Every time the Dardanelles was discussed, instead of pointing out its inherent shortcomings, he invariably dragged in his Baltic plan and the attack on Belgium. Asquith never appears to have questioned Fisher on his objections to the Dardanelles, and, had he done so, would have been convinced they were postulated to regenerate his Baltic scheme, especially as many of the monitors and other vessels built for the Baltic were now at the Dardanelles. Had Fisher attacked the operation on its inherent flaws he might have won the day and resuscitated the Baltic plan later. As it was, Asquith supported Churchill and together they persuaded him to attend the meeting. Again the sailor was outwitted by the smooth-tongued politicians. The Dardanelles Commission reported that, 'He did not criticise the attack on the Gallipoli Peninsula on its own merits. Neither did he mention to the Prime Minister that he had any thought of resigning if his opinions were overruled.' *Of course* he did not criticize the attack on Gallipoli; he fully supported it. It was the Navy-only penetration of the Dardanelles to which he objected. Churchill continued, 'I contended that both Zeebrugge and the Dardanelles scheme should be undertaken, but that if either were dropped, it should be Zeebrugge, to which the First Sea Lord seemed more particularly opposed.'[14] Asquith's letter to Venetia Stanley the same day does not support this:

> 'Another personal matter which rather worries me is the growing friction between Winston and Fisher. They came to see me this morning before the War Council and gave tongue to their mutual grievances. I tried to compose their differences by a compromise under which Winston was to give up for the present his bombardment of Zeebrugge, Fisher withdrawing his opposition to the operation against the Dardanelles. When at the Council we came to discuss the latter – which is warmly supported by Kitchener and Grey and enthusiastically by AJB, old 'Jacky' maintained an obstinate and ominous silence. He is always threatening to resign. . . . K has taken on the rôle of conciliator – for which you might think he was not naturally cut out!'[15]

Fisher had had other disagreements with Churchill over the action required as a result of the Dogger Bank engagement and attended the Council in a state of anger. He did not expect the Dardanelles to be discussed, but appears to have decided before the meeting that he would resign if it went ahead. It was, and he said 'that he had understood that this question would not be raised today. The Prime Minister was well aware of his views, yet said that, in view of the steps that had already been taken, the question could not well be left in abeyance.'[16] The Council supported a solely naval operation. Fisher rose from his seat and made for the room of the Prime Minister's Private Secretary, Bonham-Carter, to write out his resignation. Kitchener also rose, and stopped him. They stood some distance from the table, Kitchener urging Fisher to remain, saying that he was the only one present who disagreed and there were overwhelming political reasons for it. Fisher was the only responsible professional present and his views should surely have been given weight. Kitchener's motives were doubtful; Corbett says 'as a result of a study of this theatre by the General Staff, Lord Kitchener reached the conclusion that the Dardanelles was the most suitable objective',[17] but unquestionably he was thinking of his Alexandretta campaign, still kept strictly to himself. Fisher said he 'reluctantly gave in to Lord Kitchener's entreaty and resumed his seat'; another mistake, for this was the time to resign. It must have been perfectly clear to everyone present what had occurred, yet no one asked him for his objections. But, absurdly, Asquith told the Dardanelles Commission that he had no recollection of Fisher leaving the table! A wise wartime Prime Minister would in the first place have asked Fisher's views in writing, stating that the Baltic plan was not for consideration in this context. He could then have consulted the many naval officers available, when doubtless he would have been convinced of the folly of the idea and the later Gallipoli campaign never mounted.

Churchill could not leave Fisher's threatened resignation unexamined. After lunch he and Fisher met in the First Lord's room and Churchill says:

> 'I had noticed the incident of his leaving the table [He could hardly fail to; Fisher sat next to him!]. . . . I strongly urged him to undertake the operation, and he definitely consented to do so. I state this positively. We then repaired to the afternoon Council meeting, Admiral Oliver, the Chief of Staff coming with us, and I announced finally, on behalf of the Admiralty, and with the agreement of Lord Fisher, that we had decided to undertake the task with which the War Council had charged us so urgently.'[18]

Oliver did not normally attend meetings and evidently was there to provide some semblance of support in case Fisher raised any objections, but he appears to have been convinced by Churchill's plausible arguments that it was his duty to go through with the operation 'with which the War Council had charged the Admiralty so urgently'. Ever susceptible to appeals to loyalty, patriotism and duty, he may have felt he had been overruled and it was his duty to carry on.

The papers of the day indicate that the War Council, Churchill, Asquith and Balfour in particular, were so dazzled by the dubious political advantages of success that they never gave consideration to the consequences of failure and closed their minds to the possibility. Success seems to have been assumed by all the politicians and soldiers, no matter what the naval officers said. To Fisher the balance was strongly in favour of failure and the consequences appalling. The need for troops was raised at the meeting, but strongly resisted by Kitchener. After a few hours' perfunctory discussion, the War Council recorded its final decision, against the views of the acknowledged naval authority of the day: 'An attack should be made by the fleet alone, with Constantinople as its ultimate objective'.[19]

In a letter to Venetia Stanley, Asquith wrote that the War Council had dispatched Churchill to France to see French 'in order that both he and Joffre may realise the importance we all attach to being able to send at any rate two divisions to help the Servians instead of continuing to pour every available man into the north of France . . . Curiously enough it was K who suggested that he should go and pressed it hard.'[20] Was Asquith too naïve to understand Kitchener's motives? The Field Marshal had made it abundantly clear that 'we have no troops to spare anywhere'. Both Asquith and Kitchener knew French would stubbornly resist any reduction in his forces, but that Churchill's rhetoric would persuade him.

The operation went ahead in spite of Fisher, and, once committed, he did all he could to bring success. He had himself suggested that *Queen Elizabeth*, carrying out gunnery trials, could expend her ammunition on the Turks, but never contemplated her remaining after their completion. He was persuaded to agree to the operation because he was assured of its political necessity and that, if failure seemed likely, it could be broken off. The latter proved unfounded; within five days of the failure of the initial bombardment of the outer forts it was agreed that withdrawal was unacceptable. The War Council secretary's notes recorded that Kitchener pontificated on 24 February: 'The effect of a defeat in the Orient would be very serious. There could be no going back.'

The opening bombardment was to take place on 15 February, as decided by Churchill, the earliest date *Queen Elizabeth* could arrive, and he signalled Carden accordingly. He believed her 15-inch guns, the biggest in the world, would have a devastating effect. On 6 February he ordered two battalions of the Royal Marines to Lemnos, to land after the forts had been silenced, to destroy the shore torpedo tubes which were part of the entrance defences. Jackson wrote a memorandum stating in detail how the Carden plan should be executed. He proposed to anchor the bombarding ships out of range of the outer forts to save ammunition by eliminating one variable (not, as Churchill suggested[21], and a recent historian parrots, because ships' fire under way was inaccurate – their designed function!). Each ship would be provided with another to spot for her, and he detailed the best position for each bombarding ship and which fort it should attack, stressing that this was a stage-by-stage operation, each to be completed before the next could be entered. His memorandum comprised the best means of executing Carden's dubious plan, and, despite the limitations of his duties, he warned of his disapproval of the scheme without troops:

'The employment of the marine brigade must depend on the number and position of the enemy forces on the Peninsula and the Asiatic shore. If these can be held by the B`de, the work of demolition of the forts and guns may be thoroughly completed as the operations proceed, and look-out spotting stations established. Owing to the prevailing northerly winds and southwesterly current, it is probable that the fore-turret guns and starboard batteries will get an undue share of the firing. To prevent disablement of guns from this cause [i.e. from wear of the barrels] reduced charges should always be used if the range permits it. The provision of the necessary military forces to enable the fruits of this heavy naval undertaking to be gathered must never be lost sight of; the transports carrying them should be in readiness to enter the straits as soon as it is seen the forts at the narrows will be silenced. To complete their destruc-

tion, strong military landing parties with strong covering forces will be neces-
sary. It is considered, however, that the full advantage of the undertaking would
only be obtained by the occupation of the Peninsula by a military force acting
in conjunction with the naval operations, as the pressure of a strong field army
on the Peninsula would not only harass the operations, but would render the
passage of the Straits impracticable by any but powerfully armed vessels, even
though all the permanent defences had been silenced. The naval bombardment
is not recommended as a sound military operation unless strong military force is
ready to assist in the operation, or, at least, follow it up immediately the forts
are silenced.'[22]

The passages in italics were entirely omitted in Churchill's version. As far as possible in his position, Jackson had established the impossibility of the oper-ation without troops, for if only powerfully armed vessels could pass the straits, they could not then be supplied with coal, ammunition and stores. A repetition of Duckworth's catastrophe was inevitable. Yet Churchill, despite his suppres-sion of the vital passages, commented, 'There was much mixed thinking in this. The difference between "assisting in the operations" and "following it up immediately the forts are silenced" was fundamental.'[23] It was Churchill who was guilty of mixed thinking. On the 14th Richmond wrote, 'The bombard-ment of the Dardanelles, even if all the forts are destroyed, can be nothing but a local success, which without an army to carry it on, can have no further effect. ... Thirty thousand men at the Dardanelles next week would make more impression on the continental campaign than five times that number on the banks of the Yser.'[24] He wrote a paper accordingly, which Hankey described as A.1. and Fisher as EXCELLENT.[25] However, Churchill added, 'Fisher, on the other hand, was perfectly clear. He wanted the Gallipoli Peninsula stormed and held by the Army. This idea neither Lord Kitchener nor the War Council would at this time have entertained.'[26] This was not Fisher's view. He, Jackson and Richmond fully supported the attack if it was a combined operation, but not without adequate military forces. Churchill's many attempts in *The World Crisis* to suggest that Fisher changed his opinion later were false and, if 'neither Kitchener nor the War Council would have entertained' the idea, then the attempt should never have been mounted against professional advice.

The next day came the news that the German Marshal von der Goltz was strengthening the defences of the Dardanelles, and, too late, speed in mounting the attack was seen to be needed. German knowledge of British intentions is hardly surprising since security was puerile. Even the Prime Minister spread information with little regard for secrecy. He wrote to Venetia Stanley on 9 February: 'I can't help feeling that the whole situation in the Near East may be virtually transformed, if the bombardment of the Dardanelles by our ships next week *(Secret)* goes well. It is a great experiment. ... The only exciting thing in prospect (after seeing you on Friday) is what will happen in the

Dardanelles next week. This, as I said, is supposed to be a secret, and indeed it isn't known to some members of the Cabinet, though Violet heard Louis Mallet talking about it most indiscreetly at dinner one night . . . naturally I shall tell you *everything*.'[27] The same day he wrote again 'The result is – that we try the Dardanelles bombardment next week and with the French and we hope and believe the Russians, make the Serbian démarché by or about the beginning of March. This is all for *yourself alone*.'[28] Again, the next day 'A secret telegram came this morning which has only been seen by Winston, Grey, K and me, from the Admiral (Carden) that the business . . . has had to be postponed for a few days as the requisite minesweepers could not be got together sooner. . . . So far it has been on the whole a well-kept secret.[29] 'Most secrets,' wrote Esher, 'were the talk of the town.'[30]

Yet, if Asquith was right, the telegram from the admiral in command of the most important operation in progress was not apparently seen by the First Sea Lord. A well-kept secret indeed! But in fact the date of the intended bombardment was common gossip in the trenches of France.[31]

Delay, however, was unavoidable, for on 12 February *Queen Elizabeth* stripped a turbine and was reduced to 15 knots; she could not arrive at the Dardanelles in much less than a week.[32] And south-westerly gales intervened.

On her arrival Carden transferred his flag to *Queen Elizabeth* and the next day, 19 February, ominously the anniversary of Duckworth's attack, the bombardments of the outer forts took place. Carden had under his command the largest concentration of warships ever seen in the Mediterranean, fifteen British capital ships, mustering between them eight 15-inch, thirty-six 12-inch and eight 10-inch guns, with four French battleships with a total of fourteen 12-inch guns, cruisers, destroyers, minesweepers and ancillary vessels. The restricted waters compelled him to use only part of his force and he selected twelve ships, including the most modern British and all the French ships for the initial attack, the remainder held in reserve. A deliberate long-range bombardment would be followed by another at medium range and an overwhelming attack at close range. During this period the minesweepers were to clear a passage to the entrance to the straits.

The attack began just before 10 am, the slow bombardment lasting all the morning. As Cunningham said, 'It sounded just too easy; but few of us in the destroyers had all that touching faith in naval gunnery. . . . The shooting appeared to be fairly good. The forts seemed to be hit repeatedly, and made no reply.'[33] At 2 pm Carden closed to 6,000 yards and at 4.45 *Vengeance, Cornwallis* and *Suffren* closed further and the forts began to answer their fire. The light was failing and Carden ordered his ships to retire. Rear-Admiral de Robeck, Carden's Second-in-Command, flying his flag in *Vengeance*, sought permission to continue the attack, but was refused as he was silhouetted against the setting sun, an unnecessary refusal as he could bombard from outside the range of the forts.

During the whole of this languid bombardment only 139 12-inch shells had been expended, an average of less than two shells an hour for each ship! Carden's ammunition supply was limited; but the later Mitchell Committee concluded that to destroy the actual guns a success rate of not more than 2% could be expected, so few more than three guns could have been put out of action. Yet Churchill claimed the bombardment had shown it was possible to destroy the guns 'without undue expenditure of ammunition'.[34] This torpid exercise had little effect on the enemy, and demonstrated how 'just too easy' the Allies thought it was going to be. 'The net result . . . was precisely nothing, apart, perhaps from killing a few Turks. Really to knock out the forts it was necessary to get direct hits on the guns or their mounting,' wrote Cunningham.[35]

On 22 February a brief communiqué was issued by the Admiralty and a leading article appeared in *The Times,* obviously inspired, intimating that an attack of major importance had been initiated. It surveyed the political, economic and military advantages of forcing the Straits, referred to the consequences of the fall of Constantinople and opening the way to Odessa at the northern end of the Black Sea:

> 'Bombardment from the sea will not carry such a project very far unless it is combined with troops. . . . A bombardment of the entrances to the Dardanelles can only be satisfactorily developed into a combined land and sea attack, if the military strength employed is at least equivalent to the naval strength. . . . It is not enough to have plenty of battleships, for plenty of troops are required also. . . . No greater mistake could be committed than to give the fleet insufficient military support. . . . If the Peninsula of Gallipoli could be seized and safely held, the worst stage would be over!'

On the night of 19 February the weather broke, rough seas, bitter sleet and snow making further operations impossible. Carden, worried by the reaction in London, sent off a placatory and typically over-optimistic signal drafted for him by his jingoistic Chief of Staff, Commodore Roger Keyes:

> 'I do not intend to commence in bad weather leaving result undecided as from experience on first day I am convinced, given favourable weather conditions, that the reduction of the forts at the entrance can be completed in one day.' [36] This was an absurdity; 'an employment of ships of war that had been condemned by every seaman in the past'.[37]

The foul weather continued for five days and the bombardment was resumed on 25 February, continuing the next two days. 'The loss of life on both sides was small,' claimed Churchill, 'Practically no damage was done to the fleet, although the *Agamemnon* was hit six or seven times. In all only three men were killed and seven wounded.'[38] This does not agree with those on the spot. 'The ships steamed in line ahead and each took up her appointed billet for the bombardment. *Agamemnon* came to single anchor 10,000 yards from No. 1 Fort. At 10.38 the forts opened fire and hit her amidships on the main derrick-head, passing through the funnel, killing three men and wounding nine. Seeing shells falling all round her, the flagship signalled her to weigh. A large shell burst on the upper deck wounding many men, who could be heard groaning later. While weighing, shots fell just over and just short and she was hit five times. Next she was hit on S2 turret on the side armour; this shell then went right through the upper deck, and burst, splinters penetrating plating and cables, eventually landing in the Marines' barracks. The third hit went through the foremost funnel and burst on the port foremost winch, smashing it to pieces and holing the flying deck. The fourth shot hit the topgallant mast, above the foretop. The fifth, an armour-piercing shell, holed the side on the aft deck in the ship's office, passed through two cabins, through the main deck in the after hydraulic room causing a fire between two magazines. The sixth hit the 8-in. belt abreast of S3 turret and failed to penetrate it. At 1045 *Agamemnon* broke away and steamed out of range.[39]

The 'aeroplane ship' *Ark Royal*, an ugly converted steamer with a launching ramp forward, joined the fleet. She carried a motley collection of aircraft, the fastest capable of 105 mph, some unable to rise from the sea and some unable to climb above 2,000 feet. Neither pilots nor ship's officers had experience or training in air spotting. The midshipman of *Agamemnon* quoted above recorded in his diary many times 'air reconnaissance not possible', 'unable to understand your spotting corrections', 'cannot locate battery'. 'As far as *Agamemnon* was concerned, we achieved very little benefit from air spotting, although air reconnaissance was very helpful.[40]

After three days the Turks withdrew from the entrance forts, which were not their main defences. On the 26th demolition parties were sent ashore and Lieutenant Commander Eric Robinson succeeded in demolishing some of the guns, gaining a VC and promotion. Gales intervened the next day, but on 1 March demolition parties again landed and continued destruction of the outer forts.

At the conclusion of the bombardment of 25 February, an attempt was made to clear mines from the entrance, to permit bombardment of the minefield batteries and Narrows forts. Trawlers, rigged as rudimentary minesweepers had been provided to sweep mines inside the straits. The method was to sling a 2½-inch (circumference) wire between two trawlers, kept at the desired depth by two 'kites', the sweepers steaming on parallel courses, 500 yards apart, until the mine mooring wire was caught by the sweep. The mine was then dragged perilously to shallow water and exploded by rifle fire. Manned by civilian ex-fishermen, the sweepers were never intended to operate under fire and their crews, while prepared to face the peril of mines, expected to be able to deal with them in relative calm, not under gunfire, and towing the mines into shallow water in the confinement of the Dardanelles brought them right under enemy guns.

There is no tide in the Mediterranean, but many rivers, including the Danube, flow into the Black Sea and the melting snows cause a current through the Dardanelles of between three and five knots. Against this the trawlers could make little more than three knots and were sitting targets. A daylight attempt was unsuccessful, the minesweepers, unaccustomed to heavy gunfire, slipping their sweeps and escaping when fired on from both shores. 'Shell pitched all around the trawlers; but by some miracle they got away undamaged.'[41] Night-sweeping towards Kephez Point was then resorted to under the protection of destroyers. The trawlers, brilliantly illuminated by the searchlights, were again attacked, the destroyers firing ineffectually at the gunflashes and searchlights, which were immediately extinguished until the destroyers' fire ceased and then relit.

On the night of 10th–11th, supported by *Canopus*, *Amethyst* and destroyers, the trawlers steamed past Kephez Point to turn, pass their sweeps and come down with the current. *Canopus* went in first, firing at the searchlights,

> 'but for all the good she did, she might have been firing at the moon. . . . After this bombardment there was a pause for two hours to give the Turks the idea that operations had ceased for the night. The seven trawlers steamed up in line ahead, and by great good luck managed to get past Kephez Point, turn, and pass their sweeps while a searchlight was temporarily doused. The leading pair caught mines almost at once, and a trawler was blown up and sunk. The instant the explosion was heard ashore every gun that could bear opened fire. . . . There was nothing for it but to call the operation off.'[42]

The procedure was repeated the following night without a battleship, with no more success.

Keyes was a man whose personal courage and ambition far outweighed his ability. As a 14-year-old cadet he had sworn to be First Sea Lord. 'Keyes is a fine fellow but not blessed with much brains,' wrote Jellicoe.[43] Richmond called him a 'fighting blockhead – courageous, independent, but with very little brains'.[44] Keyes contemptuously accused the minesweeper crews of cowardice:

> 'To put it briefly the sweepers turned tail and fled directly they were fired upon. . . . It did not matter if we lost all seven sweepers, there were 28 more, and the mines had got to be swept up. How could they talk of being stopped by heavy fire if they were not hit? The Admiralty were prepared for losses, but we had chucked our hand in and started squealing before we had any.'[45].

Keyes suggested that the trawlers should be 'stiffened' with regular naval personnel. Each trawler was therefore given a commissioned officer in command, some armed with revolvers. Another attempt at sweeping was made on the night of 13–14 March, preceded by a bombardment by the battleship *Cornwallis* in a forlorn effort to disable the searchlights and batteries, which only prewarned the Turks. At 2 am *Amethyst* and destroyers were followed by seven trawlers and five picket boats with explosive sweeps. The enemy was ready.

> 'The Turks allowed the sweepers to get into the middle of the minefield on their way up, contenting themselves by firing a single gun. Then the searchlights went out for a moment, and flashed on again. It was evidently a prearranged signal, for at once every gun opened fire. Followed by a storm of shell, the trawlers held on to the turning point, which was roughly a mile above Kephez Point, then swung round and tried to pass their sweeps. They had pressed on with the greatest gallantry, but had already suffered severely. Two had their entire working crews killed or wounded. Hit by every sort of shell from 6-inch downwards, minesweeping kites were demolished, sweep wires cut and winches smashed. Only two were fit for sweeping and they got several mines. . . . "Kipper" Robinson had his trawler hit 84 times.'[46]

Night-sweeping had failed. The Mitchell report summed the matter up: 'The Minefield batteries had shown themselves to be so strong that the life of a trawler in a minefield was most precarious, and it was most doubtful, however determined and persistent the attacks made, whether any effective sweeping could be carried out unless the batteries were first dominated.'[47]

At home the mood was steadily changing. Almost imperceptibly, the need for troops was becoming accepted. According to Churchill, up to 28 January, 'the War Council and the Admiralty had accepted unquestioningly the basis that no troops were available for offensive operations against the Dardanelles. . . . It was on that foundation alone that all our decision in favour of a purely naval attack had been taken.'[48]

If the 'Admiralty' included Fisher, as it must, the word 'unquestioningly' is surely a terminological inexactitude. Fisher had reluctantly accepted the experiment on the premise that it could be broken off'. One merit of the scheme, Kitchener had said, was that, if satisfactory progress was not made, the attack could be called off without loss of face. Yet on 24 February he had said, 'There could be no going back'. These contradictory views were accepted by the Cabinet without demur. So Fisher's one hope of escape from disaster was closed.

It seems that Churchill, from the beginning, had every intention of luring the Army into a new expedition in the Balkans. He devotes several pages of *The World Crisis* to an attempt to justify this action and claims that the decision of the War Council on 28 January was not, as recorded by the Dardanelles Commission, simply that an 'attack should be made *'by the fleet alone* with Constantinople as its objective,'[49] (my italics) but also 'showed itself earnestly desirous of procuring some military force to influence the political situation in the Balkans'.[50] After the meeting Churchill crossed to France for his discussions with Sir John French. He then told Kitchener, to the latter's chagrin, that he had managed to persuade the Field Marshal that he could spare two divisions from the middle of March. The arguments he used are unrecorded. 'I was very much impressed with the Field Marshall's great desire to meet the wishes of the Government, even when he could not share our views.'[51] The idea of a wholly naval operation had waned even before the bombardment of the outer forts. When Churchill ordered the two battalions of the Royal Marines to Lemnos the Turks immediately moved two divisions into Gallipoli. The abandonment of the Zeebrugge plan and the bungled Turkish expedition against the Suez Canal made some other troops available. On 13 February Hankey managed to persuade Asquith that troops were essential. The latter wrote on the same day:

> 'I have just been having a talk with Hankey, whose views are always worth hearing. He thinks very strongly that the naval operations, of which you know, should be supported by landing a fairly strong military force. I have been for some time coming to the same opinion, and I think we ought to be able, without denuding French, to scrape together from Egypt, Malta and elsewhere a sufficiently large contingent. If only these heart-breaking Balkan states could be bribed or goaded into action the trick would be done with the greatest of ease and with incalculable consequences.'[52]

The action at the Dogger Bank showed that the Navy could prevent invasion, and the need for troops at home was diminished. When, on 9 February, the Salonika expedition had again been proposed to entice Greece into the war, it was agreed that first-line troops were essential and Kitchener had proposed the 29th Division. When the Greeks refused to be drawn into the conflict, the troops were available for use elsewhere; Kitchener, still hopeful of his Alexandretta project, only agreed to send them to Gallipoli with great reluctance, if troops were found essential 'at a later stage'. However, according to the Dardanelles Commission:

> 'After the meeting of the War Council on January 28 the objective of the British Government remained the same, but the views entertained as to the means of realising it underwent a gradual but profound change. The necessity for employing a large military force became daily more apparent. The idea of a purely naval operation was gradually dropped. ... General Callwell [Director of Military Operations] says it would be very difficult to assign any date at which the change took place. "We drifted," he said, "into the big military attack".'[53]

The best men on the spot were of the same opinion. 'I believe,' wrote Cunningham, 'that as early as March 3rd, Rear-Admiral de Robeck, commanding the inshore squadron, had reported that in his opinion the Straits could not be forced unless one shore or the other were occupied.'[54]

The Dardanelles Commission Report records that the naval officers, especially Fisher, 'were all along in favour of a combined attack, but not of action by the fleet alone,'[55] yet Churchill claims that 'once it began to be realised that troops in considerable numbers were becoming available Sir Henry Jackson and Lord Fisher began to press for their employment in the Dardanelles operation'.[56] Fisher certainly pressed hard, as he had done from the beginning, and so did some of the generals. The much-admired Sir William Robertson, who rose from private to field marshal, pungently questioned the wisdom of a naval attack unsupported and lacking surprise.[57]

Churchill had been working for military support much earlier:

'February 16 was a day of resolve. At a meeting of the principal ministers of the War Council, including the Prime Minister, Lord Kitchener and myself, the following decisions, eventually incorporated in the decisions of the War Council, were taken:- (1) The 29th Division to be dispatched to Lemnos at the earliest possible date, preferably within nine or ten days. (2) Arrangement to be made to send a force from Egypt, if required. (3) The whole of the above forces, with the Royal Marine battalions already dispatched, to be available in case of necessity to support the naval attack on the Dardanelles. (4) Horse boats to be taken out with the 29th Division, and the Admiralty to make arrangements to collect small craft, tugs and lighters in the Levant.'[58]

Such decisions, which should surely be taken by the Cabinet, were not even taken by the War Council, but by a select group, enabling Churchill's dialectic, with Asquith's by now convinced support, to bring pressure on the ageing field marshal. Fisher wrote to Churchill on 29 January (not 16 February, as stated by Churchill):

'I hope you were successful with Kitchener in getting the divisions sent to Lemnos *tomorrow!* Not a grain of wheat will come from the Black Sea unless there is a military occupation of the Dardanelles, and it will be the wonder of the ages that no troops were sent to co-operate with the Fleet with half a million soldiers in England. . . . Somebody will land at Gallipoli some time or another.'[59]

'Acute discussions took place at the War Council on 19, 24 and 26 February.'[60] At the first, three days after the agreement recorded by Churchill, Kitchener said he proposed to substitute the unblooded and only partly trained troops from Australia and New Zealand [Anzacs] for the 29th and retain the latter 'in readiness to proceed later to the East, if required'. Churchill expressed his disappointment and again surveyed the military and political advantages he saw in the campaign. The usual rambling discussion followed. Fisher pointed out that the transports for the Anzacs would have to be dispatched from the United

Kingdom and would take three weeks to reach Alexandria. As usual no conclusion was reached, the minutes recording 'No final decision to be taken at present with regard to the 29th Division'. At the meeting on 24 February, despite Churchill's eloquence, the conclusion was recorded: 'The decision as regards the 29th Division to be postponed until the next meeting'.[61] At the last of these meetings Churchill gave a fascinatingly optimistic picture of the Dardanelles: 'All the outer forts were now reduced, mine-sweeping had commenced, and as soon as the intervening minefields had been cleared up, the battleships would attack the forts at the Narrows.' He added, 'The military forces were not intended to participate in the immediate operations, but to enable him to reap the fruits of those operations when successfully accomplished. . . . In three weeks' time Constantinople might be at our mercy . . . the actual and definite object of the Army would be to reap the fruits of the naval success,' and, 'He believed that the moment it became clear that our fleet was likely to get through the Dardanelles, things would go with a run, and the Turkish Army would be cut off.'[62]

However, he formally recorded his dissent at the retention of the 29th in the UK, adding that 'he must disclaim all responsibility if disaster occurred in Turkey owing to the insufficiency of troops'.[63] Less than a month earlier, as Arthur Wilson told the Commission, Churchill 'kept on saying he could do it without the Army', and at the meeting of 24th Lloyd George had made the distasteful remark that 'the Army should not be required or expected to pull the chestnuts out of the fire for the navy and that, if the navy failed, we should try somewhere else, in the Balkans, and not necessarily at the Dardanelles'.[64] The War Council was far from unanimous, which accounts for the 'acute discussions' and 'gradual but profound change'.

'Winston and Fisher have, for the time at any rate, patched up their differences,' wrote Asquith, 'though F is still a little uneasy about the Dardanelles,' a gross understatement, again illustrating Asquith's misjudgment.

On 12 March Sir Ian Hamilton was appointed to command the force of British and Imperial troops and a French division of 18,000 colonial troops. His orders from Kitchener included the strict injunctions:

> 'The Fleet have undertaken to force the passage of the Dardanelles. The employment of military forces on any large scale for land operations at this juncture is only contemplated in the event of the Fleet failing to get through after every effort has been exhausted. . . . This does not preclude the probability of minor operations being engaged upon to clear areas occupied by the Turks with guns annoying the Fleet or for demolition of forts already silenced by the Fleet . . . and should as far as practicable not entail permanent occupation of positions on the Gallipoli Peninsula.'[65]

Already on 1 March five battalions of the Naval Division and the two of the Royal Marines, Churchill's private Army, had left for Lemnos. Kitchener, wanting a reliable report, sent General Birdwood, in command in Egypt, to examine the situation.

On 2 March, in response to an inquiry from the impatient Churchill, Carden, again probably under the influence of Keyes, made the unlikely forecast that, given fine weather, he expected to get through to Constantinople in fourteen days. There was no evidence whatsoever on which to base such a foolhardy prognostication. 'It sounded just too easy.'

Landing parties on 5 March suffered heavy casualties; they emphatically did not, as one author eloquently and inaccurately put it, 'roam at will across the Trojan plain and the tip of the Gallipoli Peninsula, blowing up the abandoned guns, smashing the searchlights and wrecking the enemy emplacements'. Their success was limited and Keyes was hardly complimentary about the Royal Marine Brigade:

> 'Yesterday the long awaited for landing covered by the R.M. Brigade, 'Winston's Own' took place in lovely weather. . . . They lost 19 killed and 23 wounded – 3 missing. A few bluejackets were killed in the demolition parties and boats crews. It was all over the same grounds as the pretty little fight I described to you in my last letter. . . . For several hours we watched the advanced party, cut off, trying to take shelter, but suffering severely from the enemy's rifle fire from concealed positions which we could not locate. Wounded men crawling along, then hit and killed. Some very gallant and heroic actions . . . the water along the beach where they were trying to hide behind bunches of seaweed and sand hummocks was being whipped up by bullets. . . . Most of the men were hit with explosive bullets, a very small entry and an enormous exit. . . . The R.M. Brigade is made up of pensioners of 40 to 50 – 12-year men of 32 to 40 – and boys of 19 to 22. . . . The officers are – many of them – school boys – clerks – volunteers – etc. – not much experience naturally. In fact it was the same tale as Antwerp.'[66]

The first stage had taken ten days and the obvious massing of heavy ships and the huge base of the landlocked harbour at Mudros, humming with life, made British intentions clear to the enemy who accelerated the strengthening of his defences. Local *caiques* passed to and fro ceaselessly and among them the Germans sent spies who daily informed them of every detail.

The second phase of Carden's plan had been unsuccessful, yet the attempt was made on 5 March to bombard the guns at the Narrows, over the mine-fields. Simultaneously indirect fire over the Peninsula was attempted by *Queen Elizabeth*, aircraft being used for spotting. The under-powered seaplanes, with their limited ceiling, and the lengthy period it took to reach height, were of little assistance, their problems compounded by clouds of sand, dust and smoke obscuring the targets when shells landed, by the poor quality of radio communication and inexperience of the pilots, observers and gunnery officers.

This was the first time any of them had undertaken any such exercise. The over-confidence of the airmen was demonstrated by Group Captain Williamson's letter to Professor Marder:

> 'It was of course, true, that at that time neither I, nor anyone else, had ever spotted for ships firing at a shore target. . . . But it never struck me that the spotting required would present any difficulty. With good visibility, no hurry, no interference from enemy aircraft or anti-aircraft guns, and a target that was stationary, in no wise camouflaged and very conspicuous, it would have interested me to know in what way it was thought I could go wrong.'[67]

But go wrong it did. The first aircraft's propeller broke off, the pilot of a second was wounded by a rifle bullet and the third was able to signal only one spotting correction. Keyes recorded,

> 'The seaplanes which we had relied on to give us information for the *Queen Elizabeth*'s indirect fire managed nothing. . . . They are not much use as their machines could only get up in a flat calm and take ages to get to a safe height, if they get there at all. They have only flown about four days.'[68]

The Mitchell Report confirms this:

> 'Had aeroplane [as opposed to seaplane] observation been possible there is little doubt that, *with sufficient expenditure of ammunition*, every gun might have been smashed. The forts were quite unprotected from this direction and each gun and mounting presented a maximum target. . . . Without aeroplane observation, little except moral effect would be expected, and this moral effect could be discounted unless the attack were accompanied by a simultaneous break-through of the Fleet.' (my italics).[69]

But how much ammunition? An unlimited supply would of course have achieved the object, but 'the ammunition reserve available at this time and the necessity for preserving ammunition for operations in the Sea of Marmora made economy in expenditure essential'.[70] The ammunition, mostly armour-piercing high explosive, was unsuitable for obtaining direct hits on individual guns, even if the spotting had been accurate. Indirect bombardment was continued the next day, and on 7 and 8 March *Queen Elizabeth* and the two 'Lord Nelsons' repeated direct bombardment from inside the Straits, with negligible results. Birdwood, who witnessed the attack, telegraphed home: 'I am very doubtful if the Navy can force the passage unassisted'.[71] The next day he again telegraphed, 'I have already informed you that I consider the Admiral's forecast is too sanguine, and though we may have a better estimate by 12th, I doubt his ability to force the passage unaided.'[72]

The practical realities, so long pointed out by Fisher, were now being driven home, though his view was dismissed and a soldier's realistic appreciation was at once accepted, a reflection of the weight carried by Kitchener, who would listen to his close friend 'Birdy', and the position of subordination in which the First Lord had placed the senior naval authority in the country. 'That a considerable force of troops would be wanted and wanted quickly, was becoming every day more plain to those on the spot.'[73]

On 10 March Kitchener unexpectedly announced that he would release the 29th Division and that the Allied force would amount to nearly 130,000 men and 300 guns, including 48,000 Russians with 120 guns. 'What precisely was the consideration which finally induced Lord Kitchener to cast the lot in favour of the Dardanelles is not clear.'[74]

There is so much muddying of the waters in *The World Crisis* that it is difficult to ascertain what was Churchill's real attitude. He accurately relates, for example, that Fisher offered to take command in the Dardanelles; 'Lord Fisher himself informed the Dardanelles Commissioners of this fact in a very frank and chivalrous manner,'[75] but draws from this the inference that Fisher supported a Navy-only operation. He continues:

> 'So far as the other responsible authorities cited in these pages were concerned, no sign of disagreement was manifested. Sir Arthur Wilson, Sir Henry Jackson, Admiral Oliver, Commodore de Bartolemé all were united and agreed to press on. The Ministers seemed equally decided. War Office and Foreign Office were eager and hopeful. The Prime Minister did not even think it necessary to summon a council and put the point to them. I have never concealed my opinion. I rejoiced to find so much agreement and force gathering behind the enterprise.'[76]

But the naval officers were steadfastly opposed to a Navy-only operation on tactical grounds and all had warned of the impossibility of the operation without troops, yet they had been overruled by their political master, and with a loyalty Churchill would have done better to have acknowledged, they co-operated against their own judgment and to the utmost. A dominant characteristic of Churchill was his inability to consider, or even hear, the views of others when he was convinced that his view, and only his, was correct.

On 11 March Jackson, in a memorandum to the Chief of Staff, reiterated his view that the action could only succeed with military assistance:

> 'Admiral Carden's report, No 194 of the 10th instant, on the progress of the operations in the Dardanelles shows . . . operations are now greatly retarded by concealed batteries of howitzers, and that their effects are now as formidable as the heavy guns in the permanent batteries. He also states that demolition parties are essential to render the guns useless. The enemy's military forces have prevented this work from being effectually

completed at the entrance, and they will be in an even better position to prevent it further up the Straits. . . . To advance further with a rush over unswept minefields and in waters commanded at short range by heavy guns, howitzers and torpedo tubes, must involve serious losses in ships and men and will not achieve the object of making the Straits a safe waterway for the transports. . . . I suggest the Vice-Admiral be asked if he considers the time has now arrived to make use of military forces to occupy the Gallipoli Peninsula, and clear away the enemy artillery on that side – an operation he would support with his squadrons.'[77]

Churchill wrote of this: 'This minute reveals a certain confusion of thought. No one had ever suggested advancing "with a rush over unswept mine-fields . . .". In fact the distinction between "rushing" and the "piecemeal reduction" was the whole foundation of the naval policy.'[78] That same day he sent a telegram to Carden, which he claimed enjoyed the support of all the officers on the Admiralty War Group:

'Your original instructions laid stress on caution and deliberate methods, and we approve highly the skill and patience with which you have advanced hitherto without loss. The results to be gained are, however, great enough to justify loss of ships and men if success cannot be obtained without. Turning of the corner at Chanak may decide the whole oper-ation and produce consequences of a decisive character upon the war, and we suggest for your consideration that a point has now been reached when it is necessary, choosing favourable weather conditions, to over-whelm the forts at the Narrows at decisive range by the fire of the largest number of guns, large and small, that can be brought to bear upon them. Under cover of this fire the guns at the forts might be destroyed by landing parties, and as much as possible of the minefield swept up. This oper-ation might have to be repeated until all the forts at the Narrows had been destroyed and the approaches cleared of mines. We do not wish to hurry you, or urge you beyond your judgment, but we recognise clearly that at a certain point in your operations, you will have to press hard for a deci-sion, and we desire to know whether you consider that point has now been reached. We shall support you in well-conceived action for forcing a de-cision, even if regrettable losses are entailed. We wish to hear your views before you take any decisive departure from the present policy.'[79]

Despite the plural, this could never be disguised as other than solely Churchillian, and if the English language can express a desire to 'rush' the straits and the Narrows this surely does so. It was a politician's message; the layman at home left the responsibility with Carden on the spot, yet made it almost impossible for him to refuse. Carden parried the attempt at delegation in a message cleverly designed to embarrass the Admiralty:

'Fully concur with the view of Admiralty Telegram 101. It is considered stage is reached when vigorous sustained action is necessary for success.

'In my opinion military operations on large scale should be commenced immediately in order to ensure my communication line immediately fleet enters Marmora.

'The losses in passing through the narrows may be great; therefore submit that further ships be held in readiness at short notice and additional ammunition be dispatched as soon as possible.'[80]

But how difficult it was to argue with Churchill. He returned on 15 March with another long harangue, attempting from 3,500 miles away to bully Carden into irresponsible aggression:

'You must concert any military operations with General Hamilton when he arrives. . . . We understand that it is your intention to sweep a good clear passage through the minefields to enable the forts at the Narrows eventually to be attacked at close range, and to cover this operation, whether against the forts or the light and movable armament, by whatever fire is necessary from the Battle Fleet, and that this task will probably take several days. After this is completed, we understand you intend to engage the forts at the Narrows at decisive range and put them effectually out of action. You will then proceed again at your convenience with the attack on the forts beyond, and any further sweeping operations that may be necessary. If this is your intention, we cordially approve it. We wish it to be pressed forward without hurry, but without loss of time. *We do not gather that at this stage you contemplate any attempt to rush the passage without having previously cleared a channel through the mines and destroyed the primary armament of the forts . . .*' [my italics][81]

Purporting to reiterate the Admiral's own plans, Churchill issued instructions. Pestered by this torrent of unnecessary messages, Carden replied testily enough: 'I fully appreciate the situation, and intend, as stated in my telegram of March 14, to vigorously attack fortresses at the Narrows, clearing minefields under cover of attack. Good visibility is essential and I will take the first favourable opportunity.'[82]

There are sentiments expressed by Churchill, in phrases and words also used by Keyes, which lead to the suspicion that the latter was in touch with someone at Admiralty, who passed his comments on to the First Lord. Carden, goaded by these messages, decided he must now take his big ships into the Dardanelles and finally silence the forts and minefield batteries before any attempt could be made at sweeping. The outer forts at Sedd-el-Bahr and Kum Kale were out of action, but searchlights remained at the former. The ships would approach the minefields and, over them, shell the forts and batteries in the Narrows, so that the minesweepers could clear the mines, after which the fleet would penetrate the Sea of Marmora. But this overlooked the basic problem of ships attacking forts and, even more so, land batteries. In his evidence to the Dardanelles Commission, Churchill said, 'This war has brought about many surprises. We have seen fortresses reputed throughout Europe to be impregnable collapsing after a few days attack by field armies.' This betrayed his failure to understand the difference between field guns and those of ships. He was referring to the forts at Liège, Namur and Antwerp, against which the Germans were able to place their guns wherever they wished, camouflaged even from aircraft. Out of range of the guns of the forts, they could find the range of the enemy and continue their bombardment until each fort was reduced.

> 'I do not think,' wrote Percy Scott, 'that the war brought surprises to those who knew anything about artillery fire. If the statement that all Europe thought the Belgian forts impregnable is correct, then all Europe was very ignorant. I cannot agree with Mr Winston Churchill, for I am quite sure that no officer with any knowledge of artillery fire would consider any fort impregnable from guns on land. Here we had a very wrong supposition and an even more erroneous idea, and these two wrongs were the basis for the authorities' decision that the obsolescent battleships in the Mediterranean could successfully attack the Dardanelles.'[83]

Carden had for some time been showing that his responsibility was telling on him. Pressed from above to do impossible things and from below by his rash Chief of Staff, on 16 March, 48 hours before the attack on the Narrows was due, he broke down and was obliged to surrender his command to Rear-Admiral John de Robeck, his Second-in-Command, (though Keyes' papers give us a suspicion that he wished to eschew the responsibility).[84] Wemyss, senior officer Mudros, was senior to de Robeck, but far less experienced; promoted commander for service in the Royal Yacht and again to captain for similar service, having never faced competition in his career, he had taken only 12½ years to progress from Lieutenant to Rear Admiral. Graciously, (or perhaps shrewdly) he volunteered to serve under de Robeck's orders, and set up a splendid back-up organization.

Churchill telegraphed de Robeck the next day asking him to say 'that you consider, after separate and independent judgment, that the immediate operations are wise and practicable'.[85] De Robeck replied that he was in 'full agreement', but cautiously added 'everything depends on our ability to clear the minefields . . . and this necessitates silencing the forts during the process of sweeping'.[86] He was given the acting rank of vice-admiral.

The next day, 18 March, de Robeck launched the attack in brilliant sunshine on a calm sea. Only six ships could enter the Straits abreast so the fleet was arranged in three groups, the first comprising *Queen Elizabeth* to port, *Agamemnon*, *Lord Nelson* and *Inflexible* to starboard, while *Prince George* and *Triumph* took station on the port and starboard quarters. The second group,

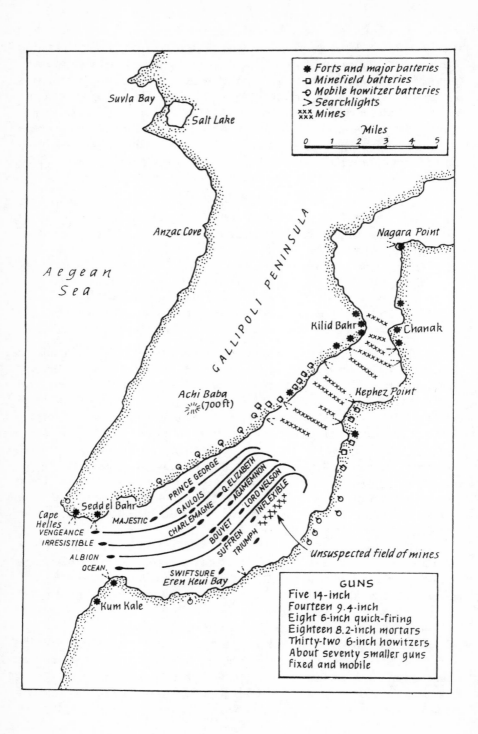

Suvla Bay

Salt Lake

Anzac Cove

*Aegean
Sea*

GALLIPOLI PENINSULA

Nagara Point

Kilid Bahr

Chanak

Achi Baba
(700 ft)

Kephez Point

PRINCE GEORGE
GAULOIS
Q. ELIZABETH
CHARLEMAGNE
AGAMEMNON
BOUVET
LORD NELSON
SUFFREN
INFLEXIBLE
TRIUMPH

Cape
Helles
VENGEANCE
IRRESISTIBLE

ALBION
OCEAN

Sedd el Bahr
MAJESTIC

SWIFTSURE
Eren Keui Bay

Kum Kale

Unsuspected field of mines

Forts and major batteries
Minefield batteries
Mobile howitzer batteries
Searchlights
Mines

Miles

0   1   2   3   4   5

GUNS
Five 14-inch
Fourteen 9.4-inch
Eight 6-inch quick-firing
Eighteen 8.2-inch mortars
Thirty-two 6-inch howitzers
About seventy smaller guns
fixed and mobile

about a mile astern, included the four French battleships, *Gaulois*, *Charlemagne*, *Bouvet* and *Suffren*, with the British *Majestic* and *Swiftsure* similarly on their quarters, while the last consisted of *Vengeance*, *Irresistible*, *Albion* and *Ocean*, with destroyers and minesweepers waiting at the entrance to the Straits.

The attack began at 11.30 am, when the morning haze lifted to reveal the Turkish forts, and the first two groups entered the straits, immediately coming under heavy fire from field guns and howitzers from both sides. The first group steamed steadily against the current until it reached a position about eight miles short of the Narrows, which both the minesweeping force, under Captain C.P.R.Coode, and aerial reconnaissance had previously declared free of mines, and from long range started a bombardment of the forts at Kilid Bahr and Chanak, the Allied ships out of range of the forts, which were hit repeatedly, and about 11.50 a heavy explosion occurred at Chanak, believed to be an ammunition store blowing up. But the ships were in range of the batteries, which inflicted considerable damage on them, and, after just over half an hour, de Robeck decided the first group should withdraw and the second, under Admiral Guépratte, should engage.

'We saw *Queen Elizabeth* hit abreast of B-turret,' wrote Midshipman Denham, 'and a big explosion near No. 13 Fort with large volumes of black and yellow smoke. A minute later a salvo fell all round *Lord Nelson* and then shots falling very near us, some close alongside, making the ship vibrate by water hammering. At 12.17 saw *Inflexible* hit on forebridge and *Lord Nelson* getting a warm time. At 12.22 salvos of three or four shots 50 yards off our port beam continued to fall all round us, probably from 8-inch howitzers which we could not locate; they burst on striking the water very close, making the ship shake like blazes. I thought the after turret was going by the board, for it lifted clean off its seating and shook everyone inside. More shots hit us; shell burst just outside our turret; saw all the flash inside and much noise; it must have been a high explosive shell. At 1.06, shot hit the conning tower, others close, but we now cleared out of range and as shots fell astern of us they started to practise [sic] on *Lord Nelson*.'[87]

Inflexible had been considerably damaged, with fires in her upperworks and a jagged hole in her side. *Agamemnon* had sustained twelve hits, though casualties were few. What was now apparent, but appears not to have occurred to the panegyrists of the operation, was the effect of the high-angle fire from the batteries and forts, resulting in shot falling at a steep angle. Thus the side armour of the ships was of little advantage, most of the enemy shells landing on the lightly armoured ships' decks, penetrating them and bursting inside.

The first group turned together to starboard and retired in line ahead about 3,000 yards off the southern shore, where there were fewer guns, but a new line of 20 mines had been laid parallel to the Asiatic shore, in Eren Keui Bay, where the enemy had noted that the fleet habitually turned. *Irresistible, Ocean* and *Bouvet* were sunk. *Inflexible* was badly damaged, with a hole 25 by 24 feet and seven collision mats out,[88] 'with her forecastle nearly level with the water and the ship's company mustered aft',[89] (to keep the bows as high in the water as possible). She had to be convoyed to Malta for repair. *Lord Nelson* and *Agamemnon* also needed repair, and *Gaulois* had to be beached on Drepano Island with bows badly damaged by gunfire. All this in only Carden's second phase, which had taken just a month and had been wholly unsuccessful. The fleet turned back well below the main minefields.

De Robeck reported the result in a cable that reached Admiralty early next morning. He was deeply distressed and thought he would be relieved of his command, but prepared to renew the attack. Churchill told the Dardanelles Commission he 'regarded it as only the first of several days' fighting. . . . It never occurred to me that we should not go on within the limits of *what we had decided to risk, 10 or 12 ships had been mentioned*.' (my italics) He failed to say that these were 'mentioned' by Fisher as a warning of the probable losses if the Navy-only attack went ahead, and certainly not as 'what we had decided to risk'.

De Robeck was much concerned at the danger from floating mines, which had been seen to be launched from a Turkish ship to float downstream, with which the moored mines in Eren Keui Bay had been confused. Later the same day, having received reports of the state of all his ships, he sent a further message to the Admiralty stating that, despite losses, the squadron was ready for immediate action, but the plan of attack must be reconsidered to deal with floating mines.

De Robeck certainly did not exaggerate; Keyes wrote to his wife:

> 'It is very obvious that all the defences are run by Germans. Their system of fire is wonderfully good and they fire in salvos. Our friends dropped salvos of three all round us, they came down from Heaven very steep and do a good deal of damage. The field guns which are concealed about, direct all their attention to killing people with shrapnel in our control positions – and our experts had many narrow shaves – one hit the wireless and some rigging and spars. . . . The *Inflexible* on the other shore had the same attentions but suffered more severely, her bridge caught on fire and blazed. Then a shell hit the forecontrol top killing or wounding everyone in it.'[90]

Ian Hamilton had arrived and almost immediately wrote to Kitchener, 'Certainly it looks at present as if the fleet would not be able to carry on at this rate, and if so, the soldiers will have to do the trick.'[91] The next day he telegraphed: 'From what I saw of the extraordinarily gallant attack made yesterday I am most reluctantly driven to the conclusion that the Dardanelles are less likely to be forced by battleships than at one time seemed probable and if the Army is to participate, its operations will not assume the subsidiary form anticipated.'[92] Again the impossibility of the operation by the Navy alone had been seen at once by a soldier, when admirals were trying to convince themselves otherwise, because the First Lord said so.

The same day (19 March) the War Council met and for once a politician, Lloyd George, asked Wilson his view, to which the latter answered the forts 'had only been temporarily silenced'. Churchill then asked the Council to agree that he should instruct de Robeck 'to use his discretion in continuing the operations', adding that he had 'information that the Turks were short of ammunition and mines'. Fisher again said that the loss of twelve battleships 'must be expected before the Dardanelles could be forced by the Navy alone'. The meeting as usual then degenerated into an indecisive discussion, rambling over the Western Front, drunkenness in munition factories and an avaricious discussion of how the spoils of a disintegrated Turkey could best be divided among the Allies, the only decision being to authorize Churchill to inform de Robeck 'that he could continue the operations against the Dardanelles if he thought fit'. Asquith asked Kitchener if plans had been worked out for a military landing, to which the Field Marshal said they must be left to Hamilton, and no discussion took place.

Privately Kitchener gave in. He replied to Hamilton's message:

> 'You know my views that the passage of the Dardanelles must be forced, and that if any large military operations on the Gallipoli Peninsula by the Army are necessary to clear the way, they must be undertaken, after careful consideration of the local defences, and must be carried through.'[93]

Yet Churchill still pressed for naval success; a message had been intercepted by Room 40 *on 12 March*, (almost a week before the attack),[94] from the Kaiser instructing Von Usedom to hold on at all costs, assuring him that ammunition would reach him. This message was handed to Churchill and Fisher on 19 March, *the day after* the attack, and in an absurdly sensational account fifteen years after the event, Captain W.R.Hall, Director of Naval Intelligence, stated that Churchill exclaimed, 'That means they've come to the end of their ammunition'. Hall described how even Fisher was enthusiastic: 'By God, I'll go through tomorrow! We shall probably lose six ships, but I'm going through.' If it were true that the Turks were short of ammunition the idea of going through the next day, before they could receive new supplies, was obviously sound, and, according to Hall, Fisher sat down to draft a message to de Robeck proposing another attack. But if the telegram from the Kaiser had been received a week earlier, Fisher's euphoria must have been a figment of Hall's imagination. His telegram to de Robeck was moderate and noncommittal.

> 'We regret the losses you have suffered in your resolute attack. Convey to all ranks and ratings Their Lordships' approbation of their conduct in

action and seamanlike skill with which His Majesty's ships were handled. Convey to the French squadron the Admiralty's appreciation of their loyal and effective support, and our sorrow for the losses they have sustained. *Queen* and *Implacable* should join you very soon; and *London* and *Prince of Wales* sail to-night. Please Telegraph any information as to damage done to forts, and also full casualties and ammunition expended. It appears important not to let the forts be repaired or to encourage enemy by an apparent suspension of the operations. Ample supplies of 15-inch ammunition are available for indirect fire of *Queen Elizabeth* across the peninsula.'[95]

De Robeck described a reorganization of the sweeping force devised by Keyes, the trawlers having now been manned entirely by volunteers from the fleet; fourteen destroyers, four torpedo boats and a flotilla of picket boats had been rigged up to assist in the minesweeping operation; fifty British and twelve French sweepers were available. He would not now attempt night sweeping and the area in which the ships would manoeuvre would be swept again, the same system of sweeping wires employed (the paravane had not been invented). 'It is hoped to be in a position to commence operations in three or four days, but delay is inevitable as new crews and destroyers will need some preliminary practice. No ship will enter Dardanelles unless everything is ready for a sustained attack.'[96]

To this Churchill wrote: 'Thus everything was so far steady and resolved. The First Sea Lord and the Admiralty War Group, the Prime Minister and the War Council, the French Minister of Marine, Admiral de Robeck and the French Admiral on the spot – all had no other idea but to persevere in accordance with the solemn decisions which had been taken.'[97]

The War Council and Fisher had left the matter to de Robeck and of the War Group only Oliver gave half-hearted support. There had never been a 'solemn decision'; Churchill had led everyone into the undertaking by his own personal action.

Hamilton decided he could not launch an attack until the 29th Division arrived; but they had only just left the United Kingdom, so this could not be before the first week in April. No one in the War Office had imagined they would immediately be required to carry out an opposed landing, nor was there any reason to suspect so; they were there to 'reap the fruits of the naval attack'. They were embarked in 22 ships, the ammunition in one, the horses in another, the harness in a third, the machine guns in the bottom of the hold in yet another, and the stores included, for use in that almost roadless, mountainous peninsula, bicycles and motor vehicles. The arrangements for the naval brigade were no better. Hamilton immediately realized that all this would have to be reorganized and signalled de Robeck that, as there were no facilities at Lemnos, he would be obliged to take the 29th Division to Alexandria, 600 miles away, for restowing, in the meantime leaving the 4,000 Australian infantry at Lemnos, together with the Royal Marines.

On 22 March a conference was held in *Queen Elizabeth* between de Robeck, Wemyss, Hamilton, Birdwood and others. Keyes, who had written to his wife the day before that he was 'spoiling to have at it again', was not present. De Robeck had been reflecting on the situation. He considered that a new assault could not be made without competent minesweepers and Keyes had estimated that the training of the new crews would not be complete until about 4 April. Hamilton thought the attack by the Army could take place about the middle of April, 'say 14th'. The delay, if the naval attack was abandoned in favour of a combined operation could be as little as ten days.

Hamilton recorded:

> 'The moment we sat down de Robeck told us that he was now quite clear that he could not get through without the help of all my troops. Before we ever went aboard, Braithwaite [Chief of Staff], Birdwood and I had agreed that whatever we landsmen might think we must leave the seamen to settle their own job, saying nothing for or against land operations or amphibious operations until the sailors themselves turned to us and said they had abandoned the idea of forcing the passage by naval operations alone. . . . So there was no discussion. We at once turned our faces to the land scheme.'[98]

The next day de Robeck telegraphed the Admiralty that the Army could not undertake operations before 14 April. To safeguard his communications, all the numerous guns protecting the straits must be destroyed, and this could not be done by naval gunfire. Landings inside the Dardanelles were not practicable, with which view Hamilton agreed. Dealing with the mines, which were a greater menace than previously thought, would take time. He therefore proposed a simultaneous attack 'about the middle of April'.[99] He was vindicated after the war when it was found that only two 14-inch guns and two or three smaller ones in the forts were destroyed; not a single gun defending the minefield had even been damaged, and the main minefield was undisturbed.

Churchill read this message 'with consternation' and presented to the Admiralty War Group a draft message to de Robeck melodramatically ordering him to renew the attack:

> 'You should dominate the forts at the Narrows and sweep the minefield and then batter the forts at close range, taking your time, using your aeroplanes and all your improved methods of guarding against mines. . . . We know the forts are short of ammunition and supply of mines is limited.'[100]

This meaningless message contributed no suggestion as to how these desirable objects were to be achieved. Churchill's assumption that the Kaiser's message indicated a shortage of ammunition has been repeated by a succession of Dardanelles encomiasts, but he admitted that there remained 271 rounds of 14-inch ammunition, 868 rounds of 9.4-inch, 371 of 6-inch QF, 720 rounds of 8.2-inch mortar and 3.706 rounds of 6-inch howitzer ammunition.[101] and the 'shortage' lasted only a few days, for the Germans rushed replenishments through Romania and Bulgaria, who turned a blind eye to their neutrality. The Baghdad Railway provided direct communication between Germany and Constantinople and 'it was very evident that modern guns and ammunition were reaching the Turkish Army in some quantity'.[102] A report from Constantinople, through neutral sources, confirmed the shortage was over before 18 March. *The Morning Post* reported that 'about 150 mines, any amount of ammunition, guns &c' had been coming through Romania from Germany. When 40 officers arrived they brought with them cases of ammunition, marked Red Cross; there was now there no attempt at concealment; 'The ammunition comes through quite openly, and there is nothing to prevent the Germans bringing in even bigger guns.'[103]

Further evidence came from Russia, and approaches from Grey to the respective Ministers in London revealed only that they had little confidence in Allied ability to defeat the Turks. In the next six weeks 200 Skoda guns were installed. The Cabinet never asked, even now, if the Balkans could ever have been united against the Turks or whether the campaign should continue.

Churchill tried to reassure de Robeck, but in a manner more likely to dismay him:

> 'Secret and Personal. Reports from various sources as to alleged transit of German artillerymen, arms and ammunition through Roumania to strengthen the Dardanelles and any rumours as to appearances of submarines in the Mediterranean or Adriatic, are being transmitted to you as a matter of routine. It should, however, be understood that this information is merely passed on by the Admiralty, and that reports of this nature are frequently discovered later to be unreliable. . . .
>
> 'Turkish ammunition – It is known that the forts on the 12th instant were short and that steps were being taken to obtain replenishments from Germany. It is not considered that these steps have as yet been successful. Is any estimate possible of the amount of ammunition expended by the forts in recent operations?'[104]

Churchill claimed Turkish morale was low, which was admitted by Von Sanders, but it had been much improved by success in repulsing the Allied fleet, and the attackers were more impressed by the volume of fire they met and their losses than by jingoistic optimism from the comfort of a London office. 'Everyone was awfully depressed after yesterday's battle,' wrote Midshipman Denham, 'and the Admiral sent some signals trying to cheer us up.'[105]

Churchill proposed to send De Bartolomé, his Naval Secretary, 'to give you our views on points of detail. Meanwhile all your preparations for renewing the attack should go forward,' effectively giving de Robeck an order, despite the War Council's decision that operations should be renewed only at his discretion. De Bartolomé and Oliver acquiesced, but Fisher, Wilson and Jackson unyieldingly opposed it. Churchill went to Asquith and Balfour, who supported his telegram, but for once Asquith supported the professional officers and, without Fisher's support, Churchill was unable to proceed. The next day (24 March) Fisher wrote to Bartolomé: 'I fully agree with First Lord at end of his proposed telegram for you to hustle out to Lemnos, *but the rest of his telegram I am dead against ! We ought to wait de Robeck's reply to telegram sent him last night.* Equinoctial gales in full blast, so nothing could be done anyway, certainly no flying!'[106]

Churchill wrote: 'I had to content myself with sending a reasoned telegram, which, while giving him the strongest possible lead, left the decision still in the Admiral's hands.'[107] Fisher emphatically protested, but Churchill asserted, 'This telegram the First Sea Lord was induced, with some difficulty, to agree to.'[108] 'It is clear that the Army should at once prepare to attack the Kilid Bahr plateau. . . . But the question now to be decided by the Admiralty is whether the time has come to abandon the naval plan . . . without the aid of a large army. It may be necessary to . . . admit that the task is beyond our powers and if you think so, you should not fail to say so. But before deciding, certain facts must be weighed: first the delay and the consequent danger of submarines coming and ruining all; second, the heavy losses, at least 5,000, which the Army would suffer; third the possibilities of a check in the land operations far more serious than the loss of a few old surplus ships. . . . These must be balanced against the risks and hopes of a purely naval undertaking. . . . the moral effect of a British fleet . . . entering the sea of Marmora.' Churchill continued to speculate that when the Turks realized the fortresses at the Narrows were not going to stop the fleet, 'a general evacuation will take place; but anyhow all troops remaining upon it will be doomed to starvation or surrender', and then forecast uprisings in Constantinople. He ended: 'What has happened since 21st to make you alter your intention? We have never contemplated a reckless rush over minefields and past undamaged primary guns. . . . We know the forts are short of ammunition. It is probable they have not got many mines. . . . I cannot understand why . . . forts like 7 and 8 should not be demolished by heavy gunfire.'[109]

This verbose message was an undisguised attempt to force de Robeck into further rash action, but on Fisher's insistence a last paragraph stated: 'You must of course understand that this telegram is not an executive order.' The key words in the whole message were 'I cannot understand'. It is hardly surprising that Fisher was only persuaded to agree 'with some difficulty'; the question is whether he ever agreed at all. It was hardly a 'reasoned telegram' reiterating all the outworn arguments for a navy-only operation, contributing nothing as to how the miracle was to be performed. Fisher was appalled and that night sent a note to Churchill: 'Although the telegram goes from you personally, the fact of my remaining at the Admiralty sanctions my connection with it, so if it goes I do not see how I can remain.'[110] But he tried to console Churchill: 'It is the right thing without any doubt whatever to send Bartolomé, and the sooner the better. . . . You are very wrong to worry and excite yourself . . . We are sure to win!!! I know I am an optimist *Always have been. . . . Hustle Bartolomé! Send no more telegrams! Let it alone!*'[111]

Bartolomé did not go. Churchill informed the Cabinet of the refusal of de Robeck and the naval staff to continue the attack without military support. Kitchener then demonstrated his ignorance of the problem. 'In a few brief sentences he assumed the burden and declared he would carry the operations through by military force.'[112] There was no discussion; the rest of the Cabinet accepted that the Great Kitchener would see the matter through. Even Churchill complained, 'The silent plunge into this military adventure must be regarded as an extraordinary episode'.[113] Kitchener imagined that the storming of Gallipoli could take place within a week and that de Robeck's attack would continue pending landings. He then and there drafted for Churchill a telegram *ordering* de Robeck to continue the attack and demanded to know from Hamilton why he could not attack before 14 April. There were further confused exchanges until at last de Robeck, in a long message, stated clearly the case against pursuing the naval attack:

'The original approved plan for forcing the Dardanelles was drawn up on the assumption that gunfire alone was capable of destroying forts. This assumption has been conclusively proved to be wrong when applied to high velocity guns. . . . Conclusions drawn from the attack on the Cupola forts at Antwerp by heavy howitzers are quite misleading. . . . To obtain direct hits on each gun has been found impracticable. . . . To destroy forts, therefore, it is necessary to land demolishing parties. To cover these parties at the Narrows is a task General Hamilton is not prepared to undertake and I fully concur in this view. . . . The mine menace being even greater than anticipated, the number of torpedo tubes . . . having been added to . . . materially increases the difficulties of clearing passage for the Fleet. . . . If the Turkish Army is undismayed by the advent of the fleet into the Sea of Marmora and the Straits are closed behind it, [the Fleet] depends almost entirely on the number of colliers and ammunition [ships] which can accompany the fleet. . . . The passage of supply ships for the fleet through the Dardanelles with the forts intact is a problem to which I can see no practical solution. . . . The delay possibly of a fortnight will allow co-operation, which would really prove factor that will reduce length of time necessary to complete the campaign in the Sea of Marmora and occupy Constantinople.'[114]

Practical experience had shown that the views expressed by Fisher and Scott before the foolhardy gamble were correct. Even Churchill admitted that 'the arguments of de Robeck's telegram were decisive'.[115]

Fisher was now more than ever alarmed at the dissipation of British Forces. There were at the Dardanelles 15 battleships, 2 battlecruisers, 6 light cruisers, 24 destroyers, 10 submarines, 3 monitors, 2 gunboats 52 minesweepers, 7 fleet sweepers, one aeroplane carrier (*Ark Royal*) 5 torpedo boats, 6 ocean tugs, 3 salvage vessels and 5 other fleet auxiliaries. On 28 March he sent a memorandum to Churchill which included the passage:

> 'With reference to a private and personal telegram sent this forenoon by the First Lord to Vice-Admiral de Robeck stating that an official telegram would be sent from the Admiralty approving his proposed action, as conveyed in his private telegram to the First Lord, my decided opinion is that before any such action, the Admiralty should have before them the report of the War Office as to the likelihood of the proposed military operations in cooperation with the fleet being so favourable as to justify the very considerable naval losses that may ensue.'[116]

In a covering note he said:

> 'If the Germans decide (as well they may) – influenced largely no doubt by [us] having so large a force away from the decisive theatre, on some big thing at home, there is (you must admit) much cause for anxiety, especially with the German and Austrian submarine menace to the yet unlanded troops and our Dardanelles fleet. What is Ian Hamilton's report as to probable success? Admiral de Robeck does not look forward to disabling the guns. Such justifiable losses for so great a political prize as Constantinople might possibly at the same time jeopardise our large margins of superiority over the German Navy in the decisive theatre – observing that the dispatch of submarines and destroyers from England today to the Dardanelles, together with those detained there . . . is a serious diminution of our required force in home waters; and that also in all directions, such as aircraft, nets, monitors repair ships and light cruisers, our home resources are being heavily drawn upon for the Dardanelles operation, but perhaps most especially in the amount of ammunition and wear of the big guns.'[117]

In a postscript he added: 'I am not blind to the political necessity of going forward with the task; but before going further forward, let the whole situation be so fully examined that success is assured while safety in the decisive theatre is not compromised.'[118]

The 'wear of the big guns' is extremely rapid and they lose accuracy to such an extent that an adjustment has to be made after every shot. When this reaches unacceptable levels the barrels have to be changed in a dockyard, which takes only a few days, but, being costly, few spares are held and as manufacture is a lengthy process, replacements could not readily be provided. The matter is not trivial.

Whether Fisher was as convinced of the political advantages as he indicates is doubtful. But political decisions he regarded as the province of the politicians, a wise attitude, for if he meddled in politics he could hardly complain when they meddled in strategy.

Churchill appears to have ignored his memorandum and three days later he sent another urgent warning:

> 'I desire now to state my definite opinion that we must stand or fall by the ships now out in the Mediterranean or on their way there. If the concerted operations now about to be taken are not successful, and we incur heavy losses either in great or small ships, we cannot afford to send any more from home waters to complete the work – not even if, by sending reinforcements, there is a possibility, even a certainty that the operations will then be successful and with only small losses – nor even if more naval force is required to extricate our Army. Further . . . if some new development decreases our margin of safety in the North Sea . . . we must be free to recall at once our ships from the Mediterranean. . . . I therefore urge that before . . . the troops [are] landed, the Dardanelles operation should again be examined . . . by the War Council. We should have before us the considered report of Sir Ian Hamilton with the remarks of the Army Council thereon; we should reconsider the position in view of the lack of damage done to the guns in the forts by the previous bombardment; we should consider the possible arrival of enemy submarines, and in a word, all the factors that might result in the next operation being indecisive or unsuccessful. . . . We can recover from an indecisive or even unsuccessful result of these operations . . . but we can never recover from a reverse to our main fleets in the decisive theatre at home . . .
>
> 'I therefore beg you to forward my previous memorandum with its accompanying letter, and this communication also, to the War Council in order that immediate deliberation may take place.'[119]

It is apparent what Fisher was calling for. The operation had never been planned; it had taken root from a seed germinated in Churchill's mind by taking a single paragraph out of context from the remaining concomitant essentials in Fisher's proposal for an amphibious operation and from Carden's sketchy ideas. From this unimpressive beginning it had grown into a huge Navy-only assault on Gallipoli and Constantinople, decided upon by politicians against the advice of the best naval expertise. Even when Kitchener grudgingly provided military support, it was in an off-hand manner, without any planning.

Still Fisher was ignored and his exasperation grew:

> 'April 2nd, 1915. We can't send another rope yarn even to de Robeck! WE HAVE GONE TO THE VERY LIMIT!!! And so they must not

hustle and should be most emphatically told that no further reinforce-ment of the Fleet can be looked for! *A failure or check in the Dardanelles would be nothing. A failure in the North Sea would be ruin.* But I do not wish to be pessimistic and let us hope that Gallipoli ain't going to be Plevna, or that de Robeck will be "Duckworthed".'[120]

News from New York provided evidence that the 21 German liners interned there might attempt to escape, convert to AMCs and attack British trade. The only ships that could match their high speed would be the battlecruisers whose detachment from the Grand Fleet would seriously weaken it. In ad-dition the French Ambassador, Cambon, had warned that there was a possibility that Holland might join the Central Powers, and on 5 April Fisher wrote, even more emphatically: 'I do not think you are sufficiently impressed by Cambon's warning as to Holland! *We ought to have every detail organized to move in a moment to Texel.* You are just simply eaten up with the Dardanelles and cannot think of anything else! Damn the Dardanelles! They will be our grave!'[121]

During the next three months, in addition to the 29th Division, there were made available from England two first-line Territorial divisions, the Royal Naval Division and a dismounted Yeomanry division; from Egypt two divisions and one brigade of Australians and New Zealanders, the Lancashire Territorial Division and an Indian Brigade; and from France two French divisions. The only voice crying for a plan was Fisher's. At every stage he called for study of the problem and at every stage he was ignored. He called for a review before the landings took place in Suvla Bay. He received no reply. Incredibly, the War Council had no meeting between 19 March and 14 May, despite the fact that disaster was staring them in the face

So the other Sea Lords, Sir Frederick Hamilton, Rear-Admiral F.C.Tudor and Captain Cecil Lambert, met. All supported Fisher, and so did the War Group in the Admiralty and the admiral on the spot – a courageous officer who tended if anything to rashness. The three Sea Lords, on 8 April, sent Fisher a memorandum initialled by all of them:

'*First Sea Lord.*

'We wish to ask you to reassure us on certain points connected with the conduct of the war.

'We will start from the ground on which there is common agreement, viz.: That the Grand Fleet should always be in such a position and in such strength that it can be at all times ready to meet the entire fleet of the enemy with confident assurance as to the result.

'Is it quite certain that we are not putting that assurance in jeopardy?

'There can be no doubt that the ideal method of deciding general questions of the larger strategy is by having one person whose decisions, based on ample advice, are final.

'That person, subject to the high points of policy, which can only be decided by the Cabinet, is, and should be, the First Sea Lord.

'If, however, he has not the final voice the result must be that the policy becomes one of compromise, which is obviously unsound, and likely to lead to mistake, and possibly to disaster.

'To go into particulars.

The attack on the Dardanelles is probably, from the point of view of high policy, quite correct.

'On that point we have not sufficient acquaintance with the political situation to enable us to form an opinion, but what we are quite certain of is that it is a very expensive policy, and is likely before we have done with it, to cost us several ships and an enormous expenditure of ammunition.

'We have already lost, or more or less demobilized, ten battleships (including *Inflexible*). It is true that they are mostly old ones, and on the other hand we have added or shall shortly add, seven.

'The Germans have lost none and have added six.

'As to the future, it is not known, so far as we are aware, what the Germans are going to do. But we do know that we are postponing battle-ship completion for the sake of arming a number of small craft, whose actual proposed use we are not familiar with, though obviously it must be something totally unconnected with the bedrock policy of maintaining the crushing superiority of the Grand Fleet.

'Another matter which is delaying battleship completion is the construction under the Admiralty of 15 'Howitzers' for purposes quite unconnected with any Fleet requirement.

'Are you satisfied with the rate of progress of Battleship completion in the light of attached statement?

'Is the prospect of obtaining supplies of ammunition sufficiently good to ensure there being enough available for the use of the Grand Fleet in the light of the expenditure involved by operations in the Dardanelles?

'These are matters about which we are uneasy, and we ask you to assure us that the whole policy has your concurrence, and that you are satisfied with it.

'If not, and you think there would be any value in the support of the Board (which still exists, at all events in name), we shall consider it our duty to give it to you.

F.T.H   C.F.L.   F.C.T.T.'[122]

The 'attached statement' comprised a calculation of the balance of naval power in home waters, detailing numbers and gunpower of big ships, showing that the Grand Fleet had been reduced to a strength perilously close to equality with the High Sea Fleet, and, if ships refitting or at the Dardanelles were deducted, inferior. Churchill referred contemptuously to the figures as 'a good example of a certain class of arithmetic and of magnifying the enemy's strength'.

It is debatable whether Fisher was wise in his response. It can be argued that his patriotism, of which there was no doubt, demanded that he seize the opportunity presented to him and confront Churchill with an ultimatum, if necessary approaching the Prime Minister direct. As it was, he demonstrated his over-generous loyalty to Churchill. His response was carefully worded to placate the Sea Lords but uphold the constitutional authority of the Cabinet, yet to express his own view and leave open the option of accepting the naval members' offer.

> 'I am in entire agreement with the fundamental principle which you seek
> to uphold. . . . It was with hesitation that I consented to this undertaking.
> . . . These high points of policy must be decided by the Cabinet. . . . I am
> of the opinion at the present time that our supremacy is secure in Home
> Waters. . . . But . . . we have reached the absolute limit . . . for we can send
> out no more help of any kind. I have expressed this view very clearly to the
> First Lord and, should there at a later period be any disposition on the part
> of the Cabinet to overrule me on this point, I shall request my naval
> colleagues to give their support in upholding my view. I agree with you as
> to the desirability for proceeding with the completion of the battleships in
> hand. . . . I am satisfied with the position at present and in the near future
> but shall of course be more satisfied when we get the battleships back from
> the Dardanelles. The supply of cordite is very far from satisfactory . . . all
> extraneous sources of expenditure must be cut off at once.'[123]

It was typical of Churchill's disingenuousness that in *The World Crisis* he should write of this memorandum: 'The position of the First Sea Lord is thus very clearly defined. He is seen to be formally and deliberately identified with the enterprise.'[124] Churchill believed that one more try to force the Narrows should be made (he would always have wanted one more try) and in the revised edition of his book, written as late as 1938, he maintained that position: 'Not to persevere – that was the crime!'

Keyes believed for the rest of his life that the Dardanelles could have been forced by the Navy alone. And Professor Marder has written:

> 'Supposing the fleet at the Dardanelles had been led by a Nelson – or even
> by a Keyes! One can envisage him saying to the Generals at the fateful
> meeting in the *Queen Elizabeth* on 22 March: 'As soon as my fast sweepers
> are ready, I am going through to Constantinople. If we don't then succeed
> in getting a peace settlement, it may be necessary for me to leave the
> Marmora and to land your army to occupy the peninsula, so that I can
> keep the fleet in the Marmora indefinitely.'[125]

But he forgets that Nelson said only a fool would attack a fort with ships.

8

THE RESIGNATION

Hamilton's belief that he could mount his attack about 14 April was not realized. He left Britain with no staff, no maps, no knowledge of the strength of the enemy or its willingness to fight, the topography of the country, whether there was water, what roads there were, whether the depth of water inshore would allow close approach, how casualties could be evacuated, whether the enemy was entrenched or prepared to fight in the open, how guns and stores could be got ashore; indeed no staff work whatever had been done. When formed, his staff were a scratch lot. Compton Mackenzie, living in Capri, used influence in Whitehall to join it, without even a uniform. The staff did not arrive in Alexandria until 11 April.

The reloading of the transports went on day and night. Hamilton found shortages of everything; guns, ammunition, hand grenades, trench mortars. He frantically telegraphed Kitchener for more. He had 75,000 men but needed more; he discovered there was a brigade of Gurkhas in Egypt and arranged for them to join him. His staff scoured the shops for tourist guides of Gallipoli.

He conferred with his generals and received differing and discouraging advice. Paris, the Royal Marine general, the best acquainted with amphibious warfare, said 'to land would be difficult enough if surprise were possible but hazardous in the extreme in present conditions'. General Hunter-Weston, in command of the 29th Division, thought the expedition should be abandoned. Hamilton lunched with the Sultan in Cairo, who told him the forts were impregnable, which was confirmed by Troubridge as early as 27 August:

> 'The German Ambassador gives out that the Dardanelles would be quite impossible to force, since the Germans have taken special measures to render them impregnable. Our ambassador says complete success would alone justify the attempt as failure means disaster at Constantinople and would have serious effects everywhere.'[1]

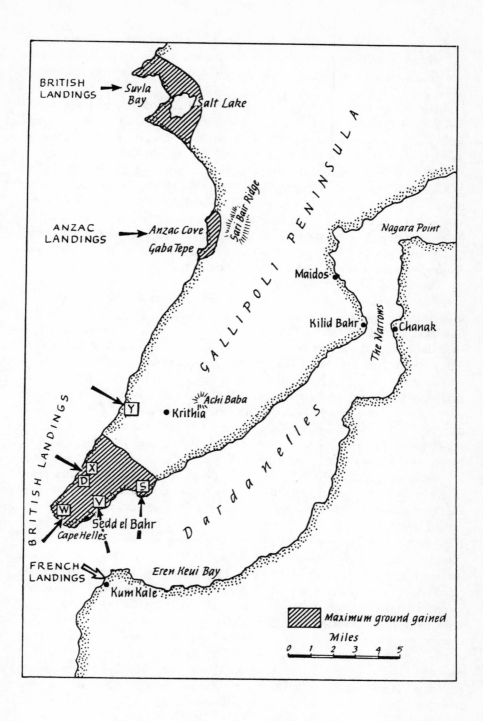

BRITISH
LANDINGS → Suvla
Bay   Salt Lake

ANZAC
LANDINGS → Anzac Cove
              Gaba Tepe

Sari Bair Ridge

GALLIPOLI PENINSULA

Nagara Point

Maidos

Kilid Bahr   Chanak

The Narrows

Achi Baba
Krithia

Y

BRITISH LANDINGS
X
D
S
W V
Sedd el Bahr
Cape Helles

Dardanelles

FRENCH
LANDINGS

Eren Keui Bay

Kum Kale

Maximum ground gained

Miles
0 1 2 3 4 5

In September the Ambassador had reported 'the Dardanelles are being every day strengthened'.[2] At the November bombardment trenches and field works had disputed the landing of the marines who were to complete the demolition of the guns.[3]

Security was totally lacking. Letters arrived from UK addressed to individuals in 'Constantinople Force, Egypt'. Like television in the Falklands and Gulf Wars, Cairo newspapers discussed precisely what troops were arriving, the chances of success and how the expedition would be handled

Press criticism rumbled in the background and Lord Charles Beresford pointedly asked in the Commons: 'Who is responsible for the operations in the Dardanelles; whether it was intended to be in the nature of combined naval and military operations, and whether the ultimate success of the operations will be considerably delayed owing to the naval attack having been delivered before the Army was landed?'[4], giving obvious notice of the projected landings. Asquith replied that it was a joint operation, but 'it was not desirable at the present stage to say anything further'.

It was decided the 29th would land at five beaches at Cape Helles, and, incredibly, it was expected the 700 foot Achi Baba, towering like the Rock of Gibraltar six miles inland, would be taken on the first day. Birdwood was to land his Anzacs thirteen miles further up the coast, just north of Gaba Tepe and to strike across to Maidos, overlooking the narrows. The Naval Division was to make a diversion at the Bulair Isthmus. The French would simultaneously land on the Asiatic side, which they believed best. The fleet would sweep the minefields and pass the Narrows, unharassed by forts or mobile batteries. 'It sounded just too easy!' The attack was fixed for 23 April, the military forces assembling in Mudros, Skyros, Imbros and Tenedos, but a gale blew and it was postponed until the 25th. On Gallipoli the enemy brought in reinforcements, dug more trenches and laid barbed wire entanglements, some under water, so that men disembarking became entangled, under merciless machine-gun fire. The landings were heavily resisted, casualties high and, though the Anzacs, fighting like tigers, made some headway – mainly because they were landed in the wrong place, a mile from their intended landing – progress was slow with every evidence of another stalemate developing. It was not going to be 'just too easy' after all. The Opposition had grave doubts, the public was worried by rumours and even Liberals expressed misgivings. Beresford again hit the bullseye, asking the PM 'whether the attack on the Dardanelles has developed a new and serious situation; whether the ships, munitions of war, and officers and men of both Services have been diverted to the Dardanelles; and whether, seeing that the Government have informed the public that every man, gun and munition that can possibly be provided are required for the campaign in Flanders, and in order to allay anxiety with regard to the strain on our resources for the new campaign in the Dardanelles, he would make a statement on the subject?'[5] Asquith parried the question on security grounds, but then Kellaway, a Liberal, asked 'whether Lord Fisher was consulted with regard to the March attack on the Dardanelles by the Fleet; and whether he expressed the opinion that the attack ought not to be made in the circumstances in which it was made?'[6] Fisher loyally drafted an answer for Churchill: 'I must decline in the interests of the proper prosecution of the war to answer this or any similar question. It cannot be permitted that all the various considerations connected with war operations should be fully discussed and some particular item selected for malignant attack. I am desired by Lord Fisher to state that he associates himself fully in this reply. If the insinuation contained in the question were correct, Lord Fisher would not now be at the Admiralty.' This generous, if not wholly truthful, answer was to rebound on Fisher when it was used as evidence of his support for the operation. In fact Churchill replied, 'The answer to the first part of the question is in the affirmative, and to the second part in the negative,' which was wholly untruthful.

The improbability of an easy victory was now being borne in on those at the scene. Keyes, who had admitted to his diary on 8 March, 'It is a much bigger thing than the Admiralty or anyone out here realised,' yet who had attempted to persuade de Robeck to renew the naval attack without military support, again began to press him. Only a small proportion of the fleet could be used to support the Army; already 19,000 soldiers had been lost and little progress was being made in the land attack. He argued that many field guns and howitzers would have been removed for use against the Army and his reorganized minesweeping force would readily clear the minefield, advocating what Fisher had proposed in February, feasible then, but now, with 500,000 Turks on the peninsula, guns and ammunition reaching them in quantity, de Robeck disagreed. He was short of ammunition (by the end of May he had only 400 rounds of 12-inch ammunition left). But Keyes insisted and de Robeck, with extreme concession to the bellicose commodore, called a conference of his three rear-admirals, who all endorsed his view. They agreed that success was possible and would help the Army, but failure would imperil it and the problem of keeping the fleet supplied remained. Keyes had a direct line to Churchill through his brother, Jack Churchill, serving with the Yeomanry, and de Robeck was acutely aware of this. He sent the Admiralty a confused message, attempting to embrace the views of his pugnacious Chief of Staff and himself making it clear that he would attempt penetration if ordered, but not on his own responsibility, ending:

'Points for decision appear to be:- First: – Can the Navy by forcing the Dardanelles ensure the success of the operation? Second:- If the navy were to suffer a reverse, which of necessity could only be a severe one, would the position of the Army be so critical as to jeopardize the whole of the operations?'[7]

The version of this message in *The World Crisis* is markedly different from the accurate one given by Martin Gilbert and includes the statement, 'The help which the Navy has been able to give the Army has not been as great as was anticipated, [though effective in keeping down the fire of the enemy's batteries].'[8]

For once Churchill hesitated. Reinforcements were on the way for the Army, Italy was about to enter the war and, to aid her, four battleships and four cruisers were to be removed from de Robeck's fleet. U-boats had been sighted in the Aegean. Jackson forecast that 'of the 16 ships that attempted to rush the straits . . . four badly injured ones might with luck return'. But Churchill longed to realize his dream of a naval penetration of the Dardanelles and, as usual, assumed numbers of ships were the deciding factor, overlooking the confined waters of the Dardanelles, and ignoring technical advice.

'I was of course, as always, in favour of renewing the naval attack. . . . I wished the fleet to engage the forts at the Narrows and thus test the reports which we had received about the shortage of ammunition. Under cover of this engagement I wished the Kephez minefield to be swept and got out of the way. These were perfectly feasible operations now that the minesweeping force was thoroughly organised and the Dardanelles fleet, although reduced, was ample for their purpose. The elimination of the Kephez minefield would in itself begin to imperil the communication of the Army the Turks were building up on the Peninsula.'[9] Churchill's logic was strange. Another attack was an expensive way of discovering the enemy's ammunition supplies. The reorganized minesweeping force had not been tested and sweeping would only marginally impair Turkish communications. The enemy could have laid an effective trap.

It was at this point in *The World Crisis* that, with his political foresight, Churchill suggested Fisher was breaking down, as he had Bridgeman:

'I could see, however, that Lord Fisher was under considerable strain. His seventy-four years lay heavy upon him. During my absence in Paris upon the negotiations for the Anglo-Italian naval convention, he had shown great nervous exhaustion. He had evinced unconcealed distress and anxiety at being left alone in sole charge of the Admiralty. There is no doubt that the old admiral was worried almost out of his wits by the immense pressure of the times and by the course events had taken. Admiral de Robeck's telegram distressed him extremely. He expected to be confronted with the demand he hated most and dreaded most, the renewal of the naval battle and fighting the matter out to a conclusion.'[10]

Such a description of Fisher is preposterous. He relished sole charge of the Admiralty, and the last sentence denies his whole life. He longed for a naval battle to fight the matter out to a conclusion; he was frustrated at the failure to use the Navy fully and pined to see it in grand action. But he had the wit to weigh the odds; he was not prepared to sacrifice the Navy in a futile expedition he knew could only end in disaster in pursuit of a politician's delusion. His formal memorandum quoted below, in the preparation of which he had Hankey's help, is surely an example of clear-sighted reason. Martin Gilbert agrees that Hankey shared Fisher's view and believed military success essential before the resumption of naval operations.[11] He nevertheless relates, in support of Churchill's claim, that Clementine Churchill recalled a bizarre incident when Fisher had warned her of Churchill's unfaithfulness while on his visits to France and that he was 'as nervous as a kitten'.[12] In the absence of documentary evidence, this story cannot be denied, but it is wholly out of character and not the sort of charge a woman would ordinarily relate against her husband; perhaps it was Clementine's attempt to support her husband's self-defensive prevarication about Fisher' state of mind.

On the morning of 11 May Churchill and Fisher discussed the operation: 'I endeavoured repeatedly to make it clear that all I wanted was the sweeping of the Kephez minefield under cover of a renewed engagement of the forts at the narrows, and that I had no idea of pressing for a decisive effort to force the straits and penetrate the Marmora.'[13]

Fisher was not deceived. This was a carbon copy of the earlier attempt to penetrate the Dardanelles by naval force alone. Later that day he wrote to Churchill: 'With much reluctance, in view of our conversation this morning, I feel compelled to send you the enclosed formal memorandum of my views respecting the Dardanelles, as it is essential that on so vital a point I should not leave you in any doubt as to my opinion.'[14] His formal memorandum made his position perfectly clear:

'I desire formally to put on record my views as to the. . . . progress of the operations . . .

'Our deliberations on the subject of these operations have been conducted either in personal conference or by the interchange of informal notes, and there is therefore no official record of the views that I have from time to time expressed. . . . [my italics] Although I have acquiesced in each stage of the operations up to the present, largely on account of consideration of political expediency and the political advantage which those whose business it is to judge of these matters have assured me would accrue from success. or even partial success, I have clearly expressed my opinion that I did not consider the original attempt to force the Dardanelles with the fleet alone was a practical operation. . . .

'This collection of forces in the Mediterranean has been carried out so gradually that it has been difficult for me to decide at what point danger was threatened in the North Sea; yet each successive increment to the fleet in the Mediterranean has appeared essential to the success of the local operations. Nevertheless I was compelled to write to you some few weeks ago that I considered we had reached finality . . .

'Yesterday evening you sent me a draft telegram for my concurrence. . . . The general tone of this telegram implied that the Board of Admiralty might be prepared to sanction the Fleet undertaking further operations against the Forts irrespective of the Army being unable to advance beyond their present positions. I made an amendment, without which I was not able to concur in this telegram being sent, inserting the words "A naval attack cannot even be considered until the Italians etc., etc.,". I have not heard from you whether this telegram, or any, has actually been sent. I presume not, as I have seen no copy. . . .

'I therefore feel impelled to inform you definitely and formally of my conviction that such an attack by the fleet on the Dardanelles Forts, in repetition of the operations which failed on March 18, or any attempt by the fleet to rush the Narrows, is doomed to failure, and moreover is fraught with possibilities of disaster utterly incommensurate to any advantage that could be obtained therefrom.'

Fisher outlined the folly of the operation, the losses suffered and forecast, pointing out that, even if the fleet got through, it could not be kept supplied and would again lose disastrously on returning. He recalled his consistent opposition to the operation ending: 'I cannot under any circumstances be a party to any order to Admiral de Robeck to make an attempt to pass the Dardanelles until the shores have been effectively occupied.'[15]

At last Fisher had formally recorded both his consistent objection to the campaign, and that there was no official record of his views. They should have been on permanent official record, but the operation had grown imperceptibly and it was always difficult to say 'enough, no more!'. He asked Hankey to represent his views. 'At Fisher's request saw the Prime Minister before lunch and told him Fisher would resign if such action was taken.'[16] Asquith said he thought this was 'a very foolish message', but instructed Hankey to tell Fisher that separate naval action would not be taken without his concurrence. Significantly, Churchill, in a breathtaking footnote, says he 'cannot trace' the draft mentioned in Fisher's fourth paragraph and surmises:

'No doubt it was to the effect that while an attempt to rush the straits could not immediately be authorised, operations should be undertaken to sweep the Kephez minefield under cover of the Fleet and force the forts to exhaust their ammunition. It seems probable that the words introduced by Lord Fisher destroyed the purpose and meaning of the telegram. It was not sent. *Nothing was ever sent without his agreement.*'[17] (my italics)

But Churchill's habit of using isolated sentences or single words out of context will be remembered. Now he jumped at Fisher's use of the word 'rush'. The same day (11 May) he wrote:

'You will never receive from me any proposition to "rush" the Dardanelles; and I agree with the views you express so forcibly on the subject. It may be that the Admiral will have to engage the forts and sweep the Kephez minefield as an aid to the military operations; and we have always agreed on the desirability of forcing them to fire off their scanty stock of ammunition. . . . We are now committed to one of the greatest amphibious enterprises of history. You are absolutely committed. Comradeship, resource, firmness, patience, all in the highest degrees will be needed to carry the matter through to victory. . . . I beg you to lend your whole aid and goodwill; and ultimately then success is certain.'[18]

Churchill's rhetoric, which Hankey described as 'rather slippery', made no change to the original Carden plan which would not assist the Army, and, in the unlikely event of success, Churchill would press for the fleet to enter the Marmora. All the objections to the attack of 18 March still stood, except for the reorganized minesweeping force, which was as yet untried.

Fisher was still not deceived. The next day he wrote to Churchill:

'Until the military operations have effectively occupied the shores of the Narrows, etc., no naval attack on the minefield can take place. But your letter does not repudiate this, and therefore, in view of our joint conversation with the Prime Minister prior to March 18, I have sent him a copy of my memorandum to you. With reference to your remark that I am absolutely committed, I have only to say that you must know (as the Prime Minister also) that my unwilling acquiescence did not extend to such a further gamble as any repetition of March 18 until the Army had done their part.'[19]

Fisher worried for the safety of *Queen Elizabeth* without protection from submarines. He had suggested her use only for the duration of her gun trials, but she was providing gun support for the military operations, proving as little value on the precipitous peninsula as he and Scott had anticipated. Britain's most modern battleship was urgently needed in the Grand Fleet. That day came the news that the 'Canopus' class battleship, *Goliath*, had been sunk at anchor by a Turkish torpedo-boat, and he insisted on *Queen Elizabeth's* return. Churchill invited Kitchener to a meeting with Fisher at the Admiralty, which proved stormy, Kitchener asserting that the Navy was deserting the Army at a critical moment, which was hardly justified since two old battleships with four 12-inch guns each and two monitors with 14-inch guns were to be substituted, all of which were at least as useful in such confined waters, and possibly more so. Finally Fisher said, 'Either the *Queen Elizabeth* left that afternoon or he left the Admiralty that night'. This decided the matter. Within a fortnight a dummy *Queen Elizabeth* was torpedoed and, before the end of the month, *Triumph*, also at anchor, with anti-torpedo nets out, and *Majestic,* anchored off 'W' Beach, were sunk by a single submarine.

But there had been many other disagreements between Fisher and Churchill. The failure at Neuve Chapelle in March had resulted in 20,000 men lost and reinforcements were needed. All acceptable were at the Dardanelles, short of ammunition, and themselves calling for reinforcements. Fisher's memoranda and notes to Churchill were either overruled, contradicted or ignored. He now sent to the Prime Minister a copy of his memorandum to Churchill, with a covering note drawing attention to the events of 28 January. 'With extreme reluctance, and largely due to earnest words spoken to me by Kitchener, I, by not resigning *(as I see now I should have done)* remained a most unwilling beholder (and indeed a participator) of the gradual draining of our naval resources from the decisive theatre of war.'[20]

During the day (12 May) discussion with Churchill went some way to placate him, and Churchill wrote to reassure the Prime Minister, who then wrote to Fisher:

> 'My dear Lord Fisher,
> 'Since receiving your letter and memorandum of to-day, I have been given to understand that an arrangement has been come to between the First Lord and yourself. I am very glad.'[21]

Fisher replied clearly that this was not so:

> 'Within four hours of the pact being concluded the First Lord said to Kitchener "that in the event of the Army's failure, the fleet would endeavour to force its way through", or words to that effect. However, with your kind assurance of no such action being permitted, I remain to do my best. . . . Still, I honestly feel I cannot remain where I am much longer, as there is an inevitable and never-ceasing drain *daily (almost hourly)* of our resources in the decisive theatre of the war. But that is not the worst – instead of the whole time of the whole of the Admiralty being concentrated on the daily increasing submarine menace in Home Waters, we are all diverted to the Dardanelles, and the unceasing activities of the First Lord, both by day and night, are engaged in ceaseless *prodding* of everyone in every department afloat and shore in the interests of the Dardanelles Fleet, . . . whose size is sufficiently indicated by their having as many battleships out there as in the German High Sea Fleet! . . . This purely private and personal letter . . . is to mention to the one person who I feel OUGHT to know, *that I feel my time is short!*'[22]

Asquith's later claim that he was not fully aware of Fisher's views is absurd, but his total ignorance of naval warfare and lack of imagination led him after the 18 March events to write, 'Winston thinks & I agree with him, that the ships, as soon as the weather clears, & the aeroplanes can detect the condition of the forts and the positions of the concealed guns, ought to make another push: & I hope this will be done.'[23] The same day a telegram came from the French Ministry of Marine that Admiral Guépratte had reported that action was contemplated against the Chanak Fort, to reach which the unswept minefields would have to be negotiated. The French did not agree. Significantly, there is no mention of this in *The World Crisis*.

Throughout 13 May Churchill attempted to persuade Fisher to renew the attack. In a long memorandum,[24] which again demonstrated his rudimentary understanding of amphibious warfare, he suggested mounting long-range naval guns on shore, which he asserted could bring accurate fire on enemy defences from positions held by allied troops. This was, of course, untrue; the flat trajectory of naval guns would be disadvantageous. Long range was not needed and the task of mounting the guns under fire beggars the imagination. He suggested building landing stages, 'of a semi-permanent character', at Sedd el Bahr and Gaba Tepe with cranes, railway lines, and 'all other facilities' for handling large and heavy traffic. How the troops hanging on by their finger-tips on narrow beaches facing steep rocky cliffs would have reacted had they seen this suggestion is unrecorded. He wanted indicator nets stretching from Imbros to Gallipoli, ten nautical miles at its narrowest point. The first storm would have dispersed them. The battleships should go in turn to Malta to be fitted with 'the best steel trellis work protection against mines which can be devised'. Whose idea this was is doubtful and merits no further thought. Any officer who had served at sea, even for a limited time, would have discounted the notion. Two Russian army corps were to be transported by rail to Archangel and shipped round to Enos (nearly 6,000 miles via the North Sea). Even Churchill apparently saw the absurdity and deleted this paragraph. He wanted 70 aeroplanes and seaplanes, including those capable of dropping 500 lb. bombs. Which area of operations was to be denuded Churchill did not say.

That afternoon he drafted a message to de Robeck, encouraging him to attempt again to sweep and penetrate the minefields, to which Fisher objected and substituted, 'You must on no account take decisive action without our permission'.[25] To this Churchill replied:

'At a moment when the Army may be committed to an attack I cannot agree to send a telegram which might have the effect of paralysing necessary naval action as judged necessary by the responsible admiral on the spot. The telegram I have drafted is quite sufficient; but I have made a small amendment in an attempt to meet your wishes. It is dangerous to delay sending the telegram and I have therefore directed the secretary to send it in this form.' [26]

Bacon calls this an 'arbitrary' minute from a First Lord to a First Sea Lord. The matter was clearly in the province of the First Sea Lord. How much Churchill knew of Asquith's assurance to Fisher is uncertain, but he had given way considerably in the face of Fisher's determination. His revised message read:

> 'We think the moment for an independent naval attempt to force the Narrows has passed and will not arise again under present conditions. The Army is now landed, large reinforcements are being sent and there can be no doubt that with time and patience the Kilid Bahr Plateau will be taken. Your role is therefore to support the Army in its costly but sure advance and reserve your strength to deal with the situation which will arise later when the Army has succeeded with your aid in its task. We are going to send you the first six monitors as they are delivered and you will find them far better adapted for this special work than the old battleships. You will later receive telegrams about increased provisions of nets against submarines, about fitting special anti-mine protection to some of your battleships and about landing heavy guns.'[27]

This message did not in any way answer the two questions on which de Robeck had asked for decisions. Fisher had succeeded in vetoing what amounted to a direct order to resume the naval attack, but the suggestion remained. 'Churchill,' says Martin Gilbert, 'had given way entirely to Fisher's demands. Three days of long argument and bitter recriminations, were, he hoped, at an end. But Fisher ignored the extent of his success, and was still determined to give the impression that Churchill had been unreasonable.'[28]

The Kilid Bahr plateau was never taken; the Army's advance was certainly costly, but far from sure, and Churchill's habit of sending messages 'From First Lord' was a transparent device to circumvent the constitution of the Admiralty; such messages should have been 'From Admiralty', implying Board approval. But Churchill's wording was authoritative and compelling; an admiral would regard it as a directive, to be disobeyed at his peril. Early the next morning (14 May) Fisher wrote to Hankey, again appealing for his tactful assistance:

> '*BURN.*
> 'My beloved Hankey,
> '*AGAIN* last evening Winston sent off another telegram to de Robeck when Bartolomé had told him I objected! So I had to go to him at 5.30 pm and say it was a *"casus belli"* and then he cancelled the telegram and sent the one I had given to Bartolomé – and then once again at 7 pm he re-asserted his conviction that after all in six weeks time the fleet would have to do it *ALONE!* "& would I remain on anyhow quiet for these six weeks!!!" *That is to say I am to aid and abet for 6 weeks?*
> 'What is one to do with such a determined mad gambler? – ask MCKENNA! SECRETLY – *and the Prime Minister says to me* "Rely on me" "*I will never fail you,*" *but Winston ignores the lot and sends the telegram from himself* – "Surely I can send a private letter to a friend without

showing it to you"!!!! That's his argument! – "A private telegram of friendship, cordiality and encouragement" (as he terms it).'[29]

The telegram, with Churchill's minute, was shown to the other Sea Lords, who collectively signed a memorandum in reply to the First Sea Lord, agreeing with his views and asking to be kept informed, so that each could decide his own attitude. But just before midnight on 13 May the Italian Naval Attaché came to see Churchill asking for certain arrangements to be effected. These had already been agreed with Fisher, so he composed a telegram accordingly, but added, 'First Sea Lord to see after action', which he later admitted he had often done before. This telegram dealt almost exclusively with the movements of ships and again was a matter for Fisher. He did not in fact see it until other events had overtaken it and Churchill's subsequent claim that this precipitated Fisher's resignation was untrue.

The same day, 14 May, a meeting of the War Council took place which Churchill described as 'sulphurous'. The shortage of shells on the Western Front had been disclosed by Repington in *The Times*; Sir John French had lost another 20,000 men in the attack on Aubers Ridge and was calling for reinforcements and ammunition. The weakness and disasters on the Russian front were becoming crucial, and at Gallipoli Sir Ian Hamilton's Army had been brought to a complete halt, was difficult to reinforce and even more difficult to withdraw. 'Intense anxiety and extreme bad temper, all suppressed under formal demeanour, characterised the discussion.'[30]

Kitchener attacked the Navy for the withdrawal of the *Queen Elizabeth* and claimed that he had only been induced to participate in the Dardanelles campaign by the assurance that the Navy would force the passage and by the presence of the *Queen Elizabeth*. 'Lord Fisher at this point interjected that he had been against the Dardanelles operation from the beginning and that the Prime Minister and Lord Kitchener knew this fact well. This remarkable interruption was received in silence.'[31]

This suggests the primacy of Kitchener, the ineptitude of Asquith and the subservient position in which Fisher was held, who appears to have been treated like an impertinent schoolboy interrupting his betters. Unless, of course, the meeting now recognized the wisdom of his words.

Kitchener turned in a pessimistic manner to survey the other theatres of war, finally falling back on the old invasion bogey, now that so many ships were at the Dardanelles, and claimed he must keep four divisions at home, compared with the two divisions that had sufficed earlier in the war.

Churchill responded convincingly. If it had been known three months earlier that 80–100,000 men would be available in May to attack the Dardanelles, the Navy would not have attacked alone. The operation did not depend solely on the disabled *Queen Elizabeth* whose contribution should not be exaggerated. He scornfully dismissed the invasion scare. (Postwar German records supported him; Germany never even considered invasion and could never have mounted one). The meeting, as was customary, broke up without decision, but its result was important, for the next day Churchill wrote to Asquith:

'I must ask you to take note of Fisher's statements today that 'he was against the Dardanelles and had been all along', or words to that effect. *The First Sea Lord has agreed in writing to every executive telegram* [my italics] on which the operations have been conducted; and had they been immediately successful the credit would have been his. But I make no complaint of that. . . . My point is that a moment will probably arise in these operations when the Admiral and General on the spot will wish and require to run a risk with the fleet for a great and decisive effort. If I agree with them I shall sanction it and I cannot undertake to be paralysed by the veto of a friend who, whatever the result, will certainly say, 'I was against the Dardanelles . . .'.

'But I wish to make it clear to you that a man who says, 'I disclaim responsibility for failure', cannot be the final arbiter of the measures which may be found vital to success.'[32]

The italicized words are transparently untrue. Many of Churchill's devotees are deceived by Admiralty procedure; the mere initialling of a document did not indicate concurrence, but only that the paper had been seen by the person concerned. Concurrence demanded a positive statement to that effect. Nor would credit for success have been Fisher's; we may be sure Churchill would have appropriated it. 'I am in no way concealing the great and continuous pressure I put on the old Admiral.'[33]

But the last paragraph is perhaps Churchill's worst; it implies that he knew better than a man with sixty years' naval experience, in nearly all the most important appointments. Churchill's administration of the Admiralty while the submissive Battenberg had been First Sea Lord was dogged with failure and he had brought back Fisher, the leading expert of his day, to save his political life. But his personal egotism and strength of character were such that even the man on whose advice he had relied before the war must give way. A later First Lord, Geddes, was to say, 'You may rely on me doing whatever is possible for a civilian to do, but naval warfare must be run by the Navy, and cannot be run by a civilian'.[34] The idea of a layman overruling the professional advice of the head of the Navy was comparable to a modern Health Minister telling surgeons how to perform an operation. The Dardanelles Commission reported:

'Mr Churchill knew of the opinions entertained by Lord Fisher and Sir Arthur Wilson and . . . the fact that the other experts at the Admiralty who had been consulted, although they assented to an attack of the outer forts of the Dardanelles and to progressive operations thereafter up the straits *as far as might be found practicable,* had not done so with any great cordiality or enthusiasm.'

Neither knew of the other's communication to the Prime Minister. About 6.30 that evening they met in Fisher's room. Crease, Fisher's Naval Assistant, said that as Churchill left he said goodnight in an affable manner and added, 'We have settled everything, and you must go home and have a good night's rest. Things will look brighter in the morning and we'll pull the thing through together.'[35] When Churchill had gone, Fisher called Crease into his room and said, 'You need not pack up just yet,' and that he had a definite understanding with the First Lord regarding the Dardanelles. 'But,' he added, 'I suppose he'll soon be at me again.' Clearly he had little hope that the understanding would last.

The next morning Fisher received four memoranda from Churchill, written late in the night. The first three related to the ideas postulated in his memorandum of 13 May (see page 173) and a scheme by Tyrwhitt for submarine and zeppelin hunting, proposing various changes in the Grand Fleet, including stationing cruisers in the Humber, all matters for the First Sea Lord, not the First Lord. The last of the four dealt with reinforcements for the Dardanelles.

'First Sea Lord.
1. The fifth 15-inch howitzer with fifty rounds of ammunition should go to the Dardanelles with the least possible delay, being sent by special train across France and re-embarked at Marseilles. Let me have a time table showing by what time it can arrive at the Dardanelles.

'The two 9.2 guns will go to the Dardanelles either in two monitors prepared for them or separately for mounting ashore. This will be decided as soon as we hear from Admiral de Robeck.
2. The following nine heavy monitors should go in succession to the Dardanelles as soon as they are ready: *Admiral Farragut, General Grant, Stonewall Jackson, Robert E Lee, Lord Clive, Prince Rupert, Sir John Moore, General Crauford* and *Marshal Ney*.

'The first six of the 9.2 monitors should also go unless the Admiral chooses to have two of their guns for work on shore, in which case the first four only will go.

'A time table should be prepared showing the dates on which they will be dispatched and will arrive. They can calibrate on the Turks. All necessary steps for their seaworthiness on the voyage should be taken.

'In the case of the 9.2 monitors it may be found better to send the actual guns out to Malta separately.

It is clear that when this large accession of force reaches the Vice-Admiral, he should be able to spare a portion of his battleships for service in Home Waters, but it may be better to see how the monitors work, and what use they are to him before raising this point.
3. Four of the 'Edgars' with special bulge protection against mines and torpedoes are now ready. They carry ten 6-inch guns each and supply the

medium armament that the monitors lack. They should be specially useful in supporting the Army at night without risk from torpedo attack. They would also be useful at a later stage in passing a shore torpedo-tube or escorting other ships that were passing.

'We have not found any satisfactory use for them here.

'It is not necessary to provide crews for them; working parties which can take them out will be sufficient. The Admiral can man them from his large fleet for any special service that may be required. They should start as soon as possible.

'Let me have a report on the manning possibilities as defined above and the time by which they can arrive.

'It will be for consideration, when these vessels are on the spot, whether a valuable ship like the *Chatham* should not be released for other duties. 4 The Third Sea Lord will make proposals for providing anti-mine protection for a proportion of the battleships employed on the lines proposed at our discussion.

5. The following increased provision will be made for the Air Service.

(DAD will supply on verbal instructions)

6. During this month five new submarines are delivered, viz., S2, E18, V2, V3, and S3. In June, the Montreal boats come in. Therefore in view of the request of the Vice-Admiral, I consider that two more 'E' boats should be sent to the Dardanelles.'[36]

The whole memorandum is breathtaking in its arrogation of the responsibilities of the First Sea Lord and its demonstrable ignorance of the practicalities of seamanship and naval tactics. De Robeck could not simply put men on board to operate the ships without time to discover their eccentricities, the location of the multitude of valves, pipes and other equipment, which vary from ship to ship, their steering characteristics, turning circles and so on. Not only were the Sea Lords being treated as mere clerks to do his bidding, but the last two clauses were a flagrant breach of the agreement reached only a few hours before, and in the first edition of *The World Crisis* Churchill omitted them. Bacon drew attention to this omission in his biography of Fisher and the two paragraphs were reinstated in an appendix in the second edition, but even then, in a foot-note, he attempts to brush the omission aside: 'For the final text of this minute see Appendix I'. There was nothing final about it; it was as he drafted it. Accompanying this memorandum, which created days of work, was a covering note which read: MY DEAR FISHER:- I send you this before marking it to others, in order that, if any point arises, we can discuss it. I hope you will agree.'[37]

Churchill knew perfectly well Fisher would not agree, and we have to ask ourselves whether this was pure tactlessness or whether he wanted to rid himself of Fisher. Crease throws light on this:

'I was working in my room at the Admiralty on the night of 14th May, when toward midnight, Masterton Smith [the First Lord's private secretary] came in with the minute and covering letter and said that the First Lord wished the First Sea Lord to have them in the morning.

'Masterton Smith asked me to read them through, and I did so. He was evidently uneasy about the minute and asked me how I thought the old man would take it. Knowing well Lord Fisher's frame of mind during the past few days and his letter to the Prime Minister of the day before, and reading that submarines were now included in the proposed reinforcements, in addition to various other ships and materials that Lord Fisher had not mentioned a few hours earlier, I had no hesitation about my reply. I said at once that I had no doubt whatsoever Lord Fisher would resign instantly if he received the minute; for these new proposals, coming at that moment, would be the last straw.

'Masterton Smith, who was also very familiar with the First Sea Lord and his ways, said he did not think Lord Fisher would go so far as that; but I repeated that I felt quite certain that he would. After some discussion, Masterton Smith said he would tell the First Lord my opinion before definitely handing me the minute to pass on. After some delay – I believe Masterton Smith first spoke to De Bartolomé on the subject before going to Mr. Churchill – he came back with the dispatch box and said it must be sent on, for the First Lord was certain that Lord Fisher would not object to the proposals; but the First Lord also added *that in any case it was necessary that they should be made.* I repeated my warning as to the consequences, and then arranged for the dispatch box to be delivered early in the morning to Lord Fisher.'[38]

Churchill's tone to a distinguished admiral was surely unacceptable. *'Let me have a timetable.'* *'Let me have a report on the manning possibilities.'* These are phrases that an admiral might use to a junior staff officer.

About 5 am on Saturday, 15 May, Fisher opened the dispatch box in the First Sea Lord's house. He read the memorandum and considered that for the second time in two days Churchill had broken his word. He at once wrote and dispatched a letter of resignation to the First Lord: 'After further anxious reflection, I have come to the regretted conclusion that I am unable to remain any longer as your colleague. It is undesirable, in the public interest, to go into details – Jowett said "never explain" – but I find it increasingly difficult to adjust myself to the increasing daily requirements of the Dardanelles to meet your views. As you truly said yesterday, I am in the position of continually vetoing your proposals. This is not fair to you, besides being extremely distasteful to me. I am off to Scotland at once so as to avoid all questionings.'[39] He sent a copy to Asquith with a brief covering letter.

Churchill immediately replied pathetically:

'In order to bring you back to the Admiralty I took my political life in my hands – as you well know. You then promised to stand by me and see me through. If you now go at this bad moment and therefore let loose on me the spite and malice of those who are your enemies even more than they are mine, it will be a melancholy ending to our six months of successful war and administration. The discussions that will arise will strike a cruel blow at the fortunes of the Army now struggling on the Gallipoli peninsula and cannot fail to invest with an air of disaster a mighty enterprise which with patience can, and will, certainly be carried to success. . . . I hope you will come and see me tomorrow afternoon. I have a proposition to make to you, with the assent of the Prime Minister, which may remove some of the anxieties and difficulties which you feel about the measures necessary to support the Army at the Dardanelles. Though I stand at my post until relieved, it will be a very great grief to me to part from you; and our rupture will be profoundly injurious to every public interest.'[40]

There are several explanations for this emotional appeal. Perhaps Churchill thought Fisher would never resign; he had often threatened to. 'I did not, however, at first take a serious view . . . he had threatened or hinted resignation . . . on all sorts of matters.'[41] He may have been attempting to get Fisher to toe the line and act as a mere aid, whose resounding name would add credibility to his schemes, especially the Dardanelles, or he may have realized that Fisher' resignation would harm his political life.

There were further sentimental letters from Churchill 'similar to those which hitherto had been effective and had caused Lord Fisher more than once to acquiesce',[42] but this time Fisher was adamant. On receipt of his resignation, Asquith demanded to see him, but he could not be found; he was probably in Westminster Abbey, where he often went for solace at times of crisis. He was determined to see no politicians who would try to persuade him to remain and whose promises he distrusted. He had taken a room at the Charing Cross Hotel, which no doubt Crease knew, and when a letter from Asquith arrived it reached him there. It was probably without equal in modern times; peremptory in tone, mediaeval in terms, it was like something out of a Victorian schoolboy story. It read:

'Lord Fisher,
'In the King's name I order you to remain at your post.'[43]

This theatrical communication was quite pointless. Had Fisher been of a truculent, undisciplined nature there were ample alternatives open to him. He could have 'remained at his post' and done nothing. He could have disregarded the Prime Minister's 'order' and gone to Scotland, or passed it to the Press. What could Asquith have done? Court-martialled the First Sea Lord, an Admiral of the Fleet and a peer, in wartime? And such a man that it would have been diffi-cult, perhaps impossible, to find officers to serve on a court. There would have been an outcry throughout the Navy and many resignations. The only benefi-ciary would have been Germany. But, partly, the absurd tactic worked. Fisher abandoned for the moment his plan to stay in Scotland with the Duke of Hamilton, who had served under him as a midshipman. Later that day he went to see Asquith. On the steps of No 10 Downing Street he met Lloyd George, who tried to persuade him to wait until the following Monday and put his case before a War Council.

> 'So far as the Council was concerned he had never expressed any dissent
> from the policy or the plans for the expedition; that though I was a
> member of the War Council and had been opposed to the venture from
> the start I had not heard one word of protest from him. . . . His answer
> was that Mr. Churchill was his Chief, and that by the traditions of the
> Service, he was not entitled to differ from him in public. On being
> reminded by me that the Council was a Council of War, and he was
> bound, as a member of that Council, to speak his mind freely to all his
> colleagues around the table, he stated that he had at the outset made an
> emphatic protest against the whole expedition to the Prime Minister
> privately, and had left to him the responsibility of communicating or with-
> holding that knowledge.'[44]

Coming from the shrewd Lloyd George, who had seen Fisher leaving the table on 28 January, this was hardly convincing, but, recognizing the vital importance of the situation, he sent a message to Asquith, who was attending a wedding, stressing the need to see Fisher at once, which he did, but was unable to shake Fisher's resolve. That evening the King told Esher, who wrote,

> 'The endless quarrels with Churchill have come to a head. Both Fisher
> and Churchill offered their resignations, and the Prime Minister refused
> to accept Churchill's. Fisher saw Churchill this afternoon, and there is
> some idea that an arrangement may have to be made. The King sees that
> Fisher's resignation at such a moment is bound to have a deplorable, if
> not disastrous, effect upon the public, not only at home, but abroad.'[45]

Fisher remained in his house refusing to enter the Admiralty or to deal with routine business. Crease sent important operational papers through to the house and he dealt with these. He sent a curious telegram to Jellicoe: 'From Lord Fisher: Personal and Private: Prevented by pressing business from answering your letters'.[46] This, Bacon believed, was a code, as Jellicoe had an arrangement that he should wire Fisher personally if he had doubt about any message received from the Admiralty. He made sure *Queen Elizabeth* had proper routing instructions to avoid submarines and dealt with other impor-tant matters. But in the evening Crease pointed out that none of the other Sea

Lords knew of his resignation and business was coming to a standstill. Fisher had thought it Churchill's business to inform them and announce the name of his successor, but Crease persuaded him to tell them, and early the next morning (Sunday) he wrote to Crease:

> 'Make three copies of the enclosed letter to Winston, and then give the original to Masterton and beg him to telegraph to Winston not to come to see me – it is so painful – and *my decision is irrevocable*. Ask the Second Sea Lord to do my work and the C.O.S to see the Second Sea Lord instead of me. . . . We shall take rooms at an hotel on Tuesday. . . . Show the Sea Lords copy of my letter to Winston, also to Hopwood [Additional Civil Lord]. Impress on Masterton the utter futility of my seeing Winston.'[47]

He replied to Churchill's unctuous appeal the same day:

> 'The Prime Minister put the case in a nutshell when he stated to me yesterday afternoon the actual fact that I had been dead against the Dardanelles operation from the beginning! How could I be otherwise when previously as First Sea Lord I had been responsible for the Defence Committee Memorandum stating the forcing of the Dardanelles to be impossible? You *must* remember my extreme reluctance in the Prime Minister's room in January to accept his decision in regard to the Dardanelles and, at the War Council held immediately afterwards, I stated in reply to a question of the Chancellor of the Exchequer that the Prime Minister knew my views, and I left the matter for him to explain. . . . YOU ARE BENT ON FORCING THE DARDANELLES AND NOTHING WILL TURN YOU FROM IT – NOTHING. I know you so well. I could give you no better proof of my desire to stand by you than my having remained by you in this Dardanelles business up to the last moment against the strongest conviction of my life, as stated in the Dardanelles Committee Memorandum. YOU WILL REMAIN and I SHALL GO – it is better so. Your splendid stand on my behalf I shall never forget when you took your political life in your hands and I have really worked very hard for you in return – *My utmost;* but here is a question beyond all personal obligations. I assure you that it is only painful to have further conversations. I have told the Prime Minister I will not remain.'[48]

Fisher's acceptance of Churchill's claim to have 'taken his political life in his hands' surely demonstrates extraordinary naïvity; the politician's career was saved by recalling the admiral, who owed him nothing on this account.

At the same time he wrote to McKenna, by now a close personal friend:

> 'I late last night at 10 p.m. got a long letter from Winston. . . . It absolutely CONVINCES me I am right in my UNALTERABLE DECISION to resign! *In*

fact I have resigned. . . . I want you kindly to tell the Prime Minister distinctly and definitely that *I am no longer First Sea Lord. There is no compromise possible.*'[49]

McKenna came to see him and attempted to persuade him to stay on; he then went to see the Prime Minister, and wrote to Fisher the same night: 'Just back. – The P.M. holds the opinion that your resignation is void until he accepts. Before he does so I am satisfied that he is bound to have your precise grounds definitely formulated in writing and presented to him. If you are up I will come and see you when I have had some food.'[50]

Crease showed the other Sea Lords the correspondence, resulting in another curious incident, for the same day they sent a memorandum to both Churchill and Fisher, stating that they believed the Dardanelles operation endangered the Grand Fleet and expressing their dissatisfaction that 'orders for controlling movements and supplies appear to be largely taken out of the hands of the First Sea Lord,' and that Fisher's resignation would be 'a national disaster' and must be averted, ending, 'Whatever differences in opinion or defects in procedure may have arisen or become apparent should be capable of adjustment by mutual discussion and concession, and we therefore venture to urge you both to consider whether the national interests do not demand that you should follow the advice we have tendered.'[51]

They sent a copy to Asquith. How they believed reconciliation possible is difficult to imagine, but Fisher had been most careful not to allow his frustration to disturb the smooth working of the Admiralty and they were certainly not fully aware of the position, though informed of much that had gone on; they knew of the repeated 'mutual discussion', always ending unsatisfactorily, despite 'understandings' and 'agreements'. Fisher responded with brief thanks and no comment. All the Sea Lords disbelieved in success in the Dardanelles and thought the Grand Fleet in danger, and had Fisher appealed to them, all would have resigned, but he scrupulously avoided drawing them in; the resignation of the entire Board would have created a national crisis. They had a duty to restore operational control to professional hands, in which they signally failed and the wishy-washy talk of 'mutual agreement' avoided the issue. That they were in a dilemma is certain; that they failed to meet it equally so. Fisher wrote to Crease the same day: 'I hope the Sea Lords clearly understand my undoubtedly correct reason for not entangling them, but I grieve they allowed themselves to be made use of and send me advice which I did not require, and it was exceedingly bad advice; and they and Sir A.K.Wilson will clearly see this when the Day of Judgment comes along and all chicanery is exposed. Was it likely that I did not know all the circumstances?'[52]

Churchill answered them on Monday 17 May:

'I am vy. much indebted to you for the loyalty to national interests wh. has in this emergency guided your action. I must however put on record

183

with regard to your minute that there is not the slightest foundation for the statement that "the method of directing the distribution of the Fleet & the conduct of the War" are largely taken out of the hands of the First Sea Lord. No order of the slightest consequence affecting the movements of the Fleet or its distribution has ever been issued except with the authority of the First Sea Lord. . . . The First Sea Lord has agreed to every step that has been taken & every order that has been sent.'[53]

But they were not as gullible as he thought:

'We wish to point out . . . that this does not fully meet our contention. . . . What we maintain is that all such orders should be initiated by the First Sea Lord and referred to you for criticism or concurrence. The difference between the two methods is obvious. We take this opportunity to ask that an assurance may be given that means shall be found to ensure that all the Sea Lords are consulted and kept more fully informed on large points of policy than has been the practice hitherto.'[54]

But the Sea Lords were no match for the great dialectician, who tried to shift the blame and fell back on the Admiralty Patent.

'I must observe that [your remarks] are a criticism of the First Sea Lord and not me. The action which I initiated, which obtained the concurrence of the First Sea Lord, was necessary for the prosecution of the war. Had I neglected to propose it in default of the First Sea Lord's initiative, injury would have resulted to vital interests. It is better that the First Sea Lord should make proposals and the First Lord criticise them or concur. But no rule can be laid down. Certainly under the patent the First Lord has the power, not only of veto but of initiation. I should never accept a system by which the First Lord, who is solely responsible to Crown and Parliament for the whole business of the Admiralty, should be deprived of the power of even bringing before his principal naval colleague & advisor his views and wishes; & I am quite sure that on reflection you will agree that this would be impossible. With regard to your last paragraph, I agree that the four Sea Lords shd. be more fully consulted on large questions of policy, as apart from the day to day running of the war, where action must proceed easily and rapidly. But neither Prince Louis of Battenberg nor Lord Fisher were in favour of this practice, considering that war plans and war policy lay wholly in the domain of the First Sea Lord, with the First Lord exercising the supreme executive power. It wd. appear desirable in future that the war situation shd. be reviewed each week by the naval members of the Board under the presidency of the First Lord. It must however be evident that in war the necessary action *must* be taken, and no rules as to consultation or agreement can be allowed to hamper the discharge of the gravest duties.'[55]

By conceding weekly meetings of the Sea Lords (which in the event never took place), Churchill appeased the Board. He had thrown all the blame for almost everything on Fisher and, with blatant misrepresentation, accused him of lack of initiative, something even Beresford in his wildest moments had never suggested. But the ruse succeeded; the Sea Lords were satisfied with the minor concession they had wrung and tamely did nothing further to support Fisher.

Fisher was inundated with advice, good and bad.

'You really must not resign under present conditions,' wrote Wilson. 'It would mean a great national disaster and you have no right to consider your private feelings in the matter while the interest of the country are so much at stake as they are now. Do change your mind and see the thing out.'[56] Esher wrote completely the opposite: 'You will never *permanently* patch up these quarrels. The only thing to be done is to revive the office of Lord High Admiral and take it yourself. Otherwise we are beaten at sea; and unless Lord K takes the war into his own hands, ditto on land.'[57]

Queen Alexandra wrote, '*Stick* to your post like *Nelson!* The Nation and we all have confidence in you and *I* and they will not suffer you to go. You are the nation's hope and we trust you!'[58]

Bonar Law, Leader of the Opposition and an old friend, had written, and, emboldened by this encouragement, Fisher replied on 17 May, heading his letter

'*Private and Personal. This letter and its contents must not be divulged now or ever to any living soul:*

In reply to your letter, after repeated refusals by him I have written to the PM to say that now my *definite decision* is I am absolutely unable to remain with WC (HE'S A REAL DANGER!) *But he is going to be kept* (so I go! *at once, TO-DAY), only they are "forking" me till Parliament rises in three weeks or more. I regret to say your AJB has been backing WC ALL THROUGH AND I have refused to have anything to do with him (AJB) in consequence! Keep this private.* I must not see you, BUT PARLIAMENT SHOULD NOT RISE TILL THE FACT OF MY GOING IS EXTRACTED. Lots of people must know – for instance see enclosed from Lord Esher. You might see him at 2, Tilney Street, Park Lane, and let his informant be your source of information. *I could not see you – I have seen no one. I have written to no one.* Yours, F.

'Don't be cajoled *privately* by the PM to keep silence. The danger is imminent and VITAL. I don't want to stay, but WC MUST go at all costs. . . . The PM will stick at nothing to keep WC. *I'm a dead dog. . . . I feel bound to tell you as leader of the Opposition, because a very great national disaster is very near us in the Dardanelles!* against which I have vainly protested and did resign long ago, but Kitchener persuaded me to stop. *I was a d———d fool to do so.* (HE ought to have resigned also).'[59]

Fisher's was not the only letter Law received that day. The shrewd Sir Henry Wilson wrote from France:

'I hear on good authority to-night we are thoroughly well "hold up" [*sic*] in Gallipoli. I hear also there is a violent attack of Invasion fever. As a result our reinforcements are not to come – At present. Now all this wants watching. A man who can pilot the Ulster pogrom plan Antwerp & carry out the Dardanelles fiasco is worth watching. He and the Govt. have got to cover up their tracks & the means employed will not be too nice. Only this line of warning.'[60]

Fisher's resignation came at a dangerous moment for Asquith. A debate was about to be held on the shortage of shell, which promised to be lively, and Bonar Law wrote to Asquith on the Monday morning:

'Lord Lansdowne and I have learnt with dismay that Lord Fisher has resigned, and we have come to the conclusion that we cannot allow the House to adjourn until this fact has been made known and discussed. . . . In our opinion things cannot go on as they are and some change in the Government seems to us inevitable . . . and if you are prepared to take the necessary steps to secure the object which I have indicated, and if Lord Fisher's resignation is in the meantime postponed, we shall be ready to keep silence now. Otherwise I must to-day ask you if Lord Fisher has resigned, and press for a day to discuss the situation arising out of his resignation.'[61]

Despite having once turned him out of office, Churchill approached Wilson to become First Sea Lord. Grossly misinformed, Wilson wrote:

'Fisher's bombshell has done us more harm than a big defeat, and I don't know yet in the least what will come of it. He sent in his resignation and left the Admiralty . . . without troubling himself to think how the work would be affected. When I saw Mr. Churchill on Sunday he told me that Fisher had gone, and asked me to take office as First Sea Lord. After a good deal of hesitation I agreed and the Prime Minister said he was very pleased, and I thought the matter would be settled the next day, but on Monday decided to postpone my decision.'[62]

Churchill wrote to Asquith: 'I have learned with great surprise that Sir Arthur Wilson yesterday informed the Naval Lords [*sic*] that, while he was prepared to serve as First Sea Lord under me, he was not prepared to do so under anyone else. This is the greatest compliment I have ever been paid. The three Naval Lords [*sic*] are also ready to serve under me. They take a vy. serious view of Lord Fisher's desertion of his post in time of war for what has now amounted to six days, during which serious operations have been in progress. They feel that should he return to the Admiralty their position would be made vy. difficult as also will those of many officers of the department who have been associated with me & will become objects of resentment.'[63]

Wilson had misunderstood Churchill, for Asquith cannot have said he was 'very pleased'; when Churchill arrived to propose the appointment, with the names of the new Board in his pocket, which Bonar Law described as 'tame', he found Asquith's solution to his problem was to invite the Unionist leaders to form a coalition Government, and he, Churchill, might not be in the Cabinet. Wilson's nomination could not be accepted. Even so, despite his views on Heligoland, Asquith described Wilson as 'our most distinguished naval strategist and tactician'.[64]

Churchill returned to the Admiralty in an extraordinary position, to hear that the High Sea Fleet had put to sea. The First Sea Lord's resignation had not been accepted; Wilson had no status. The Second Sea Lord could hardly take over until Fisher's resignation was agreed; Asquith refused to take even transient action to fill the gap. Churchill had no way to turn. Fisher too had heard the High Sea Fleet was out, but was convinced it was a mere excursion to discover whether Britain could read enemy ciphers. He kept discreetly in touch and, though he refused the First Lord's entreaty to pass along the passage from his house to the main building, he was ready to do so in a real emergency. If he returned to his office he effectively remained First Sea Lord and, except in emergency, he was determined to keep away from Churchill, whose persuasive tongue he feared would tempt him back to the office he so much hated leaving. Churchill, however, saw his opportunity. Only a miracle could save him from political disaster and the sortie by the High Sea Fleet seemed just that miracle. If he could win the new Trafalgar unaided, his reputation would not merely be restored, but he would have scored a victory which would establish his prestige forever. He spent the whole night rushing forces to meet the challenge, filling the air with streams of radio messages. The sudden vast increase in wireless traffic appeared to provide the enemy with just the information they wanted; the German fleet returned to harbour. Fisher was convinced he was right, though in fact he was wrong; the Germans never realized the British could read their ciphers.

On 17 May he wrote to the Prime Minister: 'I have remained until to-day (Monday) in accordance with your wishes and I now write to say DEFINITELY that I am unable to remain at the Admiralty with Mr. Winston Churchill, and will NOT remain after to-day.'[65]

This brought forth a reply pregnant with meaning:

'*Secret.*

'Dear Lord Fisher,

I have your letter this morning. I feel bound to tell you for your own information only that a considerable reconstruction of the Government is in contemplation, and in the public interest I trust that you will neither say nor do anything for a day or two.

Yours sincerely,   H.H. Asquith'.[66]

Fisher replied that day, 'It's very kind of you to have written to me, as it prevents my going to Scotland to-morrow morning.'[67] Then came the news of the coalition. Both Wilson and Fisher saw that this changed everything. Said Wilson,

'I then wrote to the Prime Minister to say that, although I had undertaken to serve under Mr. Churchill, I could not take up the responsibilities under a new man as I was not strong enough. Since that, nothing has been settled, except that Mr. Churchill is to go. I believe Mr. Balfour is to take his place, but I am not certain. No one knows who is to be First Sea Lord. In the meantime I am helping the Second Sea Lord to do the First Sea Lord's work.'[68]

Wilson's acceptance of the post and refusal to serve under any other than Churchill has repeatedly been quoted against Fisher, suggesting Wilson's support for Churchill, who repeated in *The World Crisis* what he had told Asquith, 'This utterly unexpected mark of confidence from the old Admiral astounded me. His reserve had been impenetrable. I had no idea how he viewed me and my work. Certainly I never counted on the slightest support or approbation from him.'[69] But Wilson's offer was to preserve continuity; it had little to do with approbation of Churchill; he was no more supportive of the Dardanelles than Fisher.

Churchill then sent a message to Fisher, offering him a seat in the Cabinet if he would stay on with himself as First Lord. Hankey said the message was brought verbally by Lambert, the Civil Lord, but Fisher's reply was to tell Churchill to go to hell. Fisher 'rejected the 30 pieces of silver.'[70] But Churchill had no authority to make the offer; Asquith was the only man who had, and in view of his plans, cannot have sanctioned it. Maurice Bonham Carter, Asquith's Private Secretary, confirmed this to Marder in 1954: 'I do not believe for one moment that Lambert was authorized by the Prime Minister to offer Fisher a seat in the Cabinet on any condition at all.'[71] (This incident is recorded by Hankey as having occurred on 19 May, but Fisher refers to it in his letter to Bonar Law on 17 May as having occurred that evening). The notion of having both in the Cabinet was unprecedented and unworkable, but Asquith's letter to Fisher indicating a reconstruction of the Government suggests that, if he had told Churchill Fisher might be offered a seat in the

Cabinet, it may have been his intention to offer him the appointment of First Lord; at Bonar Law's insistence he had already decided to drop Churchill, who may have misunderstood.

The crisis became common gossip and the Press rallied almost solidly behind Fisher. On the front page of *The Globe* a huge headline shouted LORD FISHER MUST NOT GO, and the paper asked '*Lord Fisher or Mr. Churchill? Expert or amateur?*'. *The Times* and the *Telegraph* proposed Fisher as First Lord, which was taken up by many other papers, the former stating that he was 'the only possible choice'; the *Army and Navy Gazette* listed all the former naval officers who had successfully occupied the position – Anson, Keppel, St. Vincent and Barham.[72] In the Fleet, Fisher's departure was viewed with almost universal alarm. Jellicoe wrote to him: 'I am dismayed at the prospect ahead. The Navy distrusts Mr. Churchill and Sir A.K.Wilson profoundly. I feel the question is most serious, and if I can help you in any capacity, I am ready and would put aside all personal feelings.'[73]

Beatty also wrote : 'The Commander-in-Chief told me this morning that you had resigned. I cannot believe that it is possible that the Government will accept it. It would be a worse calamity than a defeat at sea. If it is any value to know it, the fleet is numbed with the thought of the possibility . . . Please God it is *not* possible.'[74] Professor Marder finds some evidence that Jellicoe and Beatty, dreading Wilson's strategic ideas, were both prepared to resign if he succeeded Fisher.

It was this massive support that was Fisher's undoing. He was misled into believing that the Unionists insisted on his remaining, whereas they insisted on Churchill's departure. The King, too, wanted Churchill removed; he wrote to the Queen on 19 May, 'Personally I am glad the Prime Minister is going to have a National Government. Only by that means can we get rid of Churchill from Admiralty. He is intriguing also with French against K. He is the real danger.'[75]

Churchill now became seriously alarmed. He inundated influential people with letters beseeching them to aid him and swearing eternal friendship to his enemies. He wrote repeatedly over the next few days to Bonar Law, to Asquith, to Stamfordham (for the King), and even recruited Clementine Churchill to write a pathetic and beseeching letter to the Prime Minister, but to no avail. Asquith did not reply and several times read her letter out at the luncheon table with entertaining delight, describing it to Venetia Stanley as 'the letter of a maniac'.[76] On 21 May he wrote to Churchill that he must accept that he would no longer remain at the Admiralty.

But the news that Balfour, who supported the Dardanelles campaign, was to be First Lord and the rumour that Churchill would remain in the Cabinet meant the operation would continue and Fisher made perhaps the biggest mistake in his life; for he wrote to the Prime Minister a dictatorial letter laying down conditions for his return:

'If the following six conditions are agreed to, I can guarantee the successful termination of the war and the total abolition of the submarine menace.

'I also wish to add that since Lord Ripon wished, in 1885, to make me a Lord of the Admiralty, but at my request made me Director of Naval Ordnance and Torpedoes instead, I have served under nine First Lords and seventeen years at the Admiralty, so I ought to know something about it.

(1) That Mr. Winston Churchill is not in the Cabinet to be always circumventing me. Nor will I serve under Mr. Balfour.

(2) That Sir A.K.Wilson leaves the Admiralty, and the Committee of Imperial Defence, and the War Council, as my time will be occupied in resisting the bombardment of Heligoland and other such wild projects. Also his policy is totally opposed to mine, and he accepted the position of First Sea Lord in succession to me, thereby adopting a policy diametrically opposed to my views.

(3) That there shall be an entire new Board of Admiralty as regards the Sea Lords and the Financial Secretary (who is utterly useless), *New measures demand new men.*

(4) That I should have complete professional charge of the war at sea, together with the sole disposition of the fleet and the appointment of all officers of all ranks whatsoever and absolutely untrammelled sole command of all the sea forces whatsoever.

(5) That the First Lord of the Admiralty should be absolutely restricted to policy and Parliamentary procedure, and should occupy the same position towards me as Mr. Tennant MP [Asquith's brother-in-law] does to Lord Kitchener (and very well he does it).

(6) That I should have the sole absolute authority for all new construction and all dockyard work of whatever sort whatsoever, and complete control over the civil establishment of the Navy.

    19.5.15   F.

'P.S – the 60 per cent of my time and energy which I have exhausted on nine First Lords *in the past* I wish *in the future* to devote to the successful prosecution of the war. That is the sole reason for these six conditions. These six conditions must be published verbatim, so that the fleet may know my position.[77]

He attached a note giving details of the changes he wished to make in commands and in the Board of Admiralty.

The absurdity of this letter needs no elaboration. No Prime Minister could be dictated to in this manner. The exaggerated first paragraph, the arrogation of power and nomination of men to be excluded from the Government were bound to offend, even create ridicule. Had he stayed silent and waited the turn of events it is likely he would have been asked to withdraw his resignation and continue to serve under another more amenable First Lord, or have been so appointed himself. Asquith later said that, had he called on him, he could have put his view and would have been listened to. Better still he should have done nothing. He had, by this injudicious act, destroyed all chance of re-appointment.

The same day he wrote an almost equally unwise letter to Bonar Law explaining his objection to Balfour as First Lord. Balfour had supported the Dardanelles campaign and had repeatedly been closeted with Churchill in the Admiralty.

> 'It is impossible to explain by letter the chicanery in progress! To me it is absolutely incomprehensible that Winston having left the Cabinet should have been brought back into it by A.J.B. . . . I am sure you will under-stand that my position would have been both intolerable and impossible with Winston in the Cabinet circumventing me and in such close intimacy as he is with A.J.B. he would be practically his advisor instead of me.'[78]

Mackay blames Fisher's tactless letters on Esher's suggestion of the revival of the office of Lord High Admiral, but this is surely unconvincing. Had he discussed his draft with Esher he would have received sound advice. There was much sense in what he wrote, mixed up with nonsense. The sense was obscured by the nonsense.

Almost simultaneously, Selborne was writing to Balfour, 'I am very firmly convinced that you cannot improve on Fisher for First Sea Lord.' Later in the day, having heard of Fisher's letter to the Prime Minister, he wrote again, hoping that Fisher would not be excluded on this account, because he was 'the best available'. But Balfour, evidently getting his information from Churchill, replied the next day: 'I am afraid that Jacky is a little mad; he has been using, I hear, the most violent language about me. . . . I am not sure that even if Asquith consented to his remaining at the Admiralty, he (Fisher) would consent to serve under me.'[79]

Esher gave Fisher further encouragement:

> 'There is only one solution.
> Lord Fisher
> Lord K.
> Operations   To be hanged if they fail.
>   To be crowned with bays if they succeed . . .
> Stick to this.'[80]

So confident was Fisher of remaining as First Sea Lord that he sent a note to Crease instructing him to prepare a withdrawal from the Dardanelles. The Army would be taken off and landed at Haifa and all ships not required to protect the Army would be withdrawn. All the necessary telegrams were to be prepared, ready for signature. Crease was also to arrange for continuous aircraft patrols off the Humber estuary. But Crease soon heard of Fisher's letter to Asquith and went to his house to enquire about the state of affairs. Fisher showed the letter to Crease, who was astounded to find the Admiral could see nothing wrong with it.

Fisher's behaviour at this time is difficult to understand. He was convinced by Asquith's letter and by support in the Press and a mass of encouraging letters, that his retention of power, even its enhancement, was a foregone conclusion. The strain of the past few weeks, the stress of the last few days, had blurred his judgment. But Churchill's inferences in *The World Crisis* and his claims that Fisher had had a 'nervous breakdown' were undoubtedly postulated to shift attention from his own part in the affair. Men often imagine that the denigration of others enhances their own prestige. Fisher's orders to Crease were clear, well thought out and eminently sensible, certainly not the words of a man suffering from a nervous breakdown. It was Churchill's charge that gave rise to the unfounded story, reflected by Balfour, that Fisher had lost his reason; in a footnote to Kitchener on 21 May Churchill spread the rumour in even stronger language: 'Fisher went mad.'[81]

Verily, whom the Politicians wish to destroy, they first call mad!

Perhaps unconsciously, Hankey added to this fantasy by entering in his diary on 19 May, 'Fisher madder than ever'.[82] But he clearly meant this solecism in the colloquial sense of eccentric or zealous, not literally.

The mendacity of Fisher's 'desertion of his post' was written into the myth of history in Churchill's letter to Asquith concerning Wilson, no doubt to support his case for the retention of office. I have found no evidence that the other Sea Lords expressed any opinion of the matter, as Churchill claimed. Both he and Asquith described Fisher's action as 'deserting his post' and, though in his letter of resignation Fisher had expressed his intention of going to Scotland, this was on the not unreasonable assumption that his resignation would immediately be accepted. Hankey records in his diary that, far from 'deserting his post', he was so convinced that his 'six conditions' would be accepted that he had to be prized out of the Admiralty buildings.

> '*May 22nd.* In morning I saw Balfour for a short time, but spent most of the morning in getting pressure put on Fisher to go right away to Scotland, away from Journalistic influences, as he may do himself and the nation great harm by an indiscretion in his present excited state. I saw him and took the line that he ought to adopt the rôle of the 'strong, silent man', injured, but still keeping silent. I reminded him that he had given this advice to Kitchener with excellent results, and told him it was his one chance of getting back to the Admiralty. It was 12.30 before he agreed, and his train was at 2 pm. Then I remembered that, technically, as his

resignation had not been accepted, he was First Sea Lord and ought not to quit his post without leave, so I undertook to square this with the Prime Minister. Unfortunately the Prime Minister was with the King and did not get back until nearly 2 pm. He came back rather flustered and irritable, and when I broached the question of Fisher's leave he said he ought to be shot for leaving his post! This was awkward for me, as I had given Fisher a personal guarantee that I would make matters right, and it required some tact to induce Asquith to let me send a wire to Fisher approving his leave. McKenna and Crease were acting with me in getting Fisher away, which I am sure was the right course. . . . This weekend, in the middle of this desperate war, there is neither a First Lord nor a First Sea Lord at the Admiralty.'[83]

Asquith's letter, which reached Fisher later, was brief to the point of rudeness:

> '*Dear Lord Fisher,*
> 'I am commanded by the King to accept your tendered resignation of the office of First Sea Lord of the Admiralty.
> Yours faithfully,
> H.H.Asquith.[84]

Fisher was understandably deeply offended by 'a curt letter of five lines . . . not the faintest expression of regret'.

The Coalition Government took office on 25 May, with Asquith still hanging on precariously as Prime Minister. But Bonar Law insisted as a condition that Churchill should leave the Admiralty. Balfour became First Lord, while Churchill was relegated to the sinecure and uninfluential situation of Chancellor of the Duchy of Lancaster, though still with a seat in the Cabinet, a concession Asquith made 'with the greatest reluctance'. There was another concession he was obliged to make, for when he had seen the King to submit his new Government, George V urged him to form a Ministry of Munitions under Lloyd George and thus relieve Kitchener of all responsibility for the supply of ammunition. It was this feature that led him, when he saw Hankey, to be 'rather flustered and irritable'.

Balfour took office on 27 May and on that busy day Beresford called on him and demanded a peerage so that he could 'answer for the Admiralty' in the Lords. Astonishingly, Balfour recommended Asquith to comply. Beresford had evidently been canvassing this elsewhere, for Bonar Law also pressed Asquith on the matter, and his peerage was announced in the New Year's honours. It was surely asking for trouble to have both Fisher and Beresford in the Lords, but Fisher seldom attended and avoided a fight.

A week after Fisher's journey to Scotland, Jellicoe wrote again:

> 'My dear Lord Fisher,
> 'It is difficult to write when one feels so deeply. I waited first until the

question was definitely decided and then did not know what to say, but feel that I must write now.

'We owe you a debt of gratitude for having saved the Navy from a continuance in office of Mr. Churchill, and I hope that never again will any politician be allowed to usurp the functions which he took upon himself to exercise. The same thing will not occur in Mr. Balfour's case.

'I have seen Mr. Balfour and had a long interview. He seems sound, but after the Dardanelles business I mistrust anyone who in any way supported the early policy of that monument. I am glad to see that in the leading article of *The Times* of 27th, your work at the Admiralty is recognised. History will show that your six months in office there revolutionised the situation and laid the foundations of the new Navy with which the war will be fought out; only your energy and foresight could have done it. The whole Navy knows it – even your enemies admit it loudest – and I trust that you will find consolation in the fact. For myself you are the one man in the Empire.

Yours always devotedly,

J.R.Jellicoe.'[85]

Beatty wrote even more strongly, 'The Navy breathes freer now that it is rid of the succubus Churchill,' and even Wemyss, at the Dardanelles, said his name 'would be handed down to posterity as that of a man who undertook an operation of whose requirements he was entirely ignorant'.[86]

In his memoirs, Asquith wrote of the resignation:

'Lord Fisher was undoubtedly a man with streaks of genius, but he was afflicted with fits of megalomania, in one of which this extraordinary ultimatum must have been composed. I always remained on the best personal terms with him, but the whole of his conduct at this critical time convinced me that it had become impossible that he should remain responsible for the Admiralty.'[87]

'Streaks of genius' is an understatement; Fisher's whole life had prepared him for the European War, which he foresaw long before others and with greater clarity. The megalomania to which Asquith refers equally denigrates him; his greatness was beyond dispute and as First Sea Lord he would have achieved greater success and contributed much more to winning the war, had it not been for the discordant and overpowering influence of a politician who believed he had learned more in three years than Fisher had in sixty, and who snatched from him the reins of power.

Before Asquith published his book he asked Churchill for his views on Fisher's demanding letter and published Churchill's comments:

'The document is new to me and certainly it has not been made public. I knew, of course, that Fisher had demanded powers similar to

Kitchener's, but I am surprised – and now I think I may say amused – at the categorical manner in which his requirements were explained. The Submarine campaign to which he refers was, of course, the first submarine campaign. It was already thoroughly defeated, and did not appear again as a danger for more than eighteen months, and then in entirely different circumstances.

'The document seems to show that Fisher *used the uncertain course of events at the Dardanelles as a means of making a bid for supreme naval power.*'[88] (Bacon's Italics).

The italicized words indicate that Churchill had forgotten his desperate efforts to retain Fisher at the Admiralty. The submarines had not been defeated and his reference to a 'first campaign' is misleading. It was continuous throughout the war, though it waxed and waned because of measures to defeat it, counter-measures and attempts to placate neutrals. If Churchill thought it defeated he was much mistaken. Fisher had forecast its final phase long before. Nor was there anything 'uncertain' about the course of events at the Dardanelles. Churchill's conduct of the operation doomed it to failure from the beginning and, by the time he wrote, this was obvious. Many an over-ambitious politician has attempted to make his life's reputation by a rash military adventure. His desire for a political master-stroke inspired the politicians to embark on a naval operation against which all the informed military and naval opinion was unanimous. He should have heeded the dictum of the elder Moltke: 'Only humility leads to victory; arrogance and self-conceit to defeat'. Churchill himself ultimately tacitly admitted this:

'We had undertaken this operation, not because we thought it was the ideal method of attack, but because we were told that no military force was available, and in response to the appeals for help from Lord Kitchener and the Grand Duke. . . . I have asked myself in later years what would have happened if I had taken Lord Fisher's advice. . . . The Dardanelles Commissioners, studying the story from an entirely different angle, obviously felt that if there had been no naval plan in the field, there would later have been a really well conceived and well-concerted amphibious attack. . . . In cold blood it could never have been done. General Headquarters and the French General Staff would have succeeded in shattering any plans for a large diversion of force to the Southern Theatre.'[89]

Churchill's mistake was his determination that the Dardanelles operation should be undertaken and succeed against all the odds. Fisher's original concept was sound. When Kitchener refused to assist, Churchill did not recognize the problems; he just ignored them, blinded himself, persuaded himself that they did not exist and ignored the advice of the brilliant officers around him, Fisher, Richmond, de Robeck, Hankey, Jellicoe and Beatty. He cajoled, persuaded, distorted arguments and selected those parts of reports that suited his purpose; he listened to those who gave him the advice he wanted to hear.

Fisher *did* make a bid for supreme naval power. It was Churchill's appropriation of all power and his treatment of Fisher as a mere underling that created in him, with his massive naval knowledge, a desire to prevent any repetition, to restore the pendulum to the centre; and, perhaps expecting his demands to be whittled away, he swung it too far. His bid for power was to prevent another First Lord repeating Churchill's mistakes. He made his philosophy clear:

> 'There would be an end of Parliamentary Government and of the People's will . . . if experts were able to override a Government Policy. Sea Lords are the servants of the Government. Having given their advice, then it's their duty to carry out the commands of the political party in power until the moment comes when they feel they can no loner support a policy which they are convinced is disastrous.'[90]

Fisher died in 1920, before Churchill's and Asquith's memoirs appeared, so only one side of the picture was presented. Bacon's very fair biography of Fisher attempted to balance the equation. Published in 1929, it evidently alarmed Churchill and provoked his essay *Lord Fisher and his Biographer* in which he makes numerous rather small-minded attacks on both men. When Churchill's *World Crisis* appeared Crease wrote to him and pointed out certain errors of fact. Churchill had claimed Fisher's resignation was attributable to his paper dispatching cruisers to the Adriatic, and marked 'First Sea Lord to see after action', which as the action had been agreed, might be regarded as petty. Crease pointed out that this was not so and Fisher had not seen it until after he wrote his resignation:

> 'The real reason for Lord Fisher's resignation at that moment was the minute which you wrote to him somewhere about 11 pm on 14th May and which he read probably about 5 am on 15th May. . . . There are also differences in the direction of the minute and minor discrepancies in the body. I think it is necessary therefore, for the sake of Lord Fisher's reputation and for historical accuracy now to draw special attention to this minute and to the circumstances in which it was written. All the reasons you have suggested in your book for Lord Fisher's resignation on that early morning, except the telegram, were equally as valid on the night of 14th when you parted so amicably, as the morning of 15th, and, as I have said, the telegram had nothing to do with the matter. Without the powerful reason of this particular minute Lord Fisher's action in resigning would appear to be due to vacillation and indecision, if nothing worse, and a most undeserved slur is cast on his memory. . . .

> 'It was obvious to me that this minute went far beyond the agreement

regarding reinforcements of ships and materials for the Dardanelles, which Lord Fisher told me himself he reached with you earlier in the evening.'[91]

In over a century no First Sea Lord had resigned over a difference of opinion with the political head of the Admiralty. Under Churchill, of his four First Sea Lords, two had resigned; Sir Francis Bridgeman was dismissed in a manner Bonar Law described in the House of Commons as 'brutal', and Prince Louis of Battenberg had resigned, partly because of his nationality problem, which was published as the sole reason, but also because Churchill wanted Fisher's great name to be associated with his own, to save his political life.

9

THE FALL OF ICARUS

Fisher's departure brought distress to the Navy. Jellicoe wrote to Sir Frederick Hamilton, the Second Sea Lord, on 19 May: 'Lord Fisher had many enemies, more enemies than friends in the Service, but even his enemies have been saying that his presence at the Admiralty was essential, as he was the only person who could tackle the First Lord.[1]

The news that Wilson, who had proved himself quite unable to handle the politicians, was not to succeed him was greeted with relief. He was no match for Churchill, his administrative ability was abysmal, he was incapable of delegation, and his ludicrous proposals about Heligoland alarmed Jellicoe. The combination of Churchill and Wilson was a bleak prospect indeed. 'Winston Churchill,' said Jellicoe 'is a public danger to the Empire.'[2] (Yet he wrote on 29 May a sympathetic letter to Churchill, praising his work at the Admiralty.)

With great reluctance Churchill accepted that he could not remain First Lord in the new Cabinet. He had originally insisted that he would take no office but the Admiralty or the War Office, but now said he would accept even the lowest. Clearly it was better to have this potential critic in the Cabinet than as a detractor outside and he was able to write to his brother Jack that, with a seat in the Cabinet and on the War Council, he could monitor the Dardanelles. He welcomed Balfour's appointment and exulted at Fisher's removal, asserting that his policy would continue.

Balfour's first problem was to find a First Sea Lord. There was little point in considering Fisher, who blamed Balfour for supporting the Dardanelles. campaign. In this he was fully justified, for Balfour's wishful thinking reflected Churchill's:

'MR. BALFOUR suggested that, if the purely naval operation were carried out, the following results would be attained: the command of the

198

Sea of Marmora would be secured; the Turkish troops remaining in Europe would be cut off; the arsenal and dockyard at Constantinople could be destroyed; the conditions of the Turks would become worse every day they held out; the Bosphorus could be opened; a line of supply for warlike stores opened up with Russia; and wheat obtained from the Black Sea.'[3]

'Arthur Balfour always imagined that had fate decreed that he should be a soldier he would have been a great tactician. All that was necessary was to apply the principles of logic and you pulverised the enemy.'[4] Thus did the classical mind work, ignoring the possibility that the enemy might also apply the principles of logic!

Queen Alexandra wrote to the King on 23 May expressing her distress at the turn of events, asserting, 'It is all that stupid young *foolhardy* Winston C's fault,' and supporting Fisher: '*he* is the man in the Navy'.

Misunderstanding Wilson's refusal to serve under any other and hoping to influence events, Churchill tried to persuade him to serve under Balfour, but Selborne strongly advised the latter to look elsewhere. Jellicoe was a favourite, but no obvious successor could be found for him in the Grand Fleet, except Callaghan, who was past his best. Beatty was insufficiently experienced. This left only Jackson, who at least would give continuity.

The Churchill-Fisher combination had failed because two fiery enthusiasts had been paired, and there cannot be two men at the helm. Now there was the opposite. Balfour had personal charm, a reputation for a penetrating intellect, 'easily the most acclaimed statesman on the Unionist side of the House.'[5] He had been founder chairman of the CID and developed a great interest in defence matters. Yet, despite Fisher's view, he avoided Churchill's mistakes and accepted that he must be guided by the professionals, which suited him, since he was not an energetic man, however intellectual. 'He lacked the physical energy . . . for the administration of the Admiralty.'[6]

Jackson too was an intelligent man of sound common sense, with a scientific bent, a Fellow of the Royal Society, but uninspired and uninspiring, pessimistic, possessing little personality, morose and uncommunicative. He lacked Fisher's forceful enthusiasm and his ability to listen to and use the brains of others. He had already proved himself a sound staff officer, having been head of the War College and Chief of the Staff but had little sea service as an admiral and tended to deal in minutiae. He insisted that every paper, no matter how unimportant, was referred to him. As a wartime First Sea Lord, he dealt personally with the case of a Lieutenant-Commander who had run up a large wine bill and a simple case of a wireless set transferred from one trawler to another.

Like Geddes later, and unlike Churchill, Balfour said, 'A First Lord who insisted on running the Admiralty without regard to naval opinion would be a serious danger'. But his lethargy and Jackson's irresolution were the complete opposite of the fire and vigour of their predecessors. The whirlwind of the Churchill-Fisher era was replaced by a passive calm. 'When Mr. Churchill and Lord Fisher left the Admiralty,' wrote Keyes, 'papers had resumed their habit of drifting leisurely down their peacetime channels.'[7] A combination of Balfour and Fisher could have produced outstanding results; one of Churchill and Jackson might have produced disaster.

After the hectic six months at the Admiralty, at the age of 74, Fisher needed rest. At first he was content to be out of the centre of things, enjoying the peace of the countryside. He wrote to Jellicoe on 3 June, 'McKenna and others seem perfectly sure I shall return to the Admiralty. . . . *But I have no illusions!* for I do not think the politicians on either side will EVER permit me to get back into office.'[8]

Soon his restless spirit rebelled and on 5 June he misguidedly wrote to Balfour that, as Jackson, whose health was doubtful, wanted to serve at sea, he was willing to serve under the new First Lord. Balfour was politely negative. Two days later Fisher wrote to the King apologizing for failure to pay the customary call on leaving the Admiralty, to which he received a courteous reply:

> 'I was unaware of the circumstances to which you allude and certainly would have been glad to see you before you left London. Nobody regrets more than I do that a situation should have arisen at the Admiralty which resulted in changes which have now taken place. I wish to express my appreciation of the great services which you have rendered to the Navy while you have been at the Admiralty. I am so pleased to hear that it is your desire that there should be no controversy with regard to those services having now come to an end.
>
> Believe me, Very sincerely yours,   George R.I.'[9]

It was a pity Fisher did not leave the matter, but replied with an unnecessarily long letter enclosing a list of the 593 vessels ordered since his arrival at the Admiralty the previous October.[10]

But Churchill's influential friends and political allies subjected Fisher to a vicious campaign of vilification. Ian Hamilton wrote to Churchill from Gallipoli,

> 'My dear friend, what a tragedy has been enacted, the old, old tragedy of the husbandman who brought a snake in from the outer cold and warmed it in his bosom! Of all the sorrows and anxieties which have rained down upon me since the start of this show, your departure from the Admiralty has been the most cruel. By a side wind I heard of a secret conference between your snake and a military officer in high place (*not* Lord K), a few days before his resignation, and in my humble opinion, a blacker-

hearted or more unscrupulous rogue has rarely wormed his way across the pages of our history.'[11]

Lady Wemyss, in her biography of her husband, devoted successive pages to uninformed and bitter attacks upon Fisher. He husband's ill will was so intense that little else could be expected. He had written of his departure for Mudros:

'It was whilst in the Naval Secretary's room, after having said good-bye to the First Lord, that I met Lord Fisher for the last time. Now, I had not spoken to Lord Fisher since the year 1908, when he had proposed to me that I should become Naval Secretary, plainly indicating . . . that I should have to pay for it by being his creature. I had written a letter to him indignantly refusing to accept the appointment under such conditions, though at that time it was the one which I wished for most and since then all communication between us had been severed. "Why, it's Wemyss," exclaimed Lord Fisher, as if it were the most extraordinary thing that I should be there, and as if he had suddenly come across his dearest friend. "Yes, Sir, it's Wemyss," I replied, ignoring his outstretched hand. "How are you, my dear Wemyss? It's ages since I saw you," he went on, still keeping his hand outstretched towards me. "Very well, thank you, Sir," I replied, still ignoring his hand. But this would not satisfy him. Once more he repeated, "How are you my dear Wemyss?", thrusting his hand still further towards me and almost seizing mine, which till now had remained limp by my side. It was impossible for me, under the circumstances, to attempt to maintain my attitude of reserve. After all he was First Sea Lord and I a junior rear-admiral, and there was a mighty war raging, so I took his hand and could not help laughing as I said, "Well, the war brings funny people together".[12]

He appears to have had no intention of calling on the First Sea Lord. It was surely understandable that Fisher would expect loyalty from the Naval Secretary and Wemyss's gross ill manners, largely attributable to his social vanity, were boorish. But he was by no means the worst.

Lady Cynthia Asquith, eldest daughter of the 11th Earl of Wemyss, wrote in her diary on 27 May:

'I lunched at the Admiralty with the "setting sun" minister. . . . Clemmie said she had always known it would happen from the day Fisher was appointed, and Winston said that, if he could do things over again, he would do just the same with regard to appointing Fisher as he says he has done really great organising work. I think his nature, though he may be unscrupulous and inclined to trample on susceptibilities of sailors, or whomever he may have to deal with, from eagerness – is absolutely devoid of vindictiveness, unlike the half-caste Fisher who really runs amok with malevolent spleen and is now saying he will tell the Germans where all our ships are.'[13]

Many officers of the Beresford school spread venom against Fisher, often because they were badly misinformed about the circumstances of his resignation. Admiral Sir Cecil Colville, whom Fisher had criticized for lethargy in pursuing the defences of Scapa Flow, wrote to the King, a personal friend, that the Navy was relieved to be rid of Churchill and pleased at Balfour's appointment, but that Fisher leaving the Admiralty in wartime without waiting for his successor was 'criminal'.

But the newspapers, with better judgment than social chit-chat, continued to agitate for Fisher's return, yet in some cases blamed him for the breach. *John Bull* published a leading article entitled *Lord Fisher – Striker!*: 'Is it too late to appeal to Lord Fisher to repent his hasty action? . . . There is only one pardon and the path of reparation leads straight back to Whitehall. There Lord Fisher would still be warmly welcomed, and by the nation at large his reinstatement would be hailed with joy. Again we insist that his King and Country need him. What is his reply?'[14]

After encouraging letters from Robert Donald of the *Daily Chronicle* and J.L.Garvin of the *Observer,* his reply was to write again to Balfour offering to serve in much the same capacity as had Wilson, to accept the Dardanelles operation as a political decision and to continue to assist it. 'So the sooner you telegraph me to come up the better I shall be pleased and the sooner will be terminated the endless accusations the daily post brings me that I am a deserter!'[15]

Any suggestion of his return was unrealistic, however, as long as Churchill was in the Cabinet and War Council, now renamed the Dardanelles Committee, but still performing all the functions of the War Council. Apart from Kitchener, who was a member by virtue of his ministerial status, not a single service officer was a member, strategic and professional operational decisions being made entirely by politicians. Though without ministerial responsibility, Churchill used his membership to express his voluble views on how the war should be fought. The minutes show that he spoke more often and more loquaciously than any other. Balfour was not even accompanied by Jackson, so, if Fisher had replaced him his position would have been worse than before. Churchill was firmly in the Cabinet, 'always circumventing me'.

This was not all. On 29 May, with no authority whatsoever, Churchill wrote a long letter to Masterton Smith demanding copies of the Dardanelles telegrams daily, with the daily intelligence reports. and the *Pink List*, a highly secret daily list of the location and condition of all HM Ships, even in peacetime treated with strict security, always kept under lock and key.[16]

The Dardanelles Committee met on 7 June and decided that Ian Hamilton must be reinforced with three divisions of the new armies. Churchill at once wrote to Kitchener suggesting more. By the end of May, after three months' hard fighting, the Allied troops at Helles were still three miles from the hills Hamilton had said he would reach on the first day; the Anzacs had reached only 1,000 yards from the beach which was so crowded that there was no room for more men to land. They were by now desperately short of ammunition, while the Turks seemed plentifully supplied. A comparable problem existed for the Navy. There were already more big ships than could be used, could enter the Straits or bombard the coast.

At a meeting on 17 June Balfour said escorts could not be provided for re-inforcements before the end of August, which Churchill challenged and suggested two territorial divisions should be held at Malta or Alexandria as a reserve – a far cry from his belief that the fleet could penetrate the Dardanelles without troops. Another letter from Hamilton reversed his former belief that shellfire from the Asiatic shore was merely a nuisance. An attack there would, he said, 'relieve our backs and right flank from this cursed Asiatic firing, which is going on at the moment as I write to you – one heavy gun per 30 seconds. Men killed in hospital and officers killed in their dug-outs.'[17]

Ellis Ashmead-Bartlett, who had served in the Army in the Boer War and subsequently became a war correspondent with the Japanese in the Far East, with the Italians in Libya, the Turks and the Serbians in the Balkan wars, and was now with the Allies in Gallipoli, wrote an article for publication at home; Hamilton censored it and refused his vigorous protests, so he came home to avoid censorship. But before publishing, displaying a rare sense of responsi-bility, he called on Asquith and gave him 'a full account of the situation in the Gallipoli Peninsula, which was not altogether agreeable'. Asquith asked him to put his views in writing and on 11 June he submitted a lengthy and reasoned memorandum, expressing his deep concern:

'For the time being the Fleet can play no active part in the reduction of the Straits. In fact, our ships can never attempt to go beyond Tott's Battery. The enemy's minefield is intact, the damage to the forts at the Narrows has been made good, and the existence of concealed torpedo tubes on shore is perhaps the most serious obstacle of all. . . .

'It is a fundamental error to assume any longer that, if we are able to occupy the southern extremity of the peninsula so as to embrace Kilid Bahr and the European shore of the Narrows, we have opened the gate to Constantinople for the Fleet. The enemy has been engaged for two months in fortifying the longer reach of waters stretching from the Narrows to the entrance of the Sea of Marmora by placing heavy guns in field works on both shores, in preparing new mine-fields and torpedo tubes; . . . Therefore, even with the Kilid Bahr plateau in our possession, we shall have to tackle the longer reach of waters beyond. . . .

'The Australians at Anzac hold the most extraordinary position in which an army has ever found itself, clinging as they are to the face of a cliff. . . . The position at Anzac is a complete stalemate. . . .

'We should eliminate any idea of active assistance from the fleet, except submarines, and regard the situation merely from the military standpoint. The whole of the Gallipoli Peninsula has, in fact, been transformed into an immense fortress. We are supposed to be besieging it, but instead of cutting the enemy's communications and consequently stopping his supplies, we are endeavouring to force a way forward through the entire length of his successive lines of works. This must be wrong, judged from almost any military standpoint. Therefore, there is only one alternative plan, namely to concentrate all our efforts to get astride the peninsula either at, or rather north of, Bulair.'[18]

In response to Ashmead-Bartlett Churchill wrote a memorandum to Asquith, Balfour, Bonar Law and Curzon, notably excluding Kitchener, refuting the suggestion that the Bulair Lines should have been taken at the outset of the campaign, stating that their seizure would not have been decisive, because the Turks could hold the forts at the Narrows with a small force supplied from the Asiatic shore and could attack both sides of the Bulair Isthmus. The Narrows would still have been closed to the fleet and the army was not strong enough to operate except on restricted ground.[19] This again contradicted his earlier view that the Fleet could penetrate the Dardanelles without an Army.

Ashmead-Bartlett's memorandum alarmed Asquith, who began to see the naval and military facts of life. He convened a meeting of the Dardanelles Committee, which, after the usual rambling discussion, decided that Kitchener would telegraph Hamilton for his view of the memorandum. Hamilton immediately recognized some of the phrases and dismissed it with haughty contempt.

Even Jack Churchill was less optimistic. The Royal Naval Divisions were demoralized, with no further drafts to call on. Backhouse's brigade was reduced to 800 men. The 29th was much reduced. The Bulair lines might be difficult to hold.[20]

Churchill still maintained his purblind optimism and wrote to his brother (19 June) that intelligence reports indicated low morale and anxiety in Constantinople. Yet less than four weeks earlier Maurice Brett had written to his father, Lord Esher, that one of the secretaries at the American Embassy there had told him the city was absolutely quiet and peaceful and there seemed no chance of internal trouble, unless there was disaster on the Peninsula. The Turks had withdrawn from the reach of ships' guns and dug in, with much reduced losses and had regained confidence. The campaign was now similar to the Western Front, but more difficult owing to the terrain, and, unless help came from the Russians, would go on for months. The Army had been much improved by the Germans. 'The scenes during the landing were dreadful. The wounded were taken back on board the ships, but when these became full, had to be taken back again to the beach where they were slowly killed by the Turkish machine guns. The water was red for hours after the fight.'[21]

On 21 June Carson wrote to Churchill, with analytical logic, that expectations had all been disproved by events and he did not want the obvious advantages of success to influence judgment, miscalculating the difficulties.[22]

Throughout the rest of June and July the Dardanelles Committee procrastinated. On 3 July Jack Churchill suggested to his brother, half in jest, that he should visit Gallipoli to report on the situation, a proposal Churchill jumped at.

The next day Balfour invited Fisher to become chairman of the Board of Invention and Research. Churchill protested vehemently to Balfour, who told him Asquith had approved, to whom Churchill also protested. Asquith informed him he was now reconciled to Fisher, so Churchill wrote him an angry letter, absurdly heaping blame on Fisher and adopting the attitude of one betrayed, and untruthfully claiming Fisher had given no reason for his resignation and that the only current matters of policy were of little consequence.[23] He wisely refrained from sending this petulant and vindictive letter, but instead wrote to Balfour repeating the arguments and adding two short paragraphs betraying his real purpose: He was afraid Fisher might ultimately be appointed First Lord, the post he most desired himself. He drew attention to the newspaper campaign for Fisher's return and repeated his slander of Fisher's insanity.[24]

The Board of Invention and Research was to coordinate the flood of ideas coming in from the Service and the general public, many as countermeasures against submarines. It included Sir J.J.Thomson, President of the Royal Society, Sir Charles Parsons, Sir George Beilby, a great chemist, and a number of others prominent in the world of science and engineering, co-opted as advisers. Though Fisher was flattered and enthusiastic about the new appointment, which he thought 'promises to be a very big affair', he was diffident as he felt his scientific knowledge inadequate.

The U-Boat campaign which Churchill had said was 'thoroughly defeated' was now the main menace to commerce. At first the Germans had attempted to comply with the Hague Convention, but this soon proved impracticable and, as the hatreds of war grew, they became less circumspect. Until the end of January, 1915, only 7% of British merchant ship losses were attributable to submarines, but on 1 February Bethmann-Hollweg proposed, and the Kaiser approved, that the waters surrounding the British Isles should be declared a 'war zone' in which all merchant ships would be sunk, without necessarily giving warning. Though Germany only possessed 22 U-boats, by the end of April 39 merchant ships had been sunk, almost 80% of the tonnage sunk by

Emden and *Karlsruhe,* which had caused so much panic, and on 7 May, while Churchill was still very much in charge, *Lusitania* was sunk with the loss of 1,198 lives, including 128 Americans. Fisher's prewar paper on U-boat warfare was proving horribly accurate, despite Churchill's disbelief.

Rudimentary methods were employed to combat submarines: detector nets which set off a carbide flare when U-boats ran into them, barrier nets across the Straits of Dover, elementary boom defence systems. But this was the world's first experience of submarine warfare and the Admiralty was groping for a solution to a new problem only one man had foreseen accurately. The main deterrence came from neutral protest, especially from Americans, whose antagonism Germany was anxious to avoid.

Before the war a committee had existed to deal with the problem, but so little importance did Churchill's Board attach to submarines that it was disbanded on the outbreak of war. From Fisher's Submarine Attack Committee came the hydrophone, an underwater microphone that could detect the beat of a ship's propeller. It was tried out with a shore operator controlling charges which could be set off when the location of the U-boat had been determined, though only one was sunk. More successful was that mounted in ships, but this was not in service until early 1917. Depth charges were developed early in the war, but were ineffective unless exploded very close to the U-boat, the first success being achieved in March, 1916. The 'A'-sweep, such as used in the Dardanelles against mines, was adapted for use against submarines, an 80-pound charge attached to the wire. From this was developed a single wire bearing a number of charges along its length, towed by an anti-submarine vessel and fired electrically. But it proved unwieldy and ineffective. The committee was unable to contribute much to the progress of the war. Asking to be furnished with details of successful attacks against submarines they were unaccountably refused. Yet, by May, 1916, a 'submarine detector', forerunner of the Asdic, now known as 'Sonar', had been developed. They asked for a submarine on which to carry out full-scale trials and were again refused. After pressure from Fisher, they were condescendingly told one would be made available 'when not required for other duties', in the event meaning never. A year passed while the idea was kicked around the Admiralty; then a competing idea was tried on a laboratory scale and the whole matter was dropped because no one could decide between the two. The 'loop detector system' was developed which appeared to Fisher to be very simple. It was turned down, but two years later, when the German submarine campaign was reaching alarming proportions, it was vigorously adopted with, Fisher claimed, 'astoundingly successful results'.

Fisher's own contribution was a scheme for a 'submarine dreadnought' armed with a 12-inch gun. He offered to return to the Admiralty as Third Sea Lord for six months to get the design completed and building started. Balfour was wary, and said with justice, 'If once you put your foot inside the Admiralty, where should we all be?'[25] Modern submarines are, of course, larger than the battleships of those days, so Fisher was far ahead of his time, though it is doubtful if their contribution would have justified the resources employed. It is hardly surprising that Fisher soon lost his enthusiasm when everything he suggested seemed to be kicked into touch, and, in October, 1915, he asked Asquith for more useful employment, as he was 'doing nothing at all'.

The Dardanelles Committee continued to expand into an unwieldy monster, whose discussions meandered over every subject, nothing ever being concluded, every member having his say and then wandering on to another topic, Asquith seldom interrupting. The meetings contained some gems of the English tongue, such as, for example, that of Lord Crewe, who, on 24 July, 'asked if it was not difficult to legislate for the future until we knew what happened'. At last, in July, Jackson joined the Committee, but appears merely to have been brought along by Balfour, as Churchill had Fisher, as a consultant, to advise his master, who then delivered the Admiralty view. He did not attend meetings on 19 or 20 August, 3 or 23 September. He attended on 27 August, 6, 7, 11, 14, 21 and 25 October, but in all these meetings uttered two sentences, one of 13 and the other of 31 words.

Jack Churchill's suggestion that his brother should visit Gallipoli had taken root in Churchill's mind; he thirsted for some activity and floated the idea to Asquith, who approved, subject to Balfour's and Kitchener's agreement, which was given, though the latter was concerned to safeguard against another Antwerp and ensure reports were unbiased. Churchill drafted a telegram to Hamilton which stated that he was representing the Cabinet and was to watch operations. He would bring one officer and a secretary with him.[26] The officer was to be Freddie Guest, his cousin, and the secretary Eddie Marsh. But Kitchener modified the telegram that he was going out to confer with Hamilton and would report to the Cabinet. Kitchener was guarded and reminded Hamilton of his responsibility to himself, stating Churchill had no authority to interfere. To this Hamilton replied that he 'had hoped we were too far off for visitors, but you know that in all the circumstances you can rely on my loyalty to you'. But this did not satisfy Kitchener and he asked Asquith to send Hankey 'to bring back an independent report'. 'Very awkward position for me,' wrote Hankey in his diary, 'as, in a sense, I am intended as a check on Churchill.'

But Curzon overheard Asquith's Liberal colleagues wishing Churchill goodbye and demanded to know where he was going. On being told, he immediately informed his Conservative friends in the Cabinet. Bonar Law objected emphatically and the visit was cancelled; Hankey went alone. Esher wrote in his diary: 'Lord K told me this morning; he laughed over it a good deal, and admitted he would not have been sorry to get rid of Winston for a while.'[27] Kitchener had every reason for his misgivings, for already Churchill had told his insurance agent he might 'have to visit the Balkan States,' and he wrote to Asquith:

'The two reasons wh. have led me to undertake this journey are first: in case the coming attack does not succeed, or succeeds only partially, I wish to be able to advise the Cabinet with the fullest knowledge upon the new and grave situation wh. will then arise. I can acquire this knowledge only upon the spot, & no one else will have the same advantages for acquiring it. Secondly, if a decisive victory is won, I shall be at hand shd. the Government decide to send a special mission to Sofia or Athens, in order to reap to the fullest extent the fruits of the victory.'[28]

Having heard that it was hoped to have a number of submarines in the Marmora to intercept Turkish supplies, on 22 July Churchill complained to Balfour, 'with a persistence which annoyed rather than convinced,' that aircraft were being inadequately used and seriously suggested that submarines could carry fuel supplies for them and perform minor repairs. To those of us who have launched and recovered Walrus aircraft in choppy seas the thought brings pallor to our cheeks! Submarine and aircraft would both roll and heave while a technician trained in aircraft repairs, an extra body in a crowded submarine, struggled to carry out minor repairs under shellfire.

On 30 July Churchill drafted a telegram to Hankey at Gallipoli that the general should not hesitate to ask for more ammunition, which was available at home. Kitchener intimated that three train-loads were on the way, but Churchill wrote to Masterton Smith asking him the date and route by which they were sent, 'Creedy [Kitchener's private Secretary] could tell you on the telephone or General Callwell or even Glyn [Liaison Intelligence Officer between the War Office and GHQ France]'.[29] On 3 August he wrote again to Masterton Smith for Balfour's benefit, advising him on the use of Fisher's monitors at the Dardanelles. He had concluded that four were inadequate and more should be sent. In the event, these ships, designed for the Baltic, were quite unsuitable for the confined waters of the Dardanelles and were not used after their 3,500-mile journey.

A new attack on Suvla Bay took place on 6 August. The strategy was to take Hill 60 and Sari Bair ridge, from which the Army would descend on the Dardanelles, enabling the fleet to penetrate the Narrows, unhindered by gunfire from the European shore. The Turks' German leaders saw the idea at once and poured men and ammunition onto the ridge. For five days the raw British troops were slaughtered attempting to take the steep peak. The attack failed. On 19 August, at a meeting of the Dardanelles Committee, it became plain that some members were beginning to discredit Churchill's everlasting optimism; Bonar Law said that Hamilton was 'always *nearly* winning' and when Churchill tried to point out his friend Hamilton's difficulties, Grey said curtly, 'We should deal with facts and accept them'. Asquith said that Hamilton had lost 23,000 men and yet was still confident. The reason was 'not easy to see'. Churchill pressed for even more reinforcements and said Hamilton was contemplating a further attack, 'to save the situation', to which Law responded acidly that a further attack would be a useless sacrifice of life. During this discussion Kitchener was absent in France and another meeting was held the next day when he was present. With customary feebleness it was decided: 'That it was not possible to send out the large divisional units asked for, since a joint operation was contemplated in France, but that it was hoped that, with the reinforcements in Egypt and the drafts from lesser reinforcements which were on their way from England, Sir Ian Hamilton would be able to carry out the operations he had in hand.'[30]

A further attack took place on 21 August against the dominating Scimitar Hill and Hill 60. On the first day, of the 14,300 men, 5,300 were killed or wounded. Fighting continued for seven days when it was evident that the exhausted troops were making little progress, the Turks remaining in control of Sari Bair Ridge, and therefore the Peninsula. Hamilton coolly asked for another 95,000 men to renew the attack, though he must have known Kitchener would never agree.

Keyes' thirst for a new Navy-only attack was by no means dispelled, despite the expressed decision of de Robeck supported by his three rear-admirals. With total disregard for security, Keyes had made a practice of writing long letters to his wife, which she was enjoined to keep as a diary and show to influential people. On 17 August:

> 'Since 6th we have had 26,000 wounded – and I suppose 6000 or 7000 killed. . . . I had a long talk with Admiral Wemyss this evening. I believe I persuaded him. I said more than I have ever said before to de R. on Saturday – and he paid more attention but he doesn't agree yet. . . . My submarines go up [the Dardanelles] with an even money chance of never coming back. They have the only thing that matters: a *spirit* which will risk anything for so great a prize . . . I am sure the majority of us would get through – once through – with the Army in position to gather the fruits of victory – the end would be very soon – and a most glorious page would be added to our naval history'.[31]

Keyes invited his wife to show this letter to Hedworth Meux, no doubt hoping his views would reach the King. But his ambition was controlling his utterances rather than his brain. The nearly total defeat of the Army, its state of exhaustion, the lack of replacement troops, the failure to sweep the minefields, the untried new sweeping force, the reinforcement of the Turks from Germany, their now ample supplies of ammunition and above all the shortage of ammunition on the Allied side for both Services, made a new attempt to penetrate the Dardanelles, without the guns being taken from behind, no more hopeful than before. There was not a single soldier with the Dardanelles in his sight.

Keyes now wrote a memorandum to de Robeck reviewing the military operation, which he admitted had failed, and suggested a new naval attack. De

Robeck disagreed. Keyes's 'plan' was little more than a repetition of the attempt of 18 March and he made numerous assumptions supported by little evidence. De Robeck, an admiral with a reputation for dash and courage, understood the principles of war much better than his subordinate. He did not underestimate the enemy, he refused to believe the unsupported rumours of enemy shortage of ammunition, low morale and revolutionary prospects; he was sceptical of the 'new' minesweeping force and asked the simple question 'What were 3 or 4 ships to do in the Marmora?' But neither pinpointed another problem. The Germans too had brought aircraft to the area; balloons would have been destroyed with ease and aircraft engaged in dog fights instead of concentrating on the careful task of spotting.

On 20 August, with the obvious intention of pre-empting criticism and freeing de Robeck's hand, Balfour sent a message to the Admiral: 'If you still think your old battleships could make any really decisive or important contribution to success of land operations you will be supported in any use to which you may think it desirable to put them.'[32]

Brigadier-General Cecil Aspinall-Oglander, the official military historian of the Gallipoli campaign and biographer of Keyes, claimed this message 'was the completest sanction for the immediate introduction of the Keyes plan'.[33] It was nothing of the sort; it gave the Admiral freedom to make his own decision and he had already made it against Keyes's bombast.

Surely no coincidence, four days after Keyes had prepared his memorandum, on 21 August, Churchill again proposed a renewal of the naval attack on the tortuous reasoning that, because the losses in the attack of 18 March had been slight in comparison with those of the Army, a new attempt held out a prospect of success. He added that a squadron of ships in the Marmora would starve out the Turkish Army, the squadron need not now be so strong, because *Goeben* and *Breslau* were in a dilapidated state and the monitors were 'protected against torpedoes by their structure' and of shallow enough draught to pass over the minefields, both of which statements were erroneous. He wrote a memorandum to Asquith and Balfour. 'Naval opinion on the spot,' he said, 'was confident of success in the operations to force the Dardanelles begun on March 18th,' another interesting example of Churchillian sophism, since de Robeck and his three rear-admirals were opposed to it, which left only Keyes and perhaps a few more junior officers without full knowledge of the facts and possibly persuaded by Keyes. There are echoes of Keyes's memorandum throughout Churchill's: 'We know from the secret information that the Turkish forts were short of heavy shell and that the enemy viewed the resumption of a purely naval attack with the utmost anxiety. This is certain.'[34]

At a meeting of the Dardanelles Committee on 27 August Balfour firmly rejected another naval attempt and the campaign came under attack, especially from Carson, who said, 'The slaughter which had gone on was no success,' and inquired if it were to be continued, and from Bonar Law, who asked 'if Sir Ian

Hamilton was supposed to be acting on the defensive, or if he was going to continue his course of sacrificing men without a chance of success?' Later he said, rather illogically, that his view was that the operations should be carried on, on the understanding that 'we cannot win the peninsula'. For the first time the question of withdrawal was broached when Carson 'asked for a definite statement of policy as to whether we were to hold on or to withdraw', but the meeting was again inconclusive. Hamilton was to hold the ground he had gained and would be asked his opinion as to future policy.

Three days later Hankey circulated a report on his visit, which, for a man normally displaying military wisdom, was over-optimistic, advocating further reinforcements and a 'great push' by the Navy. Kitchener pointed out that the French wished to mount another offensive in France, so reinforcements would not be available and the discussion ambled aimlessly, until Lloyd George firmly said that one or the other operation should be attempted, but not both together. He favoured the Dardanelles, 'where we already had some superiority'. His reasoning seems questionable.

Carson had brought a spark of decisiveness to the Cabinet and was 'appalled by the way in which important war business was conducted. He disliked the casual way in which his colleagues brushed aside carefully prepared arguments, and resented too strong or emotional an appeal on some major war question. Churchill too felt the indecisiveness of the Cabinet and Committee, though he contributed much to the confusion. Carson wrote to him on 9 September describing Cabinet meetings as 'useless'. Francis Stevenson recorded in her diary a conversation between Churchill, Lloyd George and Curzon. The last said that the Tories could no longer tolerate the state of things. They would demand the resignation of Kitchener as incompetent. Lloyd George and Churchill said they would join him and his friends, the former saying that he could no longer be a party to the shameful mismanagement and slackness. 'He says things are simply being allowed to slide, and it is time some one spoke out.' But he mistrusted Churchill 'when it comes to a matter of personal interest'.

Carson wrote again to Churchill: 'Are we going to allow everlasting drift on the policy of the Dardanelles? . . . no one is held more responsible for the Dardanelles policy than yrself! Now if the clear policy of certain victory at any cost is adopted by the Cabinet, I will adopt it, but it must be no narrow margins nor estimates framed "to do the best we can" & for Generals who are only looking to see how far they can please.'[35]

Many still blamed Churchill for all the naval problems of the first year of the war – the loss of the three cruisers and other ships, Antwerp and Coronel, and now the Dardanelles – and recognized that nothing had gone right until Fisher's arrival at the Admiralty. Churchill's political position was perilous and he asked Asquith to publish the documents relating to his administration of the Admiralty. He received no reply and returned to the attack. He had prepared papers about Cradock and the three cruisers and asked for their publication.

Asquith recognized that the papers were selective and edited. Failing to gain his support, Churchill circulated the documents round the Cabinet, Later he showed these confidential documents to C.P.Scott, editor of *The Manchester Guardian.*

On 6 October Churchill wrote to Balfour urging renewal of the naval attack and at a Cabinet that day Asquith agreed to set up a naval and military committee, under Jackson's chairmanship, to examine the relative merits of the Western Front and Gallipoli. Set up at the outset of the campaign, before any naval bombardment, with secrecy and a combined staff to work out details, this could have yielded an amphibious attack such as Fisher had proposed. Over the weekend they studied the matter and on the Monday morning reported that the Army should concentrate on the Western Front. But events overtook their deliberations, for that day the Germans and Austrians entered Belgrade. Already, on 7 October, at the insistence of Bonar Law, Kitchener had agreed that a scheme for evacuating the Peninsula should be prepared. Now Bulgaria mobilized against Serbia, Greece refused to join the Allies, Rumania, beleaguered on all sides, dared not abandon her neutrality.

In spite of the rapidly developing situation, Churchill, at a Dardanelles Committee meeting on 11 October, again pressed for 'Naval domination of the Sea of Marmora' and Kitchener said, 'Abandonment [of Gallipoli] would be the most disastrous event in the history of the Empire. We should lose about 25,000 men and many guns'. Egypt, he said, was imperilled, the dangers of abandonment were very grave, but he would like to 'liquidate the situation'. Again Churchill gave way to his customary wishful thinking, suggesting that the Turkish position could be taken and the whole Turkish Army on the plateau captured or destroyed. Ignoring failure to penetrate further than the Narrows, he claimed that the fleet, once in the Sea of Marmora, would prevent all German movement.

Carson asked what British forces in Gallipoli were supposed to do? Hold on and resist the Bulgarians, Turks and Germans? Asquith, with a contradiction that denied his vaunted logic, said he was 'of an open mind' but that two of Carson's proposals were 'out of the question', including evacuation. The Committee decided that a suitable general should be dispatched to the near east to report 'as to which particular sphere and with what particular objective, we should direct our attention'. The ball was kicked into touch again. A War Office memorandum had been circulated to the Committee advocating sending a further 150,000 men to Gallipoli, but Carson was told by a member of the General Staff that the proposal had not been in the memorandum when it left them and must have been inserted later. Carson resigned.

Frances Stevenson recorded in her diary that Lloyd George was 'sick with Churchill, who will not acknowledge the futility of the Dardanelles campaign. He prevents the Prime Minister from facing the facts too, by reminding him that he too is implicated in the campaign & tells him that if the thing is acknowledged to be a failure, he (the PM) as well as Churchill will be blamed.' So political expediency and retention of office were more important than the deaths, mutilation and misery of the men at Gallipoli.

De Robeck's rejection of his proposals did not dissuade Keyes from prodding for another naval offensive. On 23 September he had forwarded to de Robeck yet another version of the naval plan, this time prepared over Captain J.H.Godfrey's signature. Though it gave the impression of careful thought, it differed little from Keyes's plan, consisting of either a surprise rush at dawn or a repetition of the deliberate bombardment so unsuccessful in the past. With extraordinary fairness, de Robeck consulted three captains, D.L.Dent (later admiral), J.W.L.McClintock (later vice-admiral) and A.Heneage (later admiral), none of whom appear to have been convinced. But Keyes continued to press de Robeck, writing on 12 October to his wife: 'I went for a walk with the Admiral the other evening – I do most evenings at Kephalo – and tackled him again about my project. Finally I asked him to put it to the Admiralty, he flatly refused.'[36] Again on 17 October: 'I had been feeling very unhappy about the situation for some days. My memo to the Admiral of 23rd September had fallen flat. . . . I went for a walk with the Admiral determined to have it out. . . . I felt that I was nearer persuading him than at any previous time. So much so that just before we got down to the beach, "Then you will telegraph and ask for reinforcements and put the general scheme to the Admiralty and ask for their decision." But he shut up like a book and I felt I was beat.'[37]

When reinforcements were cancelled in favour of the Salonika expedition and a further attack on the Western Front, Keyes again raised the idea of renewing the naval plan. Bulgaria had declared war on Serbia on 14 October; 800 Allied troops a day were being evacuated from sickness alone; no army unit was better than half its strength and ammunition was now so depleted that guns were rationed to two rounds a day. 'I have only two rounds left in my battery,' one officer signalled, 'Am I to let them be fired, or keep them against an emergency?'[38]

The Government were now in a state of complete confusion. Their attempts to woo the Balkan countries had hopelessly failed and Germany's diplomacy had proved far superior. Jackson wrote bitterly to de Robeck on 9 October: 'On October 7th the "War Council of the Cabinet" came to the conclusion that they did not know what to do and perhaps it might be worthwhile asking their professional naval and military advisers as to what they ought to do. This is the first time, *I believe,* since the outbreak of war that they have taken any advice except through Heads of departments.'[39] Yet even so, in spite of the conditions, he favoured pressing on to Constantinople![40]

Kitchener telegraphed Hamilton asking for an estimate of casualties to be expected in the event of evacuation, an almost unanswerable question, and Hamilton hedged; he thought it might cost him half his force, but it could be more or less! This vague answer gave the Government an opportunity to find a scapegoat in Hamilton, who was ordered on 16 October to surrender his command. He left Gallipoli the next day. His over-optimism and failure to take firm charge of operations would have justified this action much earlier, but it was primarily the indecisive and unrealistic behaviour of the Government that had led to the disaster. General Charles Monro, a convinced 'Westerner' who had much experience in France and Flanders, and believed the only way to win the war was 'killing Germans', was appointed to relieve Hamilton, Birdwood taking command in the interim.

The day Hamilton left, Keyes wrote yet again to the Admiral, and asked: 'Would you allow me to go home for a week to lay the plan of attack before the Admiralty. . . . Letters and telegrams are an unsatisfactory means of communication, and I feel sure I could persuade the Admiralty to send reinforcements which would enable you to deliver an attack on a scale which could not suffer defeat.'[41] De Robeck read Keyes's memorandum that evening. He was in a difficult position; well aware of Keyes's under-cover communication with Churchill, Meux and others, and tired of his persistent opposition; he knew that if he refused his request he would be accused of failing to listen to a constructive proposal, the inspired ideas of a junior. The next morning Keyes went to see him before breakfast. He spoke curtly, 'Well, Commodore you will go home with the King's Messenger.' He added that Keyes was only doing his duty, as he was doing his in giving his opinion against it. 'He said he would give me a fair field to state my case. All he would say was that he did not agree and if they wanted it done they had better send someone out who believed in it, could approach it with a fresh mind.'[42]

To what extent de Robeck was influenced by Keyes's dealings with politicians at home is difficult to assess. Most admirals of his generation would have been deeply offended by the actions of his Chief of Staff, but, with extraordinary generosity, he sent with Keyes a letter to Balfour in which he explained his position:

'I send this letter by Commodore Keyes – my excellent chief of staff – who will give you all information about the naval situation in the Dardanelles. He will put before you a scheme for a plan of attack by the Fleet on the Turkish defences of the Dardanelles and I hope every consideration will be given to the proposals.

'My chief reason for sending my Chief of Staff is that I differ profoundly from him as to the chances of success of the scheme – as I do not think it would achieve the object we desire. I do not propose in this letter to criticise the plan beyond saying that if carried out it would, in my opinion be a most costly and desperate effort whether successful or otherwise and further that it would lead to no definite result.

'Please do not think that there is any ill will between us over this difference of opinion; on the contrary there is none whatever. I have always encouraged officers under me to state their views in the most candid manner possible and as Commodore Keyes is an officer of so much experience, I think it is desirable he should personally lay his views before you . . .

'To my mind the only possible solution is the absolute destruction step by step of the forts and defences of the Dardanelles and this can only be done with the assistance of the Army.

'Again – if this attack, carried out on the lines proposed, fails, the loss of personnel and ships must be great. One cannot expect that if ships are sunk in the minefield or near the forts at the Narrows many of the crews will be saved.[43]

Thus de Robeck had defined two of the most important aspects of a renewed attack: the need to take the guns from behind, and the probable losses of trained naval personnel needed to man the new ships, a point Fisher had emphasized, but which never seems to have penetrated Churchill's mind. It was no sentimental attachment to old ships, which he had so unworthily attributed to the admirals, it was the losses in men who took many years to train. The reserves (RNR and RNVR) were a mere shadow of what they became in the Second World War, and there were few trained men to turn to. It was the regular officers and men on whom the Navy had to rely. The events at the Dardanelles and Gallipoli, and de Robeck's expression of them, proved how accurate Fisher's assessment had been when the undertaking without troops and with ample warning to the enemy had been embarked upon against his firm advice.

Keyes arrived home the day Monro arrived at Gallipoli and immediately set about a tour of all the influential people he could contact in an effort to persuade them to renew the naval attack. He saw Jackson, Oliver, Commodore A.F.Everett (later Admiral Sir Allan), Naval Secretary, Balfour ('I must say when I left him on Friday evening I felt almost beat and I went out feeling like a boy leaving the "head master"'), then was examined by all the Sea Lords. On Monday he lunched with Meux, who later refused to support him. On Wednesday Bartolomé told him Balfour wished him to see Churchill ('but I did not want to see him as I felt it would be very awkward') and Kitchener ('who was awfully bitten with my scheme'). Kitchener then produced a fantastic proposal to land 40,000 troops at Bulair (where only a narrow strip of land was possible) who would supply the fleet in the Marmora with coal, ammunition and stores overland! Even Keyes saw the absurdity, but Kitchener was so taken with Keyes scheme that Balfour was obliged to reconsider the possibilities. Keyes responded with a lengthy memorandum to the First Lord,[44] differing widely from his discussions with de Robeck,[45] with rhetoric worthy of Churchill, reiterating all the old ideas of the naval attacks and adding some even more ludicrous suggestions, such as 'Coal – As much as possible,' and carrying fuel for submarines in the battleships' oil tanks (not impossible, but technically extremely complicated). 'If the preliminary rush through the straits is successful, the reduction of the forts at the Narrows and the opening of the Straits cannot be long delayed if an attack . . . is vigorously pressed.'[46]

Keyes, despite protestations of loyalty, subtly undermined de Robeck:

> 'I have said nothing about de R., but at every interview with him [Balfour] and Sir Henry [Jackson] and Oliver his (de R's) disapproval of the scheme was discussed. I said that I felt sure that if he (de R) was approaching the thing with a fresh mind – as when he came from Cruiser Force I – that he would be *for it,* but that he was weary and in need of sleep – suffered from insomnia – and had authorised me to say he was in want of rest – in fact he wrote to Sir Henry. I also told Mr. Balfour about his having origi-nally written to him saying that if they accepted my scheme they must get someone else to do it. . . . Mr. B. said his opinion of de R. was higher than ever. After hearing this I told him R.W. [Wemyss] was *for it* and begged that he might be given the job if de R. came home.'[47]

On 9 November de Robeck wrote to Limpus, the man who knew the Dardanelles best, 'The Admiralty probably on the advice of Roger Keyes are evidently anxious that we should again attack the Dardanelles with the Fleet. I am perfectly determined to do nothing of the sort, as it would probably lead to a colossal disaster. . . . Unless we can clear the mines away and destroy the torpedo tubes it is madness, fancy bringing these old battleships into the Narrows to be torpedoed. It is like sending an unfortunate horse into the bull ring blindfolded!'[48]

Limpus replied:

> 'You are absolutely right. It wants an independent and strong man to tell the Admiralty so. I am horrified that they even contemplated such an operation. . . . Heaven forbid that we are smitten by madness again and allow ourselves to exhibit a visible disaster to our Fleet to the world. . . . I believe that an attempt by the Fleet to rush the Dardanelles would provide us with the biggest disaster of the whole war. Imagine my thank-fulness that – this time – we have a man who is strong enough to say NO.'[49]

Balfour telegraphed de Robeck suggesting he should come home for a rest: 'In making arrangements for your substitute during your absence please bear in mind that an urgent appeal from the Army to cooperate with them in a great effort may make it necessary for the Fleet to attempt to force the Straits. The admiral left in charge should therefore be capable of organising this critical operation and should be in full agreement with the policy.'[50] Seldom can there have been a stronger hint to an admiral that he was about to be ordered to haul down his flag. But there was more sense in the Admiralty than Keyes, the 'fighting blockhead', imagined. Jackson wrote on 7 November to de Robeck,

'Keyes has not made much impression except perhaps on K. However, he has given up plenty of information.'[51]

Monro arrived at Gallipoli on 28 October. It took him only three days to reach the obvious conclusion. Aspinall-Oglander writes contemptuously of his rapid decision and though admittedly a convinced westerner, a new mind made the position clear.

> 'Fresh from France, with its peaceful harbours and docks. and its staff cars awaiting the Channel steamer, Monro was quite unprepared for the scenes on 'W' beach. The cramped space, the crazy piers, the landing of stores by hand from bumping lighters, the strings of kicking mules, the heavy sand, the jostling crowds of fatigue parties within range of the enemy's guns, filled him with blank amazement. At Anzac, where the conditions were even more difficult, his wonder only grew. To Aspinall, walking beside him, he said with a whimsical smile: "It's just like Alice in Wonderland – curiouser and curiouser." '[52]

Monro at once sent a telegram to Kitchener that he could see no military advantage in staying in the Peninsula, stating that the health of all the troops had seriously deteriorated and they were incapable of heavy physical exertion. and added two days later, 'The longer the troops remain on the Peninsula, the less efficient they will become'. He wrote a long report to Kitchener in the same sense. This was discussed at a meeting of the Dardanelles Committee on 4 November and it was suggested that Kitchener should go to Gallipoli to judge the situation for himself. At least in part, this was a ruse to get Kitchener out of the way so that he could be displaced.

On 21 October at a Cabinet meeting, Crewe taking the chair as Asquith was sick, it was unanimously decided that the war should be managed by a very small committee, probably of three. After the meeting all the members remained behind, except Kitchener, when Balfour said he could not serve on a committee of three with Kitchener and it was agreed that he must be dismissed. It was, of course, for Crewe to inform Asquith of the result of the meeting, yet Churchill drafted a letter to the Prime Minister outlining the proceedings, urging Kitchener's removal and advocating a competent *civilian* [my italics] Secretary of State for War sustained by the strongest General Staff possible. This transparent bid for office was emphasized by a threat to resign from the Cabinet if Kitchener was not dismissed, but Churchill thought better of it and the letter was withheld. Asquith, fearing he might be forced to appoint Lloyd George, which would undermine his own position, refused to dismiss Kitchener but abolished the Dardanelles Committee and formed a new Cabinet War Committee of three – himself, Kitchener and Balfour, the last immediately changing his mind and agreeing to serve with Kitchener. This committee was what Kitchener had wanted a year before, with Fisher as the third member, which would have provided two professionals under the

chairmanship of a theoretically impartial civilian. There was certainly no justification for the appointment of a civilian Minister for War; war is much too
serious a business to be left to politicians.

By November the Dardanelles Committee had swelled to Asquith, Crewe,
Lansdowne, Curzon, Bonar Law, Balfour, Kitchener, Sir Archibald Murray,
Churchill, Selborne, Grey and Lloyd George, with Hankey as Secretary and an
Assistant Secretary, Lieut-Col. Swinton. Others like Jackson, Austen
Chamberlain and Sir Edmund Barrow often attended. Apart from Jackson, not
a single member had any naval experience. But Asquith's attention was force-
fully drawn to the Committee's unwieldy nature in a letter written after the
meeting of 4 November by Lords Cromer, Loreburn, Midleton, Milner,
Morley, St Aldwyn and Sydenham, objecting to the inclusion in any new
committee of any minister who had a responsibility for undertaking the
Dardanelles operation, and indicating that they would raise the matter publicly.

Though this made no mention of naval or military representation, it implied
that Churchill, Balfour, perhaps Kitchener, and even Asquith, himself should
be excluded. Bonar Law wrote to Asquith on 5 November that the position in
Gallipoli was 'untenable' and the delay in reaching a conclusion 'a fatal error'.

Yet the Committee met again the next day and still made no decision. With
Balfour's and Kitchener's agreement, the Field Marshal was sent off to
Gallipoli, suspecting intrigue and taking the seals of his office with him in his
pocket. 'There were not many who believed in his return.' It took him little
time, after consultation with Birdwood, the three corps commanders and de
Robeck, to agree with Monro. Evacuation, he thought, could be achieved with
fewer casualties than had been supposed. Simultaneously, the General Staff on
London reached a like conclusion, suggesting that casualties might be 50,000,
but would release 140,000 men for France. As he left the Peninsula he told
Aspinall-Oglander: 'I don't believe a word about those 25,000 casualties. Carry
on just as you are doing; and when the order does arrive, as it will, you'll just
slip off without losing a man, and without the Turks knowing anything about
it.'[53] Six weeks later this is exactly what happened; one man was wounded.
Churchill, supported by some generals and a few naval officers, notably
Wemyss and Keyes, continued to express optimistic views on the ease with
which the Dardanelles could be penetrated and Constantinople taken.

De Robeck went home on 25 November and Wemyss assumed command
in his stead. The former wrote, with unwarranted trust, to Limpus the next
day: 'I hate running away even for a day, but Rosie Wemyss is such a good
fellow, he will not be induced into any foolish action by R.Keyes. The latter
the most capable and best of C.O.S, but at present he is obsessed with the
idea of forcing the Straits with the Fleet and is quite incapable of weighing
the consequences in case of failure.'[54] He was wrong; the moment his back
was turned Keyes persuaded Wemyss to make a personal appeal to Monro,
who was non-committal, so Wemyss telegraphed Balfour stressing the

dangers of evacuation and the chance of success in a combined operation. But to Keyes's and Wemyss's disappointment the order to evacuate reached them on 7 December.

On his return, the over-tolerant de Robeck wrote to Limpus in a different sense.

'They pulled off a great performance here and every credit is due to those who did it and Wemyss and Keyes and Keyes especially. They were certainly very foolish and sent many telegrams that showed they had no true appreciation of their responsibilities, however all's well that ends well. R.W. is off as C-in-C Egypt and I have [had] a heart to heart talk with R.Keyes and told him that he must in future be C.O.S. and not "leader of the opposition"! I had not the heart to send him away.'[55]

At home, Carson's resignation and pressure for the dismissal of Kitchener created a problem for Asquith, already struggling with the argument on conscription, which many Ministers believed the only fair way in which the manhood of the nation could take an equal share of the horror, but Kitchener stubbornly argued against it. Almost alone, he believed in a volunteer army, increasing his isolation. Asquith parried this agitation by introducing the Derby Scheme, by which every man between the ages of 18 and 41 attested to his willingness to serve when his 'group' and 'class' was called. There were two classes, married and unmarried, and each was divided into groups by age.

Churchill made another desperate bid for power by writing a memorandum on his creation of the Royal Naval Air Service, with the underlying suggestion that a third Service should be formed and implying he should be the Minister. He sent it to Balfour, no doubt hoping the First Lord would raise the matter with Asquith, but he was disappointed; Balfour returned it through Masterton Smith, telling him that he had no objection whatever to 'Winston making any use of it he intends'. Churchill dropped the matter. He made one more attempt to press for another naval attack at the Dardanelles, repeating his ignoble view that 'mere sentiment in regard to the loss of vessels is exercising an altogether undue influence'. He got no reaction. He then produced an extraordinary scheme for 'recovering the initiative in the Near East', involving an Anglo-Franco-Russian attack on Turkey and Bulgaria, the Russians to be armed with Japanese rifles provided by Britain. It was ignored. At last he realized that there was no hope of his return to power and he sent in his resignation to Asquith. The latter, still anxious to retain Kitchener, who still commanded public confidence, asked Churchill to withhold his resignation, though he recognized that political pressure might force his hand.

On 11 November Asquith formed his new Cabinet War Committee, though with five members instead of three. It consisted of himself, Lloyd George, Balfour, Law and McKenna. Neither Kitchener nor Churchill was included and not a single Service officer. Churchill resigned again. He asked, to Balfour's amusement, to be made Governor and Commander-in-Chief, East Africa, with some support from Bonar Law. Asquith refused.

In his resignation speech he attempted to justify his conduct at the Admiralty, claiming that he 'did not receive from the First Sea Lord, either the clear guidance before the event or the firm support after, which I was entitled to expect'.[56] Since he had firmly rejected the clear guidance he received and yet was given support, this was hardly fair. He continued: 'If the First Sea Lord had not approved the operations, if he thought they were unlikely to take the course that was expected of them, if he thought they would lead to undue losses, it was his duty to refuse consent. No one could have prevailed against such a refusal. The operation would never have been begun.'[57] Fisher did not approve the operations, he was convinced they would fail, he had refused his consent and Churchill had prevailed against him; the operation was begun. Churchill continued: 'All through this year I have offered the same counsel to the Government – undertake no operation in the West which is more costly to us in life than to the enemy; in the East, take Constantinople; take it by ships if you can; take it by soldiers if you must; take it by whichever plan, military or naval, commends itself to your military experts, but take it, and take it soon, and take it while time remains.'[58]

Churchill's character assassination of Fisher was complete. In a pathetic letter of sympathy and adulation, Violet Asquith wrote, '*How* thankful I am you said what you did about that wicked old lunatic'.[59]

But Spender wrote to Esher:

'Winston was less mischievous than was expected &, if the egotism can be pardoned, the performance was effective though essentially unfair to Jackie & the experts. It is all very well to say "discussions were frequent & no adverse opinions were expressed", but we all know who discussed & what happened to the exponents of adverse opinions.'[60]

When Churchill considered resignation in August he had sounded Asquith on being given command of a division in France. His belief in his own military ability was unabated and he considered himself entitled to high military rank, but despite his suggestion of the rank of Lieutenant-General at Antwerp, Kitchener now point blank refused. Although no longer an active army officer, since resigning his commission as a subaltern, Churchill held a commission as a major in the family regiment, The Queen's Own Oxfordshire Hussars, with which he had to be content, though he was promised, and given, early command of a battalion, with the rank of lieutenant-colonel. Sir John French was prepared to make him a brigadier, but was superseded before this could take effect.

10

VINDICATION

To instil more vigour into the Board, Fisher wanted to be a member of the new Cabinet War Committee, though Crease said that by this time his age and the trauma of the May crisis were telling on him. Hamilton, Second Sea Lord, had turned against him since his 'desertion of his post' and mounted a calculating campaign to frustrate him, with the support of Jellicoe, whose ineffectual policy of waiting in Scapa Flow for the enemy to take the initiative was totally opposed to Fisher's aggressive views. Jellicoe was afraid he might be forced to mount the Baltic plan and wrote to Hamilton, 'I am fully aware of his totally wrong strategical notions and so are others to whom I should write'.[1]

In response to Churchill's tasteless resignation speech Fisher was expected to initiate a vitriolic attack in the Lords, but instead the next day he made his maiden speech, in a 'resounding quarter-deck sort of voice':

> 'I ask leave of your Lordships to make a statement. Certain references were made to me in the other House yesterday by Mr. Churchill. I have been sixty-one years in the service of my country, and I leave my record in the hands of my countrymen. The Prime Minister said yesterday that Mr. Churchill had said one or two things which he had better not have said, and that he necessarily, and naturally, left unsaid some things which will have to be said. I am content to wait. It is unfitting to make personal explanations affecting national interests when my country is in the midst of a great war.'[2]

Without waiting, he strode out of the Chamber. His speech was received with admiration, the result far greater than a bitter attack on Churchill. The effect of his dignified refusal to respond to Churchill's attempt to make him a scapegoat was immense. James Douglas, a journalist, wrote to Pamela McKenna:

'I never witnessed anything so dramatic in my life. The effect has been tremendous. I was lunching at the Reform Club today, and the opinion there was unanimous in admiration of the speech. As for the speech generally, the revulsion of feeling is remarkable. I note particularly the change in the tone of the *Manchester Guardian*, which yesterday as usual was strongly pro-Churchill. Today it comes right round.'[3]

Typical of Press reaction was that of the *Daily News* who said Fisher 'firmly declined to be drawn into an unseemly personal wrangle. This is not the least of the great services Lord Fisher has done for the country.'

The months passed and, though his standing had been restored, he was obliged to witness powerlessly the mismanagement of the war. Not the cautious Jellicoe, nor the lethargic Balfour nor the unimaginative Jackson, nor even the vainglorious Beatty could see any way of achieving the second Trafalgar. The outnumbered and out-gunned High Sea Fleet remained safely in harbour, making occasional sallies into the North Sea, threatening the East Coast, but quickly scurrying back to safety as soon as any possibility of meeting the Grand Fleet arose, hoping always to overpower small isolated units and slowly reduce Jellicoe's superiority.

Jellicoe, frustrated by submarines and apprehensive of being drawn over mines, was acutely aware of his shortage of destroyers and handicapped by their short endurance – twenty hours' steaming from the Bight, they could not accompany him for long without returning to port to fuel. He still corresponded with Fisher, to whom he poured out his troubles, complaining in January, 1916, that the 18-inch-gunned *Furious* was 'hopelessly delayed' and that destroyers due to complete in October had still not arrived. He put the average delay at between three and nine months, while 'for several months I have not been allowed to send ships to home yards to refit, on the plea that I am delaying new construction.'[4]

Asquith, his respect for Fisher restored, asked for his views on the possibility of the Germans having adopted 17-inch guns in new battleships. Fisher was unable to give a definite answer, but took the opportunity to pass on Jellicoe's complaints, without mentioning the C-in-C, and added that the 18-inch guns he had ordered when First Sea Lord had been cancelled. His advocacy of the larger guns was dubious, for their extended range could only be used in very clear weather. Without better methods of finding and holding the range over the horizon, like good air spotting, the maximum useful calibre was 15-inches, and this the Admiralty reported to Asquith. The enemy would not benefit from 17-inch guns, fewer of which could be mounted and then only at the sacrifice of speed or armour.

On destroyer deliveries the Admiralty was less convincing. They compared prewar construction periods of $20\frac{1}{2}$ months with wartime averages of $12\frac{1}{2}$ months, without mention that this included those delivered during the Fisher régime, since when delivery had slowed, though they admitted a shortage, and claimed shipyard capacity was full, which was seriously reduced by Kitchener's unhelpful policy of massive recruiting in the shipyard areas, many skilled workers being employed as infantrymen in the mud of Flanders.

Stalemate on the Western Front was matched by stalemate in the North Sea. The Admiralty were devoid of new ideas, Jackson in particular, who could think of nothing but persuading the High Sea Fleet to commit suicide by giving battle to a superior force. 'I wish you could entice them out from Heligoland to give you a chance,' he wrote to Jellicoe in September, 1915, 'Have you any ideas for it ? I wish I had.'[5] By January Balfour was turning to Fisher's Baltic scheme: 'Have you, by the way, given much thought to a possible naval offensive against Germany in the Baltic or elsewhere?'[6] But Jellicoe was negative. He claimed the passage of the Great Belt, 'the only possible route', was now obstructed by mines and was 'practically prohibited'. He was prepared to consider strengthening the submarine force in the Baltic, but that was all. Neither he nor Jackson considered an unobtrusive investigation of the supposed minefields; Denmark was neutral, smarting over the loss of Schleswig, and it should not have been impossible to gain the information that there were no mines in the Kattegat, Skagerrak or the Great Belts. As we know, Tirpitz confirmed this after the war.

Balfour came back to the charge, suggesting the use of the old battleships returning from the Dardanelles, and Jellicoe showed his cautious hand again. Unless the force, together with the Russians, was comparable with the High Sea Fleet it would be annihilated. 'We should be forced to send dreadnoughts through.' A possible stratagem would be to use old battleships as a bait to draw the High Sea Fleet into a submarine trap, into which he himself refused to be drawn. But in any case, the same result, he believed, could be achieved in the North Sea, perhaps by a feint against Borkum or Sylt. Clearly he was thinking solely in terms of a fleet action; the Fisher Baltic scheme never entered Jellicoe's head. Both Jellicoe and Jackson could see all the difficulties, but sought no solution. Here was where a properly trained naval staff could have worked out plans, found means of overcoming the difficulties, and here Fisher has to accept his share of the blame, though far smaller than his detractors have suggested. At a War Committee meeting on 17 February, 1916, attended by Jellicoe, the Baltic scheme was again raised, but again abandoned on the grounds that mines and submarines made success impossible. There was little attempt to overcome difficulties, no suggestion of seeking intelligence or making plans, and the meeting passed on to consider alternative offensive operations, each of which was given cursory examination and cast aside. Once again there were 'no troops to spare'; improved artillery now made storming a coastal island impracticable; merchant ships could not be spared as blockships, so the closing of enemy ports was ruled out; mining them was equally 'out of the question' until the High Sea Fleet had been defeated, (which would seem to make the operation rather superfluous!) because close watch could not be kept to ensure mines were not swept. Nothing could be done but lure the German fleet out against its will. Fisher's ninepins again knocked each other over.

The next day Hankey wrote to Richmond:

> 'I am always hammering at the distribution of the allied fleets and am received with the kindest of bland smiles & charming hospitality but *cannot get a move on*. I have always been hammering hard about the demoralising want of offensive, and even succeeded in bringing a distinguished personage to London from a great distance. It is no good. The Navy has completely lost the spirit of offensive! I cannot find a trace of it in any flag officer except Bacon! We shall have a shock one of these days I am certain.'[7]

Corbett, Richmond and Hankey proposed an expedition to Alexandretta which met with opposition from Jellicoe on the grounds that the Salonika expedition was already denuding the Grand Fleet, and the War Office opposed it because the Westerners still wanted every available man for the trenches of France. Monro told Keyes that 'every man not employed in killing Germans in France and Flanders is wasted'.

Corbett was depressed. 'I can give you no comfort.' he wrote to Richmond, 'The soldier square-heads have got hold of the war solid and refuse to do anything except on the Western Front, damn it!'[8]

So naval initiative was left with the enemy and increasingly so when Scheer took over from Pohl in January. Indeed he followed the same policy of luring out his enemy as the Grand Fleet, but with greater chance of success. By submarine attacks on merchant shipping, mining, aerial warfare and raids on the British Coast he would goad Jellicoe into sending out *part* of his fleet, which would provide him with opportunities for attrition leading to equality. His first attempt yielded little, though he came as far south as Texel in the hope that British naval forces would come out against zeppelins sent ahead to bomb England.

In March an attempt was made by Tyrwhitt to entice the Germans out with an air attack on the zeppelin base at Hoyer, opposite Sylt, with five aircraft from the seaplane carrier *Vindex* while Beatty stood off Horns Reef. Enemy ships were expected to come to attack Tyrwhitt's force, which was to fall back on the Grand Fleet, cautiously remaining north. Hipper came to sea, but never got closer than 60 miles of Beatty. The only result was the loss of three aircraft, the discovery that there were no aircraft sheds at Hoyer anyway and damage to several British ships due to collision in atrocious weather. At last Jackson showed a spark of aggression: 'It looks as though your best chance to get at them is to go for them . . . instead of acting entirely on the defensive according to existing war standing orders, as very little seems to result.'[9] Jellicoe was negative. He wrote to Beatty in April:

'There is a feeling in the Admiralty which I think may lead to their trying to persuade me into what is called a "more active policy". . . . The real truth to my mind is that our policy should be to engage them *not* in a position close to their minefields and therefore close to their S.M., T.B.D., and aircraft bases, but to accept the position that we must wait until they give us a chance in a favourable position. Patience is the virtue we must exercise. I am still trying to devise a means of drawing them further out, but I am bound to say that I don't think air raids will do it. What do you think?'[10]

Marder describes Beatty's reply as 'of the greatest interest and importance':

'You ask me what I think? Well, I think the German Fleet will come out *only* on its own initiative when the right time arrives . . . But it is certain that he will *not* come out in Grand Force when we set the tune, i.e. to fight the great battle we are all waiting for . . .

'Your arguments re the fuel question are unanswerable and measure the situation absolutely. We cannot amble about the North Sea for two or three days and at the end be in a condition in which we can produce our whole force to fight to the finish the most decisive battle of the War; to think it is possible is simply too foolish and tends towards losing the battle before we begin.

'As I said, my contention is that when the Great Day comes it will be when the enemy retakes the initiative; and I think our principle business now is to investigate the North Sea with minesweepers so that we can have a clear and fairly accurate knowledge of what waters in it are safe and what are not; so that when he does take the initiative we can judge fairly accurately in what waters we can engage him. I think we can be quite sure that it will not be north of Lat. 56° [The Forth].

'What I am disturbed about is that 'there is a feeling in the Admiralty, etc. to persuade me into a more active policy – and being pressed to plan another'. This is truly deplorable.'[11]

Thus Beatty, for all the post-war arguments, was little more aggressive than Jellicoe and seems to have had no more idea of devising offensive operations, without which 'investigation' by minesweepers would seem pointless.

On 25 April Scheer made another sortie, a minor bombardment of the East Coast, to coincide with the Easter rising of the Irish Nationalists, planned in collusion with the Germans. An intercepted signal warned the Admiralty the day before of Scheer's intention to proceed to sea. At 3.50 pm the Grand fleet was ordered to come to two hours' notice and at 7.05 pm ordered to sea. An hour later another intercepted signal disclosed that Scheer's target was Yarmouth. The Harwich force under Commodore Tyrwhitt (later Admiral Sir Reginald) proceeded up the coast and at 3.50 am was sighted by the enemy battlecruisers' screen. He immediately signalled Beatty and Jellicoe, while he retired southward, attempting to draw the enemy away from Lowestoft, which the Germans, ignoring Tyrwhitt's invitation, proceeded to bombard, causing damage and casualties. Tyrwhitt again turned towards the enemy to keep in touch, but with cruisers on his starboard bow and battlecruisers ahead was obliged again to retire south, sustaining considerable damage to his flagship *Conquest.*

Believing Tyrwhitt had superior speed and unsure of other forces, Scheer allowed the Harwich Force to escape and retired to harbour. He had achieved his main objective of harassing the British coast and suggesting that Germany might still invade, but missed an opportunity to advance the policy of attrition.

The Grand Fleet was on its way south against heavy seas, without its destroyers, which had become dispersed in the severe weather. Jellicoe had only three cruisers as a screen and, on receiving Tyrwhitt's report of enemy in sight, was off Cromarty, about 350 miles away, while the battlecruisers were about 220 miles from Terschelling. Again the remoteness of Scapa Flow and Rosyth were a major factor in another opportunity lost. The enemy still had their destroyers in company.

Despite Jellicoe and Beatty's antagonism to the air raid at Hoyer, a similar attempt was made early in May. Two seaplane carriers from Rosyth, accompanied by the 1st Light Cruiser squadron and sixteen destroyers, attacked the zeppelin shed at Tondern. The operation was a more realistic attempt to trap the High Sea Fleet. By dawn on 4 May the battle fleet was stationed off the Skagerrak with the battlecruisers further south. Seven submarines were stationed off the northern end of the Bight and minefields were laid on the enemy's most probable course. Only one aircraft succeeded in bombing its objective. This was enough, it was hoped, to bring Scheer out, but he held back. Just after midday the Admiralty signalled Jellicoe that the Germans did not appear to know British forces were in the area and at 2 pm Jellicoe turned for Scapa, shortage of fuel being one of the reasons he gave in his report. The High Sea Fleet came out at 3 pm and went north to Sylt. But Jellicoe had gone home. His trap had sprung, but he missed his quarry by little more than an hour.

Beatty was disappointed. Believing the Admiralty responsible for the decision to give up the operation, he wrote to Jellicoe roundly abusing them: 'I had husbanded my destroyers' fuel and they were well able to have had a good period at full speed the next day and get home at 15 knots if required. You can understand my disappointment when we were ordered to return to base. Why cannot Admiralty leave the situation to those on the spot?'[12]

A fortnight later he still blamed the Admiralty. He had discussed the Lowestoft raid with Tyrwhitt and wrote to Jellicoe: 'The system of water-tight compartments has reached its climax. The Chief of the War Staff has priceless information given to him which he sits on until it is too late.'[13]

At least their failure brought some new thinking. The Grand Fleet at Scapa was out of touch with the enemy, over 500 miles from the German bases, which were half that distance from the British coast and 400 miles from Dover. It was surely dull reasoning to suppose that a great battle could be staged by enticing out an unwilling adversary when he could slip across the North Sea and be home again before his opponent had arrived at the scene of his depredations. Fisher had wanted the Grand Fleet based on the Humber, almost exactly the same latitude as Wilhelmshaven. The Admiralty, compromising, now wanted it based in the Forth, but the advantage in distance was only 70 miles, about 3½ hours, and Jellicoe argued that there was insufficient room, that the outer anchorages below the bridge were unsafe from submarines and that the fleet might be 'mined in'. He refused Beatty's suggestion that the 'Queen Elizabeths', the fastest battleships in the fleet, should be moved to Rosyth on the grounds that 'The stronger I make Beatty, the greater is the temptation for him to get involved in an independent action',[14] surely a vote of no-confidence in his subordinate.

The matter had been raised by the Admiralty in February, 1916, not for the first time, and Jackson, Jellicoe and Beatty had engaged in a dilatory correspondence on the subject extending over two inconclusive months. Under public pressure, the Admiralty now asked the C-in-C for proposals, which resulted in a new command under Rear Admiral E.E.Bradford, based on the Swin, consisting of the old 'King Edward VIIs' and the 1st Cruiser Squadron, *Defence, Warrior, Duke of Edinburgh* and *Black Prince*. Little more than a public relations exercise, the public saw through it. The Press scathingly rejected a defensive policy which provided no strategic advantage. Said *The Times*; 'Only once did our rulers voluntarily adopt an attitude of passive resistance as an exchange for one of active, resolute opposition, and then the Hollander came up the Medway and destroyed the ships off Chatham.'

Jackson, Jellicoe and Beatty met at Rosyth to resolve the problem, and at last decided that as soon as the defences of the Forth were improved, Rosyth would become the main base for the whole Grand Fleet. But the defences were not completed until 1917 and even then the Battle Squadron did not move there until April, 1918, a torpid programme indeed.

Small wonder that there were calls for Fisher's restoration. He chafed at enforced inactivity and maintained a colourful correspondence with friends. Through Arnold White he ventilated his views. Calls for him to be given a more responsible post came from the *Manchester Guardian* in a leading article on 7 February, though it did not specify exactly in what capacity:

'Nothing must be taken for granted in war, and least of all in naval war. We need for the direction of our naval policy every ounce of our energy, every counsel of experience, and, above all, every impulse of restless ingenuity and of the spirit of innovation in which the British genius excels. It is notorious that our full store of these qualities is not being drawn upon. . . . Lord Fisher's immense experience, energy and driving power are not used in such a position [as BIR Chairman], and the nation cannot afford to waste them.'[15]

The Press seemed unsure how best he could be employed and the suggestions were various. Some, perhaps still believing him a 'materialist', wanted him appointed as overlord of naval construction, with absolute powers, a view supported by Lloyd George. Others wanted him to join the War Committee, but the largest number wanted him as First Lord; again it was pointed out that in all the most desperate moments of history Britain had been saved by a naval officer as First Lord and all the examples, Barham, St Vincent *et al*, were again cited. Comparisons were made with Kitchener's appointment. If a soldier, why not a sailor? *The Naval and Military Record* wanted a sailor in any case, even if it was not Fisher.

Some of the Conservative Press were against him and his old antagonist Admiral Sir Gerard Noel, supported by Sir Arthur Moore, argued, with some justice, that he was too old. But, with less fairness, they claimed that he had created so much bitterness that his appointment would impair the loyalty of the Service, who, in any case, had confidence in Balfour and Jackson, which was not true. *The Morning Post* illogically criticized his reforms of 1904–1910 and attacked him for 'deserting his post ' in May, 1915. The King, under the influence of Meux and probably Wemyss, joined the anti-Fisher campaign.

More serious and discreditable was the agitation by Sir Frederick Hamilton, Second Sea Lord, who, it will be remembered, had signed the joint memorandum supporting Fisher against Churchill. Subtly avoiding becoming personally involved, he used Hall, the DNI, as a front man, persuading him to convince the Fleet Street editors that the movement was damaging. When C.P.Scott brought Lord Loreburn into the discussion, a committee of peers was formed to press the matter. The Duchess of Hamilton, a loyal and trusted friend of Fisher. used her considerable influence with men of importance, entertaining them to 'tea and propaganda'. Some activities of Fisher's supporters, however, embarrassed him; a shop in St. Martin's Lane showed a portrait of him in the window with an invitation to passers-by to sign a petition for his appointment to the Cabinet. Fisher himself, knowing the King's opposition, was 'dead set' against the agitation and had little faith in his returning to responsibility, but characteristically was already thinking of what he would do in that event. He decided on Jellicoe as First Sea Lord and Madden as C-in-C Grand Fleet, a combination that might have worked well.

On 29 January, 1916, Jellicoe confided in Fisher, 'In August last it was anticipated that I should have received by now an addition of 17 new destroyers. I have actually got 2 and the rate of delay is a progressive one. The case is almost worse in light cruisers, and is equally bad as regards submarines. Of course battleships are also delayed . . . but my most pressing need is and *has always been* destroyers and *minesweepers*. The latter don't come at all. I don't want to go behind the back of the Board, or I would write to the Prime Minister.'[16]

Beatty, less circumspect, did write to the Prime Minister, with a copy to Jellicoe. He described Jellicoe as 'perturbed and despondent'. To the depletion of labour through Army recruitment had now been added the demands of Lloyd George's Ministry of Munitions also drawing men from the shipyards: 'No doubt you are aware of this . . . but what you cannot be aware of is the very serious view of the situation taken by the Commander-in-Chief.'[17]

Jellicoe was invited to a War Committee meeting, when it was accepted that the need for light vessels was urgent, but the meeting, in Jellicoe's opinion, descended into 'a mere rambling conversation'. He therefore tried to record his views in a memorandum to the Prime Minister, for which he earned a rebuke from Jackson: 'Your views are now known to all responsible and you know the situation as regards new construction, etc . . . and how anxious we are to hasten it. Don't you think it is time the matter was dropped?'[18] He suggested Jellicoe should make the best of the tools he had, quoting 'the spirit of the true seamen of old', which provoked a reasoned reply from the C-in-C: 'As regards my paper to the Prime Minister, I sent it because the secretary's notes of the meeting did not represent what I said or intended to say . . . the conclusions reached seemed to ignore the points on which I laid stress. Surely it is best to try and get the new construction pushed on.'[19]

C.P.Scott talked to three Cabinet Ministers about the meeting, all of whom believed Jellicoe had been satisfied by the Admiralty and his visit to the War Committee had ended in a 'fizzle'. Scott came to see Fisher and told him what he had heard and that A.K.Wilson had attended. Asquith's purpose was obvious. Wilson's incoherence would enable the smooth-tongued politicians to run rings round him and claim his support. Fisher was irritated, perhaps partly because he felt excluded, but more because he believed Jellicoe had been fobbed off. He therefore sent a letter to Asquith reiterating his views, sending it first to Jellicoe and Hankey for comments, both of whom supported him fully, except that Jellicoe disagreed on one minor point, mainly of semantics.

When Balfour introduced the Navy Estimates on 7 March, he tried to persuade the House that all was well with the Navy, that, with the single exception of armoured cruisers, Britain was superior to the enemy, that the shipbuilding industry was working to capacity, the only limitation being shortage of labour, and added, with less than the truth, that there had never been the 'smallest difference of opinion' between the Board and the admirals afloat.

Churchill, who returned from Flanders to take part in the debate, rose to speak. He had shown his speech to Fisher whose advice to reduce its length and make it more pithy he had accepted. The House expected an attack on Fisher, who sat in the Peers' gallery. Churchill enunciated, as only he could, the first rule of war: 'In naval war particularly, you must always be asking about the enemy – what now, what next? You must always be seeking to penetrate what he will do, and your measures must always be governed and framed that he will do what you would least like him to do.'[20]

He pointed out that the Germans would certainly have completed every ship they had planned before the war. He attacked the First Lord's reference to the limits of labour in the shipbuilding industry, the negative attitude of the present Board, and, though he rather spoilt his case by claiming that the U-boats, which Balfour had not even mentioned, had, 'up to date been a great failure, and . . . will probably continue to be a failure,' he added, with more prescience, 'here again you cannot afford to assume that it will not present itself in new and more difficult forms and that new exertions and new inventions will not be demanded.' He added that his Board would certainly not have been content with an attitude of 'pure passivity'. He ended his speech, to the 'stupefaction and bewilderment' of his hearers:

> 'There was a time when I did not think that I could have brought myself to say this, but I have been away for some months, and my mind is now clear. The times are crucial. The issues are momentous. . . . The existence of our country and our cause depend upon the Fleet. We cannot afford to deprive ourselves or the Navy of the strongest and most vigorous forces that are available. . . . There is [in the Admiralty] a lack of driving force and mental energy. . . . I urge to First Lord of the Admiralty without delay to fortify himself, to vitalise and animate his Board of Admiralty by recalling Lord Fisher to his post as First Sea Lord.'[21]

But Churchill made no mention of this in *The World Crisis*. There was a moment's stunned silence and then the House broke into cheers, mingled with cries of dissent. Fisher rose and departed from his place and many members broke the rules of the House by cheering him as he left.

Reaction in the country was mixed. The anti-Fisher school claimed to believe Balfour's statement without question and attacked Churchill's support of Fisher as an attempt to regain power by destroying Balfour's credibility, surely an underestimate of Churchill; there was no chance of his return to office at that juncture, especially in conjunction with Fisher; their disagreements and the circumstances of their departure from the Admiralty were still fresh, and he was discredited by the Dardanelles tragedy. By advocating Fisher's return he was destroying his own chances, but this did not stop the *Spectator's* unseemly remark: 'To watch this fevered, this agonised struggle to regain the political fortune which the arch-gambler threw away is to witness one of the great tragedies of life.' Nor did it prevent Admiral Colville's even more offensive remark, 'Surely Winston Churchill must be going off his head like his father did?'

There was a wave of support for Fisher. Even *The Times*, normally very anti-Fisher, admitted that Churchill's speech 'will certainly command a good deal of attention, because it expressed very vividly the vague popular anxiety which has lately been prevalent about our general naval position,' though Repington, the military correspondent, recorded in his diary that he had dined with Lady Randolph when Churchill had said, 'He still thinks Fisher worth all the rest of our admirals, but I advised him not to harness himself to a corpse'.[22]

The next day Balfour replied to Churchill in a masterly speech, though it obscured much of the truth. He was in a dilemma; not only was he forced, from a personal and party point of view, to defend his political reputation, but it was undesirable to expose British weakness. He suggested that Churchill's views were unjustified and for security reasons should not have been ventilated, though he admitted the slow-down in construction, attributing delays to shortage of labour and asserting that skilled men were being recalled from the trenches, overtime was being increased and labour dilution agreed with the Unions. Again admitting all was not well, he said, 'Every effort is being made by the Admiralty to bring about a better state of things'. Then he went on to lash Churchill with his own words. In November he had complained that he had not received from Fisher the cooperation to which he considered himself entitled: 'Why does he suppose that Lord Fisher should behave differently to me . . . ? Is it my merits? Am I more gifted in the way of working with people than my Right Hon. Friend?' He praised Jackson with the exaggerated statement that he was of 'outstanding character, ability and experience. . . . The Right Hon. gentleman was not fortunate enough to get the guidance and support of the First Sea Lord when he was in office. I have had a happier fate. I have received both guidance and support from the present First Sea Lord.'[23]

Churchill liked to prepare his speeches carefully in advance and on this occasion he had no opportunity to do so. His reply was wholly ineffectual, though the affair drew public attention to the need for a naval officer in the Cabinet. *The Naval and Military Record* put the matter succinctly: 'The truth is that the Navy is represented practically nowhere. The Navy is not important in the Cabinet, as the other Allied fleets are represented in the Allied Cabinets; it is almost without voice in the two Houses of Parliament; and it is apparent that in the matter of the blockade, the expansion of our military forces, and the grievances under which officers and men suffer, the Admiralty today exercises little influence.'

During the debate a row of sandwichmen in Whitehall proclaimed 'GIVE US BACK FISHER' and 'GIVE US BACK THE MAN WHO WON THE FALKLANDS ISLANDS BATTLE', one of the placards stating (correctly) 'Lord Fisher knows nothing of this, he has not been consulted, the need of the nation is great, modes of expression are few'; while at one of the London theatres a song included a chorus *'Give us back our Jacky'*.

At the insistence of Lloyd George, Fisher was now invited to attend a meeting of the War Committee. He handed over a memorandum advocating the appointment of 'some suitable person . . . placed in dictatorial command of the whole building programme with unrestricted powers and untrammelled by anyone whatsoever,' and continued, 'Every possible means should be taken to accelerate all vessels in hand and others should be laid down and pushed forward with all rapidity in every vacant building slip in the country'. He went on to press for the return 'without a moment's delay' of the fleet and all auxiliaries from the Mediterranean, which he said could safely be left to the French and Italian fleets, who were immensely superior to the Austrians. 'I have not been wrong hitherto and I am not wrong now in predicting a naval disaster unless drastic action is taken, and I repeat, never has the existence of the British Empire been so menaced as at the present juncture, because of the possible German naval surprises in store for us.'[24]

Arthur Pollen, now an embittered and vicious opponent of Fisher, poured cold water on his performance, calling it a 'dismal failure':

> 'His main point was that the dates of his programme of construction had not been kept. The Admiralty had no difficulty in showing that his dates were meaningless or dishonest. He had practically forced the builders to promise deliveries months before delivery was possible – a thing they were perfectly willing to do if all the penalties for non-delivery were waived, as in fact they were. Before the thing was over Fisher lost his temper hopelessly and tried to brush the Admiralty objections to one side. All the War Committee are, I hear, agreed upon his failure, and he will probably not be asked to attend again, so that the whole intrigue has really fizzled out this time.' [25]

As Pollen was not present and had no knowledge of the subject, it is difficult to understand how he came to this conclusion. His version is transparently untrue. Fisher's record of getting ships built in incredibly short times – *Dreadnought*, the Schwab submarines, the landing craft, monitors and 'Queen Elizabeths' – spoke for itself. Hankey, a knowledgeable and impartial witness, was impressed and said he had 'exactly the right effect of dotting the "i"s and crossing the "t"s of Jellicoe's evidence. I cannot overstate my own gratitude to you, not only for coming yesterday, but for the persistence with which you have by letters and personal interviews compelled the War Committee to probe these matters to the bottom.'[26]

Asquith, far more concerned at his increasingly precarious political position than the progress of the war, was nervous of the effects of the agitation for Fisher's return. When C.P.Scott went to see him that afternoon to press him to recall Fisher, the Prime Minister was disparaging:

> 'He was silent and grim . . . the war council had heard what Fisher had to say. What did it amount to? . . . Then he broke out on them both [Fisher and Churchill], rising in his seat and marching to and fro. As for Churchill's speech, it was a piece of the grossest effrontery. . . . "I admit

that [Fisher] has valuable qualities. He is a constructor, very fertile and ingenious; he is not a strategist; he would be no use in command of a fleet . . . he has no doubt what the Americans call 'hustle'", and then went on to say that there was nothing extraordinary about him in this, and that others 'could do and were doing quite as well.'[27]

This short passage betrayed both Asquith's ignorance and his failure to understand either the urgency of the situation or his own inability to get to grips with it. Fisher and Jellicoe had drawn attention to facts that were of the greatest urgency; it 'amounted' to a great deal! Fisher was not merely a constructor; his ships from the *Dreadnought* to landing craft were devised for specific strategic and tactical purposes, and though he himself would be the last to claim the technical expertise of design, his ships showed his understanding of war and its developments. He had already shown his ability in command of a fleet and, though there might be better tacticians, there had perhaps never been a better Commander-in-Chief. 'Hustle' was surely what was needed, and to assert that others were doing as well is absurd.

Lloyd George was more realistic. Though not unduly impressed with his presentation of his case, he was decidedly so with his 'hustle'. 'If I were faced with a sudden emergency, I should feel, if Fisher were at the Admiralty, that everything would be done that could be done.'[28]

As long as Asquith remained Prime Minister Fisher would be given no responsible post. Asquith still enjoyed his afternoon bridge parties, his almost daily dinner parties and continued to write to Venetia Stanley during Cabinet meetings, allowing the argument to go on round him and then announcing, 'So-and-so is decided,' after which there was no further discussion.

Fisher was out in the cold and would remain there. He was deeply worried by the conduct of the war, the number of ships in the Mediterranean, the retention of half a million men in Egypt and Salonika. where they faced only two Austrian divisions, men who could be employed far more effectively elsewhere, and the number of merchant ships supporting them. He was still one of the very few who understood the threat of submarine warfare and the menace of zeppelins, which could now reach altitudes of 15,000 feet, and could, in clear weather, keep the German Command informed of British fleet movements, as well as spotting. Though he slightly exaggerated the qualities of zeppelins, the latest, *L.30*, was capable of 17,400 feet and had a speed of 62 mph. Beatty was as anxious as he:

'We cannot go on as in the past. . . . Our Zeppelin construction, about which the Chief of the War Staff wrote me 3½ months ago that they were building, but they would be no use *this war*!! How long do they take to build and how long do the War Staff think the war is going to last? Presumably about another three months!!'[29]

Fisher continued to correspond with many loyal friends. In November, 1916, when the U-boat campaign was obviously succeeding, he wrote to George Lambert (Civil Lord in Fisher's time, later Viscount):

'*Please burn all enclosed.* I arranged to make a speech of seventeen words in the House of Lords, and sent it to McKenna; but he entreats me not to do so, as it would have an absolutely fatal effect on our Allies. I rather think he showed my letter to Asquith. *Please burn this.* I heard from Jellicoe Last night; very pessimistic as to German submarines.'[30]

Lambert later commented:

'This letter is important. If Lord Fisher had not been dissuaded by McKenna from making that speech, it is more than probable that Lord Fisher would have been backed by Lord Northcliffe as First Sea Lord. The date was just before the fall of the Asquith Government and Northcliffe was all-powerful then.'[31]

Bacon believed it was fortunate that Fisher was not recalled, for by then his age made him unfit to cope with the immense load that fell on a wartime First Sea Lord, though he believed that, if he had been limited to strategic work, and the routine dealt with by others, his talents might have been utilized. If McKenna had again become First Lord, such an arrangement might have been come to, but it seems unlikely that Fisher's still vast energy could have been curbed and his field of activity restricted.

When Jellicoe became First Sea Lord, all chance of Fisher's return vanished, though Jellicoe seriously considered his re-employment as Third Sea Lord and consulted many of their mutual friends, who all agreed that the strain would be too much for a man of 75. 'Age was undoubtedly telling on Lord Fisher; his judgment was not what it had been; he himself felt as young as ever, but he was not the Fisher of 1904, or even of 1910.'[32]

The report of the Dardanelles Commission was published in 1917, and included:

'There can be no doubt that at the two meetings on 28th January Mr. Churchill strongly advocated the adoption of the Dardanelles enterprise. . . . Mr. Churchill knew of the opinions entertained by Lord Fisher, and Sir Arthur Wilson assented to an attack on the outer forts and to progressive operations thereafter up to the straits as far as might be found practicable, [but] had not done so with any great cordiality or enthusiasm. He ought, instead of urging Lord Fisher, as he seems to have done at the private meeting after luncheon on 28th January, to give a silent but manifestly reluctant assent to the undertaking, not merely have invited Lord Fisher and Sir Arthur Wilson to express their views freely to the Council, but further to have insisted on their doing so.'

The Minority Report of Walter Roch was even more explicit:

'The War Council concentrated their attention too much on the political ends . . . never had before them detailed staff estimates of men, munitions and material or definite plans showing them what military operations were possible.

'The War Council also underestimated without any real investigation the strength of the Turkish opposition . . . rejected without further consideration all previous opinions against a purely naval attack on forts. . . .

'Mr. Churchill failed to present fully to the War Council the opinions of his naval advisers, and this failure was due to his own strong personal opinion in favour of a naval attack. Mr. Churchill should have consulted the Board of Admiralty before such a large and novel departure in naval policy was undertaken.'[33]

Fisher spoke in the House of Lords for the second and last time:

'With your Lordships' permission I desire to make a personal statement. When our country is in great jeopardy, as she now is, it is not the time to tarnish great reputations, to asperse the dead and to discover our supposed weaknesses to the enemy; so I shall not discuss the Dardanelles Reports – I shall await the end of the war, when all the truth can be made known.'[34]

Fisher's dignity in both his speeches, his refusal to enter into ungracious slanging matches in wartime is to his credit and belies the malicious slander that his mind had given way. It was as clear as ever and, for a man of his age, lucid and brilliant. No man can be discredited by age, but reputation can be destroyed by those who write 'history' with a personal interest. Churchill wrote after the war: 'Generals and Admirals mutter "To break away from first-class war that only comes once in a hundred years, for an amphibious strategico-political manoeuvre of this kind" is nothing less than unprofessional.'[35]

Of this Bacon says, 'Few more inaccurate statements have ever been made in books on the war'. It was Churchill who, in the face of Kitchener's refusal to provide troops, attempted an absurd gamble using the Navy alone instead of amphibious war and one wonders if he ever re-read his words after the magnificently planned Normandy landings in 1944. If he had confined his arraignment to Kitchener it might have been fair, but to include Fisher is turning history on its head. Fisher passionately believed in amphibious warfare where it could be effective, not 3,500 miles away in some unplanned expedition against mountainous shores, whose success would have been a miracle, whose effect, if successful was conjectural and of whose pending execution the enemy had been amply warned. As Bacon put it:

'Let us, however, imagine ourselves in his place. He remembered his past successes: his phenomenal career, and his time as First Sea Lord when he had introduced his reforms, triumphed over objections and trampled on all obstructions. He appreciated to the full that he had returned to the Admiralty when disaster seemed to be rampant everywhere, by half a dozen telegrams and by the exercise of his indomitable personality, he had turned disaster into victory. He firmly believed that a great strategic coup could still be brought off, by using the Navy and the Army in conjunction, to threaten the north coast of Germany and force the enemy to detach a large number of men to deal with the threat. He saw the whole of the force he had built up for this purpose being dissipated in secondary operations, instead of being used in a concentrated attack close to home.'[36]

It was ironical that his plan for a landing on the north German coast was adopted by the enemy and on 28 March, 1917, he wrote to Lloyd George:

'I desire to call your earnest attention to the four enclosures herewith in reference to the imminent danger of the German High Sea Fleet convoying a large number of transports and taking a German army into the islands of Riga by sea, into the vicinity of Petrograd, thereby endangering the Russian capital – a deadly blow to Russia; and our Grand Fleet, with its unchallenged supremacy, condemned to be a passive spectator of such an appalling catastrophe.'[37]

This was quoted by George Lambert in the House of Commons and caused a stir, more than one member asking if Fisher's greatness was being wasted and whether his talents could not be of use to the country. Fisher knew how the war should be fought; he had been proved right time and time again. Age and damage to his reputation, from malice in some quarters and from the need for a scapegoat in others, kept him from active employment; he could only vent his frustration in writing letters to friends, former colleagues, members of the Government and the newspapers. He wrote again to Lloyd George urging that his scheme for attacking Antwerp from the sea should be reconsidered. He bombarded him with ideas on how to deal with submarines, how to use aircraft, how to entice the High Sea Fleet out to fight. All his ideas were realistic, though to those who did not know and understand him, his unfortunate habit of imitating in writing the exaggerated hyperbole he used in speech made them appear far from coolly thought out plans. At the end of July, 1917, he wrote:

'Had my recent letter of 12th June to the Prime Minister been acted upon at once, the late successful German attack on the Yser would have been forestalled and the disastrous catastrophe that befell us (in the loss of thousands of our brave troops) then would have been avoided. But Alas! this war from the very beginning has been waged on a political basis, and no far-flung strategic scheme has ever been elaborated and pertinaciously adhered to. The principle has been lost sight of that the decisive theatre of the war was in the North and that the Baltic shore was the key to the war. . . . No war scheme that involves a year's preparation stands a chance! Some new political fad turns up and wrecks it! And yet it is only by the long and studious preparation of a huge, rapidly, specially built Armada that the Navy can come into the war and finish the war . . . It is just exasperating that with our really astounding naval supremacy the Admiralty policy should be to "hold the ring". And now we have the whole American Fleet to help us! . . . So far as the British Navy is concerned the British Army might as well be in Timbuctoo! And yet never in history was the opportunity so great as in the present war for a great amphibious operation in northern waters, and one so absolutely certain to end the war! But politics have guided the war and sent our expeditionary force in 1914 to France and Mons instead of Antwerp and Victory!'[38]

Robin Prior has shown that *The World Crisis* was written as self-justification, not as history.[39] In particular the events of 1914–15 are related with a view to exculpation for the mismanagement of the war and especially the Dardanelles fiasco, by selective quotation, omission of passages detrimental to Churchill, and by the clever use of ambiguity to lead the reader to draw conclusions that were not justified by the facts. But Churchill's talent in the use of English and his retention in private hands of official documents give an impression of scholarly impartiality which has caused many historians to use the book as a primary source. At the time he wrote, much of the documentation was inaccessible to the public and fact could not be disentangled from fiction. In the meantime a huge volume of material has repeated the Gospel according to Churchill and has then been requoted to support his views, so that the incestuous nature of historical writing has led to its acceptance as unimpeachable fact.

Many of the leading figures were still living when Churchill and his disciples wrote, and the libel laws made it inadvisable for writers to represent fully the parts they played. Others, too, wrote self defensive memoirs, claiming innocence or laying the blame on others. It was the dead on whom most of the blame could be laid with impunity. Kitchener and Fisher stand out in this respect. Kitchener's death in 1916 and that of Fisher in 1920 left the field clear for calumny.

For a maritime nation to fail to use its greatest asset, sea power, and outflank its enemy, to concentrate on a continental war of attrition was, from a national point of view, a mistaken policy. It was largely due to the dominating influence of the Army in political and social circles. When, during the Agadir Crisis, Henry Wilson presented his plan for fighting on the French left, pushing the enemy back like a rugby scrum, to where they came from, and 'killing Germans', he presented a *fait accompli* without consulting the Navy on the way in which the Services could work together. Arthur Wilson's incoherence and failure to present any detailed plans to achieve his ill-considered ideas for the occupation of Borkum and the capture of Heligoland, his failure to develop the Baltic scheme, left only the French strategy. and the politicians failed utterly to perform their basic duty, to consider the various schemes put before them and ensure that the best went forward. When Haldane threatened resignation unless a staff was created in the Admiralty he did so, not to achieve mutual cooperation, but to force the Admiralty merely to provide a service for the Army. Even after the Battle of the Marne, when trenches ran from Switzerland to the sea, only Fisher produced realistic strategies, one of which was cast aside by Churchill in his obsession with the Dardanelles, a scheme rendered hopeless by Kitchener's refusal to cooperate and even more so by Churchill's determination, against sound expert advice, to achieve it without troops.

Fisher too must take a share in the blame for his failure to create a staff. He trusted no staff, and, as we have seen, he had good reason : Hulbert, Campbell and others, some still unidentified, had proved disloyal, and Wemyss's refusal to accept a confidential post on a confidential basis was a classic example of the attitude of the day. Fisher had modernized the Navy, taken away the privilege, glitter and glory, and substituted hard graft; he had gone a long way to replace nepotism by promotion by merit alone and by so doing had lowered the social status of a Service that was becoming a parasitic tentacle of the rich and noble. Every effort was made to destroy his power and influence, so that the Service could preen itself in the glory of its paintwork and polish. It is doubtful if Fisher could have achieved a full staff organization no matter how hard he tried, for, as Vice-Admiral K.G.B.Dewar, who described Fisher's reforms as 'half-baked', so bitterly complained, no effective attempt at training staff officers had been made even after Fisher started the Staff College at Portsmouth, since there was little real talent available to run courses, and what there was was required in operational posts. If Fisher could have devoted more time to the matter, things might have been different, but the huge volume of reforms he introduced were enough to occupy any man to the full.

Churchill emerges as the only politician with an active determination to fight the war on Allied terms, rather than merely by sheer weight on the Western Front. He saw the stalemate like many others, but tried to do something about it. He supported Fisher's Baltic scheme and went on doing so even when the Dardanelles operation was in full swing. He saw the strategic value of Antwerp and, though he much overrated his own ability, at least he tried to save the city. He saw the danger to Ostend and, with the approval of both Fisher and French, he tried to achieve a flanking attack. His greatest mistake was in taking out of context one paragraph of Fisher's Dardanelles plan. In January there were only 9,000 Turks defending Gallipoli and, without the warning bombardment, it could then have been taken by the Army and Navy together. If the guns and forts had been taken from behind, the Navy could have penetrated the Dardanelles and a combined attack on Constantinople might have changed the course of the war. By the time Churchill succeeded in forcing Kitchener to agree to a military operation it was too late; the attack could never then have been anything but a dismal failure.

Who do we blame for the horrors of Gallipoli? The greatest blame must inevitably be placed on the politicians whose assumption of polymathy led them to treat with contempt the opinions of those whose specialist knowledge was much greater than theirs, and even to consider the First Sea Lord's protest at the crucial meeting of the War Cabinet as a 'remarkable interruption'. By far the largest single share must be borne by Asquith. He never appreciated until far too late that the war was a serious business that transcended party politics. Like many another, he believed it would 'all be over by Christmas'. His ineffectual failure to take charge of his ministers, his failure as a chairman of Cabinet and War Council meetings, his preoccupation with his social life and political future, all contributed in no small measure to the terrible failure. He knew Fisher's views at an early stage, but preferred to ignore them, and neither demanded that the First Sea Lord should be heard nor tried to explain them himself. Indeed there is evidence that he tried to conceal them so as to avoid a breach with his impetuous young colleague. Of necessity, the buck stopped with him. His Cabinet colleagues share the blame, for anyone present at the War Council meeting in 28 January, 1915, could hardly fail to know that Fisher violently disagreed. Their duty was to probe his opinions. None did.

But out of the ruins, the misery, the incompetence came benefit in the long term. When Churchill became Prime Minister in 1940 he had learnt much from his experience in the First World War. He put politics aside, formed a coalition Government, introduced real security and inter-service planning, by perhaps mistakenly substituting a Ministry of Defence for a Minister for Coordination of Defence, becoming his own minister. Though his first choice was a bad one, he ultimately chose the right man as Chief of Combined Operations. Above all, he gave the country the leadership so desperately needed.

And Fisher was his tutor.

11

EPITAPH

When he left the Admiralty in 1915 Fisher's wish to get away from London led him to seek shelter with the Duke of Hamilton at Lennoxlove, in Lothian. The Duke asked him to become a trustee of the Hamilton estates, which had become much run down, a situation complicated by the late Duke's will. Fisher took on the task with a vigour that would take his mind off public affairs.

During the final period of his life he wrote repeatedly to *The Times* denouncing, in his inimitable style, the policies of the Government and the Admiralty. The letters became known as the 'Scrap the Lot Letters'. But almost everything he suggested was realized, though in some cases not until the latter half of the twentieth century.

Fisher lost his wife in July, 1918, after 52 years of happy marriage. She had been of immense support to him throughout his turbulent years and had always effaced herself to enable him to progress in his remarkable career, encouraging and succouring him. He at once took on the responsibility of nursing her until her death and her loss affected him deeply.

At Christmas, 1919, Fisher organized a party of friends to visit the South of France. At Monte Carlo he felt unwell and returned home, where three operations were performed. He wrote, characteristically, before the first: 'No mourning, no flowers and the nearest cemetery'. His life dragged on for six months and he died on 10 July, 1920.

Even his last wish was denied him, though perhaps he would have been pleased, for he was given a state funeral and service in Westminster Abbey, to which he had so often retreated in times of crisis and misgiving to consult his God, in whom he had utter faith, and to seek His guidance. No one deserved the honour more. Even if the politicians and some fellow naval officers derided him, conspired against him, frustrated him, the British public recognized how much they owed him. Every inch of the way was thronged with people who stood bareheaded in silent respect as the coffin was hauled on a gun carriage by the sailors he loved and who loved him, from St James's Square, along Pall Mall, past the palace of the three monarchs he had served so well, down the Mall, through Admiralty Arch, past the offices in which he had made so many momentous decisions, past the column bearing the effigy of the man who had inspired him since boyhood, whose biography he had read at the age of 12, past the Cenotaph, in place, but not yet unveiled, through Parliament Square to the Abbey.

The pallbearers included Jellicoe, Jackson, Bridgeman, King-Hall, Henderson, Moore, Thursby and Bacon, who had all shared so much of his triumphs and disasters. *The Times* of 14 July wrote:

> 'Yesterday morning the mortal remains of Admiral of the Fleet Lord Fisher of Kilverstone, GCB, OM, GCVO were borne in solemn state to Westminster Abbey, where in the presence of a vast congregation representing all that is most eminent in national life, an august ceremonial celebrated the passing of a great spirit from the earthly scene of its stupendous labours.
>
> 'And yesterday morning the British public showed that it loved and mourned one 'Jacky Fisher'. There is no surer test of public feeling than the size and the behaviour of the crowd in the streets. Till the last weeks of his long and bellicose life, Lord Fisher was a stormy petrel, bringing the tempest he rejoiced in. Behind him he had, at first, no one; behind him, he had, in those later years the whole solid affection and admiration of the people. And yesterday morning the people, in its silent, stolid, reverent British way, wrote its affection and admiration for 'Jacky Fisher' upon the social history of our time.'

And 'the Viscount Jellicoe of Scapa freely and unmistakably wept'.

Fisher's remains were buried in the little local churchyard at Kilverstone next to those of his wife. There is no statue in London, no memorial in Westminster Abbey nor in St Paul's. The Duchess of Hamilton put one in the little church at Berwick St. John, near the Duke's property at Ferne House in Wiltshire, but the nation has not bothered to honour the man who served his country so long and so well, without whom Jellicoe would certainly have 'lost the war in an afternoon'. Epstein made a magnificent bust of the man, with all his characteristics; it is housed in Glasgow, not in London, that knew him so well.

Jacky Fisher joined the Navy in the days of sail, for steam was then only an auxiliary. The guns were still the old smooth-bores, cast iron or bronze, loaded down the muzzle, recognizable to Nelson, who died less than half a century before, and even to Drake. There had been minor improvements in sighting, but essentially ships' gunnery consisted in pointing the guns in the general direction of the enemy and hoping. Ranges had not increased at all. It was

Fisher who changed all that; it was he who saw how things were to go. It was he who as captain of *Excellent*, dragged the Navy into the nineteenth century. It was he who as Director of Naval Ordnance, Controller, Second Sea Lord and First Sea Lord painfully lashed it into the twentieth. It was he who unleashed Percy Scott to change gunnery from guesswork into a science, and Dreyer to continue that work. It was he who saw the effect all this was to have on tactics, who not only foresaw, but engineered the change to the fast all-big-gun battleship, who designed the new fleet. As a gunnery officer he saw the influence the mine and torpedo were to have and achieved, almost by brute force, a separate specialization. He fired the Navy and the Admiralty with enthusiasm and despite bitter opposition, despite Custance's tortuous arguments against change, Beresford's vainglorious manoeuvrings for power and magnificence, despite the pompous outpourings of peacetime admirals, most of whom had never seen a shot fired in anger, many of whom reached their high rank through patronage and nepotism, or even on the retired list, and pontificated that the navy was going to the dogs because gunnery took precedence over paintwork. He had inspired and achieved the introduction of the turbine and oil fuel against vested interests and bitter arguments. He had recognized the need for technological personnel of a high order and in equality with the 'military' officer, whose education he changed from haphazard ignorance, at least to some learning. He had swept away privilege, the atmosphere of a gentlemen's club in which it was bad taste to study the profession of naval warfare, the supercilious attitude of the wealthy and well-connected classes, who regarded the Navy, as much as the Army, as a spare-time occupation to provide amusement for those they thought had a God-given talent for leadership because of their social position.

Fisher stands out like a mountain on a plain of ordinary men. He had seen all his prophetic prewar reasoning fulfilled, his foresight realized. He had identified the submarines as weapons of the future when other men thought them playthings, had foreseen the German U-boat campaign and recognized that war would be fought in bestial ways which other men believed impossible, but in a few years dwarfed in brutality by the murder of men, women and children, because they did not belong to a 'master race'. He had foretold, years ahead, the date of the outbreak of war, to within two months. He had manoeuvred to get Jellicoe to command the Grand Fleet exactly on time – not perhaps the ideal man, but undeniably the best available in those amateurish days. He had worked out a simple method of striking at the heart of Germany, which could have brought the war to an early end. His support for a combined operation at the Dardanelles as second best had been unstinted, but his opposition to the campaign as a navy-only operation was vindicated by events. Few knowledgeable naval and military historians have failed to condemn the Dardanelles adventure and the Gallipoli campaign that stemmed from it. Even Churchill admitted in the end:

'Looking back, with after-knowledge and increasing years, I seem to have been too ready to undertake tasks which were hazardous or even forlorn.[1]

'. . . as a mere politician and civilian, I would never have agreed to the Dardanelles project if I had not believed in it, I would have done my utmost to break it down in argument and to marshal opinion against it. Had I been in Lord Fisher's position and held his views I would have refused point blank. There was no need for him to resign. *Only the First Sea Lord can order the ships to steam and the guns to fire.*' (my italics)[2]

Stephen Roskill says that 'Churchill's admiration for the elder Pitt . . . and his study of his ancestor Marlborough's campaigns and strategy probably contributed to his lively and enduring interest in amphibious operations and in "peripheral strategy".'[3] Perhaps. But Churchill met Fisher four years before he became First Lord, and Fisher's admiration for Pitt and belief in amphibious warfare had developed while Churchill was 'still in his cradle'. The Army was a 'projectile to be fired by the Navy'. It was Fisher more than anyone else who convinced Churchill of this philosophy of war.

Fisher had been derided, insulted, conspired against by those who thought they had a divine right to high places, often because they hated change merely because it was change. But it took the politician Churchill to damage his reputation more permanently. Fisher's management of the Admiralty as First Sea Lord was dictatorial, but the opposition could only be overcome by such means. He was not guilty of being wrong; he was guilty of a much worse offence – he was right. So he had to be destroyed. The stature of the man was too great for this. So other means to discredit him had to be found. Balfour wrote: 'Winston has written a book about himself and called it *The World Crisis*'. It was primarily Churchill in his book about himself that discredited Fisher.

Like most other naval officers, Fisher was politically naïve. He was impatient, blunt, ruthless and artless to the point of foolhardiness, and made enemies; he never suffered fools gladly. His judgment of character was outstanding (one of Churchill's weakest points). He sought no honours; in his latter years he had as many as the most ambitious could seek, even though his desire for a Viscountcy might indicate otherwise. But it will be remembered that he dropped the matter very quickly.

On top of the great sadness of losing his wife came the final insult. When the German fleet surrendered and made its way to Scapa Flow, many of the great figures prominent in the allied cause were invited to witness the unique ceremony. Fisher, the chief architect of that surrender was, like Jellicoe, not invited.

Fisher never sought to justify himself nor did he even carry out his threat to comment on the Dardanelles Report after the war had ended, 'when all the truth can be made known'. He started to prepare his papers for his memoirs but soon lost interest. The Duchess of Hamilton, who believed in his greatness, persuaded him to write two books, *Records* and *Memories,* but neither was a systematically prepared volume. Both were mere ramblings dictated at odd moments to the Duchess, who attempted, against his wishes to turn them into some sort of order. Beresford died while they were being prepared and Fisher at once expunged all references to his old antagonist; *de mortuis nil nisi bonum.*

'Oh Jacky! – well Jacky is splendid – simply splendid!'

SOURCE NOTES

Chapter 1. J'Ordonne, ou Je Me Tais. (pp 1–26)

1. Admiral Sir Reginald Bacon, *Lord Fisher,* p.103.
2. Marder, *Fear God,* Vol II, p.218–9.
3. Churchill, *The World Crisis,* p.54–5.
4. Gretton, Vice-Admiral Sir Peter, *Former Naval Person,* p.70.
5. Cited in Marder, *Fear God* Vol. II , p.297.
6. Bacon, *Fisher,* Vol. II, p.119.
7. Cited in Marder, *Fear God* Vol. II, p.298.
8. Fisher, *Memories,* p.195.
9. Ibid, p.200.
10. Bacon, *Fisher,* Vol. II, p.126.
11. *Ibid.*
12. Archer-Shee, a cadet at Osborne was wrongly accused of stealing. His father won a court action on his behalf and the resulting stir was an embarrassment to the Government.
13. Bacon, *Fisher,* Vol. II, p.128.
14. *Ibid,* p.133.
15. *Ibid,* p.134.
16. Hankey, *Supreme Command,* p.87.
17. Dreyer, *The Sea Heritage,* p.52.
18. Maurice, Major-General Sir Frederick, *Haldane,* p.283.
19. Churchill, *The World Crisis,* p.985.
20. Gretton, Vice Admiral Sir Peter, *Former Naval Person,* p.86.
21. Gardiner, *The Royal Oak Courts Martial,* p.18.
22. Bacon, *Fisher,* Vol. II, p.137.
23. Brock, Michael and Eleanor, (Ed.). *H. H. Asquith, Letters to Venetia Stanley,*
24. Churchill, Randolph, *Winston S. Churchill,* Vol. II, p.531–2.
25. *Ibid,* p.533.
26. *Ibid,* p 534.
27. Churchill, World *Crisis,* p.42–46.
28. Churchill, Randolph, *Winston S. Churchill,* Vol. II, p.535–6.
29. Haldane, *Autobiography,* p.
30. Lee, *King Edward VII: A Biography,* Vol. II, p.534.

31. Churchill, World *Crisis*, p.53.
32. Churchill to Fisher, 25 October, 1911, *Lennoxlove Manuscripts*, 534.
33. Fisher to Esher, 29th October 1911 Fisher, *Memories*, p.206.
34. *Ibid.* 9th November, 1911.
35. Churchill, Randolph, *Winston S. Churchill*, Vol. II, p.546.
36. Sturdee papers, cited in Gretton, *Former Naval Person*, p.71.
37. Churchill, World *Crisis*, p.56.
38. Fisher to Esher, December1911, Fisher, *Memories*, p.207.
39. Hart, Liddell, *A History of the World War, 1914–18*, p.63.
40. Fisher to Esher, 20th September, 1911, Fisher, *Memories*, p.203.
41. *Ibid.*
42. Kemp, *Fisher Papers*, (NRS) Vol. II, p.358.
43. Repington, *The First World War 1914–1918*, Vol. I, p.11–12.
44. Ellison, Lieutenant-General Sir Gerald, *The Perils of Amateur Strategy*, p.5–6.
45. Tirpitz, Grand Admiral Von, *My Memoirs*, Vol. II, p.368–9.
46. Roskill, *Churchill and the Admirals*, p.93.
47. Churchill, Winston, *The Second World War*, Vol. I, p.363–4.
48. *Ibid*, p.364.
49. *Ibid*, p.550–2.
50. Churchill, Randolph, *Winston S. Churchill*, Vol. II, p.530.
51. Churchill, World *Crisis*, p.32.
52. Briggs, *Naval Administrations*, p.189–90.
53. *Spectator*, 24 October, 1911.
54. Esher, *Journals*, Vol. III p.74.
55. Lord Riddell, *War Diary*, 5 December 1912.
56. Churchill, *World Crisis*, p.51.
57. Churchill, Randolph, *Winston S. Churchill*, Vol. II, p.628.
58. de Chair, Admiral Sir Dudley, *The Sea is Strong*, p.142.
59. Churchill, *World Crisis*, p.65.
60. Ranft, B. McL. (Ed.) *Beatty Papers*, (NRS) letter to his wife, 27 May 1912, p.46.
61. Marder, Dreadnought Vol. I, p.254.
62. Sandars to Balfour, October 1912, Balfour papers.
63. Jellicoe's autobiographical notes Addl. MSS 49038.
64. Marder, *Dreadnought* Vol. I, p.255.
65. de Chair, *The Sea is Strong*, p.140–49.
66. Churchill, *World Crisis*, p.60.
67. *Ibid*, p.56–7.
68. Cited in Marder, *Fear God* Vol. II , p.417–8.
69. *Ibid*, p.419.
70. Fisher to Esher, *Memories*, p.207.
71. Cited in Marder, *Fear God* Vol. II , p.418.
72. *Ibid*, p.416.
73. *Ibid*, p.425.

Chapter 2. Cicerone (pp 27–49)

1. Marder, *Dreadnought,* Vol. I, p 266.
2. Churchill, *World Crisis,* p.69.
3. Corbett, Julian, *Naval Operations,* Vol. I, p.18.
4. Churchill, Randolph, *Winston S Churchill,* Vol. II, p.601–2.
5. Cited in Marder, *Fear God* Vol. II. p.402.
6. Buller's defeat in a frontal attack to relieve Ladysmith.
7. Cited in Marder, *Fear God* Vol. II. p.451–2.
8. *The Times,* 2nd March, 1912.
9. Cited in Marder, *Fear God* Vol. II. p.458.
10. Churchill, Randolph, *Winston S Churchill,* Vol. II, p.567.
11. Ranft, (Ed) *The Beatty Papers,* (NRS) Vol. 1 p.45.
12. Bacon, *Fisher,* Vol. II, p.152–3.
13. *Ibid,* p.153.
14. Fisher, *Records* , p.192.
15. Cited in Marder, *Fear God* Vol. II p.482–3.
16. *Royal Commission on Oil Fuel: First Report with Proceedings,* 24 September, 1912 to 14 January, 1913, pp. 386–403.
17. Churchill, Winston, *The Second World War,* Vol. V, p.516.
18. Cited in Marder, *Fear God* Vol. II. p.352.
19. Bacon, *Fisher,* Vol. II, p.127.
20. Cited in Marder, *Fear God* Vol. II. p.469.
21. Mackay, *Fisher,* p.443.
22. *Lennoxlove Papers* 413.
23. Cited in Marder, *Fear God* Vol. II. p.485.
24. *Ibid,* p.486.
25. *Ibid,* p.489, Note.
26. *Ibid,* p.488–9.
27. *Ibid,* p.486.
28. *Lennoxlove Papers* No 4290.
29. Mackay, *Fisher,* p.449–50.
30. *Ibid,* p.450.
31. Cited in Marder, *Fear God* Vol. II. p.492.
32. *Ibid,* p.494–5.
33. *Lennoxlove Papers,* 763.
34. Keyes, *The Naval Memoirs,* Vol. I, p.53.
35. Churchill, World *Crisis,* p.692–3.
36. Cited in Marder, *Fear God* Vol. II. p.499, Note.
37. Mackay, *Fisher,* p.453.
38. Cited in Marder, *Fear God* Vol. II. p.504–5.
39. Mackay, *Fisher,* p.453.
40. Cited in Marder, *Fear God* Vol. II. p.507.
41. *Lennoxlove Papers,* 794, 10 February, 1914.
42. Marder, *Dreadnought* Vol. I , p.261.

43. Churchill, Randolph, *Winston S Churchill*, Vol., II, p.645–6.
44. *Ibid*, p.630.
45. Gretton, *Former Naval Person*, p.93.
46. Marder, *From the Dreadnought to Scapa Flow*, Vol. I , p.259.
47. Churchill, Randolph, *Winston S Churchill*, Vol., II, p.501.
48. Dreyer to Jellicoe, 23 July, 1916, CID Historical section.
49. Churchill, Randolph, *Winston S Churchill*, Vol. II p.611.
50. *Ibid*, p.612.
51. Cited in Marder, *Fear God* Vol. II, p.420.
52. Churchill, *World Crisis*, p.95.
53. *Ibid*, p.172, Note.
54. *Ibid*, p.95–96.
55. Churchill, Randolph, *Winston S Churchill*, Vol. II, p.611.
56. Cited in Marder, *Fear God* Vol. II, p.403.

Chapter 3. The Wicked Folly of it all (pp 50–66)

1. Esher, *The Tragedy of Lord Kitchener*, p.18.
2. *Ibid*, p.20.
3. The German *Official History of the War at Sea*.
4. Churchill, *World* Crisis, p.159–60.
5. de Chair, *The Sea is Strong*, p.158–9.
6. Churchill, *World Crisis*, p.166.
7. Jordan, Gerald (Ed.), *Naval Warfare in the Twentieth Century*, p.68.
8. Van de Vat, *The Ship that Changed the World*, p.650 and Churchill, World *Crisis* p.180.
9. Churchill, *World Crisis*, p.180.
10. *Ibid*, p.181.
11. *Ibid*.
12. Tirpitz, *My Memoirs*, Vol. II, p.349.
13. Churchill, *World Crisis*, p.182.
14. *Ibid*, p.183.
15. *Ibid*.
16. Tirpitz, *My Memoirs*, Vol. II, p.349.
17. *Ibid*, p.350.
18. Jordan, Gerald (Ed.), *Naval Warfare in the Twentieth Century*, p.68.
19. Tirpitz, *My Memoirs*, Vol. II, p.350.
20. Esher, *The Tragedy of Lord Kitchener*, p.29.
21. Taylor, A J P, *The First World War: an Illustrated History*, p.29.
22. Ibid.
23. Esher, *Journals*, Vol. III, p.175.
24. Kemp, (Ed) *Fisher Papers* (NRS) Vol. II, p.350–1.
25. Castlereagh, *Memorandum on a Maritime Peace* .
26. Churchill, World *Crisis*, p.299.
27. Hankey, *Supreme Command*, p.203.

28. Brock, Michael and Eleanor, (Ed.) *Asquith Letters to Venetia Stanley.*
29. Churchill, *World Crisis*, p.307.
30. Esher, *The Tragedy of Lord Kitchener*, p.67.
31. Hankey, *Supreme Command*, p.204.
32. Martin, Hugh, *Battle; the Life Story of the Rt. Hon. Winston S. Churchill*, p.110.
33. Beaverbrook, *Politicians and the War*, p.45–6.
34. Brock, Michael and Eleanor, (Ed.) *Asquith Letters to Venetia Stanley.*
35. Beaverbrook, *Politicians and the War.* p 45.
36. Hankey, *Supreme Command*, p.194.
37. Brett, *Journals and Letters of Viscount Esher*, Vol. III, p.184.
38. Churchill, *World Crisis*, p.330.
39. Marder, *Portrait of an Admiral*, p.111–2.
40. Marder, *Dreadnought*, Vol. II, p.84.
41. *Ibid.*
42. Brock, Michael and Eleanor, (Ed.) *Asquith Letters to Venetia Stanley*, p.275.

Chapter 4. *Lui Seul* (pp 67–86)
1. Churchill, *World Crisis*, p.331.
2. Dan Foley, Coastguardsman, former Chief Yeoman of Signals to the Author in private conversation.
3. Churchill, *World Crisis*, p.350.
4. *Ibid*, p.276.
5. Keyes, Admiral of the Fleet Sir Roger, *The Naval Memoirs*, p.77.
6. Churchill, *World Crisis*, p.276.
7. *Ibid*, p.276–7.
8. Gretton, *Former Naval Person*, p.175.
9. Churchill, *World Crisis*, p.277.
10. *Ibid*, p.278.
11. *Ibid*, p.279.
12. Repington, *The First World War, 1914–1918*, p.46–47.
13. Marder, *Portrait of an Admiral*, p.110.
14. Brock, Michael and Eleanor, (Ed.) *Asquith Letters to Venetia Stanley*, p.253.
15. Marder, *Portrait of an Admiral*, p.109.
16. Keyes, Admiral of the Fleet Sir Roger, *The Naval Memoirs*, p.110.
17. Brock, Michael and Eleanor, (Ed.) *Asquith Letters to Venetia Stanley*, p.290.
18. Churchill, *World Crisis*, p.357.
19. Marder, *Dreadnought* Vol. II, p.85.
20. Cited in Marder, *Fear God* Vol. II, p.302.
21. Hamilton MSS.
22. Cited in Marder, *Fear God* Vol. III, p.100.
23. Churchill, *World Crisis*, p.360.
24. *Ibid*, p.361.
25. Ranft, (Ed), *The Beatty Papers* (NRS) Vol. I ,p.153.
26. Callwell, Major General, *Experiences of a Dug-Out, 1914–1918* p.121–22.

27. Brock, Michael and Eleanor, (Ed.) *Asquith Letters to Venetia Stanley*, p.290.
28. *Ibid*, p.294.
29. Ranft, (Ed), *The Beatty Papers* (NRS) Vol. I ,p.151.
30. Wemyss, *The Life and Letters of Lord Wester Wemyss*. p.186.
31. Beaverbrook, *Politicians and the War*, p.105.
32. Churchill, *World Crisis*, p.361–2.
33. Bacon, *Fisher*, Vol. II, p.160–61.
34. Brock, Michael and Eleanor, (Ed.) *Asquith Letters to Venetia Stanley*, p.305.
35. Bacon, *Fisher*, Vol. II, p.172.
36. Marder, *Dreadnought*, Vol. II, p.106.
37. *Ibid.*
38. *Ibid.*
39. Churchill, *World Crisis*, p.366–7.
40. *Ibid*, p.367–8.
41. *Ibid*, p.368–9.
42. Marder, *Dreadnought*, Vol. II, p.110.
43. Churchill, *World Crisis*, p.371.
44. Brock, Michael and Eleanor, (Ed.) *Asquith Letters to Venetia Stanley*, p.309.
45. Ranft, (Ed), *The Beatty Papers* (NRS) Vol. I, p.159.
46. Marder, *Portrait of an Admiral*, p.113.
47. Bennett, *Naval Battles of the First World War*, p.90.
48. *Ibid*, p.91.
49. Churchill, *World Crisis*, p.388.
50. Bacon, *Fisher*, Vol. II, p.177.
51. Bennett, *Naval Battles of the First World War*, p.112.
52. Marder, *Portrait of an Admiral*, p.130.
53. Brock, Michael and Eleanor, (Ed.) *Asquith Letters to Venetia Stanley*, p.340.
54. Bennett, *Naval Battles of the First World War*, p.112–3.
55. *Ibid*, p.113.
56. *Ibid.*
57. *Ibid.*
58. Bacon, *Fisher*, Vol. II, p.178.
59. Fisher, *Memories*, p.136.
60. Farrere et Chack, *Combats et Bataille sur Mer.*

Chapter 5. The Old Broom (pp 87–104)

1. Jellicoe, *The Grand Fleet, 1914–1916* p.153.
2. Dreyer, *The Sea Heritage*, p.81.
3. Cmd. 83, 4 April 1910, p.66.
4. Keyes, The Naval Memoirs, p.53–55.
5. Churchill, *World Crisis*, Appendix B, p.1383.
6. Aspinall-Oglander, *Roger Keyes*, p.104.
7. Churchill, *World Crisis*, p.410.
8. *Ibid.*

9. Hough, Richard, *Former Naval Person*, p.53.
10. Churchill, *World Crisis*, p.411.
11. *Ibid*, p.412.
12. *Ibid*, p.413.
13. Ibid.
14. *Ibid*, p.702-03.
15. Bradford, Admiral Sir Edward, *Admiral of the Fleet Sir Arthur Knyvet Wilson*, p.235-238.
16. *Ibid*, p.493.
17. Hankey, *Supreme Command*, p.170.
18. Repington, *The First World War, 1914–1918*, Vol. 1, p.25–26.
19. Bacon, *Fisher*, Vol. II, p.188.
20. Mackay, *Balfour, Intellectual Statesman*, p.271.
21. Hankey, *Supreme Command*, p.194.
22. Kemp, (Ed.) *Fisher Papers*, (NRS) Vol. II, p.349–50.
23. Esher, to Oliver Brett, 5 September, 1914, *Journals*. III, p.184.
24. Esher, *The Tragedy of Lord Kitchener*, p.12.
25. Grey, *Twenty-five years*, p.68–9.
26. Churchill, *World Crisis*, p.479.
27. *Ibid*. p.480.
28. *Ibid*.
29. War Council Minutes, 4th Meeting, December 1st 1914.
30. Bacon, *Fisher*, Vol. II, p.192.
31. Churchill, *World Crisis*, p.480.
32. Kemp, (Ed.) *Fisher Papers*, (NRS) Vol. II, p.347–9.
33. James, *A Great Seaman: the Life of Admiral of the Fleet Sir Henry Oliver*, p.137–8.
34. *Ibid*, p.144.
35. Churchill, *World Crisis*, p.484–5.
36. *Ibid*, p.485–6.
37. Ellison, *The Perils of Amateur Strategy*, p.5–6.
38. Bacon, *Fisher*, Vol. II, p.194.
39. *Ibid*, p.193.
40. Tirpitz, *Memoirs*, Vol. II, p.368–9.
41. *New York Times*, 30 June, 1919.
42. Tirpitz, *Memoirs*, Vol. II, p.373 Note 1.
43. Roskill *Churchill and the Admirals*, p.93.
44. Churchill, Winston, *The Second World War*, Vol. I p.363–4.
45. *Ibid*, p. 364.
46. *Ibid*, Appendix G, p.550–2.

Chapter 6. Breaking the Deadlock (pp 105–127)
1. Churchill, *World Crisis*, p.501.
2. Cited in Marder, *Fear God* Vol. III, p.124.
3. Churchill, *World Crisis*, p.501–2.

4. Fisher, *Memories,* p.124.
5. Churchill, *World Crisis,* p.288.
6. Brock, Michael and Eleanor, (Ed.) *Asquith Letters to Venetia Stanley,* p.284.
7. Beaverbrook, *Men and Power,* p.151.
8. *Hansard,* 4th Series. vol. LXVIII, Col. 1594–5.
9. Brock, Michael and Eleanor, (Ed.) *Asquith Letters to Venetia Stanley,* p.285.
10. *Morning Post,* 19 October, 1914.
11. Brock, Michael and Eleanor, (Ed.) *Asquith Letters to Venetia Stanley,* p.387–8.
12. Churchill, *World Crisis,* p.486.
13. *Ibid,* p.450.
14. Cunningham of Hyndhope, Admiral of the Fleet Lord, *A Sailor's Odyssey,* p.59.
15. Cited in Marder, *Fear God* Vol. III, p.107.
16. Somervell, *The Reign of King George the Fifth, and English Chronicle,* p.121.
17. Corbett, Julian, *Naval Operations,* Vol. II, p.67.
18. Churchill, *World Crisis,* p.488.
19. Hindenburg, Marshal Von, *Out of My Life,* p.294.
20. Churchill, *World Crisis,* p.527.
21. *Ibid,* p.528.
22. *Ibid.*
23. *Ibid,* p.529.
24. *Ibid.*
25. *Ibid,* p.529–30.
26. Corbett, *Naval Operations,* Vol. II, p.64.
27. Bacon, *Fisher,* Vol. II, p.202–3 and Churchill, World *Crisis,* p.530–31.
28. Churchill, *World Crisis,* p.530.
29. Bacon, *Fisher,* Vol. II, p.203.
30. Cited in Marder, *Fear God* Vol. II p.84.
31. Churchill, *World Crisis,* p.531.
32. *Ibid.*
33. Corbett, *Naval Operations,* Vol. II, p.65.
34. *Ibid,* p.105.
35. Macksey, Piers, *The War in the Mediterranean,* p.160–1.
36. *Ibid,* p.176–7.
37. Chatterton, E Keble, *Dardanelles Dilemma: The Story of the Naval Operations,* p.114.
38. ADM. 116/208. NMM
39. Marder, *Anatomy ,* p.156.
40. Churchill, *World Crisis,* p.533.
41. Bacon, *Fisher,* Vol. II, p.206.
42. Churchill, *World Crisis,* p.533.
43. *Ibid* p.534.
44. *Ibid.*
45. Hankey, *Supreme Command,* p.261–2.
46. Churchill, *World Crisis,* p.540.

47. *Ibid.*
48. *Ibid,* p.541–2.
49. *Ibid,* p.542.
50. Hankey, *Supreme Command,* p.265.
51. *Ibid,* p.265–6.
52. *Dardanelles Commission Report,* I par. p.53.
53. Churchill, *World Crisis,* p.543.
54. War Council, Secretary's notes, *Cabinet Papers* 22/1.
55. Hankey, *Supreme Command,* p.267.

Chapter 7. The Dardanelles (pp 128–163)
1. Churchill, *World Crisis,* p.551.
2. *Ibid.*
3. *bid,* p.552.
4. *Ibid,* p.549, Note.
5. Cited in Marder, *Fear God* Vol. III, p.133.
6. *Ibid,* p.141–2.
7. Roskill, *Hankey Man of Secrets,* Vol. I, p.374.
8. *Hansard,* 5th series, Vol. XCI, Col. 1762,
9. Churchill, *World Crisis,* p.581.
10. Ibid, p.582–3.
11. *Ibid,* p.553.
12. Cited in Marder, *Fear God* Vol. III, p.147–8.
13. *Ibid,* p.149.
14. Churchill, *World Crisis,* p.589.
15. Brock, Michael and Eleanor, (Ed.) *Asquith Letters to Venetia Stanley,* p.405.
16. *War Council Minutes,* 28 January, 1915.
17. Corbett, *Official Naval History.*
18. Churchill, World *Crisis,* p.591.
19. *Dardanelles Commission Report* I, Par. 90.
20. Brock, Michael and Eleanor, (Ed.) *Asquith Letters to Venetia Stanley,* p.407.
21. Churchill, Winston, *World Crisis,* p.671.
22. *Ibid* p.602.
23. *Ibid.*
24. Richmond Papers.
25. *Ibid.*
26. Churchill, *World Crisis,* p.602.
27. Brock, Michael and Eleanor, (Ed.) *Asquith Letters to Venetia Stanley,* p.422–3.
28. *Ibid,* p.424.
29. *Ibid,* p.426.
30. Esher, *The Tragedy of Lord Kitchener,* p.76.
31. *Ibid,* p.99.
32. Corbett, *Naval Operations,* II, p.126.
33. Cunningham, *A Sailor's Odyssey,* p.60.

34. Churchill, *World Crisis*, p.613.
35. Cunningham, *A Sailor's Odyssey*, p.61.
36. Moorehead, Alan, *Gallipoli*, p.56.
37. Richmond, *Statesmen and Sea Power*, p.266.
38. Churchill, *World Crisis*, p.613.
39. Denham, *Dardanelles,: A Midshipman Diary, 1915–16*, p.33–34.
40. *Ibid*, p.26.
41. Cunningham, *A Sailor's Odyssey*, p.62.
42. *Ibid*, p.63.
43. Patterson, A. Temple, (Ed.) *The Jellicoe Papers* (NRS) Vol. I, p.187.
44. Gardiner, *The Royal Oak Courts Martial*, p.151.
45. Keyes, Admiral of the Fleet Sir Roger, *The Naval Memoirs, 1910–15*, p.212.
46. Cunningham, *A Sailor's Odyssey*, p.64.
47. *Report of Committee Appointed to Investigate the Attacks Delivered on, and the Enemy. Defences of the Dardanelles Straits*, 1919, CB. 1550, 10, October 1919, printed in April, 1921. (Commodore F.H.Mitchell, President,) (Naval Historical Library). (Hereafter Mitchell Report), p.58.
48. Churchill, *World Crisis*, p.595.
49. *Dardanelles Commission Report*, I, par. 90.
50. Churchill, *World Crisis*, p.600.
51. *Ibid*, p.601.
52. Brock, Michael and Eleanor, (Ed.) *Asquith Letters to Venetia Stanley*, p.429.
53. *Dardanelles Commission Report*, I, par. 95.
54. Cunningham, *A Sailor's Odyssey*, p.63..
55. *Dardanelles Commission Report*, I, par.67.
56. Churchill, *World Crisis*, p.602.
57. Esher, *The Tragedy of Lord Kitchener*, p.100.
58. Churchill, *World Crisis*, p.603–4.
59. *Ibid*, p.602.
60. *Dardanelles Commission Report*, I, par. 99.
61. War Council, Secretary's notes, 24 February 1915.
62. *Ibid*, 26 February 1915.
63. *Ibid*.
64. *Dardanelles Commission Report*, I, par. 101.
65. *Ibid*, par. 56.
66. Halpern, (Ed.) *The Keyes Papers*, (NRS), Vol. I, p.100–1.
67. Marder, *From the Dardanelles to Oran*, p.9.
68. Halpern, (Ed.) *The Keyes Papers*, (NRS), Vol. I, p.103.
69. Mitchell Report I, p.49.
70. *Ibid*, p.73.
71. Bacon, *Fisher*, Vol. II, p.220.
72. *Ibid*.
73. Corbett, *Naval Operations*, Vol. II, p.169.
74. *Ibid*, p.202.

75. Churchill, *World Crisis*, p.632.
76. *Ibid*, p.633.
77. *Ibid*, p.628-9.
78. *Ibid*, p.629.
79. *Ibid*, p.633.
80. *Ibid*, p.634.
81. *Ibid*.
82. *Ibid.* p.635
83. Scott, *Fifty Years in the Royal Navy*, p.328.
84. Halpern, (Ed.) *The Keyes Papers*, (NRS), Vol. I, p.108-09.
85. Churchill, *World Crisis*, p.636.
86. *Ibid*, p.637.
87. Denham, H.M., *Dardanelles: A Midshipman Diary, 1915–16*, p.64.
88. *Ibid*, p.67.
89. Cunningham, *A Sailor's Odyssey*, p.66.
90. Halpern, Paul G. (Ed.) *The Keyes Papers*, (NRS), Vol. I, p.111.
91. *Dardanelles Commission Report* I, Par. 114.
92. Bacon, *Fisher*, Vol. II, p.221.
93. Hamilton, Ian, *Gallipoli Diary*, p.41.
94. Marder, *From the Dardanelles to Oran*, p.15, Note 22.
95. Gilbert, Martin, *Winston S Churchill CV III*, p.718-9.
96. Churchill, *World Crisis*, p.646.
97. *Ibid.*
98. Hamilton, Ian, *Gallipoli Diary*, p.41.
99. Churchill, *World Crisis*, p.647.
100. *Ibid*, p.648.
101. *Ibid*, p.672.
102. Fremantle, Admiral Sir Sydney, *My Naval Life*, p.211.
103. *Morning Post*, 25 March, 1915.
104. Admiralty to de Robeck, 22nd March, 1915.
105. Denham, *Dardanelles,: A Midshipman Diary, 1915–16*, p.69.
106. Cited in Marder, *Fear God* Vol. III, p.168.
107. Churchill, *World Crisis*, p.649.
108. *Ibid*, p.653.
109. Ibid, 640-653
110. Cited in Marder, *Fear God* Vol. III, p.169.
111. Churchill, *World Crisis*, p.653.
112. *Ibid*, p.665.
113. Ibid..
114. *Ibid*, p.662-3.
115. *Ibid*, p.664.
116. Bacon, *Fisher*, Vol. II, p.221.
117. *Ibid*, p.222-3.

118.*Ibid*, p.223–4.

119.Bacon, *Fisher*, Vol. II, p.225–7 and Cited in Marder, Fear God Vol. III, p.179–181.

120.Cited in Marder, *Fear God* Vol. III, p.183. During the Russo-Turkish war the Russian advance on Constantinople was held up for five months by stubborn Turkish resistance at Plevna.

121.Churchill, *World Crisis*, p.713.

122.Cited in Marder, *Fear God* Vol. III, p.188–90.

123.*Ibid*, p.190–1.

124.Churchill, *World Crisis*, p.714–5.

125.Marder, *From the Dardanelles to Oran*, p.26–7.

Chapter 8. The Resignation (pp 164–197)

1. Lumby, E.W.R, (Ed.), *Policy and Operations in the Mediterranean, 1912–14*, (NRS). p.451.
2. ADM. 137/19. NMM
3. Price, *With the Fleet in the Dardanelles*, p.21.
4. *Hansard*, 5th Series, Vol LXXI, Col. 398–9. 22 April 1915.
5. *Hansard*, 5th Series, Vol LXXI, Col. 969 4 May, 1915.
6. *Hansard*, 5th Series, Vol.LXXI, Col. 969.
7. Churchill, *World Crisis*, p.743.
8. Gilbert, *Winston S Churchill, CV III*, p.855. The words in square brackets do not appear in the original and only in *The World Crisis*..
9. Churchill, *World Crisis*, p.743–5.
10. *Ibid*, p.745.
11. Gilbert, *Winston S Churchill*, Vol. III p.420.
12. *Ibid*, p.419.
13. Churchill, *World Crisis*, p.745.
14. *Ibid*.
15. *Ibid*, p.746–748.
16. Hankey, *Supreme Command*, p.314.
17. Churchill, *World Crisis*, p.747, Note.
18. *Ibid*, p.748–9.
19. Cited in Marder, *Fear God* Vol. III, p.219.
20. *Ibid*, p.220.
21. Bacon, *Fisher*, Vol. II, p.244.
22. Cited in Marder, *Fear God* Vol. III, p.220–1.
23. Brock, Michael and Eleanor, (Ed.) *Asquith Letters to Venetia Stanley*, p.506
24. Gilbert, *Winston S Churchill*, Vol. III, p.427–8, reproduces the memorandum almost in full.
25. Bacon, *Fisher*, Vol. II, p.246.
26. *Ibid*.
27. Churchill, *World Crisis*, p.753.

28. Gilbert, *Winston S Churchill,* Vol. III p.429.
29. *Ibid.*
30. Churchill, *World Crisis,* p.754.
31. *Ibid,* p.755.
32. *Ibid,* p.756–7.
33. Bacon, *Fisher,* Vol. II, p.218.
34. Chalmers, Rear-Admiral W.S, *The Life and Letters of David Beatty, Admiral of the Fleet,* p.450.
35. Bacon, *Fisher,* Vol. II, p.251.
36. Churchill, *World Crisis,* Appendix I, p.1420.
37. *Ibid.*
38. Bacon, *Fisher,* Vol. II, p.254–5.
39. *Ibid,* p.256.
40. *Ibid,* p.256–7.
41. Churchill, *World Crisis,* p.762.
42. Bacon, *Fisher,* Vol. II, p.259.
43. *Ibid,* p.260.
44. Lloyd George, *War Memoirs,* p.135.
45. Brett, *Journals and Letters of Viscount Esher,* Vol. III, p.235.
46. Bacon, *Fisher,* Vol. II, p.260.
47. *Ibid,* p.261.
48. *Ibid,* p.257–8.
49. Cited in Marder, *Fear God* Vol. III, p.231–2.
50. *Ibid,* p.232.
51. Bacon, *Fisher,* Vol. II, p.262.
52. *Ibid,* p.263..
53. Gilbert, *Winston S Churchill,* CV. III, p.899.
54. *Ibid,* p.903.
55. *Ibid,* p.907–8.
56. *Lennoxlove papers,* 1009.
57. *Ibid,* 1008.
58. *Ibid,* 2351.
59. Cited in Marder, *Fear God* Vol. III, p.237. The facsimile of this letter reproduced by Richard Hough is of course a rough draft.
60. Gilbert, *Winston S Churchill,* CV. III, p.894.
61. *Asquith Papers,* cited in Gilbert, *Winston S Churchill,* CV. III, p.897–8.
62. Bradford, *Admiral of the Fleet Sir Arthur Knyvet Wilson,* p.243–4.
63. Gilbert, *Winston S Churchill,* CV. III, p.919–20.
64. Asquith, *Memories and Reflections,* p. 97.
65. Cited in Marder, *Fear God* Vol. III, p.236.
66. *Ibid,* p.239.
67. *Ibid., Note.*
68. Bradford, *Admiral of the Fleet Sir Arthur Knyvet Wilson,* p.244.

69. Cited in Marder, *Fear God* Vol. III, p.773.
70. *Ibid,* Vol. III, p.238.
71. *Ibid,* , Note.
72. Marder, *Dreadnought* Vol II p.281.
73. Cited in Marder, *Fear God* Vol III, p.246.
74. *Ibid,* p.247.
75. Gilbert, *Winston S Churchill,* CV. III, p.911.
76. Soames, Mary, *Clementine Churchill,* p.123.
77. Bacon, *Fisher,* Vol. II, p.268–9, and Cited in Marder, *Fear God* Vol. III, p.241–3.
78. Bonar Law Papers. 50/3/1
79. Add. MSS. 4970B
80. Lennoxlove Papers, 1025.
81. Gilbert, *Winston S Churchill,* CV. III p.928,
82. *Ibid,* p.914,
83. Hankey, *Supreme Command,* p.317–8.
84. Bacon, *Fisher,* Vol. II, p.272.
85. *Lennoxlove papers,* 1041.
86. James, Robert Rhodes, *Churchill, Four Faces and the Man,* The politician, p.76.
87. Asquith, *Memories and Reflections,* p.94.
88. Bacon, *Fisher,* Vol. II, p.274–5.
89. Churchill, *World Crisis,* p.593.
90. Fisher, *Memories,* p.70.
91. Churchill, *World Crisis,* (Second Edition) Appendix I, p.1419.

Chapter 9. The Fall of Icarus (pp 198–220)

1. Marder, *Dreadnought* Vol. II, p.281.
2. *Ibid.*
3. Soames, Mary, *Clementine Churchill,* p. 123.
4. Gilbert, Martin, *Winston S Churchill,* CV. III, p. 926.
5. Minutes of the War Council, 26 February, 1915.
6. Ponsonby, *Recollections of Three Reigns,* p.74.
7. Lloyd George, *War Memoirs,* p.604.
8. *Ibid,* p.607.
9. Keyes, *The Naval Memoirs,* II, p.116.
10. Cited in Marder, *Fear God* Vol. III, p.253.
11. *Ibid,* p.258.
12. *Ibid,* p.260.
13. Gilbert, *Winston S Churchill,* CV III, p.952.
14. Wemyss, *The Life and Letters of Lord Wester Wemyss,* p.197–8.
15. Gilbert, *Winston S Churchill,* CV III, p.956–7.
16. *John Bull,* 12 June, 1915.
17. Cited in Marder, *Fear God* Vol. III, p.262.

18. Gilbert, *Winston S Churchill,* CV III, p.961–2.
19. *Ibid,* Vol. III, p. 500.
20. Gilbert, *Winston S Churchill,* CV III, p.1004–8.
21. *Ibid,* p.1003.
22. *Ibid,* p.1072.
23. *Ibid,* p.941–1.
24. *Ibid,* p.1043.
25. *Ibid,* p.1081–2.
26. *Ibid,* p.1084.
27. Marder, *Dreadnought,* Vol II p. 281.
28. Gilbert, *Winston S Churchill,* CV III, p. 1096.
29. *Ibid,* Vol. III, p. 514.
30. *Ibid,* p. 512.
31. *Ibid.* p. 515.
32. *Ibid,* CV III, p. 1149.
33. Halpern, (Ed.), *The Keyes Papers,* (NRS) Vol. I, p.186.
34. *Ibid,* p.171.
35. *Ibid.*
36. Cabinet Papers 42/3.
37. Gilbert, *Winston S Churchill,* CV III, p. 1179–80.
38. Halpern, (Ed.), *The Keyes Papers,* (NRS) Vol. I, p.210.
39. *Ibid,* p.216.
40. Aspinall-Oglander, *Roger Keyes,,* p.176.
41. Rodger, (Ed.), *The Naval Miscellany,* Vol. V. (NRS), p.476.
42. Jackson, Admiral H.B., First Sea Lord, and Murray, Lieut-Gen. A.J., CIGS, *An appreciation of the existing situation in the Balkans and Dardanelles with remarks as to the relative importance of this situation in regard to the general conduct of the War,* PRO ADM 137/1145.
43. Aspinall-Oglander, *Roger Keyes,* p.176.
44. Halpern, (Ed.), *The Keyes Papers,* (NRS) Vol. I, p.216.
45. Rodger, (Ed.), *The Naval Miscellany,* Vol. V. (NRS), p.478–9.
46. Halpern, (Ed.), *The Keyes Papers,* (NRS) Vol. I, p.235–40.
47. *Ibid.* p. 235, Note
48. *Ibid,* p. 239.
49. *Ibid.* p. 227.
50. Rodger, (Ed.), *The Naval Miscellany,* Vol. V. (NRS), p.481.
51. *Ibid,* p.481–2.
52. Moorhead, *Gallipoli,* p.321.
53. Rodger, (Ed.), *The Naval Miscellany,* Vol. V. (NRS), p.480.
54. Aspinall-Oglander, *Roger Keyes,* p.182.
55. *Ibid,* p.194.
56. Rodger, (Ed.), *The Naval Miscellany,* Vol. V. (NRS), p.483.
57. Prior, *Churchill's 'World Crisis' as History.*

58. *Hansard,* 5th series, LXXXV, Col. 1514.
59. *Ibid.*
60. *Ibid,* Col 1518.
61. Gilbert, *Winston S Churchill,* Vol. III, p.570.
62. *Ibid,* p.569.

Chapter 10. Vindication (pp 221–239)
1. Marder, *Dreadnought,* Vol. II, p.384.
2. *Hansard,* 5th Series. Lords, Vol. XX., Col. 336–7.
3. Cited in Marder, *Fear God* Vol. III p.273
4. *Ibid,* p.386.
5. *Ibid,* p.417.
6. *Ibid,*
7. Marder, *Portrait of an Admiral,* p.200-01.
8. *Ibid.* p.205.
9. Marder, *Dreadnought,* Vol. II, p.422.
10. *Ibid.*
11. *Ibid,* p.423–4.
12. *Ibid,* p.428.
13. *Ibid,* p.432.
14. Patterson, A.Temple, *The Jellicoe Papers,* (NRS) Vol. I, p.225.
15. *Manchester Guardian,* 7 February 1916.
16. *Lennoxlove Manuscripts,* cited in Patterson, A. Temple, (Ed.) *The Jellicoe Papers* (NRS) Vol. I p.205.
17. Addl. MSS 49008.
18. Addl. MSS 49009.
19. Patterson, A Temple, (Ed.) *The Jellicoe Papers* (NRS) Vol. I, p.226.
20. Churchill, *World Crisis,* p.1083.
21. Marder, *Dreadnought,* Vol. II, p.399.
22. Repington, *The First World War, 1914–1918,* Vol. I p.192.
23. Marder, *Dreadnought,* Vol. II, p.401.
24. Cited in Marder, *Fear God* Vol. III p.321, Note.
25. Marder, *Dreadnought,* Vol. II, p.403.
26. *Ibid,* p.402–3.
27. *Ibid,* p.403.
28. Riddell, *War Diary,* p.165.
29. NMM Beatty MSS, BTY/13/22/10 14 April, 1916
30. Bacon, *Fisher,* Vol. II, p.292.
31. *Ibid,*
32. *Ibid.* p.295.
33. Dardanelles Commission, *Minority Report,* Para. 53.
34. Fisher, *Records,* p.87.
35. Churchill, Winston, *The Aftermath,* p.447.
36. Bacon, *Fisher,* Vol. II, p.295.

37. *Ibid*, p.297.
38. *Ibid*, p.300.
39. Prior, *Churchill's 'World Crisis' as History*.

Chapter 11. Epitaph (pp 240–244)
1. Churchill, *World Crisis*, p.273.
2. *Ibid*, p.592.
3. Roskill, *Churchill and the Admirals*, p.26.

BIBLIOGRAPHY

Admiralty Orders in Council, February 1903 to December 1907 (Admiralty, 1908).

Altham, Captain E., *Jellicoe*, (Blackie, 1938).

Ashley, Maurice, *Churchill as Historian* (Secker and Warburg, 1968.

Aspinall-Oglander, *Roger Keyes; A Biography* (Hogarth Press, 1951).

Asquith, Earl of Oxford and, *Memories and Reflections, 1852–1927* (Cassell, 1928).

Aston Major General George, *Memories of a Marine*, (Murray, 1919).

Bacon, Admiral Sir Reginald, *The Life of Lord Fisher of Kilverstone, Admiral of the Fleet*,
   2 Vols, (Hodder and Stoughton, 1929).
   The Life of John Rushworth, Earl Jellicoe, (Cassell, 1936).
   From 1900 Onward (Hutchinson, 1940).
   The Jutland Scandal (Hutchinson, 1925).

'Barfleur',
   Naval Administration, (*Blackwood's Magazine*, May 1905).
   The Battle of Tsu Sima, (*Blackwood's Magazine*, February 1906).
   Naval Policy: A Plea for the Study of War, (Blackwood, 1907).

Bayly, Admiral Sir Lewis, *Pull Together!* (Harrap, 1939).

Beaverbrook, Lord, *Politicians and the War, 1914–1916*, (Doubleday, Doran & Co, NY.,
   1928).

Beckett, Ian and Gooch, John,
   Politicians and Defence: Studies in the Formulation of British Defence Policy, 1845–1970.
   (Manchester University Press, 1981).

Bennett, Geoffrey,
   Naval Battles of the First World War, (Pan Books, 1974).

Bonham Carter, Violet, *Winston Churchill as I Knew Him*, (Eyre and Spottiswood, 1965.

Bradford, Admiral Sir Edward, *Admiral of the Fleet Sir Arthur Knyvet Wilson*, (Murray,
   1923).

Brett, Maurice, *Journals and Letters of Viscount Esher*, 3 Vols (Nicholson & Watson,
   1934).

Briggs, Sir John, *Naval Administrations 1827 to 1892* (Sampson Low, 1897).

Broad, Lewis, *Winston Churchill: The Years of Preparation* (Sidgwick and Jackson, 1963).

Brock, Michael and Eleanor, (Ed.). *H. H. Asquith, Letters to Venetia Stanley,* (OUP, 1982).

Brodie, Bernard, *A Layman's Guide to Naval Strategy,* (Princeton University Press, 1942).

Brown, David K, *A century of Naval Construction; The History of the Royal Corps of Naval Constructors,* (Conway Maritime Press, 1983).

Brownrigg, Rear-Admiral Sir Douglas, *Indiscretions of the Naval Censor,* (Cassell, 1920).

Bülow, Von, *Imperial Germany 1914.*

Cable, James, *Britain's Naval Future,* (Macmillan, 1983).

Callender, Geoffrey, *The Naval Side of British History,* (Christophers, London, 1924).

Calvocoressi, Peter, and Wint, Guy, *Total War,* (Penguin Books, 1972).

Carew, Anthony, *The Lower Deck of the Royal Navy, 1900–1939* (Manchester University Press, 1981).

Chalmers, Rear-Admiral W S, *The Life and Letters of David, Earl Beatty* (Hodder & Stoughton, 1951).

Chamberlain, Austen, *Politics from Inside,* (London, 1936).

Chatfield, Admiral Lord, *The Navy and Defence,* (Heinemann, 1942).

Chatterton, E. Keble,
  Dardanelles Dilemma: The Story of the Naval Operations, (London, 1930).
  The Big Blockade (Hurst & Blackett, nd).

Churchill, Randolph S, *Winston S Churchill* (Heinemann 1967), Vol. I & II.

Churchill, Winston S.,
  The World Crisis, 1911–1918 (London 1923). 3 Vols.
  The World Crisis, 1911–1918, Revised Edition (Odhams, 1938). 4 Vols.
  Great Contemporaries, (Macmillan, 1937 and the Reprint Society, 1941).
  The Second World War (Cassell, 1951)

Clarke, Lt-Col. Sir George, and Thursfield, James, *The Navy and the Nation,* (Murray, 1897).

Clausewitz, Carl Von,
  On War (Trans. Colonel J J Graham; Kegan, Paul, 1908).
  On War (Trans. Anatol Rapoport; Penguin, 1968),

Coles, Alan, *Three Before Breakfast,* (Kenneth Mason, 1979).

Colomb, Vice-Admiral P H, *Memoirs of Sir Astley Cooper-Key,* (Methuen, 1898).

Compton-Hall, Commander P. R, *Submariners' World* (Kenneth Mason, 1983).

Corbett, Sir Julian,
  Naval Operations, (Longmans, Green & Co., 1929).
  Some principles of Maritime Strategy, (Conway Maritime Press, 1972).

Corbett, Sir Julian, and Newbolt, Sir Henry,
  History of the Great War, Naval Operations, (Longmans Green & Co., 1920–31). 5 Vols.

Cork and Orrery, Admiral of the Fleet Lord, *My Naval Life* (Hutchinson, 1942).

Cramb, J A.
  Germany and England (A series of lectures at Queen's College, London), (Murray, June 1914).

Cunningham, Admiral of the Fleet Viscount, *A Sailor's Odyssey.* (Hutchinson, 1951).

Custance, Admiral Sir Reginald, See 'Barfleur'.

Dardanelles Commission, *First Report, Comd 8490; Second Report Comd. 8502.*
de Chair, Admiral Sir Dudley, *The Sea is Strong,* (Harrap, 1961).
d'Eyncourt, Sir E Tennyson, *A Shipbuilder's Yarn* (Hutchinson, 1948).
Denham, H M, *Dardanelles: A Midshipman's Diary,* (Murray, 1981).
Doenitz, Admiral Karl, *Memoirs: Ten years and Twenty days,* (Weidenfeld & Nicolson, 1959).
Dewar, Vice Admiral K G B, *The Navy from Within,* (Gollancz, 1939).
Dictionary of National Biography.
Dixon, Norman F, *On the Psychology of Military Incompetence,* (Cape, 1976).
Domville, Admiral Sir Barry, *Look to Your Moat,* (Hutchinson, nd).
Dreyer, Admiral Sir Frederic C, *The Sea Heritage,* (Museum Press Ltd., 1955).
Duff, David, *Alexandra, Princess and Queen* (Collins, 1980).

Eade, Charles, (Ed.). *Churchill by His Contemporaries* (Hutchinson, 1953).
Eardley-Wilmot, Rear-Admiral Sir Sydney, *An Admiral's Memories,* (Sampson Low, nd).
Ellison, Lieut-General Sir Gerald, *The Perils of Amateur Strategy,* (Longmans, Green, 1926).
Esher, Viscount, *The Tragedy of Lord Kitchener,* (Murray, 1921).
Farrere et Chack, *Combats et Bataille sur Mer.*
Fisher, Admiral of the Fleet Lord,
  Memories, (Hodder & Stoughton, 1919).
  Records, (Hodder & Stoughton 1919).
Fisher, Admiral Sir Frederic, *Naval Reminiscences* (Muller, 1938).
Fisher, H A L, *A History of Europe* (Edward Arnold, 1936).
Fremantle, Admiral Sir Sydney, *My Naval Life,* (Hutchinson, nd).
Frewen, Oswald, *Sailor's Soliloquy,* (Hutchinson, 1961).

Gardiner, Leslie, *The Royal Oak Courts Martial,* (Blackwood, 1965).
Gerard, James W, *My Four Years in Germany,* (Hodder & Stoughton, 1917).
Gilbert, Martin, *Winston Churchill,* 1914–1916, (Heinemann, 1971). Vol. III and CV III.
Goodenough, Admiral Sir William, *A Rough Record,* (Hutchinson, nd).
Goodspeed, D J, *Ludendorff,* (Hart-Davis, 1966).
Gretton, Vice-Admiral Sir Peter, *Former Naval Person,* (Cassell, 1968).
Gretton, R H, *A Modern History of the English People,* (Secker, 1929).
Grey, Viscount, of Falloden, *Twenty-Five Years,* (Hodder & Stoughton, 1925).

Haldane, R B, *Autobiography,* (Hodder & Stoughton,1929).
Halpern, Paul, (Ed.), *The Keyes Papers,* 2 Vols. (NRS 1979–82).
  A Naval History of World War I. (US Naval Intitute, 1994; UCL, 1994).
Hamilton, General Sir Ian, *Compulsory Service,* (London, 1920).
  Gallipoli Diary, (London, 1920).
Hankey, Baron, *Supreme Command,* 2 Vols. (Allen & Unwin, 1961).
Hart, Liddell, *A History of the World War, 1914–1918,* (Faber, 1930).

Hatch, Alden, *The Mountbattens,* (1966).

Hazlehurst, Cameron, *Politicians at War, July, 1914–May 1915* (Cape, 1971).

Hickling, Vice-Admiral Harold, *Sailor at Sea* (William Kimber, 1965).

Hickey, Michael, *Gallipoli* (John Murray,1995).

Hindenburg, Marshall Von, *Out of My Life* (Trans. F A Holt. New York, 1921).

Home, William Douglas, and Jennifer Brown, *The Prime Ministers: Stories and Anecdotes from No 10,* (WH Allen, 1987).

Hough, Richard,
   Former Naval Person, (Weidenfeld & Nicolson, 1985).
   First Sea Lord, George Allen & Unwin, 1969).

Howard, Michael, *The Causes of War,* (Unwin Paperbacks, 1983).

Hurd, Archibald,
   Naval Efficiency: The War Readiness of the Fleet, (Chapman & Hall, 1902).
   Who Goes There? (Hutchinson, 1941).

Jackson, G Gibbard, *The Ship Under Steam,* (Fisher, Unwin 1927).

James, Admiral Sir William,
   A Great Seaman: The Life of Admiral of the Fleet Sir Henry Oliver (Witherby, 1956).
   The Eyes of the Navy: A Biographical Study of Admiral Sir Reginald Hall, (Methuen 1956).

James, David, *Lord Roberts,* (Hollis & Carter, 1954).

James, Robert Rhodes,
   Churchill: A Study in Failure, 1900–1939 (Weidenfeld & Nicolson, 1970).
   The British Revolution: British Politics, 1880–1939, (Hamish Hamilton, 1977).
   From Asquith to Chamberlain, 1914–1939, (Hamish Hamilton, 1977).

Jameson, Rear-Admiral Sir William, *The Fleet that Jack Built,*

Jellicoe, Admiral Viscount, *The Grand Fleet, 1914–16,* (Cassell, 1919).

Jordan, Gerald (Ed). *Naval Warfare in the Twentieth Century,* (Croom Helm, London, 1977).

Keegan, John,
   The Price of Admiralty, (Hutchinson, 1988).
   A History of Warfare, (Hutchinson, 1993).

Kemp, Lieut-Comdr P K, *The Papers of Admiral Sir John Fisher,* 2 Vols. (NRS, 1960 and 1964).

Kerr, Mark, *Prince Louis of Battenberg* (Longmans Green & Co 1934).

Keyes, Admiral of the Fleet Sir Roger, *The Naval Memoirs, 1910–15, 1916–18,* (Eyre & Spottiswood, 1934–5).

King-Hall, L. (Ed.). *Sea Saga: The Naval Diaries of Four generations of the King-Hall Family,* (Gollancz, 1935).

King-Hall, Stephen, *My Naval Life,* (Faber, 1951).

Laffin, John, *Damn the Dardanelles: the Agony of Gallipoli,* (Alan Sutton, 1989).

Lean's Royal Navy List, (Witherby, 1902).

Lee, Sir Sydney, *King Edward VII: A Biography,* 2 Vols. (Macmillan, 1925–27).

Leslie, Sir Shane, *The Film of Memory*, (1938).

Lewis, Michael, *The Navy of Britain*, (Allen & Unwin 1948).

Liddle, Peter H, *The Sailor's War, 1914–18*, (Blandford Press, 1985).

Lipson, E, *Europe, 1914–1939*, (Black, 1945).

Lloyd George, David, *War Memoirs of David Lloyd George*, 2 Vols. (Nicholson & Watson, 1934.

Lumby, E W R, *Policy and Operations in the Mediterranean, 1912–14*, (NRS, 1970).

Lutz, Hermann, *Lord Grey and the World War*, (Trans. E W Dickes; Allen & Unwin, 1928).

Maber, Lt-Comdr John, *The Ironclad Huascar*, (Journal of Naval Engineering, Vol 28, No 3).

Mackay, Ruddock F.

  Balfour, Intellectual Statesman, (Oxford University Press, 1985).

  Fisher of Kilverstone, (Clarendon Press, Oxford, 1973).

Macksey, Piers, *The War in the Mediterranean*, (London, 1957).

Magnus, Philip, *King Edward VII*, (Penguin Books, 1967).

Mahan, Captain A T, USN, *The Influence of Sea Power upon History*, (Sampson Low, 1889).

Manning, Frederic, *The Life of Sir William White*, (Murray, 1923).

Marder, Arthur J.

  The Anatomy of British Sea Power; A History of British Naval Policy in the Pre-Dreadnought Era, 1880–1905, (Alfred A Knopf, New York, 1940). Published in Britain as *British Naval Policy, 1880–1905: The Anatomy of British Sea Power*, (Putnam, 1941).

  Fear God and Dread Nought, The Correspondence of Admiral of the Fleet Lord Fisher of Kilverstone. 3 Vols. (Cape, 1952–59).

  From the Dardanelles to Oran; Studies of the Royal Navy in War and Peace, 1915–1940, (Oxford University Press, 1974).

  From the Dreadnought to Scapa Flow, 5 Vols. Oxford University Press, 1961–70).

  Portrait of an Admiral: The Life and Papers of Sir Herbert Richmond, (Cape, 1952).

Marriott, J A R, *Europe and Beyond*, (Methuen, 1921).

Martin, Hugh, *Battle: The Life Story of the Rt. Hon. Winston S. Churchill*, (Sampson, Low, Marston, nd).

Mathew, David, *The Naval Heritage*, (Collins, 1944).

Maurice, Major-General Sir Frederick, *Haldane*, (London, 1937).

Mitchell, *Report on the Dardanelles*, MOD, Naval Library.

Moorehead, Alan, *Gallipoli*, (Hamish Hamilton, 1956).

Navy Lists, 1834–1979 (HMSO).

Newbolt, Henry, *A Naval History of the War, 1914–1918*, (Hodder & Stoughton, nd).

Nicolson, Harold, *King George the Fifth: His Life and Reign*, (Constable, 1952).

Orders in Council and Acts of Parliament for the Regulation of the Naval Service (HMSO 1856 and 1908).

Padfield, Peter,
   Aim Straight: A Biography of Sir Percy Scott, (Hodder & Stoughton, 1966).
   Doenitz, the Last Führer (Gollancz, 1984).
Patterson, A Temple, (Ed.).
   The Jellicoe Papers, 2 Vols. (NRS, 1966).
   Jellicoe: A Biography, (Macmillan 1969).
Penn, Geoffrey,
   Up Funnel, Down Screw! (Hollis & Carter, 1955).
   Snotty: The Story of the Midshipman, (Hollis & Carter, 1957).
   HMS Thunderer: The Story of the Royal Naval Engineering College, Keyham and Manadon, (Kenneth Mason, 1984).
Pollen, Anthony, *The Great Gunnery Scandal*
Ponsonby, Sir Frederick, *Recollections of Three Reigns,* (Eyre and Spottiswood, 1951).
Price, William Harold, *With the Fleet in the Dardanelles,* (Andrew Melrose, nd).
Prior, Robin, *Churchill's 'World Crisis' as History,* (Croom Helm, 1983).

Raft, Bryan,
   Beatty Papers, (NRS 1993).
   Technical Change and British Naval Policy, 1860–1939, (Hodder & Stoughton, 1977).
Repington, Lt-Col. C A'Court, *The First World War, 1914–1918,* (Houghton Mifflin Co., New York 1921).
Richmond, Admiral Sir Herbert,
   The Invasion of Britain, Methuen, 1941).
   Statesmen and Sea Power, (Clarendon Press, 1946).
Robertson, C Grant, *Bismarck,* (Constable, 1918).
Robinson, Commander Charles N, *The British Fleet,* (Bell, 1894).
Rodger, N A M
   (Ed). *The Admiralty* (Terence Dalton Ltd., 1979).
   The Naval Miscellany, Vol, V, (NRS, 1984).
Roskill, Stephen W,
   Admiral of the Fleet Earl Beatty, (Atheneum, New York, 1981).
   Churchill and the Admirals, (Collins, 1977).
   Documents Relating to the Naval Air Service, Vol. I 1908–18, (NRS, 1969).
   Hankey, Man of Secrets, 3 vols. (Collins, 1970–74).

Schofield, B B, *The Story of HMS 'Dryad",* (Kenneth Mason, 1977).
Scott, Admiral Sir Percy, *Fifty Years in the Royal Navy* (Allen & Unwin, 1919).
Schurman, D M, *The Education of a Navy,* (Cassell, 1965).
Seymour, *Diplomatic Background of the War.*
Smith, Vice-Admiral Humphrey Hugh, *A Yellow Admiral Remembers,* (Edward Arnold 1932).
Somervell, D C, *The Reign of King George the Fifth, and English Chronicle,* (London, 1935).
Spender, J A,
   A Short History of Our Times (Cassell, 1934).
   Life, Journalism and Politics (Cassell, 1927).

Steinberg, Jonathan,
  Yesterday's Deterrent: Tirpitz and the Birth of the German Battle Fleet, (Macdonald, 1965).
Sumida, Jon Tetsuro, *The Pollen Papers* (NRS) (Allen & Unwin, 1984).
Sydenham, Baron, of Combe, (See also Clarke). *My Life's Work.*
Sydenham, and others, *The World Crisis, by Winston Churchill, a Criticism* (Hutchinson, nd).

Taylor, A J P, *The First World War: an Illustrated History,* (Hamish Hamilton, 1963).
Taylor, A J P, and others, *Churchill, Four Faces and the Man,* (Allan Lane, the Penguin Press, 1969).
Tirpitz, Grand Admiral Von, *My Memoirs,* 2 Vols. (Hurst & Blackett Ltd. nd).
Trevelyan, G M, *Fifty Years: a Composite Picture of the Period 1882–1932,* (Thornton Butterworth, 1932).

'Undistinguished Naval Officer', *The British Navy in the Present Year of Grace,* 3 Vols. (Hamilton Adams, 1885–1886).

Van de Vat, Dan, *The Ship that Changed the World,* (Hodder & Stoughton, 1985).

Wemyss, Lady Wester, *The Life and Letters of Lord Wester Wemyss* (Eyre & Spottiswood, 1935)
Wemyss, Admiral of the Fleet Lord Wester, *The Navy in the Dardanelles Campaign,* (Hodder & Stoughton, nd).
Williams, Hamilton, *Britain's Naval Power,* 2 Vols (Macmillan, 1896).
Winton, John, *Convoy,* (Michael Joseph, 1983).
Wyatt, H F and Horton-Smith, L G, *The Passing of the Great Fleet,* (Sampson Low, 1909).

INDEX

Abrolhos, 78, 81, 82
Achi Baba, 110, 122, 166
Admiralstab, 51, 53, 57
Aeroplanes, 105, 106
Agadir Crisis, 8, 11, 19, 237,
    CID Meeting, War Office
    and Admiralty plans differ,
    9
Aircraft, 105–108, German,
    209
Air raids, 105–108
Air spotting, 138, 144
Alexandra, Queen, 185,
    condemns Churchill,
    supports Fisher, 199
AMCs, enemy, in New York,
    161
Ammunition, 145, British
    shortage, 148, 203, 213;
    Turkish shortage, 153,
    154, 156, 166
Anglo-Persian Oil Company,
    34
Anti-submarine vessels, 93
Anson, Lord George, 189
Antwerp, 18, 62, 102, 149,
    224, 238, Fisher on, 61,
    meeting with Kitchener,
    Churchill, Battenberg,
    Grey, 62–63;
    Southborough on, 63;
    Grey on, 63; Esher on, 63;
    reinforcements for, 64; fall
    of, 65–66; Churchill to
    French on, 66; Richmond
    on, 66; Beatty on, 66;
    Marder on, 66; Asquith
    on, 64; Churchill assumes
    'command', 64; asks to
    surrender office to
    command, 64; short of
    food, 63; Scheldt closed,
    63; naval brigades at, 63;
    Richmond on, 66; Hankey

on, 64; Beatty on, 66;
    Marder on, 66; Asquith
    on, 66
ANZACS disembark in Egypt,
    115
Archer-Shee, Martin, 7
Army and Navy Gazette,
    supports Fisher as First
    Lord, 189
Army disembarkation
    transferred to St Nazaire,
    61
Asdic, 206
Ashmead-Bartlett, Ellis, 203;
    returns home to avoid
    censorship, 203; reports to
    Asquith, 203;
    Memorandum 203–204
Aspinall-Oglander, Brigadier
    General Cecil, 210, 217
Asquith, Herbert Henry, *See*
    Oxford and Asquith
Asquith, Lady Cynthia, 201
Asquith, Violet, 73, 136, 220
Aubers Ridge, 175
Augagneur, Victor, French
    Minister of Marine, 130
Austria, building dreadnoughts,
    6; ultimatum to Serbia, 50;
    declares war on Serbia, 51

Battlecruisers, 1, 86
'Bacchante' Class, 68
Bacon, Admiral Sir Reginald
    Hugh Spencer, 48, 79,
    173, 181, 196, 234, 235;
    on War Council 75, on
    Fisher, 236
Baghdad Railway, 115, 156
Balfour, 1st Earl of, 6, 12, 13,
    19, 36–37, 38, 111, 133,
    188–193, 205, 214–219,
    222; supports Dardanelles
    operation, 126–7; warned

of need for troops at
    Dardanelles, 129; succeeds
    Churchill as 1st Lord, 193;
    as First Lord, 198–200;
    frees de Robeck's hand,
    210; rejects further naval
    attack, 210; rebuffs Keyes,
    215; hints de Robeck will
    haul down flag, 217;
    considers Baltic Scheme,
    223; claims all well with
    Navy, 231
Ballard, Admiral George
    Alexander, 15
Baltic Scheme, 9, 10, 15, 17,
    18, 97–99, 109, 109, 223;
    brief discussion, 110;
    imitated by Germany, 102,
    236; in Second World
    War, 18
Barham, Sir Charles
    Middleton, Lord, 189, 228
Barrow, Sir Edmund, 218
Battenburg, Prince Louis
    Alexander of (See Milford
    Haven)
Bayly, Admiral Sir Lewis, 94
Beatty, Admiral of the Fleet
    Earl, 21, 31, 68, 88, 199,
    222, 224, 225, 226, 227;
    on Clementine Churchill,
    22; on Battenburg, 45; on
    Fisher's restoration,
    73–74; 'Mining-in' in
    Forth and Humber, 89; on
    Baltic scheme, 103;
    Fisher's resignation a
    'calamity', 189; on
    Churchill's departure, 194;
    little more aggressive than
    Jellicoe, 225; writes to
    Prime Minister, 229
Beaverbrook, 1st Baron, on
    Churchill at Antwerp, 65;

Beaverbrook, 1st Baron
(continued)
on breach between
Churchill and Fisher, 74
Beilby, Sir George, 205
Belgian neutrality, 1839
guarantee, 51
Belgrade occupied, 51
Beresford, Lord Charles, 3, 39,
44, 46, 74, 242; Member
of Parliament, 2; enemy of
Fisher, 2; ambition to be
First Lord, 2; Beresford
inquiry, 3, love of
splendour, 4; attempts to
remove McKenna, 7; 'War
Lord' scheme, 11; wants
executive authority for
Staff, 27; comes to Fisher's
aid, 111, 166; demands
Peerage, 193, 244
Beresford school vilifies Fisher,
201
Bethmann-Hollweg, Theobald
von, Chancellor of
Germany, 7
Birdwood, Field Marshal Lord,
115, 213; sent to Gallipoli,
144; pessimistic about
naval attack, 145; in
temporary command, 214
Birkenhead 1st Earl, 23
Bismarck, Otto Edward
Leopold von, Prince Duke
of Lauenburg, 99
Black Sea, 137
Blank cheque, 50
Blockade, 28; by submarines,
36, 40
Board of Invention and
Research, 205–206
Board of Admiralty, 20
Bombardment of Black Sea
ports, 110
Bombing of King's Lynn,
Yarmouth and
Sheringham, 108
Bonar Law, Andrew, 44, 185,
186, 187, 210; objects to
Churchill's visit to
Gallipoli, 207 Gallipoli
untenable, 218
Bonham-Carter, Sir Maurice,
132, 188
Borkum, 13, 17, 96, 99, 100,
101, 223
Bowles, Thomas Gibson,
Conservative MP, 69
Bradford, Vice-Admiral Sir
Edward Eden, 227
Braithwaite, General Sir
Walter, Hamilton's Chief
of Staff, 155, 113
Brett, Maurice, Constantinople
quiet and calm, 204
Bridgeman, Admiral Sir
Francis Charles, 5, 25, 26,
36, 43–44; 168

Briggs, Admiral Sir Charles
John, 25, 42
British Petroleum Company,
34
British ultimatum to Germany,
51
Brock, Rear-Admiral Frederic,
29
Brown, Cyril, U.S. journalist,
102
Brunsbüttel, 8, 97
Bulair lines, 110
Bulgaria, declares neturality,
109
Buller, Sir Redvers, VC, 131
Bülow, General Carl Wilhelm
Paul von, 61
Burmah Oil Company, 33, 34
Burney, Admiral of the Fleet
Sir Cecil, 87
Burns, John, resigns on
declaration of war, 51

Cabinet favours neutrality, 51;
meetings disorganized, 51;
asks for views of service
officers, 213
Cabinet War Committee, 220;
no Service officers
included, 220
Callaghan, Admiral of the Fleet
Sir George Astley, C-in-C
Home Fleet, 51, 199
Callwell, Major General Sir
Charles Edward, 73, 141,
208
Campbell, Admiral Sir Henry
Hervey, 238
Cambon, Paul, French Foreign
Minister, 161
Cape Verde Islands, 84
Captain Supervising Modified
Sweeps, 91
Carden, Admiral Sir Sackville,
122; 126; 160; reply on
attack on Dardanelles,
122; proposes four-stage
operation, 124; his further
plan, 125; opens attack,
136; expects to reduce
forts in one day, 137;
forecasts reaching
Constantinople in fourteen
days, 144; demands
troops, 147–48, pressed by
Churchill, 147–48; his
reply 148; plans attack of
18 March, 148; nervous
breakdown, 149;
surrenders command to de
Robeck, 149
Carson, Edward, 111, 205,
210, 211, 218; attacks
conduct of war, 211–12;
resigns 212, 219
Casltereagh, Viscount, 61
Catton Hall, 1
Chamberlain, Sir Austen, 218

Chanak fort, 122
Channel Ports, 67
Charing Cross Hotel, 180
Chief of War Staff, 27
Childers, Hugh, 1st Lord, 20,
23
Christian, Rear-Admiral
Arthur, 68
Churchill, Clementine, on
Fisher's warning, 169;
writes on behalf of
Winston, 189
Churchill, Jack, 167, 204, 205
Churchill, Lady Randolph, 69
Churchill, Randolph, 13, 21,
30, 46, 48, 103
Churchill, Winston Spencer, 5,
13, 97; on Fisher, 5;
opposes naval expenditure,
6; opposes British building
programme, 8; Home
Secretary, 6, 11; changes
view, 11; attempts to
dislodge McKenna, 12,
writes to Asquith, 12;
forecasts events of war, 13;
1st Lord 12; consults
Beresford, 14; compared
with Childers, 20;
discusses new board with
Fisher, 25; views on staff,
24; sacks Wilson, 24;
considers recalling Fisher,
25; consults Beresford, 14;
supports Baltic scheme,
18; domineering, 20;
misinterprets Admiralty
Patent 20; approaches sea
warfare as cavalry officer
21; Jellicoe on, 22–23;
lectures flag officers, 23;
cruises in Enchantress, 24;
discusses new board with
Fisher, 25; views on staff
23; under pressure to from
staff, 27; improves sailors
pay, 28, 29; threatens
break with Lloyd George,
29; reforms naval
discipline, 29;
appointments of Meux,
Milne and Custance, 29;
meets Fisher in Naples,
30; on oil fuel, 31; on
Pluto pipeline, 35; on
submarines, 35; obtains
copy of Paper intended for
CID, 39; disbelieves in
submarine warfare, 40;
Poore incident, 42–43;
letter to Limpus 43– 44;
supports declaration of war
51; suggests Fleet should
not be demobilized, 51; at
Cromer July, 1914, 52;
sends preparatory signal,
52; confused signalling,
53–54; French on, 66; asks

to surrender office to command at Antwerp, 64; 'Private Army', 64; sends messages 'from First Lord' 67; suggests battlecruisers for Board Fourteens, 68; political position impaired, 71; installs 'War Group', 75; misjudges condition of *Canopus*, 77; signal to Cradock, 78; limits construction to completion in six months, 89; claims submarines, mines and torpedoes 'overcome', 91; misgivings on score of expense, 93; presses recapture of Belgian ports, 94; supports Baltic scheme, 97; memorandum to Asquith on Baltic scheme, 101; proposes Baltic scheme in WW2, 103; visits Constantinople (1909), 110; on seizure of Gallipoli with Greek troops, 110; memo on Balkans, 114; expounds on naval professional matters, 111; attracted by Dardanelles, 114; rejects combined operation against Gallipoli, 120; picks out naval element from combined operation at Gallipoli, 120; asks Carden his view, 123; 'High authorities', 123, 133; gives orders for attack, 125; reveals Dardanelles plan to War Council, 126; confirms Dardanelles to Grand Duke, 128; suggests dropping Zeebrugge in favour of Dardanelles, 132; visit to French to explain Dardanelles, 141; over-optimism, 143; message to Carden, 147; misunderstands naval gunnery, 149; on shortage of ammunition, 155, 156; suggests Fisher breaking down, 168; suggests mounting naval guns ashore, 173; memoranda of 15 May, 1915, 177–78; asks A.K. Wilson to replace Fisher, 186–87; misunderstands Wilson, 186–88; campaigns for support, 188; offers Fisher seat in Cabinet, 188; alarmed at own position, 189; spreads rumours of Fisher's insanity, 191; appointed Chancellor of

Duchy of Lancaster, 193; could monitor Dardanelles, 198; tries to persuade Wilson to serve under Balfour, 199; asks for copies of Dardanelles signals and *Pink List*, 202; refutes Ashmead-Bartlett, 204; angry letter to Asquith, 205; projected visit to Dardanelles, 207; proposes fuel for aircraft in submarines, 208; proposes renewal of naval attack, 210; defensive memorandum to Asquith, 211; efforts to dislodge Kitchener, 216–17; resigns, 219; resignation speech, 220; character assassination of Fisher, 220; goes to France as Lieut-Colonel, 220; calls for Fisher's resinstatement, 229–30; on Generals' and Admirals' resistance to change, 235; only politician to attempt offensive war, 239; tacitly admits error of Dardanelles, 243;

Clarke, *See* Sydenham
Coal firing, 32–3
Coaling ship, 32
Coalition Government, 193
Colenso, 30, 131
Collard, Vice Admiral Bernard, 11
Colville, Admiral Hon Sir Stanley, 72, 202
Combined operations, exercies in, 9
Committee of Imperial Defence, 5, 7, 8, 15, 17, 19
Conference in *Queen Elizabeth*, 155
Contemptible Little Army, 109
Continental warfare, 8, 10, 15
Coode, Captain Charles Penrose Rushton, 151
Copenhagen, 1807, 121
'Copenhagen' operation, 51, 91, 121
Corbett, Sir Julian, 15, 28, 39, 109, 129, 132, 224; disbelieves unrestricted submarine warfare, 40; on Fisher's doubts about Dardanelles, 118; on unwisdom of Naval attack on Dardanelles, 120
Cork, Admiral William Henry Dudley Boyle, 12th Earl of Cork and Orrery, 18, 103
Coronel, Battle of 78–80, 87
Cradock, Rear-Admiral Sir Christopher, 76–80

Crease, Commander (Acting Captain) Thomas Evans, 177, 178–9, 181, 191, 192; corrects Churchill's record of events, 196–97
Cresswell, Captain, John, 57
Crewe, Lord, 217, 218
Crimea, 10, 121
Cromarty Inadequate U-boat defences, 75
Cunningham, Admiral of the Fleet, 1st Viscount, 114, 136, 137
Curzon, George Nathaniel, Marquess, 207
Custance, Admiral Sir Reginald, 6; 29; 30, 39, 52, 59, 242

D-Notice system, 11
Dacres, Vice-Admiral Sir Sydney, 20
Daily Chronicle, 202
Daily News, 222
Daily Telegraph, proposes Fisher as First Lord, 189
Danzig, 9
D'Arcy, W. Knox, 33, 34
Dardanelles, 110, 113, 120–21, 136, bombardment 3 November, 1914, 113–14; naval attack postponed, 136; fails, 137; evacuation, 'out of the question', 212; evacuation order, 219; Kitchener asks for estimate of likely casualties, 214
Dardanelles Commission Report, 131, 140, cabinet drifted into military attack, 141, 142, 149, 176, 234–35; minority report of Walter Roth, 235
Dardanelles Committee, 202, 207, 208; decides on reinforcements for Dardanelles, 203; 205; Jackson attends, 207; Balfour rejects further naval attack, 210; swelled to twelve, 218; abolished, 218
Dardanos, fort, 122
de Bartolomé, Admiral Sir Charles, Churchill claims support for Dardanelles, 146; to report on Dardanelles, 155–56; visit cancelled, 157
De Chair, Admiral Sir Dudley, 23, 52
De Robeck, Admiral of the Fleet Sir John, 141, 172, 196, 213; in command, 149; launches attack, 149; reports failure to Admiralty, 152; given discretion, 153; 161;

De Robeck, Admiral of the Fleet Sir John (continued) confused message to Admiralty, 167; reorganizes sweepers, 154; proposes combined operation, 155; refuses action without Army, 158–59; sends letter home with Keyes, 214

Denham, Captain Henry, 151, 156

Depth charges, 206

Derby, 15th Earl of, 121

Derby scheme, 219

Destroyers, shortage of, 222

Dewar, Vice Admiral Sir Kenneth Gilbert Balmain, 238

Dickens, Admiral Sir Gerald, 18, 103

Djemal, Ahmed, expedition against Egypt 117

Donald, Robert, Editor, Daily Chronicle, 202

Donaldson, Admiral Leonard, 91

Douglas, James, on Fisher's maiden speech, 221–2

Drake, 241

Drax, Admiral The Hon. Sir Reginald, 18, 103

Dreyer, Admiral Sir Frederic, 46, 47

Drummond, Captain John, 68

Duckworth, Admiral Sir John, 120; penetration of Dardanelles, 121, 135, 136

Dunkirk naval air stations, 62

Durnford, Admiral Sir John, 25

'Edgar' class paid off, beyond repair, 92

Edward VII, King, 3, 6, 8, 15; death of, 6 May 1910, 6

Egerton, Admiral Sir George, 25, 29

Elbe, 9

Elijah, 4

Ellison, Lieut-General Sir Gerald, 17, on Baltic scheme, 101, 103

Emden, 100

Enchantress, Admiralty yacht, Churchill's cruises, 22, 23, 30, 39, 89; visit to Naples, 31

Enemy AMCs in New York, 161

English Bank, 78

Enver Pasha, 54; attempt to take Caucasus, 116–117

Epstein bust, 241

Esher, 2nd Viscount, 3, 7, 11, 14, 17, 21, 26, 30, 35, 59; 204, on Staff, 60–61; on Fisher's strategy, 65, 96;

on Kitchener, 97; on security, 136; told by King of Fisher's resignation, 181; advice to Fisher, 185, 191

Evacuation of Calais, Boulogne, Dieppe, Havre and Rouen, 61; Lines of Communication extended, 61

Excellent, HMS, gunnery school, 242

Everett, Admiral Sir Alan, 215

Falklands, 78; Battle of, 83; Churchill on, 86; consequences of failure, 86; proved Fisher's battlecruiser concept, 86

Fehmarn, 9

Fez, 8

Firing practices, 1

First Cruiser Squadron under Milne, 53

Fisher, 1st Baron, Admiral of the Fleet, birth, 1; enters Navy, 1; believer in steam and submarines, 1; supporter of aircraft, 4; enmity of Beresford, 2; uncanny foresight, 2; predicts date of First World War, 2, 20; forecasts German use of U-boats, 2; Director of Naval Ordnance, 3; Controller, 3; C-in-C Mediterranean, 3; Second Sea Lord, 3; British Naval representative at Hague Conference, 1899, 3; serves on Esher Committee to reform War Office, 3; 'Greatest administrator since St Vincent', 5; Churchill on, 5; retired, 6; 'instant readiness for war', 14; War plans 15–26; supports naval staff, 27; sells shares in Shell Oil Company, 31; on oil engines, 34; suggests 'Pluto' pipeline, 35; on submarines, 35–36; forecasts unrestricted submarine warfare, 35; suggests submarines make invasion impossible, 35; concern over lack of Admiralty interest in submarines, 35–38; introduces 13.5-inch guns, 45; urges Churchill to adopt 15-inch gun, 45; on 'Queen Elizabeths', 48; proposal to enter Scheldt, 65; succeeds Battenberg, 72; loyalty, 76; wanted

fleet further south, 89; presses for increased submarine building, 89; Burns Admiralty docket, 90; his construction programme, 90–93; strategic and tactical ability, 93; A.K. Wilson on his strategy, 93; presses for attack on Belgian coast, 94; Baltic scheme, 95, 97, 237, on air raids, 105–08; silent at War Council, 110, 127; suggests Sturdee for attack on Dardanelles, 118; supports combined operation at Dardanelles 118–19; memo to Tweedmouth, 120; protests at over-extension of Navy, 123; not consulted 125; reconsiders Dardanelles scheme, 128; repeatedly makes his objections clear, 129–131; formal memo to Asquith giving objections, 130; presses for troops, 142; realities supported by Birdwood, 145; offers to command at Dardanelles, 146; threatens resignation, but consoles Churchill 158; on dissipation of Naval forces, 158; calls for report from Ian Hamilton, 159; warns Churchill again, 160; ignored, 161; formal record of his views on Dardanelles, 169–170; meeting with Kitchener, 171; copy of formal record to Asquith, 172; letter to Asquith, 172; letter of resignation, 179; curious message to Jellicoe, 181; might have been offered First Lord, 188; dictatorial letter to Asquith, 189–90; objects to Balfour as 1st Lord, 190; tells Crease to prepare withdrawal, 191; Asquith accepts resignation, 193; democratic views, 196; offers to serve under Balfour, 200; vilification of, 200–202; Chairman, Board of Invention and Research, 205; asks Asquith for useful employment, 207; maiden speech in Lords, 221; wanted Grand Fleet at Humber, 227; calls for restoration, 227, 228; plans Jellicoe as first Sea Lord on re-instatement,

228; writes to Asquith, 229; public support, 231; attends meeting of War Committee, 231–32; Hankey on, 232; second speech in Lords, 235; urges attack on Antwerp from sea, 236; on adoption of Baltic Scheme, by enemy, 236; on political conduct of the war, 237; on Admiralty Staff, 238, illness and death, State Funeral, 240–41; surrender of High Sea Fleet, 243; no memorial in London, 241

Fisher, Captain William, leaves Army, 1; coffee plantation fails, 1

Fisher, Cecil, 2nd Baron, 31

Fisher, Lady, 1, death, 240

Flushing, 19

Foch, Ferdinand, Marshal of France, 8

'Formidable' class, 87, 100

Franz Ferdinand, Archduke, assassination, 50

French, John Denton Pinkstone, See Ypres

French ships in Bantry Bay, 88

Fullerton, Admiral Sir Eric, 25

Fullerton, Admiral Sir John, 25

Gallipoli defences, 110; landing plans left to Hamilton, 153

Gardiner, A.G. 35

Garvin, J.L., 202

Gas turbines, Parsons on, 34

Geddes Axe, 89

Geddes, Sir Eric First Lord, 176, 199

George V, King, suggests Meux, Jackson or Sturdee as First Sea Lord, 73; aversion to Fisher, 73; Beresfordite, 73; no supporter of Churchill, 73; tells Esher of Fisher's resignation, 181; wishes to be rid of Churchill, 189; urges formation of Ministry of Munitions, 193; letter to Fisher, 200

German invasion of Denmark, 1940, 18

German liners in New York, 88

German Official History of the War, 102

Germania, 19

Germany declares war on Belgium, France, Russia, 51; marches into Belgium, 51; adopts Baltic plan, 102

Ghent, 62

Gilbert, Martin, 168, 169, 174

Gladstone, William Ewart, 20

Globe, 43, supports Fisher, 189

Godfrey, Admiral John, 213

Goeben and Breslau, escape to Turkey, 53–59, 109

Goltz, Marshal von der, 135

Gracie, Alexander, 32

Graham-Greene, Sir William, Secretary of the Admiralty, 100

Grand fleet based on Forth, 227

Grant, Admiral Heathcoat, 82, 83

Great Belt, 95, 223

Greece Declares neutrality, 109

Gretton, Vice Admiral Sir Peter, 11, 44, 68

Grey, Edward, 1st Viscount, of Fallodon, 19, 51; contacts Russians, 156

Guépratte, French Admiral, 151, disagrees with further naval attack, 173

Guest, Freddie, 207

Guns, 17-inch, 222

Gwynne, H.A., Editor, Morning Post, calls for Churchill to be controlled, 112

Haig, Douglas, 50; questions plan to fight on French left, 60

Haldane, 1st Viscount, Secretary of State for War, 10; presses for Naval Staff, 10–11, 12, 27; drafts Official Secrets Act, 11; wants to be 1st Lord, 12, 27

Hall, Admiral Sir Reginald, 153, 228

Hall, Admiral Sydney, 36, 90

Hamburg, 97, 113

Hamilton, Admiral Sir Frederick, Second Sea Lord, 198, 209, 221, 228

Hamilton, Duke of, 181, 240

Hamilton, General Sir Ian, 110, 158, 159, 164, 207, 211; in command, troops at Gallipoli, 143; regards naval attack as failure, 152; diverts troops to Egypt, 154; inadequate staff, 164; troops halted, 175; abusive letter on Fisher, 200; dismisses Ashmead-Bartlett's memorandum, 203; surrenders command, 214

Hamilton, Lord George, 121

Hamilton, Nina, Duchess of, 228, 241, 243

Hankey, Colonel Maurice, 1st Baron, 15, 36, 95, 112, 118, 126, 167–8, 188, 192, 224; on Fisher's strategy, 65; memoranda on Baltic scheme, 95–96;

on sea power, 96; Paper on Constantinople, 115–16; warns Asquith, Kitchener, Lloyd George and Balfour of need for troops at Dardanelles, 129; persuades Asquith of need for troops, 141; warns Asquith, 170; prises Fisher out of Admiralty, 193; to visit Gallipoli as check on Churchill, 207–8; reports on visit to Gallipoli, 211; on lack of offensive, 224; impressed with Fisher's performance at War Council, 232–33

Harcourt, Sir William Vernon, 35

Hartlepool bombarded, 88

Haul-down vacancies, 2

Heligoland, 9

Heneage, Admiral Algernon, 213

Henry, Prince of Prussia, 102

High Sea Fleet, 8; 71, 243; destroyers, 88; comes out, 187, 226

Hindenburg, Paul, 115

Hipper, Admiral Franz von, 224, attacks east coast, 130

'Historical School', 2

Hood, Admiral Hon. Sir Horace, in command of monitors bombarding Channel coast, 67; maintains proper signal procedure, 67; off Belgian coast, 87

Hopwood, Sir Francis See Southborough

Hoskins, Admiral Sir Anthony, 121; on penetrating Dardanelles, 121

Hough, Richard, on Churchill's appropriation of credit, 91

Hoyer, raid on, 224

Hulbert, Captain Arthur, 238

Hunter-Weston, General Sir Aylmer, 164

Hydrophone, 206

'Interest', 4;

Ingenohl, Admiral Friedrich von, Commander-in-Chief Germany Navy, 50

Invasion of France through Belgium, 51

Invasion of Britain, 74, 87

Italy, enters war, 168

Jackson, Admiral of the Fleet Sir Henry, 73, 75, 123, 214, 216, 222, 223, 224, 227; memorandum on Dardanelles, 120–21; agrees only to attack on

Jackson, Admiral of the Fleet Sir Henry (continued) outer forts, 128; refines Carden plan, 134; stresses need for troops, 134; 142, 146–47; as First Sea Lord, 199, chairs to committee to decide priorities, 212

Jade, 9

Jellicoe, Admiral of the Fleet John, 1st Earl, 10, 22, 25, 26, 29, 36, 39, 42, 68, 73, 76, 84, 87, 181, 196, 198, 222, 223, 224, 225, 226, 227, 241, 242; on Churchill, 22; urges Fisher's good relations with Churchill, 30; disbelieves unrestricted submarine warfare, 39; on Churchill's 'meddling', 45; organizes trials against armour plate, 45–46; remains in North, 88; 'Mining-in' in Forth and Humber, 89; opposition to Baltic plan, 103, 221; on Fisher's resignation, 189; writes sympathetic letter to Fisher, 193–94; on Churchill's departure, 198; denigrates Fisher, 221; shortage of destroyers, 222; disagreement with Beatty, 227; complains of slow delivery of destroyers, etc., 229

Joffre, Marshal Joseph, 94, 120; suggests naval bombardment in support of armies, 67; prefers assault on Wytschaete Ridge and Messines, 94

John Bull, 202

Johnson, Dr. Samuel, 6

Johnson, Jack, 47

Jowett, Benjamin, Master of Balliol College Oxford, 179

Jutland Peninsula, 97

Jutland, Battle of, good shooting at, 46

Kaiser Wilhelm II, 18; 105; believes in British neutrality, 50

Kattegat, 95, 223

Kellaway, Frederick, Liberal MP, 167

Kelly, Admiral Howard, 57

Kelly, Admiral of the Fleet Sir John D, 11

Kennedy, Admiral Francis, 56, 57

Kephez Bay, 122

Keppel, Admiral Augustus, 1st Viscount, 189

Keyes, Roger, Admiral of the

Fleet, 1st Baron Keyes of Zeebrugge, 36, 39, 144, 163, 166; Staff as C-in-C Mediterranean, 11; believes unrestricted submarine warfare unthinkable, 40; on 'Live Bait squadron' 68; on sinkings 70; on submarine building, 89–90; on Baltic plan, 103; optimistic telegram after first day's bombardment 137; characteristics, 139; on minesweeping, 139; on aircraft, 145; in communication with Churchill, 148; on mines, 152; reorganizes sweepers, 154; always believed in Dardanelles, 163; presses de Robeck, 167; on Admiralty after Fisher, 199–200; thirsts for Navy-only attack, 209; uses wife to spread propaganda, 209; submits new plan to de Robeck, 209; submits further plan, 213; goes home to put his case, 214; meets Jackson, Oliver, Everett, Balfour, Meux, Churchill and Kitchener 215; unsatisfactory ideas 215; undermines de Robeck, 216; reprimanded by de Robeck, 219

Kilid Bahr, 110, 122, 174

Kiel, 8, 97

Kiel Canal, 14, 26; reopening, 50, 97

Kilverstone Hall, 6, 241

King's Lynn, 108

Kitchener, Field Marshal Earl, 59, 62, 65, 94, 95, 96, 110, 111, 115, 116, 134, 146, 172, 195, 202; 228, 235, 238, 239; appointed Minister for War, 59; character, 59–60; forecasts long war, 61; suggests rank of Lieut-General for Churchill at Antwerp, 64–65; dominates War Office, 96–97; Alexandretta plan, 115, 117; appeals for 'naval demonstration to assist Russians, 117–18; telegram to St Petersburg, 118; gives French's views on Eastern operations, 124; refuses French's advance along the coast, 126; enthusiastic for Dardanelles scheme, 126–7; warned of need for troops, 129; dissuades

Fisher from resignation, 132; contradictory views, 140; orders to Ian Hamilton, 143; releases 29th Division, 146; accepts need for Army, 153; underestimates Gallipoli, 158; agrees to preparation of evacuation plans, 212; proposal to supply fleet across Bulair, 215; moves to dismiss, 218; visit to Gallipoli, 218; recommends evacuation, 218; on conscription, 219, recruiting in shipyards, 223

Kluck, General Alexander von, 61, 102

Knorr, Admiral von, 28

Krupp armour, 45

Krupp, Gustav Krupp von Bohlen und Halbach, 37

Lambe, Sophie, *See* Lady Fisher

Lambert, 1st Viscount, Civil Lord, 32, 188, 234, 236

Lansdowne, 5th Marquess of, 186

Landings on Gallipoli, 166

Lapyrère, Vice-Admiral, French Navy, 55

Letters patent, 20

Leveson, Admiral Sir Arthur, Director of Operations, 68, 69

Liège, 149

Lighters, protected Self-Propelled, 92

Limpus, Admiral Sir Arthur, 43; Head of British Mission in Turkey, 122; Admiral Superintendent, Malta, 122; supports de Roebeck opposing new attack, 216

'Live bait squadron' 68

Lloyd George, Chancellor of the Exchequer, 12, 13, 19, 28, 97, 181, 211; 228, 231; warning to Germany, 19; paper on attack on Constantinople, 115–166; proposes attack through Adriatic, 124; opposes French, 126; warned of need for troops at Dardanelles, 129; Army pulling nuts out of fire, 143; asks A.K. Wilson his views, 153; Minister of Munitions recruits from shipyards, 229; impressed with Fisher's 'Hustle', 233; Prime Minister, 236

Londonderry, Lady, 13

London Naval Treaty, 89

Loop-detector system, 206
Lord Fisher and his Biographer, by Churchill, 196
Lowestoft, 226
Luce, Captain John, 82
Lusitania, SS, 205

McClintock, Vice-Admiral John 213
Mackay, Professor Ruddock, 36, 40, 190
McKenna, Pamela, 26, 221
McKenna, Reginald, Liberal MP, First Lord, 6, 7, 8, 11, 12, 13, 14, 22, 30, 35, 36, 76, 174, 182–3, 234
Mackenzie, Compton, 164
Madden, Admiral of the Fleet Sir Charles, 25, 228
'Majestic' class suspended, 92
Mallet, Sir Louis, 54
Manchester Guardian, 211, 222, 227, 228
Manoury, General, Commanding French 6th Army, 61
Marder, Professor Arthur, 4–5, 49, 163, 189
Marne, 1st battle of, 61, 62, 238
Marsh, Eddie, 207
Masterton Smith, James, Churhill's private secretary, 179, 182, 202, 219
Material School, 2
Meeting at Kitchener's house, 63
Memories, Fisher, 244
Mesopotamia, 110
Messines, 94
Meux, Admiral of the Fleet The Hon. Sir Hedworth, (formerly Lambton), 29, 52, 73, 210, 214, 228
Milford Haven, Marquis of, Prince Louis of Battenberg, 25, 27, 62, 68, 69, 73, 75, 78, 88, 176; appointed 1st Sea Lord, 44, cancels demobilization, 52; and German birth, 71; Beresford's opposition, 71; character, 72; resignation, 72; favours attack on Borkum, 99
Miller, Gordon, Director of Contracts, 33,
Milne, Admiral Sir Archibald Berkeley, 29; C-in-C Mediterranean, 29; failure, 52; strong command, 53; fails to give Goeben's course, 56, 57, 58
Mines carried by German cruisers, 89
Minesweeping, 138–139; night sweeping fails, 154

Ministers away for weekend, July, 1914, 52
Ministry of Munitions, 193
Mitchell Committee, 137, 145
Mitchell Report, 145
Moltke (the elder), Helmuth, Count von, 19, 195
Moltke, (the younger, nephew of the elder) Helmuth, Chief of German General Staff, 67; misses opportunity to capture Channel ports, 61; allows transport of Expeditionary Force, 109;
Monro, General Charles, relieves Ian Hamilton 214, 224; recommends evacuation, 217, 219
Mons, 61, 62, 102
Monte Carlo, 240
Moore, Admiral Sir Archibald, 42, 48
Moore, Admiral Sir Arthur, 228
Morley, 1st Viscount, resigns from Cabinet, 51
Morning Post, 228
Morocco, partition, 8
Mottistone, Major-General, 1st Baron, (John Seely), 12; resignation as War Minister, 59
Motor battleships, 34

Namur, 149
Napoleon, 114
National Review, 21
Naval and Military Committee, 212
Naval and Military Record, 228, 231
Naval brigades, Hankey on, 64; Richmond on, 64; unfit, 64
Naval review, Spithead, 1914, 51
Naval Staff, 11,
Naval War College, 11, 27
Navy estimates, 1912, 30,
Nelson, Vice Admiral, First Viscount, Horatio, 3; 72, 113, 163, 241; Band of Brothers, 4
Nepotism, 4
Neuve Chapelle, 171
News of the World, 21
Nicholas, Grand Duke, of Russia, 97, 98
Nicholson, Field Marshal Sir William, 9, 12,
Noel, Admiral Sir Gerard, opposes Fisher's restoration, 228
Northcliffe, 1st Viscount, 59, 234
Noverossiysk, 110

Observer, 202
Odessa, 110
Official Secrets Act, 11
Oil Fuel, 31; 32–4
Oliver, Admiral of the Fleet Sir Henry, 72, 146; misjudges Cradock's position, 77–78; on Sturdee, 81; attends War Council, 133; weak support for Dardanelles operation, 154
Olympic, SS, 70, 90
Oram, Engineer Vice Admiral Sir Henry, 32
Oxford and Asquith, 1st Earl of, Herbert Henry Asquith, 11, 12, 19, 20, 23, 30, 36, 40, 133, 174, 180, 191; asks for Fisher on CID, 6; breaches security, 11; and Venetia Stanley, 11; meets Fisher in Naples, 30; Irish Home Rule, 51; on sinkings, 70; supports Fisher as First Sea Lord, 73; ad hoc meetings with Churchill and Kitchener, 75; compares Fisher with Battenburg 75; on Coronel, 80; poor conduct of War Council, 111; taken in by Churchill, 112; knew views of admirals 112; calls Fisher 'unbalanced', 112; believes Baltic scheme Churchill's idea, 114; desultory conduct of war, 116; knew more of Dardanelles than pretended, 129; claims not to notice Fisher leaving the table, 133; fails to probe Fisher's views, 133; ignores security, 135; over-optimism on Dardanelles, 135; underestimates Fisher's objection to Navy only attack at Dardanelles, 129–31; 'King's Command', 180; letter to Fisher on reconstruction, 188; reconciled to Fisher, 205; abolishes Dardanelles Committee, 217; forms new Cabinet War Committee, 217; respect for Fisher restored, 222; method of conduction business, 233; failure, 239

Pakenham, Admiral Sir William Christopher, 25, 42
Paris, General Archibald, Royal Marines, 64, 164

Parsons, Sir Charles, 4th son of the Earl of Rosse, 34, believes Gas turbines impossible, 34; Member of Board of Invention and Research, 205–6
Peiho, 124
Persia, 110, oil supplies, 33
Philipp, Sir Ivor, MP, 102
Phipps Hornby on penetration of the Dardanelles, 118–19, 121
Plevna, 161,
Pluto pipeline, 35
Poë, Admiral Sir Edmond, 29
Pohl, Admiral Hugo, Commander-in-Chief, High Sea Fleet, 84, 102, 105, 224
Pollen, Arthur, amateur gunnery 'expert', 232
Pomeranian coast, 19, 95
Poore, Admiral Sir Richard, 42
Pretyman, Ernest, Financial Secretary, 33
Prior, Robin, 237
Privy Consellors' Oath, 11
Promotion, 1, 2, 4
Protected self-propelled lighters, 92
Punta Arenas, 81

'Queen Elizabeth' class, 92
Queen's Own Oxfordshire Hussars, 220

Rawlinson, General Sir Henry, at Antwerp, 64, 65
Records, 244
Reigate Priory, 13, 24
Repington, Colonel Charles A'Court, 17, 19, 30, 69, 95, 231; discloses shell shortage, 175
Riddell, George, 1st Baron, 21
Richmond, Admiral Sir Herbert, 196, 224, on Naval Brigades, 63–64, 69, 70; on Coronel, 80; on Sturdee, 81; on Dardanelles, 135; Paper on need for troops, 135; on Keyes, 139
Riga, 95
Rio de Janeiro, 81
River gunboats, 92
Roberts, Field Marshal, 1st Earl, 50; on invasion, 7; on landing in Belgium, 95
Robertson, Field Marshal Sir William, Fisher suggests to command land forces in Turkey in Asia, 118, 120; presses for troops at Dardanelles, 142
Robinson, Commander Eric, VC, 138, 140

Robinson, Vice-Admiral Sir Robert, 20
Roskill, 17, 243
Rosyth, Inadequate U-boat defences, 74 Grand Fleet moves to, 227
Royal Sovereign class, conversion to monitors, 18, 103–04
Royal yachts, promotion after service in, 2
Royal Commission on oil fuel and oil engines, 31, 32; disbanded, 41
Royal Flying Corps, 105
Royal Naval Air Service, 105, 219
Rumania, declares neutrality, 109
Russia appeals to Britain, 51; asks for assistance to counter pressure on Caucasus, 117; ammunition, 108; casualties, 108; defeat Turks at Sarikamish, 127
Russian shell shortage, 108–9

St. Paul's Cathedral, 241
St. Vincent, Admiral, 1st Earl, 189, 228
Salonika, 141
Sanders, J.S., 22
Sanders, Marshal Liman von, 54, 116–17; Commander-in-Chief, Turkish Army, 110; admits Turkish morale low, 156
Sari Bair Ridge, 208
Scapa, inadequate U-boat defences, 74, 75; too far north, 88
Scarborough bombarded, 88
Scheer, Admiral Reinhard, 46, 102, 224, 225, 226
Schillinghorn, 9
Schleswig-Holstein, 9, 15
Schlieffen plan, 51, 61
Schofield, Vice-Admiral Brian, 58
Schwab, Charles, Bethlehem Steel Corporation of America, 90,
Schwab submarines, 232
Schwab monitors, 91
Schwartzhoff, General Gross von, 19
Scimitar Hill, 209
Scott, Admiral Sir Percy, 1st Baronet, 38, 242, 170; on bombardment of Alexandria, 121; refuses to command at Dardanelles, 126; on shore and naval guns 149,
Scott, Charles, editor, Manchester Guardian, 212; discussion with Loreburn,

228; sees through Asquith's tactics against Jellicoe, 229; sees Asquith, unimpressed, 232–33
Sea Lords' joint memorandum, 161–62; Fisher's response, 163; appeal to Churchill and Fisher, 183; Churchill's answer, 183–84
Seaplanes, underpowered, 145
Security, 166
Seely, See Mottistone
Selbourne, 2nd Earl of, 1st Lord, (1900–1905), 25, 27, 33, 198; advises Balfour to restore Fisher as 1st Sea Lord, 190–1
Selborne-Fisher scheme, 26
Sevastopol, 110
Shell Oil Company, 31
Shell shortage, 175; debate on, 185
Shells, influence of weight, 45–46
Shellfire from Asiatic shore, 203
Sheringham, 108
Ships against Forts, 124–5
Shipbuilding programme, 92; curtailed, 89
Skagerrak, 95, 223
Slade, Admiral Sir Edmond, 15
Smith, F.E., 1st Earl of Birkenhead, 23
Somerset House, 19
Sonar, 206
Souchon, Rear Admiral Wilhelm, 54, 55, 56; given freedom to choose escape, 57
Southborough, 1st Baron, additional Civil Lord, 31, 182; on Poore incident, 43; on Churchill's departure for Antwerp, 63
Spectator, 20, 230
Spee, Vice Admiral Count Maximilian Graf von, 74, 76, 80, 82, 83; Germany sends battlecruisers to assist, 88
Spender, John, Editor, Westminster Gazette, 220
Spion Kop, 131
Spring Gardens, 20
Staff, 27; rigidity, 60
Staff College, 238
Staff Course, 27
Stamfordham, 1st Baron, 73
Stanley, Venetia, 11, 64, 70, 112, 135
Start, Rear Admiral Sydney, 77
Stettin, 95
Stevenson, Frances, 212
Stoddard, Admiral Archibald, 79, 80, 82
Stoking, 32–33

Sturdee, Admiral of the Fleet
Sir Doveton, 1st Baronet,
39, 68, 69, 75, 81; hoists
his flag, 82; conduct on
passage 82; reaches
Falklands, 83; expenditure
of ammunition, 84;
Fisher's signals to 84, 85;
Richmond on, 84; Asquith
on, 84; Fisher resents
adulation, 84–5, 131
Submarine Attack Committee,
91, 206
Submarine building
programme, 90; Churchill
on, 90
Submarines, 1; Soviet, 35;
Balfour on, 36–37, 40;
K and M classes, 38;
Submarine Dreadnought,
206
Sueter, Rear-Admiral Sir
Murray, 105
Sudan, 10
Sultan of Egypt, 164
Super-Dreadnoughts, 1
Swinemunde, 9
Sydenham, Colonel, 1st Baron,
17, 37; disbelieves
unrestricted submarine
warfare, 39; suggests air
attack against submarines,
39, reports on
bombardment of
Alexandria, 121
Sylt, 15, 17, 223

Taylor, A.J.P., 60
Ten Year Rule, 89
Territorial Force, 62, 74
Test mobilization, 1914, 51
The Fleet, 28
Thetford, 6;
Thomson, Sir J.J., President of
the Royal Society, 205
Times, The, 137, 175, 227, 230,
240, 241; proposes Fisher
as First Lord, 189
Tirpitz, Grand Admiral von,
17, 46, 56, 57, 58, 223; on
agreement with Italy and
Austria, 57; on Souchon's
breakthrough to
Dardanelles 58–9; on
Baltic scheme 102–3;
Skagerrak and Belts not
mined, 103
Tondern, attack on zeppelin
sheds, 226
Torpedo traps, 89
Trafalgar, 10
Trench warfare, 15, 108
Tromp, Admiral Maarten, 78
Troops found for Dardanelles,
142
Troubridge, Admiral Sir
Ernest, 53, 55, 58, 164
Troy, 110

Turbines, 1
Turkey, declares neutrality,
109; German enticement,
110; ambitions, 117
Twenty-ninth Division, to
Alexandria, 154; to go to
Dardanelles, 141, 142;
decision reversed, 142
Tyrrel, Sir William, 62
Tyrwhitt, Admiral of the Fleet
Sir Reginald, 1st Baronet,
36, 177, 224, 225, 226; on
'Live Bait squadron', 68

U-boat campaign, 205
U-boats, 67, Jellicoe and
Beatty's concern, 67;
Churchill dismisses lightly,
75; in the Aegean, 168;
measures against, 206
Usedom, Admiral von,
Commander-in-Chief,
Turkish Navy, 110,

Vivian, Captain Gerald, 41–42

Wangenheim, von, German
Ambassador to Turkey, 57
War Council, 75, 110, 116;
Bacon on, 75; no sense of
urgency, 113; discusses
Dardanelles 114; meeting
of 8 January, 124, decides
Navy to 'take' Gallipoli,
127; meeting of 28
January, 1915, 132–133;
Churchill's optimism, 143;
no meeting 19 March to
14 May, 1915, 161;
renamed 'Dardanelles
Committee, 207; absence
of Service officers, 202;
Churchill uses as vehicle
for views, 203; calls for
Fisher's recall, 230
War Group, in Admiralty, 75,
100
War Office arrogation of
authority, 10
War Office Staff, 11, 96
War, declaration, 50–51
'War Lord', 11
Washington Naval Treaty, 89
Waterford, 5th Marquess of, 2
Waterloo, 10
Wellington, Duke of, 59
Wemyss, Admiral of the Fleet,
1st Baron, 209, 238;
forecasts breach between
Churchill and Fisher 74;
ill-will to Fisher, 200–201;
assumes command at
Dardanelles, 218; supports
Keyes, 216, 218; sent to
Egypt, 219
Weser, 9
Westminster abbey, 179, 240,
241

Whitby bombarded, 88
White, Arnold, Naval
Correspondent, Daily
Mail, 6, 7, 227
Whittle, Sir Frank, 34
Wilhelmshaven, 8, 9, 97, 113,
227
Williamson, Group-Captain
Hugh, on seaplanes, 145
Wilmot-Horton, Lady; 1
Wilmot-Horton, Sir Robert,
Governor of Ceylon, 1
Wilson, Admiral of the Fleet
Sir Arthur Knyvet, VC, 3;
6, 7, 10, 11, 12, 19, 23,
73, 75, 99, 100, 101, 127,
176, 238; Member of
Committee of Imperial
Defence, 5; 'Old 'Ard
'Eart', 5; due to retire, 8;
at CID meeting on Agadir,
9–10, proposes close
blockade 9, capture of
Fehmarn, Sweinemunde,
Danzig, 9–10; failure to
finalize plans; 10; on naval
staff, 11; keeps plans to
himself, 23; paper against
staff, 24; proposes depth
charges, 39; unpaid
advisor, 74; on Fisher's
strategic scheme, 93;
favours attack on Borkum,
99; not consulted on
Dardanelles, 125; on
Churchill's belief in Navy
only operation at
Dardanelles, 143;
Churchill claims supports
Navy-only attack, 146;
appeals to Fisher, 185;
misunderstands Churchill,
187; departure greeted
with relief, 197; attends
War Committee, 229; on
Borkum and Heligoland,
238
Wilson, Field Marshal Sir
Henry, 8; 9, 19, 50, 60;
Francophile, influenced by
Foch, 8; forces adherence
to existing plan, 60, 96,
186, 237
World Crisis, The, 18, 31, 103,
129, 135, 140, 146, 168,
173, 178, 188, 192, 196,
230, 237
Wray, Captain Fawcett, 58
Wyteschaete Ridge, 94

Yarmouth, bombardment 87,
88, 108
Yarrow, Sir Alfred, 32
Ypres, Battle of, 65, 74, 94

Ypres, Field Marshal, 1st Earl of, 12, 14, 115, 120, questions plan to fight on French left, 60; proposes landing in Belgium or Schleswig, 60; presses for outflanking attack on Belgian coast, 94; move toward the Channel, 109; meets War Council, 126; agrees to spare two divisions for Dardanelles, 141
Yser, 236

Zeebrugge as submarine base, 94
Zeppelins, 105, 233
Zulu war, 10

Warships
British
Aboukir, sunk, 68, 70
Agamemnon, 137, 138; 149; damaged 151–2
Agincourt, 88
Ajax, 88
Albion, 79, 125, 151; joins Cape Station, 79
Amethyst, 139, 140
Ark Royal, 138;
Audacious, sunk 67; 88, 70, 91
Barham, 41
Bellerophon, 88
Black Prince, 53, 227
Blenheim, 129
Bristol, 79, 82; seeking *Dresden*, 84
Caesar, 125
Canopus, 77, 78, 79, 80, 82; unfit condition, 77; at Dardanelles, 125
Carnarvon, 82
Chatham, 54, 55
Comet, 88
Conqueror, 88
Cornwall, 79, 82
Cornwallis, 136, 140
Cressy, sunk, 68, 70
Defence, 53, 78, 83, 85, 227; joins Stoddart east coast of S. America, 79
Dominion, 88
Dreadnought, 1, 32, 45, 46, 48, 232, 233
Dublin, 53, 55, 56
Duke of Edinburgh, 53, 227
Edinburgh, firing trials against, 45
Erin, 88
Essex, 79
Euryalus, 67
Formidable, sunk, 94
Furious, 222
Glasgow 76, 78, 79, 82, sent round West Coast of S. America to find *Leipzig*, 79 seeking *Dresden*, 84–85
Gloucester, 53, 54, 57, 58
Goliath, sunk, 171
Good Hope, 76, 79, 82
Hannibal 125
Hawke, 70
Hermes, 41
Hibernia, 88
Hogue, sunk 68, 70
Humber, 67, 91, 100
Implacable, 154
Indefatigable, 53, 54, 125, 126, 129
Indomitable, 53, 54, 58, 76; sights *Goeben* and *Breslau*, 56
Inflexible, 53, 80, 84, 85, 87, 125, 126, 128, 129, 149; sent to South Atlantic, 81, seeking *Dresden*, 84; damaged, convoyed to Malta, 151–2
Irresistible, 151; sunk, 152
Invincible 80, 82, 84, 87, 129; to South Atlantic, 81; brickwork repairs, 81; fouls propeller, 82, 281; returns to UK, 84
Iron Duke, 46, 88
Kent, 82
King Edward VII, 88
'King Edward VII', class, 87, 88
Lion, 35
London, 154
'Lord Nelsons', 145
Lord Nelson, 149; damaged, 153
Macedonia, 79, 83
Magnificent, 125
Majestic, 151; sunk, 172
Malaya, 41
Mars, 125
Mersey, 67, 91, 100
Monmouth, 76, 78, 79, 82
New Zealand, 88
Newcastle, 77
Ocean, 125, 151; sunk, 152
Oceanic, 88
Orama, 79, 82
Orion, 46, 88
Otranto, 76, 78
Pathfinder, 70
Pegasus, 70
Prince George, 125, 149
Prince of Wales, 154
Princess Royal, 87
Queen, 154
Queen Elizabeth, 41, 47, 48, 125, 126, 128, 129, 131, 134, 136, 144, 145, 149, 171, 175, 181; hit, 151; ample ammunition available, 154; Fisher insists on return, 171; dummy torpedoed, 171
Renown, 92
Repulse, 92
Rifleman, 88
'Royal Sovereign' class, conversion to monitors, 104
Severn, 67, 91, 100
Swiftsure, 125, 151
Triumph, 25, 125, 149 sunk, 171
Valiant, 41
Vengeance, 125, 136, 151
Victorious, 125
Vindex, 224
Warrior, 53, 227
Warspite, 41
Weymouth, 53, 55
French
Bouvet, 151; sunk, 151
Charlemagne, 151
Gaulois, 151; damaged and beached, 152
Suffren, 136, 151
Japanese
Hizan, cruiser, 77
Idzumo, Japanese battleship, 77
German
Blücher, 130
Breslau, 52, 55, 109, 110, 122, 210; bombards Bône, 56
Dresden, 70, 74, 76, 78, 83, 84, 85, 89; visits Orange Bay, 78; joins *Scharnhorst*, 78; sunk by *Glasgow* and *Kent*, 85
Emden, 70, 74, 80, 205
Gneisenau 76, 77, 78, 82, 83
Goeben, 52, 54, 55, 57, 109, 110, 122, 210; bombards Philippville, 56
Hohenzollern, (Kaiser's yacht), 50
Kaiser Wilhelm der Grosse, 80
Kaiser, 45
Karlsruhe, 70, 74, 79; sunk by unstable ammunition, 89, 205
Königsberg, 70, 80
Kronprinz (renamed *Kronprinz Wilhelm*), 45, 89
Leipzig, 76; joins *Scharnhorst*, 78
Nassau, 45
Nürnberg, 76; joins *Scharnhorst*, 78
Panther, 8
Prinz Eitel Friedrich, 89
Seydlitz, 46
Scharnhorst, 76, 78, 82
Greek
Salamis, 91